HOW TO TEACH
DISADVANTAGED YOUTH

HOW TO TEACH
DISADVANTAGED YOUTH

ALLAN C. ORNSTEIN
PHILIP D. VAIRO
Fordham University

DAVID McKAY COMPANY, INC.
New York

HOW TO TEACH DISADVANTAGED YOUTH

LIBRARY OF CONGRESS CATALOG CARD NUMBER: 69–17502
MANUFACTURED IN THE UNITED STATES OF AMERICA

PREFACE

The editors are keeping the appointment that they made several years ago while teaching disadvantaged youth in the ghettos of New York City. At that time they recognized the need for a book that would not merely reiterate the current issues in American education as such, but one that would also focus on the *how* approach in teaching disadvantaged youth. No pretense is made that solutions to this problem are easy. It goes without saying that easy solutions to difficult problems are seldom found. However, it is hoped that this collection of readings may help prospective teachers, teachers, trainers of teachers, and other interested persons to at least reflect anew concerning the education of the disadvantaged.

What do we know about teaching disadvantaged youth? The editors contend that although there is a wealth of literature concerning the psychosocial factors related to the problems of the disadvantaged, there is a gap between the knowledge and its implementation in the classroom. Nevertheless, educators can no longer remain silent or give old replies to the faultfinding of the critics. It is indeed one of the tragedies of American education that so many children of the poor have been alienated from the very institution that has been the symbol of American democracy. Yet, this fact should not come as a complete surprise. Historically, the poor have always been an underprivileged group in spite of our "charity" and more recently our poverty programs. It is this group, then, whose needs must not be neglected in any program of education for democracy.

Today education—not cheap land, frontiers, or rugged individualism in the eyes of the American people—plays the important role of providing social mobility and opportunity for the "good life." Americans at great sacrifice are sending their children to school; they want their children to have the opportunity they missed. In essence, education has become the most sought commodity in American life. However, are the schools creating the atmosphere so that students coming from the ghettos and our poor rural areas can succeed? Are the universities preparing teachers who are sensitive to the needs of the ghetto people? The same life chances must be provided for our poor—for they are one of the largest segments of the American population. If the poor of our society are ignored, it indeed will be tantamount to cutting the arteries of American democracy. The mounting interest and concern afforded our less fortunate citizens in recent years give special timeliness to this undertaking.

In the last analysis, well-trained teachers are the essential ingredients if the cultural and educational levels of all citizens are to be raised. If decisive steps are to be initiated to break the cycle of cultural deprivation, the logical place to begin with is the training of teachers.

The book is organized into three parts. Part One, "Why Do Teachers of Disadvantaged Youth Fail?," points out the factors and forces that contribute to the unsuccessful attempts of ghetto-school teachers. Part Two, "How Can Teachers of Disadvantaged Youth Succeed?," explores the avenues open for successful and rewarding careers for teachers of disadvantaged youth. Part Three, "What Preparation Do Teachers of Disadvantaged Youth Need?," examines the role of teacher-training institutions in the preparation of teachers for the poor.

The editors are deeply indebted to the contributors of the essays in this volume and wish to express their appreciation. Acknowledgment is also made of the encouragement and support received from colleagues and friends. The completion of this text was due in no small measure to the patience, dedication, and encouragement of our secretaries, Mrs. Kate Marino and Miss Cynthia Van Roten.

ALLAN C. ORNSTEIN
PHILIP D. VAIRO

New York, New York
June, 1968

CONTRIBUTORS

ALLEN, VIRGINIA F.
Lecturer
Teachers College, Columbia University

BARATTA, ANTHONY N.
Professor of Education
Fordham University

CLARK, KENNETH B.
Professor of Psychology
The City College of the City University of New York

DUNN, JOAN
Teacher
New York City Public Schools

ELKINS, DEBORAH
Associate Professor of Education
Queens College of the City University of New York

FOLEY, WALTER J.
Associate Director
Iowa Educational Information Center
University of Iowa

GOLDMAN, HARVEY
Assistant Professor of Education
University of Wisconsin-Milwaukee

GREENE, MARY F.
Teacher
New York City Public Schools

HAVIGHURST, ROBERT J.
Professor of Education and Human Development
The University of Chicago

HOLT, JOHN
Consultant, Fayerweather Street School
Cambridge, Massachusetts

HUNT, DAVID E.
Professor of Psychology
Syracuse University

KLEIN, RAYMOND S.
  Research Director, Office for Comprehensive Statewide Planning
    for Vocational Rehabilitation Services
  The University of the State of New York
KOHL, HERBERT
  Director, Teachers and Writers Collaborative
  Teachers College, Columbia University
KOZOL, JONATHAN
  Teacher, Newton Public Schools
  Newton, Massachusetts
LEVINE, DANIEL U.
  Assistant Professor of Education
  University of Missouri at Kansas City
LIERHEIMER, ALVIN P.
  Director, Division of Teacher Education and Certification
  New York State Department of Education
MARTIN, DAVID W.
  Professor of Education
  University of Southern California at Los Angeles
MELBO, IRVING R.
  Dean, School of Education
  University of Southern California at Los Angeles
ORNSTEIN, ALLAN C.
  Instructor of Education
  Fordham University
PEREL, WILLIAM
  Chairman and Professor of Mathematics
  Wichita State University
RIESSMAN, FRANK
  Professor of Educational Sociology
  New York University
RIVLIN, HARRY N.
  Dean, School of Education
  Fordham University
RYAN, ORLETTA
  Teacher
  New York City Public Schools
SCHWARTZ, SHEILA
  Associate Professor of English Education
  State University College, New Paltz, New York
TABA, HILDA
  Professor of Education
  San Francisco State College

VAIRO, PHILIP D.
    Associate Professor of Education
    Fordham University
WHIPPLE, GERTRUDE
    Director, City Schools Reading Project
    Detroit Public Schools

TABLE OF CONTENTS

PART THREE / WHAT PREPARATION DO TEACHERS OF DISADVANTAGED YOUTH NEED?

Part One

WHY DO TEACHERS OF DISADVANTAGED YOUTH FAIL?

The most crucial element on which success for education depends is the teacher. All our claims and innovations, no matter how sound or well-defined they seem, depend on the person doing the job in the classroom. Hardly a day passes, however, without a statement from some educator about the failure of ghetto-school teachers. In what way and to what extent the teachers are failing are discussed by our contributors.

With vivid dialogue, the first two selections dramatize the problems and pressures of teaching the disadvantaged. On the elementary-school level, Mary F. Greene and Orletta Ryan report a confusing and chaotic classroom. The children are not learning, not growing; they are being shortchanged. The teachers seem either incompetent or indifferent. The reader cannot help but get the feeling that these children are doomed, and as they pass from grade to grade their plight will most likely be intensified, as illustrated by the next selection.

Joan Dunn describes the prospects that confront the secondary-school teacher in hall patrol, study hall, and classroom. We meet an indifferent, sullen group of scholars who spend most of their class time slouching over their desks, sleeping and snoring, tapping on their desks, reading comic books, gazing out the window, and/or ridiculing themselves and their teacher.

John Holt broadens the concept of disadvantaged to include most students, even those from well-to-do families. He observes the way the students manipulate their teachers and adopt failure strategies. Even worse, according to Holt, most teachers are unaware of their students' strategies or how they think or feel.

Harvey Goldman's discussion centers around two factors that are implicit in our schools and have a detrimental effect on teaching the disadvantaged. First, he says the schools are middle-class oriented and the teachers unwittingly discriminate against and alienate the disadvantaged. Second, the schools, and in turn the teachers, tend to favor girls and discriminate against boys, especially disadvantaged boys.

Jonathan Kozol is a sensitive, socially concerned, outraged teacher. His paper is an indictment of his colleagues, school administrators, and school board. Through incidents and conversations, which may seem one-sided and too generalized, he lampoons his colleagues: illustrating their hypocrisy and prejudices and heartless feelings toward teaching Negro children. The author's description of conducting a class in the school auditorium and the collapse of a window frame, coupled with his discharge for innovating new, more objective materials illustrate the erosion of an urban school administration and school system and of a proud city.

Sheila Schwartz and Kenneth B. Clark both point out that ghetto-school teachers anticipate failure and establish self-fulfilling prophecies of failure that bring about and reinforce their students' problems. Schwartz asserts that most ghetto-school teachers resort to cynicism, adopt failure strategies, and try to discourage those who attempt to teach. Similarly, Clark contends that the function of teaching shifts to an "emphasis on discipline."

1 THE SCHOOLCHILDREN GROWING UP IN THE SLUMS

MARY F. GREENE AND ORLETTA RYAN

Monday morning, 8:15. Teachers passing, gabbling in groups: ". . . so Saturday, Burt got in from college and from then *on*—" ". . . second inlay on the terrace but when the contractor finally got out to Jackson Heights, Joe'd read up on do-it-yourself and we decided—" ". . . so I told her, if we didn't get out there *this* weekend, it'd be gone. It was the most darling old Colonial pewter—" Hall guards, ladies with badges, are shoving children out the ——th Street entrance: "The bell ain't rung yet—" and children: "Screw you . . ."

At the stairway next to the office of Assistant Principal Zang, Edith, a beautiful woman of thirty-five from Barbados, is washing "pussy" and "f—— you" from the wall. Teachers swarm past her. Her long dark arm rises and falls patiently . . . she picks up the bucket, moves on. She does this every morning. Two policemen are knocking on Zang's door, and I follow them into the office. I too have to see Zang this morning about Danny Aguilez, an eleven-year-old who carries a compass that he uses on children and on Wednesday told me to f—— myself and threw a chair. With the help of a guard, Danny was dragged down to the office on Wednesday, where he repeated it, "f——ing bitch," in front of Zang and four others. Zang had heard of this kid before— Danny had been around the school for four years, progressively growing sicker. Zang said, "Can't we handle this tomorrow? . . ." But tomorrow never came for Mr. Zang.

Danny did not return to class, however; then the next Thursday afternoon he did appear, suddenly, alone, to terrorize the room before two grown men could remove him. Even now (I've had the boy twice before) he may be bounced back.

Mary F. Greene and Orletta Ryan, *The Schoolchildren Growing Up in the Slums* (New York: Pantheon Books, Division of Random House, 1965), pp. 3–9, 11–13, 27–28, 30–38. Copyright © 1965. Reprinted by permission of the publisher.

3

The office is mobbed. Clerks are yelling at teachers and picking up phone calls from downtown about substitutes.

· · · ·

Now some hard eye has caught the clock and "Omigod, look, kids!" purses are snatched and snapped. "Toodles!"

Exit of many teachers to john, leaving Mrs. Eineman, who comes just a few minutes before school in the morning, examines her notices, and goes on to her room, where a quiet child has prepared her cup of tea. Mrs. Eineman has taught here several years, was a chemist, is married to a biochemist (though no one knows much else about her). Permissive methods, almost narrow about them. If a child throws a chair she calmly asks why; if a teacher rebukes a child of hers in line for swearing she may say, "Let him alone, he's disturbed." "But he said—" "Well if he wants to talk that way, let him."

Every child in her room has a favorite painter whose work they study from great portfolios Mrs. Eineman provides. She gives special gifts for holidays: cactus for Easter, for Christmas a Japanese pencil with a bell. She is successful with children, in this school one of the most successful.

I get into 33B just at the bell. Feet thundering by outside, I get the window down from the top, place pile of notices and junk on desk, unlock back door—but don't make it up front in time. Kicks, sharp pounds—the door's falling open as I reach my desk. The first mass of Ricardo, Jesus, Marshall, Pablo, rolls in. Someone's playing handball with Roberto's book; he's trying to get it, a lot of screaming and yelling going on in the back.

The moment each seat is filled, we begin: salute to the flag, review of days of the week and months of the year. While I take attendance, they review sums in math notebooks. All present but Danny Aguilez. This is the norm in these schools: perfect attendance or else prolonged truancies; for we are the "highest-paid baby sitters."

· · · ·

The mere reverberation of the door unsettles them, and voices break forth. "Miss Burke, Danny Aguilez he been made a monitor!" "He cursed you, but Mr. Zang still gi' him a merit card, Miss

Burke!" "They have to. Danny gets mad like he is now." "You fulla crap, man, Danny in sixt' gra' today." Children are getting out of their seats. "*Silence,* please! Everybody in their seats. *Not another word about Danny.*" But I have to walk into the aisles beginning to fill with gum wrappers, scraps of paper. Nobody's done more than three or four problems ("I don't know these, I can'"). Some heads on desks. A few are staring moodily out at the rain. Miguel Rodriguez pulls at my skirt as I pass. "Miss Burke, my mama say tell you she wan' you to fill out those papers, them teet' t'ing I gotta—" "You'll have to come up to the desk, Miguel. . . . All right. For the what?" "For the Googy Clin'—" "For the Gug-gen-heim Clinic. Repeat it, Miguel: Gug-gen-heim." "Googy . . ."

I'm occupied, so a fight starts. Three more minutes breaking this up, two to restore order, and monitors are just passing out phonics workbooks when Mr. Spane's morning voice suddenly fills the air above us. It is time for announcements. I have to go into the aisles—the children are talking and laughing freely now, and do so throughout Spane.

"Good morning, boys and girls! This is your old friend and principal, Mr. Spane. So sit tall and hearken, all!

(Pause.) "Well, Mr. Spane made a mistake, boys and girls. He left his glasses at home, and didn't see that the first message was for the teachers."

(Class is now thumbing noses and throwing fist-and-finger signs to the amplifier. "What's he talkin about?" "I can' hear him!" "I don' wanna hear him!")

"Come on then, teachers, sit tall! Mr. Pickard, I see you! Come 'way from that shelf of yummy cakes you're baking—Mr. Spane sees you! Sit tall, Miss Skally, Mrs. Eineman! You hard-working ladies are always trying to do two things at once! *I'm talking to every teacher in our school.*"

One notice escaped me; I was busy calming children in back, trying to keep their noise from bouncing off the amplifier back into his office. Another notice bubbled away, concerning "the Law . . . well-spring of Li-ber-ty. Hearken, teachers, because all supervisors and teachers will celebrate Law Day by appropriate classroom observances . . . to foster an abiding respect for law . . . moral strength. . . . Oh, just a minute. That's not until next month. *Law Day*, teachers—but all right, forget this *for the nonce*, teachers. Just Mr. Spicer and Miss Bolby see me during the week on this—y'there, Spicer? And that's all, teachers, for the nonce.

· · · ·

By the time we've got Mr. Spane off the networks, it's 9:45. School has been in session for forty-five minutes. Phonics starts behind time, but as most children now know initial and final consonants, a slight calm descends. The faster group is at work writing, the slower working orally with me. Then another messenger. (Crash.) Every shaky kid jumps up, drops what he's doing. "Heyyy, tha' Black Angel, he in sixt' gra'," they cry.

· · · ·

Luce, who's found the right beginning page, is called on first today.[1] She is a pretty and intelligent child—stands up, rather pale this cold morning in a thin nylon dress. She wears pierced earrings like most of the little girls, a rain jacket all winter, has frequent asthma attacks, often is sniffling and sick-looking, but doesn't stay out of school. Luce takes a book home every night; privately, she has confided to me that she'd like to read well enough by the end of this semester to take home a book on nurses. "Here is Ted, here is Sally," she begins. Mutterings start at once. Hands in the air.

"You will not rudely interrupt Luce while she is reading."

"Aw, *she* can' read." "You can' read neither." "Lemme read." "Mis' Burke, I don' know what page we on." "I can' keep place, she read too fas'." "Someone stole my book, it's gone." A book is slammed shut. One kid gets up and walks out.

Luce wanders back: "Ted and Sally are going to—, to—" She looks up sadly. "Miss Burke, I read this in first grade."

"Yes, I know, dear, you've had this in your hands since first grade, but you've never learned to read it. If we had more of some other easy book in the bookroom, we'd use them, but we don't. Let's go on. . . . If you don't know the word, is there a

---

[1] The Language Arts manual says there should be silent reading and denies the value of reading aloud for its own sake. But these bilingual children with their many special problems profit from frequent reading aloud.

picture clue?" She plods ahead (through a thicket of whispers: "He cursed my mother." "This page is ripped out." "Can I go to the washroom?") because she's a sweet child; then falters, can't look at the words any longer. When her eyes lift, they contain the week-end: eight people in two rooms reeking with fried food, strangled at the end of four flights up. Babies, curses, TV mumbling, the people sitting as if drunk or dead, or else screaming shrill abuse. The stairs have trails of garbage, urine, even excrement.

Luce is now staring as in a trance, and she's permitted to sit down again this first hour. Edmund, who's been wildly waving, takes her place.

"Sally go."

"Sit down, Edmund. You're on the wrong page. Roberto." For two minutes Roberto reads beautifully, with such expression that the children listen.

"Now, who can tell what the story was about today? And how can it help us in our lives?" Hands wave, "I know, I know," and a satisfactory answer is given ("Be kind to your friends and share things"). "Good. Now we'll report on our library books. Manuel."

Manuel jumps up, dropping his book with a loud crash, on purpose. "Mis' Burke, Marshall cursed my mother." "Man, whut I say was . . ." A fight starts, kicking off noisy smaller fights across the room where children had been working quietly on their own, and for two minutes all work has to stop and "Heads down" until it's quiet.

"All right. The boys and girls who are writing may go back to their work. Marshall, tell about your book."

Thickset Marshall shoves something in his pocket, slides to his feet, giving his neighbor a kick on the way up. And stands grinning with no book.

"Sit down, Marshall. Israel."

Israel looks at the floor and scuffs his too-big shoes. "Where is your book, Israel? It's a library book. . . . Please see me after school today."

. . . .

It is now nearly 10:30 and no Mrs. Abernathy. I put the faster group on reading workbooks, her slower group on their assign-ment. Mrs. Abernathy is Corrective Reading Teacher. Mr. Yount is Reading Improvement Teacher. Both were very helpful for some time. Then Mr. Yount dropped off (he's been hiding out, studying for assistant-principal exams in his office most of the school day), and Mrs. Abernathy began coming late.

Mrs. Abernathy is conscientious, brings special teaching aids to her work, and knows the teaching of reading, but has become very uneasy toward the children since she began coming late. She has been in P.S. 200 for several years. She's hit the circle that awaits the sensitive teacher—can't take any more, will quit if she isn't let out of the classroom. She becomes a specialist or supervisor. A less competent teacher takes her place. My slower reading group is scheduled for 33J, a big classroom. Mrs. Aber-nathy is supposed to take them out of the room. But lately, her friends Miss Perez, Mrs. Rumstedt, Mr. Kaplan have taken to holding "curriculum meetings" (which develop into coffee and cigarette breaks) in 33J.

There is not much I can do. Mr. Zang drives Mrs. Abernathy to school in the mornings. She's also grown very critical. Amy Katz said, "She's been getting in on that coffeepot in 33J, that's all. That's why she's been so critical lately."

But she wouldn't look at the papers. And even though her group is reading aloud because she is late, I expect trouble this morning.

It's still some minutes before we hear her calling from the door, "Good morning, children! Are we ready to take a trip?" Books slam shut—no trouble there—as she continues, gliding briskly to the back of the room, "Yes, we're 'going to the country' with Ted and Sally, where we'll see many wonderful things we can't in the city! And someone else is going today, I believe—Ted and Sally's puppy, who'll meet a friendly new animal in the country! Are we ready for the fun? All aboard! . . . Now, who'll bring Mrs. Abernathy her chair?" Big haul of chairs on all fours, rear-ward—new diversion, which gets everyone excited. "Don' you touch my a'm, man, I warnin you." "Don't curse my mother!" "I'm bringing the chair; you brought it yesterday."

"We're on a *train* now, boys and girls! Let's lock our lips and throw the key away out the window!" Mrs. Abernathy calls, putting up primer charts "The Puppy and the Rabbit" for these eleven-year-olds, most of whom were born in the United States and started kindergarten at five years.

The hubbub begins: emotionally shaky children who can't read doing phonics in front, even shakier but slower children being told in back, "Let's open to the picture of the train getting itself all ready to leave its home, the station. It's taking Ted and Sally and Tuffy *to the country!* It's a *happy* train. How can we tell? . . . well, just look at the big smile it's wearing on its engine! Who knows what the engine does?"

"Miz' Abby, we awready had dis story today."

"Mrs. Ab-er-nathy, Marshall."

"Mis' Abio, we had about that puppy-rabbit in a country today."

"No, no, Miguel, you're thinking of another puppy we had such fun with last month. That was another book. Who can tell the name of the reader we're reading now?" The fifteen who are adding suffixes to root words are now stirring, giggling, and twisting up front, trying to fishhook their friends' eyes out of the slow group in back. Abernathy's rimless glasses seem to rotate slowly before fixing themselves on me.

"You've been through the story, Miss Burke?"

"Well, we went as far as—"

"You've conducted them far enough that initial expectation can no longer be aroused?"

"Mrs. Abernathy, there *is* no—yes . . . we have been through it."

"Well, children . . . we'll just have to start over again. Could you give me the page number, Miss Burke?"

Meanwhile they've found the initial-expectation page all right. Resistance is shaping in a solid, muttering child wall. "*I* ain' readin dis story again." "I ain' *nevah* goin look at it again." "I hate Ted, I hate ol' Sally more. Who cares about that ol' red wagon and kitten they drag aroun' in it." "I rea' it today, and rea' it in firs' gra'."

Fifteen minutes later, front: we're adding *ing* to root words. "If Ted rides, Roderigo, he is—?" "Riding." "Good. Call on another child, Roderigo." Rear: "*Frame* the word. Finger on each side. Now what do you see? What do you see?—Just a moment. Are you on the right page, Carmacita?" The room is suppressed uproar. Abernathy is wearing a smile like a tied-on bandage. No trouble about the noise, though. Noise doesn't exist. Interruptions permissively treated. "Marshall, what do *you* see?" "Mis' Abernath', Marshall took my pencil." "I *ain'* took, he *trade* for his yo-yo wi' me, Miz Abby." (Handbook: "We must give scope and understanding to that intense and growing *éthique* of the fourth-grader.") At times the back of the room seems to have swung around entirely with a big clatter of chairs, clockwise. To add to everything else, the hall door's been left open. Abernathy's girl friend, Svenson, and another teacher outside: "Yes . . . Ninety-first Street outlet . . . I hear they have some pretty good stuff there."

"Bianca, please close the door."

But Mrs. Abernathy rises, carrying today's glacial smile upward, and glides. *"Please,* Miss Burke." All the slow-group books bang shut behind her. Svenson leans in as her boss approaches. "So you need anything else, Mrs. Abernathy?"

"No, Mrs. Svenson, we're all aboard for the country—our train's just a little late pulling out.—No, I'll see you later about that whole problem. Thank you for waiting."

Teacher: "Workbooks, Mrs. Abernathy? We've needed them for a week."

Dirty look from Svenson, who lists it, however, and sends down Pablo with a note. Svenson-teacher conversation resumes outside. Carlos returns with the wrong workbooks.

"All right. We'll start with these, boys and girls. They're one grade behind us so they should be really easy. Monitors, see if you can pass these out quietly."

"We can' do this kin' work," they say immediately. "These too hard for us." "I ain' gonna work this workbook."

"No, these aren't the *right* workbooks, boys and girls, but let's use them as a little review. Let's settle down and be happy."

Mrs. Abernathy's hearing has suddenly returned to her. Long, gray raised eybrows from the back. "Really, Miss Burke, they read *very* well. Beautiful reading experience in here one day last week—let me see—Wednesday! Let's not forget to praise them when it's due, Miss Burke."

"Mrs. Abernathy, there's scarcely a child in this room who can read fifty words. Few of them work; they can't read."

"They've been *well* taught, Miss Burke. All our teachers are doing their best."

"Their files said 3.1 when I started, you mean? Then why didn't they know *a, e, i, o,* and *u?*"

All the children are now out of their seats and talking; I've let my temper slip and it's too late. But Mrs. Abernathy arm-gathers materials and glides in perfect calm to the door. "Mrs. Abernathy, there *is* a certain resistance to learning here," I say to her through the din.

"We have one or two children that don't apply themselves, but really it's a beautiful class," she firmly answers. "I'll be back on Friday, boys and girls, to hear about the library books. But Roberto, let's remember, dear, to ask the librarian if she has some other kind of story than Bible books. The story of Moses finding the baby was very colorful and exciting, but we come from many different religious backgrounds. Let's find stories we can all share."

To me: "They're underprivileged but teachable, Miss Burke. We're here for the children and for no other reason."

Miss Moyle, an O.P.T. teacher (supplementary teachers who relieve the regular classroom teacher), comes in at 11:00 for social studies. These children are scheduled to study (the syllabus says they *do* study) math, social studies, science, music, and art, although they can't read. Miss Moyle is very amiable with teachers, recently engaged, salt-and-pepper gray in her hair, and happy.

．　．　．　．

"Now put everything away and sit tall. How many children know what the Atlantic Ocean is?—Put that away.—Today we're going to play a game to learn many wonderful things about the Atlantic Ocean. Let's say that together, children . . . that's right . . . once again, rounding our lips when we say 'O-cean'—good! fine!—and about Manhattan Island on which we live. Manhattan Island is in the Atlantic Ocean. Now who knows what an eye-land is?" (Eyes not exactly where she wants them but wandering from sparkler, to dapper suited front, to graying hair.)

"Now some of us are going to come up front—no, no, not until Miss Moyle calls on just four *quiet* children who don't leave seats until she says—and join hands.

"Put that away. I want your eyes looking at *me*.

"All right: you, you, you, my dear, and you. Now a fifth child. That child is to have a very important part in our play. *We're going to make our own Manhattan Island.* I'm going to look for the very tallest and ready-est . . . Edwin! Very well, Edwin, you may come up front too. (Put that away. I don't want to speak to you again.) Edwin is going to be Manhattan Island.

"—I'm going to send you—this girl—back to your seat if you can't play your part gently. Edwin, haven't you got a hanky, dear? You should use a hanky for that.

"Again, mouse steps back and forth! Now what is it we're looking at, children in seats? What are Edwin and the four children pouring back and forth on him, showing us?"

Silence. Deep contemplation. Four answers are garnered from the room:

"Hol' hans'."

"Play house?"

"——" (in Spanish, which "elicits" big, general dirty laugh).

"Ring-aroun'-a-rosy."

Last month, one solid month, was the Community. ". . . The Community is made up of many wonderful workers. Can anyone name a worker? No one? Surely someone knows the name of *one* kind of worker. Good, I knew you did! All right, that little boy."

"Policeman."

"Good. What does the policeman do?"

"He'p us."

"Good! *Fine! How* does he help us?"

"He our fren'."

"Yes, good, but *how* is he our friend? *How* does he help us?"

Lots of trouble on this one. Much time consumed. Finally, something like "he'p a los' chil' fin' he way home," is "elicited."

"Good! *Very* good! Now let's think of some other kinds of workers. Who can name another kind of wonderful worker?"

"Policeman," answer several together.

"Yes, but still another kind! We'd have a funny kind of Community, wouldn't we, if we were *all* policemen?" Frowns, sulks, drop toward apathy again.

"Let's put on our thinking caps. *All* the kinds of wonderful workers we know. What about people who help us learn many wonderful things? What kind of workers are they?" Silence . . . "*There* goes a hand up. All right, little boy with the bandage. Can't you ask Mommy to change that bandage, dear? All right."

"Teach'."

"Good! And what good workers they are, too, your wonderful teacher here, and me, and Mr. Zang and Mrs. Abernathy—how really *hard* we work, don't we?"

Fireman, Nurse, even Jim the Friendly Street Cleaner, each in turn is elicited. Then on to a cloudier side of the subject. "What about *our own parents*, who work so hard to care for us? What kind of work do *they* do?" Many children really don't know what she's talking about. A few have fallen to dreaming again. "Well, what about *our fathers*? Don't our fathers work so *very* hard, coming home at the end of day all tired but happy, too, because they've been working to earn money for our food and clothes?" This reminds them of lunch. "Good! *I* see a hand that knows the answer!" "Miss Moily, w'en bell time?"

"Quite soon, dear. Now everyone *think*. Thinking caps on tight, pulled *way* down for a cold, cold day, down to our *ears*. *What kind of work do our fathers do?*" Not six fathers in the room do any kind of work, as Moily might know if she kept her eyes open coming along ——th Street in the morning. But on she goes, question and hint, probe and nonelicit. Finally lets it drop, provisionally.

"But *someone* in our family works, or we wouldn't *be* here with our food and clothes, would we, we wouldn't have *any*thing! Who in our family works?" Mommy. "But then, what does Mommy do, all day, what *kind* of work, when she goes away and doesn't come home until sunset time?" Three minutes produce two mommies who work in the garment district, one who works stringing jewelry. "Fine! *Very* good! How interesting and wonderful a talk we've had this morning, boys and girls. And now it's time for l—— . . . for Miss Moyle to go.

"But first, Miss Moyle wants each child to do something for her. Each child is to go home and search in the newspaper tonight for a picture of a wonderful worker. Someone in our big wonderful city on Manhattan Island, who's doing some kind of work. For example: a picture of a worker in the *garment district* working: how wonderfully and carefully she's pulling her needle in and out of the cloth that will turn into trousers for a little boy or skirt for a little girl. Take notebook paper; use one side only; paste neatly just at each corner. And one more thing. How many think they can write a nice sentence, telling what the worker in the picture is working at?" (No child in this room could write a full sentence. But every hand flies up.) "Good, *good!* I knew that's what you'd like to do for Miss Moyle. And she'll be back tomorrow at eleven o'clock"—heading for the door—"to see how intelligent you are. I know we're going to have some won——"

2 RETREAT FROM LEARNING

JOAN DUNN

Just as a chain is only as strong as its weakest link, the teacher is successful in his job only to the degree that he is successful with the dullest pupil. Teaching depends upon, lives on, and wins or loses by its students as the success of a play depends upon the audience. And the teaching carried on in a large high school simply cannot afford to register a mere *succès d'estime*. Teaching comes down to the individual child, and the individual child, when you finally meet him, is likely to be very much like this one—this boy whose shoes are armed with metal cleats, who wears a heavy, many-zippered leather jacket and a pair of gloves thrust cavalierly through the shoulder straps. The gaping pockets of his Army fatigue trousers are used to stow his school supplies—a comb, cigarettes, and a knife. He is savagely barbered, but his hair is not his only uncivilized attribute. He speaks:

"Waaaaa?"

"What are you doing in the hall?"

"Nuttin. Um gonna baetroom."

"Where's your pass? You know you need a pass to leave your class."

"Wa pass? I ain' got no pass."

"Where do you belong? Your teacher wouldn't let you leave the room without a pass."

"She din gimme no pass. She's crazy."

"All right. Back to class."

"Naaaaa. I ain' gawn back that stupid class. It's boring."

"I didn't ask for your opinion. I asked for your pass."

"I toll ya. I ain' got none."

"Don't raise your voice to me. What room did you come from?"

"One oh tree."

"I'll see you to the door."

Joan Dunn, *Retreat from Learning* (New York: David McKay Company, Inc., 1955), pp. 63–70, 99–107. Copyright © 1955. Reprinted by permission of the publisher.

"Don' do me no favors."

"The pleasure is all mine."

I am in luck. He comes, though grudgingly and with great mutterings of disgust. Hugging the wall, he slinks along behind me. He stops at the back door of a classroom.

"Wai' min. I gotta see my cousin."

"No you don't."

"Miiii. I mean it. I woon't kid ya. I gotta cousin."

"I don't doubt it, but this is not the time for family chats."

"Chats? Chats? Wazzat? I gotta talk ta him."

"Come on. Stop stalling."

"Look. Wha's wrong? I just stan' here, and when the bell rings, I meet my cousin. You don' needa wait. I won' make no noise."

"Don't try to make a deal with me. I'm taking you back to class."

"Why? Ha? Jus'tell me why."

"Because you're out without a pass."

"Since when ya needa pass to leave this class? Where am I—a concentration camp?"

"No. You're in school."

"You're tellin *me*."

"I certainly am."

"You won' lemme stay here—nice and quiet?"

"No."

"Ya don' trus' me."

"Absolutely not."

"I gotta go back?"

"Most emphatically."

"Yeah?"

"Yes."

He shrugs. We start again. I walk a little faster; he walks a little slower. Suddenly, he starts to sing.

"*Stop that noise.*"

"That ain' noise. I'm singin."

"Listen. I'm losing my patience. I want you to keep still and come with me. And not another sound out of you. Understand?"

"But—"

"And *no more arguments.* That's final."

"Ahright. Ahright. Don' get mad."

We start again.

"Just a minute. I gotta comb my hair."

He wets his comb at a drinking fountain. His classroom is right around the corner, and he hopes the bell will ring before I deliver him to the door.

"Now what are you doing?"

"I tol' ya. I'm just gonna comb my hair."

He moves to the door of the nearest classroom, and, using the pane of glass as a mirror, rearranges his startling coiffure.

"Get away from that door. And get into your own room. Quick."

"I donno where it is."

"It's right there. And if I see you in the hall again without a pass, I'll report you to the dean. Now, *get in*."

"Ahright. Ahright. Don' yell."

I open the door. The teacher looks at us inquiringly.

"I found this boy in the hall without a pass."

The teacher looks crestfallen. He had hoped "this boy" would be gone all period.

But let's look further. There is also, in every large city high school, a classroom or auditorium known as the Study Hall. Here is opportunity to observe how proficient some of our students are in interpreting social situations (*pace* Dewey), and how accurately they adapt themselves to differing personalities.

Our Study Hall was held in the school auditorium, located on the first floor just opposite the main entry—making it ridiculously easy to walk from "study" straight out the front door. There were five exits all told, not counting the wings of the stage. Into this hall were thrown one hundred and fifty students and two teachers for forty minutes a day, five days a week. But even this impossible situation had its amusing side, though most of the amusement is apparent only in retrospect. We were aware of Arthur before we discovered Mr. Belknap, so let him be introduced first. Arthur interpreted the social situation in the Study Hall immediately upon arriving and within a few days had organized his clique, all dilettantes like himself who never cut Study Hall, for where Arthur was, there their hearts were also. It was apparent that he was going to play the part for all it was worth when he made his first entrance through the side door at the front of the hall, wearing baby-blue pistol pants, a gray Homburg, and an undershirt. He had a mane of yellow hair that combined with his staring eyes and slack mouth to give him a distressingly vague look. He was recognized immediately by his following, and there welled up a great tribal shout of joy, to which Arthur responded by opening his arms in a fond paternal gesture and shouting, "Um here. Um here."

Most of us in charge of the hall waged a constant battle with him (he disrupted the group every time he appeared, he argued about everything that we said whether it concerned him or not, and, worst of all, he *was* funny) that left us verging on nervous exhaustion but did not bother Arthur in the least. He adapted to us by ignoring us.

Arthur and Co. came to study every day because they were having so much fun. A typical period would be one in which Arthur arrived five or ten minutes late (thereby giving his audience time to arrive, get settled, glance at *The News*) and then proceeded, in a loud voice, to volunteer numerous excuses for not being on time. This exchange was always audible to the front rows of the Hall, and so his *bons mots* were passed back with successive howls of appreciative laughter until the place echoed with it. Such sallies as "My wife made me wash the dishes," or "I wuz dreamin' about ya, Mrs. Beal, an I didn' wanna wake up," were always well received. After about five minutes of preliminary jokes, he would flop down into a seat, hang his legs over the chair in front, burrow down until his head rested on the back rest—and sing. Arthur's songs were always of the melancholy, she-done-me-wrong persuasion, and it was easy to see why. He was unkempt and walked with a peculiar flat-footed gait. He was everybody's funny friend, a great shaggy dog. If you spoke to Arthur tactfully about the advantages of silence or about keeping his feet off the chair in front of him, he would banter with you, and his favorite reply, delivered in slurred speech from his lounging position, was "You're a doll." If you persisted in this serious attempt to silence him and he saw that he could not charm you into abandoning your stand, he might say, simply, "O.K. I be good," draw his hat down over his face, and sleep again, still draped over the furniture. For the rest of the period there would be silence, except when Arthur snored or let out a great belch. This endeared him to his following (they liked to think he had the common failings), and they would hoot so appreciatively that the great man would awaken, look around groggily, and shift his position. Once in a while he would call loudly for food—"Um hongry!"—and one of his lackeys would fetch potato chips or a sandwich to satisfy him. Add to Arthur one hundred and forty-nine other children in various degrees of disorder, and you get the picture.

It was shortly before Arthur left us. (I believe he was traded to another high school. The State Education Law prevents children from leaving high school until they are seventeen, when they may do so with their parents' consent, and consequently two schools frequently exchange one "character" for another. The gain is always mutual.) We teachers who were assigned to the Study Hall had approached the administration for another teacher to help us. Arthur alone consumed all our energy, and a few of his following must have been practicing at home, for they showed signs of picking up where Arthur left off. We learned with amazement that there had been another teacher assigned with us since the beginning of the term—Mr. Belknap, a short, wizened old man who taught one of those practical courses supposed to fit adolescents for the future, in which they spent successive terms learning to distinguish one kind of clothing material from another, and mastered other practical, nonacademic skills. Well, we decided to look for Mr. Belknap, and a few days later we found him, sitting behind a newspaper at the rear of the auditorium where he had been keeping his daily vigil in solitary and supreme indifference. He was annoyed but not embarrassed at being discovered, and he excused himself by saying, "I was told by someone higher up that I could take it easy this term." Once flushed out of his cover, Mr. Belknap agreed to take the roll occasionally, but his heart was not in it. He returned to his retreat in the back of the room, lowering his newspaper only occasionally to chuckle at a remark of Arthur's that particularly amused him.

The day Arthur left us was a great occasion. The school orchestra was rehearsing on the stage, and while earnest young musicians rushed in and out with music stands, an ingenious child was putting a key in the electric switch so that every few minutes the lights would dim and then come up again. The teacher leading the orchestra would rap for attention, and just then down would go the lights and the kids would shout and stamp as people do when the movie projector breaks down. Bear in mind that Study Hall was still in session amid this confusion and we were calling the roll—nearly shouting ourselves over the din. Then in stamped Arthur, paper in hand, hair tossing, and announced to the world at large that he was being "signed out" of study. He sincerely mourned our loss.

"Um leavin. Um goin. Will ya miss me? Sure ya will. For who will be wit ya when Um far away, when Um far away from you? Good-by. Good-by."

He leaped onto the stage and called his last words to us over the mournful sound of tuning up. "God bless you all," he cried, and accompanied his farewell with a flourish of his gray Homburg and many blown kisses.

. . . .

The bell sounded loudly, and there was a rush to stand up all at once.

"Don't leave this room until 'America' is sung."

There were groans from the class. It was not a desire to be strict that prompted my demand; it was an attempt to establish order. I did not want them to shoot into the hall while they were still slightly hysterical, for this spirit would stay with them all day long. They stood reluctantly, awkwardly, and sang feebly; the children in my first class were already piling up outside the door, peering in quizzically—they loved to see another class being punished. As soon as the stanza was finished, my perfect class bolted for the doors, and in the split second while the room was empty between shifts, I caught a glimpse of it, vacant and disordered as if it had lain in the path of a stampede. Motes of dust danced in the higher bars of sunlight, and there was not one straight row of chairs in the room. Sam dashed in the back door, down the aisle, seized his books, and raced out the front door, nearly colliding with a slight, serious-faced boy on his way in. They backed away from each other in silence.

"Get rid of the dog?" I shouted after Sam.

"Yeah," he called back.

The small boy seated himself, stacked his books neatly on the rack under his seat, folded his hands on the desk, and grinned. All the while he was doing these things, he kept his eyes riveted on me.

"Good morning, Louis. How's the world treating you today?"

"Swell, tanks."

"How's the girl friend?"

The grin extended.

"Swell, tanks."

"Good."

He continued to watch me. Suddenly, he said, "Oh, I forgot," got up, unzipped his padded cotton jacket, heaved it off his shoulders, and hung it over the back of his chair. I had to smile. He was the only one in this class who ever, willingly and without an argument, did anything I said, suggested, or demanded in the various realms of learning, behavior, or personal appearance. This was English 62G, the worst class I had this term. The rest of the indifferent scholars were now clanking in, a small group, to be sure, but a lively one. They sat down, sprawled into the aisles or hunched over the desks or extended back stiffly, preparatory to sleep; some looked dully out the window, a few made faces at one another, one or two looked indifferently at me and at the preparations I was trying to make for the lesson. I was writing a column of words on the board for vocabulary drill, but my progress was impeded by a knot of boys gathered in a front corner of the room, talking softly and seriously among themselves.

"Na, he don' know nuttin about it."

"Dat's not what I heard."

"I only tol' ya what my fren' said."

"Listen, stupid, if you can't keep ya fat mout' shut, so help me, I'll break ya head."

"I din' tell him, Frank, I *sweah* I din'."

"Don' gimme dat."

The bell rang.

"Sit down, please, gentlemen."

In this first word to the class, just as in all subsequent words, there was no sarcasm in my voice. I spoke to them formally, brightly, coaxingly, as if they were children to be enticed into entering an exciting adult world. It was only through the use of an idiom completely unknown to them, delivered in a calm, soft voice, that the barest control could be exercised; when I yelled, they knew I was truly angry. I spoke my language to them. They spoke theirs to me.

"In a minute, ha?"

"Now."

"Um talkina my fren'. Whatsa harm, ha?"

"None, just sit down."

The principal speaker sighed elaborately and turned to dismiss his cronies: "See yez later." The group dispersed, walking slowly and emphatically on cleated soles to their seats.

"Quiet, please. Take out your notebooks and put them on the desk. Take out your pens as well. We're going to have a little vocabulary drill today."

Not a movement was made. Louis was the only one in the class who carried a book, and his was already on the desk. This was all part of the game we played, E62G and I. We pretended to be teacher and students; everyone in the class was a serious disciplinary problem and would tolerate teachers only if they spoke softly and demanded nothing.

I pointed to the word at the top of the list.

"Can anyone pronounce this word?"

The boy in the last seat in the second row stretched his arms above his head, yawned deeply, closed his eyes, and sank back upon his spine.

"Does anyone know what the word means?"

One boy hissed at another, "Wha'time?" and got the leisurely answer, "Nine oh tree. Half hour to go." The questioner started tapping on his desk with a key.

"Stop the noise, Medina."

Medina exhaled loudly.

"Does anyone *care* what the word means?"

Louis grinned.

"Do you care, Marvin?"

"Wa?"

"Get your head off the desk and maybe you'll hear something."

"Ha?"

"Wake up, Marvin, and tell me what you think about the word up there. Are you awake?"

"Yeah."

"All right. What about the word?"

"Whea?"

"There."

"*That woid?*"

"*That* woid."

"Nuttin!"

"That isn't the word."

"Yeah. I know. That's what I tink."

There was loud, exaggerated laughter. Marvin, pleased, rubbed sleep out of his eyes.

"Well, now, we're on the right track. You're thinking. Now think about that word—that one."

"O.K."

"Good man."

"I can't say it."

"Do you want me to say it for you?"

"Yeah."

"Yes, Miss Dunn?"

"Yes, Mrs. Dunn."

"*Ex*-quisite."

He continued to stare at the board uncomprehendingly.

"*Ex*-quisite, Marvin."

"Oh."

"Yes."

A pause.

"Ya *sure?*"

I laughed. "Yes, I'm sure."

Another pause.

"Ex*quis*ite." A long silence. "Dat's da ting ya put fires out wit'," he announced with finality.

They howled. Someone yelled, "Sure, a fire ex*quis*ite like dey got in da hall. What a jerk!"

"Don't be so quick to comment, O'Rourke. He tried harder than you did."

"He's stupid."

"He might say the same thing about you someday."

"Let him try. I'll *drop* him."

"While you're waiting, why not try the next word."

"Na, I don' know it."

Marvin had gone to sleep again, and O'Rourke had gone sullen. He resumed his pencil-tapping.

"And put that pencil down."

He slammed it on the desk.

We glared at one another as I walked to the front window and pushed it open. I stayed there, at the side of the room, for it occasionally calmed them down if they did not see a teacher in front of them.

"Come on now, wake up, all of you. Pay attention. Shumacher, take the next word."

"I caen' see da woid."

"Turn around and look at the board. It's not out the window."

"I caen read ya writin."

"Stop stalling Shumacher. You can read a comic book at forty paces. Spell it out."

"Ac-c-om-pli-sh. Uhcomplish."

"Well?"

"Well, what?"

"Know what it means?"

"No."

"I'll use it in a sentence for you. 'The tired worker could not accomplish his task.' It's a verb."

"So what?"

"Do you know what a verb is, Schumacher?"

"No."

"It shows action," Louis sang out.

"Listen to the fruit," said O'Rourke viciously.

"And I'm sick of listening to you and your language, O'Rourke. One more word out of you, just *one more word,* and I'll get you into more trouble than you've ever seen before. Understand?"

He muttered something under his breath and sank lower in the seat.

"I asked you a question. Do you understand how I want you to behave in here, O'Rourke?"

"Yeah."

"Yes, Miss Dunn."

"Yes, Miss Dunn."

"Now, look, Anthony. Pay attention to me. If the man is tired, he cannot work as hard as he could if he were not tired. He can't accomplish what he sets out to do. What is a word meaning the same thing as accomplish?"

"Woik?"

"Well, not quite. It's nearer the idea of trying to complete something, to finish it."

"Stupid. Why do we hafta learn big woids? Whyncha say 'do'? Means the same thing."

"Not quite."

"So who cares? I say a woid like dat an all my fren's laugh at me. *Nobody* know what dat woid means."

"I do."

"You're a teacher."

"Too true. But I know more than that. I know, for instance, that Mr. Santangelo at the rear of the room has a comic book under the desk and is trying to read it. Pay attention here, August. English is a fascinating study."

"Ha?"

"Never mind. Just put the jokes away."

"Hey, Miss Dunn. I know whatta woid mean. Accomplish is a thing tha tells ya the direction when ya lost inna woods."

Marvin had not slept at all, it now appears, but had sprawled there all this while, hunched over his desk, still thinking. In attempting to repeat his victory of earlier in the period, he had been successful beyond his wildest imaginings. Heads were flung back, feet stamped on the floor, and that was the end of the vocabulary drill. Too little interest had turned into too much.

I had planned to read for the second half of the period. A quick glance at the clock (I could see it through the glass pane in the back door) told me that there were fifteen minutes left in the period, and for a moment I did not know if it was worth the effort to begin. But then, if not that, what? The mayhem could not continue.

"Sam and Ira. Give out the books please."

"Oh, *no.*"

"Oh, yes. Come on. On the double."

"Yes, sir, Captain Dunn, sir."

"Less comedy and more action, Ira."

He got up and walked to the back of the room, trailing his fingers along the desks as he went.

"All right, now. Calm down, gentlemen."

But the restlessness that was concentrated in separate parts of the room, the boredom and the indifference obvious in individuals, had coalesced during the sportive vocabulary drill. As far as work was concerned, the period was already over. But they had to do something; if it turned out to be something constructive, so much to the good. My two monitors were gleefully tossing books on desks.

"Hey, Louie, catch."

"Don' trow school property, stupid."

"Ya caen' read anyhow."

"I might loin some day."

"Shut up."

"Quiet, please."

"Yeah, stupid, yabotherna teacher. Ain he a joik, Miss Dunn?"

It was about 9:15 A.M., and I was already weary. Banging the ruler on the desk a few times, I continued to call for quiet. Called for and did not get. I picked up my copy of the book, opened it to the right place, and stood, waiting. Finally, everyone had a book placed before him on the desk.

"Open to page 104."

"Do we *hafta* read this?"

"Yes. Page 104."

"Why?"

"Why what?"

"*Why* do we hafta read this?"

"Because I say so."

For the rest of the period, I read to them from a book called *Son of the Middle Border,* an ornately written, detailed story of life on a Midwestern farm during the Civil War period. Most of the class considered the hero a "creep." The rest were not aware that there was a book being read.

The bell finally rang. For the first time, they were all looking at me, expectantly.

"All right. Pass the books to the back of the room and go."

They got up in one noisy bloc and made for the doors.

3   HOW CHILDREN FAIL

JOHN HOLT

I can't get Nell out of my mind. When she talked with me about fractions today, it was as if her mind rejected understanding. Isn't this unusual? Kids often resist understanding, make no effort to understand; but they don't often grasp an idea and then throw it way. Do they? But this seemed to be what Nell was doing. Several times she would make a real effort to follow my words, and did follow them, through a number of steps. Then, just as it seemed she was on the point of getting the idea, she would shake her head and say, "I don't get it." Can a child have a vested interest in failure? What on earth could it be? Martha, playing the number game, often acts the same way. She does not understand, does not want to understand, does not listen when you are explaining, and then says, "I'm all mixed up."

There may be a connection here with *producer-thinker* strategies. [We used the word *producer* to describe the student who was only interested in getting right answers, and who made more or less uncritical use of rules and formulae to get them; we called *thinker* the student who tried to think about the meaning, the reality, of whatever it was he was working on.] A student who jumps at the right answer and misses often falls back into defeatism and despair because he doesn't know what else to do. The thinker is more willing to plug on.

It is surprising to hear so many of these kids say, "I'm dumb." I thought this kind of thing came later, with the bogey, adolescence. Apparently not.

My room group did fairly well today at the number game. [At certain periods, two-thirds of the class was away at art or shop classes, and the rest stayed with me for "room period," a special class, invented by Bill Hull. We met in a small room just off the classroom. There we played various kinds of intellectual games,

John Holt, *How Children Fail* (New York: Pitman Publishing Corporation, 1964), Chapter I. Copyright © 1964. Reprinted by permission of the publisher.

did puzzles, and held discussions in a way as little like ordinary classroom work as possible. On this occasion we played a game like Twenty Questions, in which the teacher thinks of a number, and the students try to find it by asking questions to which the teacher may answer "Yes" or "No."] Laura was consistently the poorest asker of questions. It happened that on several occasions her turn came when the choice of numbers had been narrowed down to three or four, and she guessed the number. This made her feel that she was the official number-guesser for the day. In one game she made her first guess at an individual number when there were still twelve numbers left to choose from—obviously a poor move. Once she guessed, others started doing the same, and wasted four turns on it. Later on Mary got the idea that she was a mind reader, and started trying to guess the numbers from the beginning. The rest of her team became infected with this strategy for a while, before they went back to the plan of closing in on the number.

On the whole they were poised and collected and worked well as a team, though they didn't eliminate enough numbers at a turn. Thus, knowing that the number was between 250 and 300, they would say, "Is it between 250 and 260?" instead of taking a larger bite.

Nancy played well; but after a point the tension of the game got to be too much for her, and her mind just stopped working. She didn't get frantic, like Nell or Martha, or make fantastic guesses; she just couldn't think of anything to say, and so said nothing. A safe policy.

Intelligence is a mystery. We hear it said that most people never develop more than a very small part of their latent intellectual capacity. Probably not; but *why* not? Most of us have our engines running at about ten percent of their power. Why no more? And how do some people manage to keep revved up to twenty percent or thirty percent of their full power—or even more?

What turns the power off, or keeps it from ever being turned on?

During these past four years at the Colorado Rocky Mountain School my nose has been rubbed in the problem. When I started, I thought that some people were just born smarter than others and that not much could be done about it. This seems to be the official line of most of the psychologists. It isn't hard to believe, if all your contacts with students are in the classroom or the psychological testing room. But if you live at a small school, seeing students in class, in the dorms, in their private lives, at their recreations, sports, and manual work, you can't escape the conclusion that some people are much smarter part of the time than they are at other times. Why? Why should a boy or girl, who under some circumstances is witty, observant, imaginative, analytical, in a word, *intelligent,* come into the classroom and, as if by magic, turn into a complete dolt?

The worst student we had, the worst I have ever encountered, was in his life outside the classroom, as mature, intelligent, and interesting a student as anyone at the school. What went wrong? Experts muttered to his parents about brain damage—a handy way to end a mystery that you can't explain otherwise. Somewhere along the line, his intelligence became disconnected from his schooling. Where? Why?

This past year I had some terrible students. I failed more kids, mostly in French and Algebra, than did all the rest of the teachers in the school together. I did my best to get them through, goodness knows. Before every test we had a big cram session of practice work, politely known as "review." When they failed the exam, we had post-mortems, then more review, then a make-up test (always easier than the first), which they almost always failed again.

I thought I knew how to deal with the problem: make the work interesting and the classroom a lively and enthusiastic place. It was, too, some of the time at least; many of these failing students actually liked my classes. Overcome children's fear of saying what they don't understand, and keep explaining until they do understand. Keep a steady and resolute pressure on them. These things I did. Result? The good students stayed good, and some may have got better; but the bad students stayed bad, and some of them seemed to get worse. If they were failing in November they were still failing in June. There must be a better answer. Maybe we can prevent kids from becoming chronic failers in the first place.

Observing in Bill Hull's Class

In today's work period three or four people came up to you for help. All were stuck on that second math problem. None of them had made any effort to listen when you were explaining it at the board. I had been watching George, who had busied himself during the explanation by trying, with a pencil, to ream and countersink a hole in the side of his desk, all the while you were talking. He indignantly denied this. I showed him the hole, which silenced him. Gerald was in dreamland; so for the most part was Nancy, though she made a good recovery when asked a question. Unusual for her. Don listened about half the time, Laura about the same. Martha amused herself by turning her hand into an animal and having it crawl around her desk.

Watching older kids study, or try to study, I saw after a while that they were not sufficiently self-aware to know when their minds had wandered off the subject. When, by speaking his name, I called a daydreamer back to earth, he was always startled, not because he had thought I wouldn't notice that he had stopped studying, but because *he* hadn't noticed.

Except by inflicting real pain on myself, I am never able to stay awake when a certain kind of sleepiness comes over me. The mind plays funny tricks at such times. I remember my own school experience of falling asleep in class while listening to the teacher's voice. I used to find that the "watchman" part of my mind that was saying, "Keep awake, you fool!" would wake me when the teacher's voice began to fade. But the part of my mind that wanted or needed sleep was not so easily beaten. It used to (and still does) counterfeit a voice, so that as I fell asleep an imaginary voice continued to sound in my head, long enough to fool me until the watchman no longer had the power to awaken me. The watchman learned, in turn, that this counterfeit voice was liable to be talking about something different, or pure nonsense, and thus learned to recognize it as counterfeit. Many times, I have dozed off with a voice sounding inside my head, only to have the watchman say, "Hey! Wake up! That voice is a phoney!"

Most of us have very imperfect control over our attention. Our minds slip away from duty before we realize that they are gone. Part of being a good student is learning to be aware of the state of one's own mind and the degree of one's own understanding. The good student may be one who often says that he does not understand, simply because he keeps a constant check on his understanding. The poor student, who does not, so to speak, watch himself trying to understand, does not know most of the time whether he understands or not. Thus the problem is not to get students to ask us what they don't know; the problem is to make them aware of the difference between what they know and what they don't.

All this makes me think of Herb. I saw the other day why his words so often run off the paper. When he is copying a word, he copies about two letters at a time. I doubt whether he looks beyond them, or that he could tell you, in the middle of a word, what the whole word was. He has no idea, when he begins to copy a word, how long the word is going to be, or how much room it may take up.

I watched Ruth during the period of the Math test. At least four-fifths of the time she was looking out the window; or else she played with her pencil, or chewed her fingernails, or looked at Nell to see what information she might pick up. She did not look in the least worried or confused. It looked as if she had decided that Math tests were to be done, not during the regular test period, when everyone else does them, but during conference period on Friday, with teacher close at hand, so that if she got into a jam she could get instant help.

She seems to find the situation of not knowing what to do so painful that she prefers to do nothing at all, waiting instead for a time when she can call for help the moment she gets stuck. Even in conference period today she did next to nothing. She was trying to sneak something out of her desk. She moves rather jerkily, so every time she raised the desk lid, I saw it out of the corner of my eye and looked at her. This was rather frustrating for her; however, she kept right on trying for most of the period, not a bit abashed by being caught at it all the time.

Remember when Emily, asked to spell "microscopic," wrote MINCOPERT? That must have been several weeks ago. Today I wrote MINCOPERT on the board. To my great surprise, she recognized it. Some of the kids, watching me write it, said in amazement, "What's that for." I said, "What do you think?" Emily answered, "It's supposed to be 'microscopic.'" But she gave not the least sign of knowing that she was the person who had written MINCOPERT.

On the diagnostic spelling test, she spelled "tariff" as TEARERFIT. Today I thought I would try her again on it. This time she wrote TEARFIT. What does she do in such cases? Her reading aloud gives a clue. She closes her eyes and makes a dash for it, like someone running past a graveyard on a dark night. No looking back afterward, either.

Reminds me of a fragment of the Ancient Mariner—perhaps the world's best short ghost story:

> Like one, that on a lonesome road
> Doth walk in fear and dread,
> And having once turned round walks on,
> And turns no more his head;
> Because he knows, a frightful fiend
> Doth close behind him tread.

Is this the way some of these children make their way through life?

Memo to the Research Committee

I have mentioned Emily, who spelled "microscopic" MINCOPERT. She obviously made a wild grab at an answer, and having written it down, never looked at it, never checked to see if it looked right. I see a lot of this one-way, don't-look-back-it's-too-awful strategy among students. Emily in particular has shown instances of it so striking that I would like you to know about them.

Some time after the spelling test in question, I wrote MINCOPERT on the blackboard. Emily, and one other student, a good speller, interestingly enough, said that it was supposed to be "microscopic." Everyone found this very amusing, including Emily. She is a child who shows in her voice, look, coloring, and gestures much of what she is thinking, and she has not shown the least indication that she knows she is the creator of MINCOPERT. In fact, her attitude suggests that she rejects scornfully the idea that *she* would ever be so foolish as to spell the word in such a way.

Today she handed me, for display, a piece of tag board on which she had pasted some jokes that a friend had cut out of a newspaper. I found when I got to the last one that she had put the paste on the joke side, so that all there was to read was the meaningless fragment of a news story. I was surprised that she would paste a joke on backwards, without even looking to see whether she had it on the right way. When it was posted, and the other kids were looking at it, I said to Emily, "You'll have to explain that last joke to us; we don't get it." I thought she might look at it, for the first time, see that it was meaningless, and realize that she had pasted it on backside up. To my amazement, she smiled and said with the utmost nonchalance, "As a matter of fact, I don't get it myself." She *had* looked at it. She was perfectly ready to accept the fact that she had posted a joke that was meaningless. The possibility that she had made a mistake, and that the real joke was on the other side, did not occur to her.

I am curious about the ability of children to turn things around in their minds. One day, in room period, I asked the children to write on paper certain words that I had showed them, and then write what these would look like if seen in a mirror. I told them to be sure to write the words exactly as I did, with the same use of capital or lower case letters. First I wrote CAT. Emily wrote CAt. It didn't trouble her that two letters were capitals, and one lower case—if she noticed it at all. She assumed that seen in a mirror the order of letters would be reversed, so she wrote TaC. The lower-case *t* became capital; the *A* became lower case. The next word was BIRD. She completely forgot what she had just done about reversing the order of the letters. This time she assumed that the trick was to write each letter backwards, while keeping them in the original order. On her paper she had written BIrD. She reversed the *B* correctly, wrote the *I*, then looked at the lower-case *r*, which must have looked to her like an upside-down *L*, decided, "I must turn this right side up," and wrote *L*. Then she decided that the letters *B* and *D* should not be reversed, so her final answer was BILD. Answer to what question? She hadn't the faintest idea. Whatever task she had set out to do at the beginning had gone from her mind long before she got to the end of it; it had become changed into something else, something to do with writing letters upside down, or backwards, or something.

This child *must* be right. She cannot bear to be wrong, or even to imagine that she might be wrong. When she is wrong, as she often is, the only thing to do is to forget it as quickly as possible. Naturally she will not tell herself that she is wrong; it is bad enough when others tell her. When she is told to do something, she does it quickly and fearfully, hands it to some higher authority, and awaits the magic words, "right," or "wrong." If the word is "right," she does not have to think about that problem any more; if the word is "wrong," she does not want to, cannot bring herself to think about it.

This fear leads her to other strategies, which other children use as well. She knows that in a recitation period the teacher's attention is divided among twenty students. She also knows the teacher's strategy of asking questions of students who seem confused, or not paying attention. She therefore feels safe waving her hand in the air, as if she were bursting to tell the answer, whether she really knows it or not. This is her safe way of telling me that she, at least, knows all about whatever is going on in class. When someone else answers correctly she nods her head in emphatic agreement. Sometimes she even adds a comment, though her expression and tone of voice show that she feels this is risky. It is also interesting to note that she does not raise her hand unless there are at least half a dozen other hands up.

Sometimes she gets called on. The question arose the other day, "What is half of forty-eight?" Her hand was up; in the tiniest whisper she said, "Twenty-four." I asked her to repeat it. She said, loudly, "I said," then whispered "twenty-four." I asked her to repeat it again, because many couldn't hear her. Her face showing tension, she said, very loudly, "I said that one-half of forty-eight is . . ." and then, very softly, "twenty-four." Still, not many of the students heard. She said, indignantly, "OK, I'll shout." I said that that would be fine. She shouted, in a self-righteous tone, "The question is, what is half of forty-eight. Right?" I agreed. And once again, in a voice scarcely above a whisper, she said, "Twenty-four." I could not convince her that she had shouted the question but not the answer.

Of course, this is a strategy that often pays off. A teacher who asks a question is tuned to the right answer, ready to hear it, eager to hear it, since it will tell him that his teaching is good and that he can go on to the next topic. He will assume that anything that sounds close to the right answer is meant to be the right answer. So, for a student who is not sure of the answer, a mumble may be his best bet. If he's not sure whether something is spelled with an *a* or an *o*, he writes a letter that could be either one of them.

The mumble strategy is particularly effective in language classes. In my French classes, the students used to work it on me, without my knowing what was going on. It is particularly effective with a teacher who is finicky about accents and proud of his own. To get such a teacher to answer his own questions is a cinch. Just make some mumbled, garbled, hideously un-French answer, and the teacher, with a shudder, will give the correct answer in elegant French. The student will have to repeat it after him, but by that time he is out of the worst danger.

Game theorists have a name for the strategy which maximizes your chances of winning and minimizes your losses if you should lose. They call it "minimax." Kids are expert at finding such strategies. They can always find ways to hedge, to cover their bets. Not long ago, in room period, we were working with a balance beam. A wooden arm or beam is marked off at regular intervals and balanced on a pivot at its midpoint. The beam can be locked in a balanced position with a peg. We put a weight at a chosen point on one side of the beam, then give the student another weight, perhaps the same, perhaps heavier, perhaps lighter, which he is to place on the other side of the beam so that, when the beam is unlocked, it will stay in the balanced position. When a student has placed the weight, the other members of his group say, in turn, whether they think the beam will balance or not.

One day it was Emily's turn to place the weight. After much thought, she placed it wrongly. One by one, the members of the group said that they thought it would not balance. As each one spoke, she had less and less confidence in her choice. Finally, when they had all spoken and she had to unlock the beam, she looked around and said brightly, "I don't think it's going to balance either, personally." Written words can not convey the tone of her voice: she had completely dissociated herself from that foolish person (whoever it was) who had placed the weight on such a ridiculous spot. When she pulled the peg and the beam swung wildly, she almost seemed to feel vindicated. Most of the children hedge their bets, but few do it so unashamedly, and some even seem to feel that there is something dishonorable in having so little courage of your own convictions.

Children are often quite frank about the strategies they use to get answers out of a teacher. I once observed a class in which the teacher was testing her students on parts of speech. On the blackboard she had three columns, headed Noun, Adjective, and Verb. As she gave each word, she called on a child and asked in which column the word belonged.

Like most teachers, she hadn't thought enough about what she was doing to realize, first, that many of the words given could fit into more than one column; and secondly, that it is often the way a word is used that determines what part of speech it is.

There was a good deal of the tried-and-true strategy of *guess-and-look,* in which you start to say a word, all the while scrutinizing the teacher's face to see whether you are on the right track or not. With most teachers, no further strategies are needed. This one was more poker-faced than most, so *guess-and-look* wasn't working very well. Still, the percentage of hits was remarkably high, especially since it was clear to me from the way the children were talking and acting that they hadn't a notion of what Nouns, Adjectives, and Verbs were. Finally one child said, "Miss —, you shouldn't point to the answer each time." The teacher was surprised, and asked what she meant. The child said, "Well, you don't exactly *point,* but you kind of stand next to the answer." This was no clearer, since the teacher had been standing still. But after a while, as the class went on, I thought I saw what the girl meant. Since the teacher wrote each word down in its proper column, she was, in a way, getting herself ready to write, pointing herself at the place where she would soon be writing. From the angle of her body to the blackboard the children picked up a subtle clue to the correct answer.

This was not all. At the end of every third word, her three columns came out even, that is, there were an equal number of nouns, adjectives, and verbs. This meant that when she started off a new row, you had one chance in three of getting the right answer by a blind guess; but for the next word, you had one chance in two, and the last word was a dead giveaway to the lucky student who was asked it. Hardly any missed this opportunity; in fact, they answered so quickly that the teacher (brighter than most) caught on to their system and began keeping her columns uneven, making the strategist's job a bit harder.

In the midst of all this, there came a vivid example of the kind of thing we say in school that makes no sense, that only bewilders and confuses the thoughtful child who tries to make sense out of it. The teacher, whose specialty, by the way, was English, had told these children that a verb is a word of action—which is not always true. One of the words she asked was "dream." She was thinking of the noun, and apparently did not remember that "dream" can as easily be a verb. One little boy, making a pure guess, said it was a verb. Here the teacher, to be helpful, contributed one of those "explanations" that are so much more hindrance than help. She said, "But a verb has to have action; can you give me a sentence, using 'dream,' that has action?" The child thought a bit, and said, "I had a dream about the Trojan War." Now it's pretty hard to get much more action than that. But the teacher told him he was wrong, and he sat silent, with an utterly baffled and frightened expression on his face. She was so busy thinking about what she wanted him to say, she was so obsessed with that *right answer* hidden in her mind, that she could not think about what he was really saying and thinking, could not see that his reasoning was logical and correct, and that the mistake was not his, but hers.

At one of our leading prep schools I saw, the other day, an example of the way in which a teacher may not know what is going on in his own class.

This was a math class. The teacher, an experienced man, was doing the day's assignment on the blackboard. His way of keeping attention was to ask various members of the class, as he did each step, "Is that right?" It was a dull class, and I found it hard to keep my mind on it. It seemed to me that most students in the class had their minds elsewhere, with a mental sentry posted to alert them when their names were called. As each name was called, the boy who was asked if something or other was right answered "Yes." The class droned on. In time my mind slipped away altogether, I don't know for how long. Suddenly something snapped me to attention. I looked at the teacher. Every boy in the class was looking at him, too. The boy who had been asked if what had just been written was right, was carefully looking at the blackboard. After a moment he said, "No, sir, that isn't right, it ought to be so-and-so." The teacher chuckled appreciatively and said, "You're right, it should be." He made the change, and the class and I settled back into our private thoughts for the rest of the period.

After the boys had left, I thanked the teacher for letting me visit. He said, "You notice I threw them a little curve ball there. I do that every now and then. Keeps them on their toes." I said something in agreement. It didn't seem the time or place to tell him that when he threw his little curve ball the expression on his voice changed enough so that it warned, not only the boys, but also a complete stranger, that something was coming up and that attention had better be paid.

I've been reading over all the memos from last winter and spring. It is a curious and unsettling process, the business of changing your mind on a subject about which you had very positive convictions. After all I have said and written about the need for keeping children under pressure, I find myself coming to realize that what hampers their thinking, what drives them into these narrow and defensive strategies, is a feeling that they must please the grownups at all costs. The really able thinkers in our class turn out to be, without exception, children who don't feel so strongly the need to please grownups. Some of them are good students, some not so good; but good or not, they don't work to please us, but to please themselves.

Here is Walter, just the opposite, very eager to do whatever people want him to do, and very good at doing it. (By conventional standards he was a very able pupil, so much so that people called him brilliant, which he most assuredly was not.)

We had the problem, "If you are traveling at 40 miles per hour, how long will it take you to go 10 miles?"

Walter: 4 minutes.
JH (me): How did you get it?

W: Divided the 40 by the 10.

A quick look at my face told him that this would not do. After a while he wrote, "15 minutes." I wanted to check his understanding.

JH: If you were going 50 miles per hour, how far would you go in 24 minutes?

W (quickly): 36 miles.

JH: How did you get that?

W: Subtracted 24 from 60.

JH: If you were going 50 miles per hour, how far would you go in 30 minutes?

W: 25 miles. 30 minutes is half an hour, and half of 50 is 25.

It sounded as if he knew what he was doing at last. I thought he would have no trouble with the 24 minutes problem. But it took a long time, with some hinting from me, before he saw that 24 minutes was 2/5 of an hour, and therefore, that he would go 2/5 of 50 miles, or 20 miles, in 24 minutes. Would he have discovered it if I had not paved the way with leading questions? Hard to tell.

Most teachers would have assumed, as I would have once, that when he got the 15-minutes problem, he knew what he was doing. Even the skeptical would have been convinced when he gave his explanation about the 30-minutes problem. Yet in each case he showed that he had not really understood what he was doing, and it is not at all certain that he understands yet.

What was his strategy here? Certainly he was numeral shoving. More than that, he was making up a fairly sensible sounding explanation of how he was doing the problem. And yet, is it not possible, even probable, that in saying that in half an hour you go half of 50 miles, he was merely doing some word shoving to go along with his numeral shoving? The explanation sounded reasonable to me, because, in this case, his way of shoving the numerals happened to be the right way; but he was just as happy with his explanations when he was shoving the numerals the wrong way.

This is a disquieting thought. We say and believe that at this school we teach children to understand the meaning of what they do in math. How? By giving them (and requiring them to give back to us) "explanations" of what they do. But let's take a child's-eye view. Might not a child feel, as Walter obviously did, that in this school you not only have to get the right answer, but you also have to have the right explanation to go with it; the right answer, and the right chatter. Yet we see here that a "successful" student can give the answer and the chatter without understanding at all what he was doing or saying.

Observing in Bill Hull's Class

Of all I saw and learned this past half-year, one thing stands out. What goes on in class is not what teachers think—certainly not what I had always thought. For years now I have worked with a picture in mind of what my class was like. This reality, which I felt I knew, was partly physical, partly mental or spiritual. In other words, I thought I knew, in general, what the students were doing, and also what they were thinking and feeling. I see now that my picture of reality was almost wholly false. Why didn't I see this before?

Sitting at the side of the room, watching these kids, not so much to check up on them as to find out what they were like and how they differed from the teen-agers I have worked with and know, I slowly became aware of something. You can't find out what a child does in class by looking at him only when he is called on. You have to watch him for long stretches of time without his knowing it.

During many of the recitation classes, when the class supposedly is working as a unit, most of the children paid very little attention to what was going on. Those who most needed to pay attention, usually paid the least. The kids who knew the answer to whatever question you were asking wanted to make sure that you knew they knew, so their hands were always waving. Also, knowing the right answer, they were in a position to enjoy to the full the ridiculous answers that might be given by their less fortunate colleagues. But, as in all classes, these able students are a minority. What of the unsuccessful majority? Their attention depended on what was going on in class. Any raising of the emotional temperature made them prick up their ears. If an argument was going on, or someone was in trouble, or someone was being laughed at for a foolish answer, they took notice. Or, if you were explaining to a slow student something so simple that all the rest knew it, they would wave their arms and give agonized, half-suppressed cries of "O-o-o-o-oh! O-o-o-o-oh!" But most of the time, when explaining, questioning, or discussing was going on, the majority of children paid little attention or none at all. Some daydreamed, and no amount of calling them back to earth with a crash, much as it amused everyone else, could break them of the habit. Others wrote and passed notes, or whispered, or held conversations in sign language, or made doodles or pictures on their papers or desks, or fiddled with objects.

There doesn't seem to be much a teacher can do about this, if he is really teaching and not just keeping everyone quiet and busy. A teacher in class is like a man in the woods at night with a powerful flashlight in his hand. Wherever he turns his light, the creatures on whom it shines are aware of it, and do not behave as they do in the dark. Thus the mere fact of his watching their behavior changes it into something very different. Shine where he will, he can never know very much of the night life of the woods.

So, in class, the teacher can turn the spotlight of his attention, now on this child, now on that, now on them all; but the children know when his attention is on them, and do not act at all as they do when it is elsewhere. A teacher who is really thinking about what a particular child is doing or asking, or about what he, himself, is trying to explain, will not be able to know what all the rest of the class is doing. And if he does notice that other children are doing what they should not, and tells them to stop, they know they have only to wait until he gets back, as he must, to his real job. Classroom observers don't seem to see much of this. Why not? Some of them do not stay with a class long enough for the children to begin to act naturally in their presence. But even those who are with a class for a long time make the mistake of watching the teacher too much and the children too little. Student teachers in training spend long periods of time in one classroom, but they think they are in there to learn *How To Teach*, to pick up the tricks of child management from watching a *Master At Work*. Their concern is with manipulating and controlling children rather than understanding them. So they watch the teacher, see only what the teacher sees, and thus lose most of what could be a valuable experience.

There should be more situations in which two experienced teachers share the same class, teaching and observing the same group of kids, thinking, and talking to each other, about what they see and hear. Schools can't afford to support this; they can barely pay the one teacher in each class. I should think foundations might be willing to support this kind of work. They seem ready at the drop of a hat to spend millions of dollars on grandiose projects which produce, in the main, only publicity and doctoral dissertations. Perhaps they feel that to have two teachers learn a great deal more about children than they knew before is not worth spending money on. If so, I think they're wrong. When I think what this year's experience has revealed about children's work, behavior, and thought, what avenues of exploration and speculation it has opened up, I can only wonder what extraordinary discoveries about learning might be made if other teachers in other places could work in this way.

It has become clear over the year that these children see school almost entirely in terms of the day-to-day and hour-to-hour tasks that we impose on them. This is not at all the way the teacher thinks of it. The conscientious teacher thinks of himself as taking his students (at least part way) on a journey to some glorious destination, well worth the pains of the trip. If he teaches history, he thinks how interesting, how exciting, how useful it is to know history, and how fortunate his students will be when they begin to share his knowledge. If he teaches French, he thinks of the glories of French literature, or the beauty of spoken French, or the delights of French cooking, and how he is helping to make these joys available to his students. And so for all subjects.

Thus teachers feel, as I once did, that their interest and their students' are fundamentally the same. I used to feel that I was guiding and helping my students on a journey that they wanted to take but could not take without my help. I knew the way looked hard, but I assumed they could see the goal almost as clearly as I and that they were almost as eager to reach it. It seemed very important to give students this feeling of being on a journey to a worthwhile destination. I see now that most of my talk to this end was wasted breath. Maybe I thought the students were in my class because they were eager to learn what I was trying to teach, but they knew better. They were in school because they had to be, and in my class either because they had to be, or because otherwise they would have had to be in another class, which might be even worse.

Children in school are like children at the doctor's. He can talk himself blue in the face about how much good his medicine is going to do them; all they think of is how much it will hurt or how bad it will taste. Given their own way, they would have none of it.

So the valiant and resolute band of travelers I thought I was leading toward a much-hoped-for destination turned out instead to be more like convicts in a chain gang, forced under threat of punishment to move along a rough path leading nobody knew where and down which they could see hardly more than a few steps ahead. School feels like this to children: it is a place where *they* make you go and where *they* tell you to do things and where *they* try to make your life unpleasant if you don't do them or don't do them right.

For children, the central business of school is not learning, whatever this vague word means; it is getting these daily tasks done, or at least out of the way, with a minimum of effort and unpleasantness. Each task is an end in itself. The children don't care how they dispose of it. If they can get it out of the way by doing it, they will do it; if experience has taught them that this does not work very well, they will turn to other means, illegitimate means, that wholly defeat whatever purpose the task-giver may have in mind.

They are very good at this, at getting other people to do their tasks for them. I remember the day not long ago when Ruth opened my eyes. We had been doing math, and I was pleased with myself because, instead of telling her answers and showing her how to do problems, I was "making her think" by asking her questions. It was slow work. Question after question met only silence. She said nothing, did nothing, just sat and looked at me through those glasses, and waited. Each time, I had to think of a question easier and more pointed than the last, until I finally found one so easy that she would feel safe in answering it. So we inched our way along until suddenly, looking at her as I waited for an answer to a question, I saw with a start that she was not at all puzzled by what I had asked her. In fact, she was not even thinking about it. She was coolly appraising me, weighing my patience, waiting for that next, sure-to-be-easier question. I thought, "I've been had!" The girl had learned how to make me do her work for her, just as she had learned to make all her previous teachers do the same thing. If I wouldn't tell her the answers, very well, she would just let me question her right up to them.

Schools and teachers seem generally to be as blind to children's strategies as I was. Otherwise, they would teach their courses and assign their tasks so that students who really thought about the meaning of the subject would have the best chance of succeeding, while those who tried to do the tasks by illegitimate means, without thinking or understanding, would be foiled. But the reverse seems to be the case. Schools give every encouragement to *producers*, the kids whose idea is to get "right answers" by any and all means. In a system that runs on "right answers," they can hardly help it. And these schools are often very discouraging places for *thinkers*.

Until recently it had not occurred to me that poor students thought differently about their work than good students; I assumed they thought the same way, only less skillfully. Now it begins to look as if the expectation and fear of failure, if strong enough, may lead children to act and think in a special way, to adopt strategies different from those of more confident children. Emily is a good example. She is emotionally as well as intellectually incapable of checking her work, of comparing her ideas against reality, of making any kind of judgment about the value of her thoughts. She makes me think of an animal fleeing danger—go like the wind, don't look back, remember where that danger was, and stay away from it as far as you can. Are there many other children who react to their fears in this way?

It doesn't take the children long to figure out their teachers. Some of these kids already know that what pays off with us is plenty of talk, lots of ideas, even if they are wild. What can we do for the kids who may like to think but don't like to talk?

In my math classes I am on the horns of another dilemma. I want the kids to think about what they are doing. If I make the questions too hard, they begin trying to read my mind, or, as they did this morning, they throw out wild ideas, taking all too literally my statement that a wrong idea is better than none. If, on the other hand, I break the subject down into little lumps, so that when I ask a question most of the class will be able to answer with confidence, am I not doing what I found I was doing for Ruth last year, doing most of their thinking for them?

Perhaps there is no middle position, and what I must do is ask hard questions some of the time, easy questions other times.

What the sixth-grade teachers said the other day suggests that some of our last year's strategists have not reformed. Let's not be too discouraged about this. Given these children whose strategies are short-sighted and self-defeating, these answer-grabbers and teacher-pleasers, we can to some extent, and over a long period of time, create situations in which some of them may be willing to use their minds in better ways. Some of these, in turn, may even carry these new ways of thinking into a new situation; but we can't expect that they all will. Most of them will probably drop back into the strategies with which they are most familiar and comfortable.

Not many children, in one school year, are going to remake their whole way of dealing with life. With luck, we can give some of them a feeling of what it is like to turn one's full intelligence on a problem, to think creatively, originally, and constructively instead of defensively and evasively. We can hope that they will enjoy the experience enough to want to try it again; but it is only a hope. To put it another way, we can try to give them a glimpse of an intellectual foreign country, and even persuade them to visit it for a while; but it would take more time than we have to make them citizens of that country.

There's no telling what might be done with children if, from their very first days in school, we concentrated on creating the conditions in which intelligence was most likely to grow. Of course, setting up the conditions under which good thinking can be done does not always mean that it will be done.

Take Sam. He seems temperamentally ready to think well, but he rarely does. The other day I had some number series on the board, and asked the class to tell me any relationships they could see in them. Sam's first two or three observations were of this order: "There's a one in the top line and a one in the middle line, and there's a two in the third number and a two in the fifth number. . . ." Very trivial, very local, no generality among them at all. Then, in the middle of all this, he came up with a very powerful generalization that I had not even seen myself.

The funny thing is that I don't think he felt that one of these ideas was any better than another. He might one day say that horses and cows were similar in that they were domestic farm animals that ate grass; and the next day that they were alike because he had never ridden on either, or something like that. How can we help him to see that some ways of looking at things, ordering things, are more useful than others?

We have to convince the children that they must not be afraid to ask questions; but further than that, we must get across the idea that some questions are more useful than others, and that to the right kind of question the answer "No" can be as revealing as "Yes." Here is where Twenty Questions, the card game, the balance beam, all come in handy. The scientist who asks a question of nature—*i.e.* performs an experiment—tries to ask one such that he will gain information whichever way his experiment comes out, and will have an idea of what to do next. He asks his questions with a purpose. This is a subtle art. Can fifth graders learn some of it?

When Nancy and Sheila worked the balance beam last year, they were often close to the truth, but they could never hang onto it because they could never express their ideas in a form they could test with an experiment. Once one of them said, "Things weigh more further out." This was a big step; but they couldn't think of a way to check or refine this insight, they couldn't ask themselves (to use their terms) how much more things weigh when they get further out.

Some of our strategists at work:

Atlas Paper #2 asks the students, "What two key words on each index page of the Atlas tell at a glance which names can be found on that page?" The students are supposed to notice that the first and the last place names on any page are printed in larger type at the top of the page—as in a dictionary. The other day, Abby and Jane could not understand what the instructions were asking them to do, largely because they were too busy thinking about the answer to be able to think about the instructions. We studied the examples given in the paper, but to no avail. Finally I told them to sit at their desks and think about it some more. A minute or two later Jane appeared at the door and said indignantly, "Are you *sure* that it isn't those two words at the top of the page?" Having said no such thing, I was taken aback, and said with some surprise, "When did I say that?" She immediately turned to Abby, who was waiting outside the door, and said, "Write it down!" She had all the clues she needed.

Here are some of the children working on the balance beam experiment. One child has placed the weight where he thinks it will balance the beam; the others are being asked to predict whether it will balance.

Abby: It might move a little to one side—not much.
Elaine: It might teeter a little, then balance, but not really. (She really is covering all the possibilities.)
Rachel: It might balance.
Pat: It will balance pretty much.
Elaine: Teeter totter a teeny bit, then balance.
In this next example, 4 x 5" means that we put four weights five inches out on the beam. 2 x ? means that we gave the child 2 weights to place. In this case, 2 x 10" would have made the beam balance.
4 x 5"; 2 x ? Elaine put them at 2", then at 1", then at 9". I asked, "Is that your choice?" She said, "Yes, but I don't think it will balance." The object of the experiment was to make it balance! She decided to leave the weights at 9".
Asked if it would balance, Hester said, "Somehow I think it might."
8 x 2"; 4 x ?
Rachel (moving the weights back and forth without conviction): Probably won't balance.
Barbara: Put them where you think it *will*. (Barbara is one of our few positive strategists, and is so in everything she does.)

Rachel puts the weight at 1″. Needless to say, the beam did not balance.

3 x 2″; 6 x ? Hester scattered the six blocks all over the beam, as if in the hope that one of them might hit the magic spot.

Barbara's turn. Everyone will predict that the beam will balance.

2 x 3″; 1 x ? First she put them at 5″. She is counting out lines instead of spaces. Then she saw her mistake, and put them at 6″. Everyone except Hester said that the beam would balance.

1 x 10″; 2 x ?

Barbara: 2 x 5″. Then she said confidently but with some excitement in her voice, "It's going to do it!"

Elaine: You put a block here (1″), it makes it lighter; here (5″) makes it heavier.

When his turn came, Garry said, "I think it's just going to go down—that's safer."

1 x 10″; 1 x ? Betty put the weight at 10″.

Gil: May go down a little and then come back up.

Garry: It will be about even.

Betty: I sort of think it's going to balance.

4 x 6″; 4 x ? Ralph put them at 6″. But two members of the group predicted that it would not balance; then Betty spoke up: "I'll say it will, just in case it does, so we won't get too low a score." Talk about Minimax!

Our way of scoring was to give the groups a point for each correct prediction. Before long they were thinking more of ways to get a good score than of making the beam balance. We wanted them to figure out how to balance the beam, and introduced the scoring as a matter of motivation. But they outsmarted us, and figured out ways to get a good score that had nothing to do with whether the beam balanced or not.

4 x 9″, 4 x ? Sam put them at 9″. Ralph said, "He didn't trust me, but I'm going to trust him, because that's where I would have put it."

Later, Sam said to another player, "Do what you think is right." To which Betty, usually a positive character, said, "Play safe."

At about this point Betty figured out that the way to get a good score was to put the weights in what you know is a wrong place and then have everyone on your team say that it is wrong.

Thus they will each get a point for predicting correctly. Later, Nat said, "Are *no* votes just as good as *yes* votes?" It was a good question; we should have made *yes* votes count much more.

Another group working.

4 x 8"; 4 x ? Tony put them at 7", then said, "Get ready to disagree." Then he changed them to 8". All predicted *yes*, but Nat hedged.

Later, when it was his turn to predict, Nat said, "Too bad you have to be so specific."

Here are some notes from the other day, when the fourth graders were playing Twenty Questions.

Many of them are very anxious when their turn comes to ask a question. We ask them to play Twenty Questions in the hope that, wanting to find the hidden thought, they will learn to ask more informative and useful questions.

They see the game quite differently: "When my turn comes, I have to ask a question." They are not the least interested in the object of the game, or whether their question gains useful information. The problem is simply to think of a question, any old question. The first danger is that you will just be sitting there, unable to think of a question. The next danger is that when you ask a question, other kids will think it is silly, laugh at it, say, "That's no good."

So the problem becomes not just thinking up a question, but thinking up a question that will sound good. The best way to do this is to listen to kids that you know are pretty sharp, and ask questions that sound like theirs. Thus, a child who found in one game that "Is it water?" was a useful question, went on asking it in game after game, even when other questions had established that the information sought for had nothing to do with water.

Many of our kids play the same way. Pat, Rachel, and some others never have any idea what the object of the game is, or what information has been gained by questions already asked. All they want, when their turn comes, is to have a question that won't be laughed at. Jessie plays it even safer than that. She just refuses to ask a question, says, "I pass," and looks very pleased with herself after she says it, too.

Another popular strategy is the disguised blind guess. When kids first play this game, every question is a guess. Then some of them see that it is silly to guess right at the beginning, and that the sensible thing to do is narrow down the possibilities. They criticize very severely teammates who start guessing too soon. So the trick becomes to ask a guessing question that doesn't sound like a guess, like Nat's classic, "Was he killed by Brutus?" This has become something of a joke in his group. Still, every question he asks conceals a guess.

One day we were using the atlas, and the field of the game was geographical locations. Sam wanted to ask if it was Italy, but that was a guess, so he said, "Does it look like a boot?" Every time it is his turn, he says, "Can I make a guess?" The strategy of narrowing down possibilities has not occurred to him, or if it has, he does not know how to make use of it.

Betty makes multiple guesses. Thinking of either Corsica or Sardinia, she asked, "Does it begin with *C* or *S*?" Another time she said, "Does it begin with *B, D, C, P* or *T*?" This is not bad strategy. On another occasion she said to a cautious teammate, "Don't say 'Could it be?'; say 'Is it?' " She's a positive little critter.

Sometimes we try to track down a number with Twenty Questions. One day I said I was thinking of a number between 1 and 10,000. Children who use a good narrowing-down strategy to find a number between 1 and 100, or 1 and 500, go all to pieces when the number is between 1 and 10,000. Many start guessing from the very beginning. Even when I say that the number is very large, they will try things like 65, 113, 92. Other kids will narrow down until they find that the number is in the 8,000's; then they start guessing, as if there were now so few numbers to choose from that guessing became worthwhile. Their confidence in these shots in the dark is astonishing. They say, "We've got it this time!" They are always incredulous when they find they have not got it.

They still cling stubbornly to the idea that the only good answer is a *yes* answer. This, of course, is the result of their miseducation, in which "right answers" are the only ones that pay off. They have not learned how to learn from a mistake, or even that learning from mistakes is possible. If they say, "Is the number between 5,000 and 10,000?" and I say *yes,* they cheer; if I say *no,* they groan, even though they get exactly the same amount of information in either case. The more anxious ones will, over and over again, ask questions that have already been answered, just for the satisfaction of hearing a *yes*. Their more sophisticated teammates point out in vain that it is silly to ask a question when you already know the answer.

4 THE SCHOOLS AND THE DISADVANTAGED

HARVEY GOLDMAN

It has in recent years become rather commonplace for those concerned with the future of our nation to expound upon "the central role of the public schools within our society." Such presentations tend to place major emphasis on the rapidity of change within our society and the significance of that change for the educational establishment with respect to ensuring that our populace is capable of adapting to evolving conditions within our social, economic, and philosophic spheres.

It has also been evident that a sizable minority of Americans (forty to fifty million) have not had the quality of their lives significantly enhanced during this same period in which the standard of living for the majority has been characterized by numerous qualitative improvements. In fact, the quality of the lives of those living in our urban centers has regressed in relative terms. Bagdikian,[1] one commentator on our contemporary social scene, has expressed the fear that a class of permanently poor people is being created and that those encased in this "cycle of poverty" will continue to find escape impossible without a massive infusion of resources—human and monetary—from both the public and private sectors of our economy.

In particular, concern has been expressed over the inability of our schools to deal effectively with the problems in our urban centers. Conant [2] has pointed out that youth in our urban centers, and particularly Negroes, find it increasingly difficult to obtain employment. This is as true for those possessing high school diplomas as it is for those who leave school prior to graduation.

Melby [3] has pointed out the extent to which elementary students become increasingly dissatisfied with the schools as they progress

Harvey Goldman, "The Schools and the Disadvantaged," Harvey Goldman (ed.), *Education and the Disadvantaged* (Milwaukee: School of Education, University of Wisconsin-Milwaukee, 1967), pp. 111–126. Reprinted by permission of the author and publisher.

through the grades; their self-concepts tend to be diminished rather than enhanced as a result of their experiences in class-rooms.

This paper constitutes an examination of two factors, both integrally related, that contribute to this disaffection that our disadvantaged youth express toward the schools at such an early age. The first factor to be examined will be the middle-class nature of our school systems as they currently exist within and outside of our urban centers. The second factor to be considered will be the blatant manner with which educators tend to disregard the differential nature of the two sexes.

The Middle-Class Nature of the Public Schools

The first public schools in our country were the colonial grammar schools. These institutions served both college preparatory and religious functions. Thus, the existence of a well-trained and adequate clergy was assured at all times. A major function of the colonial grammar school "was to establish a common base of religious leadership in the whole population. . . ." [4] Although designed in a manner which ensured that only a select few would pass through its hallowed halls, the grammar school served a broader purpose than at first appeared evident. That is, those who received their education in the grammar schools were expected to transmit their knowledge to the townspeople and, in this way, facilitate the development of a common culture (albeit a religious one).

The academy, the development of which followed that of the grammar school, was an institution designed to serve a broader base of clientele and also to meet a very different set of needs. As envisioned by Benjamin Franklin, the academy was to be an instrument for the preparation of the rising middle class in terms of civic and occupational skills. It is obvious that the academy was originally established to meet the needs of those comprising the middle class at a time when the types of skills required by our society were in a state of rapid transition. The need for skilled personnel had become acute. That this ideal (the provision of occupational skills for all aspiring to middle-class status) was not fully carried out was the result of a compromise deemed necessary at the time.

It is particularly interesting to note that no classical languages were offered in the first publicly supported high school opened in Boston in 1821. Yet subjects such as surveying and navigation were included in the curriculum along with literature and composition, mathematics, history, science, and philosophy. Again, the implication is clear that the publicly supported high schools were to serve a practical function; that those completing the program offered were to be capable of "carrying their own weight" within the society.

Speaking of the public schools as they exist today, Krug [5] has pointed out that contemporary American education is based on and committed to three major ideals: 1) that it should be free; 2) that it should be popular (meeting the needs of the people); 3) that it should be universal.

One cannot escape the realization that the schools in our country have historically been the agents for the promotion of a common culture—one that encompassed the vast majority of the populace. Even the colonial grammar schools, selective in nature and educating only the intellectually capable, served the ultimate purpose of providing the community with a common culture. In retrospect, an examination of the early academy and the public high schools brings to light substantial evidence of the middle-class nature of these schools. The inclusion of vocational and other "practical" courses in their curricula is quite noticeable. During the period when public high schools were increasing in number, the traditional classical curriculum offered by many private schools was increasingly viewed with disdain by the general public.

The question arises as to whether or not the public schools as we now know them continue to retain their middle-class bias—a bias which ensures that those not committed to a middle-class value pattern are excluded from equal educational opportunities in a systematic manner through a subtle, but ever-present, form of discrimination. The major question to be answered at this time is whether or not such discrimination does exist even though, in many cases, the same curriculum, texts, buildings, and percentage of certified teachers are available to all students throughout a school system regardless of social class membership.

A study conducted by Sims [6] clearly indicates that teachers consistently perceive themselves as members of the middle or upper-middle class. In addition, they exhibited extremely conservative views with respect to political and economic issues.

The majority of the teachers showed little sympathy with labor and laboring people, generally considered themselves a "cut above" skilled workers and, to a lesser extent, above other "white collar" workers.[7]

The attitudes of teachers, as described by Sims, indicate a desire on the part of those teachers to maintain the *status quo*. At a time when the liberal segment of our society is espousing the need for the federal government to make available massive sums of money for programs to assist the disadvantaged in breaking their "cycle of poverty," teachers are expressing their desire for a traditional approach to the economic, political, and social problems that confront our nation. The type of social, economic, and political order that they see as desirable is disconcertingly similar to those of the highly conservative, *status quo* oriented, influential businessmen and bankers described by Kimbrough.[8]

Another study[9] clearly points out the extent to which the middle-class oriented teachers manifest their internalized prejudices in terms of discriminatory behavior which prevents disadvantaged children from taking full advantage of the educational opportunities offered them. The evidence clearly implied that teachers' behavioral patterns indicated a rejection of lower-class students on their part. The data indicated that students from the lower socio-economic class generally received lower grades than did those who were members of the middle or upper classes. It was also quite interesting to note that students from the lower socio-economic class received more severe punishments than did students from the other socio-economic classes *for the same disciplinary offenses*. Finally, the data made evident the fact that those students whom we currently term "disadvantaged" were not accepted socially by their teachers.

Teachers[10] tend to manifest an obvious inconsistency when attempting to justify their rejection of disadvantaged students. Their justifications defy logic and can only be viewed as gross rationalizations in defense of their inability to effectively deal with the problems facing them. This investigation showed that teachers consistently perceive students from the lower socio-economic class as being "morally unacceptable" because they smoke, drink, swear, or are occasionally involved in sexually immoral acts. Behavior of this type was considered by the teachers to be both undesirable and unnecessary. On the other hand, the same behavior, when manifested by students from the middle or upper socioeconomic classes, was casually excused by the teachers who explained these students' indiscretions with such terms as "it wasn't their fault," or "they've been terribly spoiled," or "it won't happen again." Clearly, a double standard is in effect, and it is the disadvantaged students who consistently receive "the short end of the deal." The same teachers, when asked their opinions about their roles as professional educators, stated that the same subject matter and teaching techniques are appropriate for all children. Once a teacher is able to adopt (and, perhaps, even believe) this position, he or she is nearly automatically relieved of all responsibility for the failure of some children to achieve in school. The next "logical" step is the statement that it is not the teacher's fault if the student did not learn what was "taught." At the same time we can be quite certain that these teachers would reject any statement that implied that, if teaching consisted merely of presenting a predetermined body of subject matter to students in a relatively routine fashion, we would be better off eliminating all teachers and employing various forms of programmed instruction on a massive scale. Such a suggestion would immediately evoke from the teachers numerous platitudes describing the many unique characteristics of each individual and the fact that only a thinking human being—in this case, a teacher—is suited to deal with them since the number and the complexity of the relationships among those characteristics could not be effectively dealt with by a machine. Again, the inconsistency of their statements is evident; they imply that the teaching act and the nature of the content dealt with are relatively routine, yet rebel when confronted with a statement that asserts that routine acts are best dealt with by machines built expressly for that purpose.

Although we would like to think of our schools as places in which the finest possible education is provided to every student in attendance, it appears quite clear that this ideal state has not yet been attained. The evidence also seems to indicate that, to a considerable extent, a determination of the socio-economic class to which a student belongs can serve as a rough guide indicative

of the quality of education accessible to that student and that the
most desirable teaching-learning situations are most often available to students from the middle and upper socio-economic classes
while being systematically withheld from those students classified
as "lower-class."

The Differential Nature of the Sexes and the School Program

It is amazing to note the almost total disregard with which we,
as educators, tend to dismiss the significance of inter-sex differences among our students. Not only is this disregard evident in
the manner by which we develop curricula, but it is also quite
obvious when one examines the tests—both standardized and
teacher-made—that are utilized in the school. Few, if any, so-called
"ability tests" used commonly in the schools (other than individual tests like the WISC or WAIS) provide norms for both
males and females. Only a very few reading tests (like the Gray
Oral Reading Test) provide differential norms for the sexes. And,
aside from the Differential Aptitude Tests, almost none of the
standardized achievement tests make such norms available.

In terms of school curricula there is very little differentiation
of activities between the sexes. This is particularly true in the
first through at least the third grade and, quite often, through
the sixth grade. Boys and girls read together, write together, have
art and music lessons together, and even have the dubious pleasure
of sharing the same gym classes. The one area in which the
schools have finally admitted that differences between boys and
girls are of importance is with regard to reading interests. Many
of the newer reading texts designed for elementary schools contain stories geared to the interests of young boys. It should be
noted, however, that this differential is in terms of materials and
has no effect upon the nature of the activities with which the
students are faced. The fact that most elementary teachers are
female very probably has had a significant impact on the nature
of the teaching-learning activities that have historically become
an integral aspect of the elementary curriculum, but this will not
be considered at this time since female teachers could, if they
so desired and if they felt it was necessary, devise and utilize differential activities for boys and girls during at least a part of each
school day.

Two factors must be considered at this time. The first is the extent to which differences exist between boys and girls that would necessitate the development of differential activities. And the second is an examination of the extent to which any differences that do exist between the social classes tend to result in a diminishing of the quality of education provided disadvantaged students.

Young girls from both the middle and lower socio-economic classes have many things in common.

Parents, particularly mothers, tend to keep young girls dressed in clothes that can be considered "pretty" or "cute." They are often admonished to "keep clean," "stay neat," and to "act like a young lady." This is not to imply that the clothes worn by young girls from the two social classes are necessarily of the same quality or that they are available in the same quantity; it is only to say that there is a type of clothes that young girls often wear and a set of adult expectations regarding the behavioral patterns of the young girls when wearing those clothes.

In both cases there are some distinct similarities regarding the type of play activities in which the girls engage. They tend to play games that require role-playing, often acting out such roles as "mother," "nurse," "teacher," and "actress" (all of which are realistic roles that depict people whom they will meet throughout their lives). In addition to the fact that these activities require a relatively sophisticated approach to role-playing, they are also of a rather passive nature, usually requiring a minimal amount of physical exertion. They are also activities that the girls find it possible to carry out within spatial areas of limited size. A third common characteristic of these activities is that they involve a high degree of verbalization. The girls talk to their dolls or to the other girls playing with them. The girl playing the role of mother, nurse, or teacher must explain to the other participants what is expected of them. Nevertheless, there very definitely appears to be a qualitative differential in the language patterns manifested by girls from the two social classes. To a great extent this differential can be accounted for by the differences in the quality of language utilized by the parents, and particularly the mothers, who serve as models for the girls.

Within their families, even as youngsters, the girls often enjoy certain advantages over their male counterparts. First of all, there is a tendency for the mother, who spends the most time with the youngsters during the day, to favor the girls; this tendency is exaggerated by the fact that the high degree of contact permits the girls to study and internalize the female role that their mothers carry out during the day—a role that involves the establishment of behavioral norms in a variety of areas (dress, cooking, cleaning, relations to others, etc.).

For the most part, the female model presented through the mass media describes women involved in activities similar to or related to those that the young girls view as common to the female role. They are also roles that the girls know will be open to them in later years. They are seen cleaning house, cooking, and caring for children. Even in those cases where women undertake an occupational role in the movies or on television, they usually retain their ladylike manner.

Now let us examine the situation in which young boys from the middle and lower socio-economic classes spend their childhood years.

The young boys from both social classes, too, tend to be dressed similarly. The neat, pressed slacks and clean white shirts are usually reserved for "dress-up" occasions. And for "every-day" wear the young boys can be found wearing T-shirts, sweat-shirts, dungarees, sneakers, and other articles of clothing of a similar nature. Rather than being admonished to "keep clean," "stay neat," and to "act like a young lady," the boys are told to "go out and play," "stay out of trouble," and to "act like a young man." Again, the implication cannot be made that the boys from the two social classes possess the same quantity or quality of clothes, only that there is a common type of clothes in which young boys tend to spend a considerable amount of time. As was also true for the girls, the type of clothing worn and the nature of the admonishments directed to them by their parents tend to convey to the boys a set of parental expectations that give direction to the type of behavioral patterns that they manifest.

The play activities of boys tend to be action-centered rather than role-playing centered. They tend to become involved in games of baseball, football, handball, stick-ball, running, swimming, volleyball, and others of a like sort. All of these are action-centered and also involve whole-body muscle activity; they involve the use of large muscles for body control. Those role-playing activities in which the boys do engage (such as cowboys, soldiers, and firemen) do not describe models that are realistic with respect to our society, are not sufficiently common for the boys to observe and internalize the behavior common to them, and are usually not open to the boys in later years. Those activities in which the boys from both classes prefer to engage generally require large amounts of space and can not usually be effectively carried out within the limited confines of a single room. Another common characteristic of these activities is that they rarely require a high degree of verbalization. Instead, they often involve staccato-like verbal activity (such as "Bang, you're dead," "Hit the ball," and "Run"), which is of limited use as they engage in interaction with others outside the immediate situation. There does exist a qualitative differential regarding the quality of language expressed by boys from the two classes which can only be accounted for by consideration of a wide range of influential factors. As was also true for the girls, the quality of the language patterns utilized by the parents (and particularly the mothers) differs with social class membership. Among the middle-class families, it is a common practice for the parents to spend a considerable amount of time speaking and reading to the children, a practice which is not so common in those families characterized by lower social class membership. Thus, those children from the lower socio-economic class do not listen to or utilize formal language to the extent required of children with middle-class parents.

The boys from both socio-economic classes tend not to have a male model in their homes all day to observe and emulate. Among the boys from the lower socio-economic class this problem is exaggerated by the fact that there is a higher incidence of female-headed homes that deprives these children of contact with a consistent male model (or one with a desirable behavioral and attitudinal pattern) for even a short time every day. Thus the boys have considerably fewer opportunities than the girls to observe and internalize the behavioral and attitudinal patterns of those whom they must emulate in later years. Even when the male heads of the families are available, the boys have little chance to observe them at work and to understand the nature of the activities in which they engage daily.

In direct contrast to what existed for the girls, the mass media (particularly television and the movies) tend to bombard the boys with a preponderance of models that depict males as either bungling fools easily manipulated by and subservient to their female mates or as daring he-men who go through life destroying or killing all who interfere with their plans. Neither of these models can be said to be worthy of emulation.

Conclusions

When seen from both a historical and a contemporary point of view it is clearly obvious that the public schools in our country were designed as instruments of the middle class; as a means of meeting their needs and at the same time facilitating the development of a more highly trained working class in an evolving society. This middle-class orientation is observable in terms of both the purposes of the institution and the personnel employed to maintain it.

An examination of those experiences and situations common to boys and girls from the middle and lower socio-economic classes also leads to the inescapable conclusion that the schools are best suited for educating only certain segments of the total student population. The facts leading to this conclusion are as follows:

1. Girls are better prepared throughout their childhood for the type of clothing that must be worn in school; particularly with regard to its maintenance.

2. The admonishments to which girls are subject ("be careful," "be neat," "act like a young lady") are more in line with those of the school than those to which the boys are subjected.

3. The behavioral patterns that females in our society are expected to manifest are more similar to those required by the school than are those of the boys. (Thus, the girls are used to passive activities, confinement to smaller spatial areas for long periods of time, more extensive verbalization, neatness, and following instructions.)

4. Disadvantaged students are handicapped in school as a result of their limited training in the use of formal English. This handicap is particularly evident for disadvantaged boys. Since

they do not receive sufficient training in the formal use of English either through their play activities or within their families, they are largely unprepared to meet the demands of the school.

5. Since the middle-class boy has received sufficient training in the use of formal English to permit him some degree of success (whether he likes school or not), it is usually unnecessary for him to resort to aggressive behavior in order to attain recognition.

6. The boy from the lower socio-economic class, disliking school and severely limited in terms of opportunities for success, often finds aggressive behavior his only means of obtaining recognition in school.

7. Within the school largely populated with disadvantaged youth, the girls, as a result of their previous training and experience, manifest behavioral and attitudinal patterns that permit them a greater degree of success and recognition than is available to the boys.

8. The discriminatory behavior and attitude of middle-class oriented teachers consistently operate to the disadvantage of lower-class students.

In summary, it is evident that students from homes in which the parents are representative of the lower socio-economic class are at a disadvantage in the schools, and this poses especially severe problems for disadvantaged boys.

It is of particular importance to note that, as currently operated, the schools are essentially institutions for girls; the activities in which the students must engage and the expectations by which their behavior is regulated are familiar to the girls as a result of their prior experiences, but are largely unfamiliar to the boys as they enter school.

As a result, it can be anticipated that the disciplinary problems that boys currently create within the schools will continue to increase in number and severity, and that the problem will be most severe in those schools with higher proportions of disadvantaged boys.

It is suggested here, as it has been many times, that the schools must initiate instructional and operational patterns designed to promote the maximum development of every individual. Related to this is the fact that teachers must receive a more thorough training, one that will better prepare them for the role of determining which teaching-learning conditions are best for each student and, also, to provide those situations.

It may be necessary for the schools to reexamine their instructional programs in terms of the problems posed by the differential expectation and behavior patterns that boys and girls bring to school. Perhaps, for some subjects, it would be preferable for the schools to provide instruction for boys and girls in separate classes. There is also a strong possibility that, in some cases, boys might spend an entire year in school without having girls mixed into their classes.

As pointed out earlier it is the disadvantaged students, and particularly the boys, who bear the brunt of the inequities built into the present system. Therefore, it is in schools with a significant percentage of disadvantaged boys that this modification of operational and instructional patterns should be initiated first.

We, as educators, have always recognized our responsibility to provide special programs for "exceptional" children. To that end, specialized programs have been provided for gifted and retarded children, for those who could not hear and for those without sight, and for those with psychological problems as well as for those with physical disabilities. We must now take another step toward professional maturity and recognize that the disadvantaged student is also an "exceptional" child and requires the services of a highly trained teacher to carry out a specially designed educational program.

Some day, when teachers attain a considerably greater degree of professional maturity than is currently the case, it will be apparent that every child is "exceptional" and requires a specialized program designed to meet his particular needs. Until that time we must be content with a slow but, hopefully, steady rate of progress.

NOTES

1. Bagdikian, Ben H. *In the Midst of Plenty* (New York: New American Library, 1964), p. 160.
2. Conant, James Bryant. *Slums and Suburbs* (New York: New American Library, 1961), p. 128.
3. Melby, Ernest O. "The Contemporary Scene," Lecture delivered to Mott Inter-University Clinical Preparation Program for Educational

Leadership on September 30, 1964 at the Mott Leadership Center in Flint, Michigan.

4. Krug, Edward A. *The Secondary School Curriculum* (New York: Harper and Row, Publishers, 1960), p. 16.

5. *Ibid.*, p. 1.

6. Sims, Verna M: "The Social Class Affiliations of a Group of Public School Teachers," *School Review*, 59:331–38 (September 1951).

7. *Ibid.*

8. Kimbrough, Ralph B. *Political Power and Educational Decision-Making* (Chicago: Rand McNally and Company, 1964), p. 297.

9. Abrahamson, Stephen. "Our Status System and Scholastic Rewards," *The Journal of Educational Sociology*, 25:441–50 (April 1952).

10. Beecher, Howard S. "Social-Class Variations in the Teacher-Pupil Relationship," *The Journal of Educational Sociology*, 25:451–65 (April 1952).

5   DEATH AT AN EARLY AGE

JONATHAN KOZOL

"Someday, maybe," Erik Erikson has written, "there will exist a well-informed, well-considered and yet fervent public conviction that the most deadly of all possible sins is the mutilation of a child's spirit."

If that day ever comes, American educators may be able to reflect with some horror upon the attitudes and procedures that have been allowed to flourish within a great many urban public schools.

It is a commonplace by now to say that the urban school systems of America contain a higher percentage of Negro children each year. More than anywhere else, it is here within these ghetto systems that the mutilation of which Erikson speaks becomes apparent. My own experience took place in Boston, in a segregated fourth-grade classroom. The Boston school system is not perhaps the worst offender, but it provides a clear example of the kind of education being offered the disadvantaged children of many cities. There are, admittedly, in Boston a cluster of unusually discouraging problems, chief among them the school administration's refusal for a great many years to recognize that there *was* any problem. Only slightly less troubling has been the exceptional virulence of the anti-Negro prejudice, both among teachers and the general public. Yet Boston's problems are not much different from those of other cities, and the solutions here as elsewhere will have to await a change in attitude at all levels of society.

Stephen is an eight-year-old pupil in the Boston public schools. A picture of him standing in front of a bulletin board on Arab bedouins shows a little light-brown person staring with unusual concentration at a chosen spot upon the floor. Stephen is tiny,

Jonathan Kozol, *Death at an Early Age* (New York: Houghton Mifflin Co., 1967), excerpts from pages 1–207. Copyright © 1967. Reprinted by permission of the publisher.

desperate, unwell. Sometimes he talks to himself, or laughs out loud in class for no apparent reason. He is also an indescribably mild and unmalicious child. He cannot do any of his schoolwork very well. His math and reading are poor. In third grade his class had substitute teachers much of the year. Most of the year before that he had substitute teachers too. He is in the fourth grade now, but his work is barely at the level of the second.

Nobody has complained about Stephen's situation because he does not have a real family. Stephen is a ward of the Commonwealth of Massachusetts, and as such has been placed in the home of some very poor people who do not want him now that he is not a baby anymore. He often comes to school badly beaten. If I ask him about it, he is apt to deny it because he does not want us to know what a miserable time he has. He lied to me first when I asked him how his eye got battered, claiming that it was an accident. Later, he admitted that his foster mother had flung him out onto the porch.

Although Stephen did poorly in his schoolwork, there was one thing he could do well: he made delightful drawings. They were not neat and orderly and organized, but random and casual, messy, somewhat unpredictable. For these drawings Stephen received terrific and steady embarrassment from the art teacher. *

The art teacher was a lady no longer very young who had a number of fixed opinions about children and teaching. Her most common technique of instruction was to pass out mimeographed designs, which the pupils then were asked to color according to a dictated or suggested plan. An alternate approach was to stick up on the wall or the blackboard some of the drawings that had been done in previous years by predominantly white classes. These drawings, neat and ordered and very uniform, would serve as models for the children. The neatest and most accurate reproductions would receive the greatest applause.

---

* Our school was assigned a number of experts in different subject areas, which was the result of our participation in the Boston version of a compensatory program for Negro children. The compensation involved was, in fact, of a questionable nature. When Boston lost $2 million in federal aid for compensatory education, the reason given was that the federal government did not consider Boston's program to be offering any kind of legitimate compensation. It should be added, of course, that experts, teachers, and administrators described in this article are composites.

Stephen was unable to cope with a teacher of this sort. He turned off his signals when she was speaking and withdrew into his own private world. With a pencil, frequently stubby and bitten, he would scribble and fiddle, and he would cock his head and whisper to himself. After a while, he would push aside his little drawings and try the paint and paper that he had been given, usually using the watercolors freely and a little defiantly, and he would produce paintings that were very full of his own nature.

If Stephen began to fiddle around during a lesson, he and I and the children near him would prepare for trouble. The art teacher would rush at his desk and would shriek at him, "Give me that! You've made a mess! Look what he's done! He's mixed up the colors! I don't know why we waste good paper on this child!" Then: "Garbage! Junk! He gives me garbage and junk! And garbage is one thing I will not have!"

I do not know a great deal about painting, but the art teacher did not know much about it either, and furthermore, she did not know or care at all about the way a human being can be destroyed. Stephen, in many ways already dying, died many more times before her anger.

Much of Stephen's life, inwardly and outwardly, involved a steady, and as it turned out, losing, battle to survive. Like many defenseless humans, he had to use whatever little weapons came to hand. Acting-up at school was part of it. He was granted so little attention that he must have panicked repeatedly about the possibility that with a few slight mistakes, he might simply stop existing or being seen at all. This is why, I imagine, he seemed so often to invite a tongue-lashing or whipping. Outside school, he might pull a fire-alarm lever and then have the satisfaction of hearing the sirens and seeing the fire engines, and knowing that it was all his doing, so that at least he could have proof in this way that his hands and arm muscles and his mischievous imagination did count for something measurable in the world. It must have seemed better than not having any use at all.

One time, seeing him curled up in one of the corners, I tried to get him to look up at me and smile and talk. He refused, and remained shriveled and silent, and so I said to him: "Stephen, if you curl up like that and will not even look up at me, it will just seem as if you want to make me think you are a little rat." He looked down at himself hurriedly, and then up at me, chuckled grotesquely, and said, with a pitiful little smile: "I *know* I couldn't be a rat, Mr. Kozol, because a rat has got to have a little tail."

When I later repeated this to a child psychiatrist, he suggested that the absence of a tail was all that remained to convince Stephen that he had not yet become a rat. Although this comment might smack a bit of psychiatric dogmatism, I do not really think it carried the point too far. For Boston schoolteachers for years have been speaking of their Negro children as "animals" and the school building that houses them as a "zoo." The repercussions of this attitude probably affected Stephen more than other children, but the price it exacted was paid ultimately by every child, and in the long run, I am convinced that it was paid by every teacher too.

Stephen's misery at school was only partially caused by the psychological harassment that I have been describing, for Stephen was also subjected to corporal punishment regularly, in spite of the fact that he was obviously mentally unstable and had very little control over his behavior. Corporal punishment is still sanctioned in the Boston public schools and takes the form of beatings on the hand with a thin bamboo whip or rattan.

I don't know exactly how many times Stephen underwent these whippings, but unquestionably they occurred at least as often as once a month, and probably more often, closer to once or twice a week. They happened frequently when the class was having math instruction, and this, I came to believe, was connected with the unfriendliness that the math teacher felt toward Stephen. She spoke of it on more than one occasion, yet she was also aware of his mental instability, and she was the first to acknowledge it.

I remember when she discussed this with me, snapping out the words with sureness: "The child's not in his right mind." When I asked her whether she had thought of recommending psychiatric help for him, she replied that it was no use, since he would only tell the psychiatrist that all the teachers were prejudiced. A few days after this conversation, Stephen was sent to the cellar for another rattaning, and her comment, in accusation, not diagnosis or sympathy, was that he was "not in his right mind."

I would like to describe how Stephen behaved when he went downstairs to take his beating. I have said how little he was. Sixty pounds isn't very heavy, and he couldn't have been more than four feet tall. He had terrified tiny hopeless eyes. He had on a Red Sox baseball jersey, baggy corduroy pants, and baseball sneakers which looked a few sizes too large. His hair had oil in it, and it had been shaved down almost to the scalp. He was standing near the men's smoke room. Above were the pipes of the cellar ceiling, nearby the door to the basement boys' toilet. Out of that doorway came the stink of urine. His elbows froze at his sides. The teacher who administered the whipping gave the order to hold out his hands. He wouldn't respond. Again the teacher, standing above him, passed down the order. To no effect. The teacher, now losing patience, ordered it a third time. And still he wouldn't answer or comply. A fourth time. Still this frozen terror. So the decision is made: he will get it twice as many times.

He can't hold out forever. Finally he breaks down and stops resisting. The teacher who gives the beating may, in all other instances, seem a decent man. Even in giving this beating he may do it absolutely as he is supposed to. Yet, properly done or not, and whatever the man's intent, the tears still come, and the welts are formed upon the light-brown hand.

One obvious question immediately comes to mind. Why would *any* teacher whip a child for acts that the teacher has already acknowledged, both to himself and to others, to be beyond the child's ability to prevent? Perhaps a partial explanation lies in the fact that segregated schools seem to require this kind of brutal discipline because of the bitter feelings which are so often present in the air. The children—enough of them anyway—are constantly smoldering with a generally unrecognized awareness of their own degradation. The resulting atmosphere is deeply threatening to teachers and administrators.

Possibly in most cases, this is the entire story. Thinking of some of the teachers, however, I am convinced that something else was happening at times, and once you had watched it, you would know exactly what it was and would never deny that it was there. "This hurts me," goes the saying, "more than it hurts you." Yet there are moments when the visible glint of gratification becomes unmistakable in the white teacher's eyes.

White Bostonians sometimes argue that corporal punishment did not begin with Negro children, that it is, in fact, a very old tradition within the school system. I have never found this a convincing argument. The fact that a crime might have been committed with impunity in the past may make it seem more familiar and less gruesome, but surely does not give it any greater legitimacy. Whether Irish children were once whipped by Yankee teachers, or Jewish children, in turn, by Irish, is immaterial. What does matter is that corporal punishment today is being used by whites on Negroes, and being used in too many cases to act out, on a number of persuasive pretexts, a deeply seated racial hate.

If just any tough teen-ager is beaten on the fingers by his teacher, one can assume that school officials will be able to pass it off as discipline. But when a sixty-pound mentally ill fourth-grader is whipped for acts that are manifestly crazy, and when the teacher who prepares the punishment has, not ten days before, been speaking calmly of the niggers down South, or the little bastards causing trouble up there in Room Four, then even the administrators of the system are going to have to admit that something has gone wrong.

The room in which I taught my fourth grade was not really a room at all, but the corner of an auditorium. Three or four blackboards, two of them unstable, made the area seem a little bit set apart. The first time I approached that classroom I noticed a huge torn stage curtain, a couple of broken windows, and about thirty-five bewildered-looking children, most of whom were Negro. At the other end of the auditorium there was a classroom similar to mine.

The room was relatively quiet during the first hour of the morning. Not until ten o'clock did the bad cross fire start. By ten thirty it attained such a crescendo that the children in the back rows of my section couldn't hear my questions, and I couldn't hear their answers. The room, being large and wooden, echoed every sound. Sometimes the other fourth-grade teacher and I would stagger the lessons in which our classes had to recite aloud. But this makeshift method meant that one class had to be induced to maintain an unnatural rule of silence during major portions of the day. We couldn't always do it anyway, and usually the only solution was to try to outshout each other, so that both of us often left school hoarse or wheezing.

Hours were lost in this manner, yet that was not the worst. Soon after I came into that auditorium, I discovered that our two fourth grades were also going to have to share the space with the glee club, with play rehearsals, special reading, special arithmetic, and at certain times a third- or fourth-grade phonics class. I began to make head counts of the numbers of pupils:

Seventy children from the two regular fourth grades before the invasion.

Then ninety with the glee club and remedial arithmetic.

One hundred and seven with the play rehearsal.

One day the sewing class came in with their sewing machines, and then that became a regular practice in the hall. Once I counted one hundred and twenty people, all talking, singing, yelling, laughing, reciting. Before the Christmas break it became apocalyptic. Not more than half of the planned lessons took place throughout that time.

One day a window whose frame had rotted was blown right out of its sashes by a strong gust of wind. I had noticed several times before that it was in bad condition, but so many other things were broken in the school building that I had not said anything about it. The principal and custodians and other people had been in that building for a long time before me. I felt they must have known the condition of the window. If anything could have been done, I assumed they would have done it.

First there was a cracking sound, then a burst of icy air. The next thing I knew, a child was saying: "Mr. Kozol—look at the window!" As I turned, it was starting to fall in. I was standing, by coincidence, only about four or five feet off and was able to catch it. But the wind was so strong that it nearly blew right out of my hands. A couple of seconds of good luck kept glass from the desks of six or seven children and very possibly saved several of them from being injured. I soon realized that I was not going to be able to hold the thing up by myself, and I was obliged to ask one of the stronger boys in the class to give me a hand. Meanwhile, as the children beneath us shivered in the icy wind, and as the two of us now shivered also since the mercury was hovering close to zero, I asked one of the children in the front row to run down and fetch the janitor.

When he asked me what he should tell him, I said, "Tell him the house is falling in." The children laughed. It was the first time I had ever said anything like that when the children could hear me. I am sure my reluctance to speak out more often must appear odd to many readers, for at this perspective it seems odd to me as well.

Certainly plenty of things were wrong within that school building, and there was enough we could have joked about. The truth, however, is that I very seldom talked like that, nor did many of the other teachers. Unless a teacher was ready to buck the system utterly, it would become far too difficult to teach in an atmosphere of that kind of honesty. It was a great deal easier to pretend as much as possible that everything was OK.

Some teachers carried out this posture with so much eagerness, in fact, that their defense of the school ended up as something like a hymn of praise. "You children should thank God and feel blessed with good luck for all you've got. There are so many little children in the world who have been given so much less." The books are junk, the paint peels, the cellar stinks, the teachers call you nigger, the windows fall in on your heads. "Thank God that you don't live in Russia or Africa! Thank God for all the blessings that you've got!"

After the window blew in on us, the janitor finally came up and hammered it shut with nails so that it would not fall in again, but also so that it could not be opened. A month passed before anything was done about the missing glass. Children shivered a few feet away from it. The principal walked by frequently and saw us. So did the various lady experts who traveled all week from room to room within our school. At last, one day the janitor came up with a piece of cardboard and covered over about one quarter of that lower window so that no more wind could come it, but just that much less sunshine too. I remember wondering what a piece of glass cost in Boston, and thought of going out and buying some and trying to put it in myself. That rectangle of cardboard covered our nailed-shut window for half of the term, and it was finally removed only because a television station was going to

visit in the building and the school department wanted to make
the room look more attractive. But it was winter when the window
broke, and the repairs did not take place until the middle of the
spring.

Other schools in the ghetto were no better than my own, and
some were worse. One of the most unfortunate, acording to those
who made comparisons, was the Endicott School, also heavily
imbalanced. Endicott, I learned, had become so overcrowded
that in some classes the number of pupils exceeded the number
of desks and the extra pupils had to sit in chairs behind the
teacher. A child absent one day commonly came back the
next and found someone else sitting at his desk. These facts
had been brought out in the newspaper, but nothing had been
done. When the parents of the Endicott children pressed the
school department to take action, a series of events transpired
which told a large part of the story of segregation in a very
few words.

The school department offered, in order to resolve the problem,
to buy a deserted forty-year-old Hebrew school and allot about
$7000 to furnish it with desks and chairs. Aside from the indignity
of getting everybody else's castoffs (the Negroes already lived in
former Jewish tenements and bought in formerly Jewish stores),
to buy and staff this old Hebrew school with about a dozen
teachers would cost quite a lot more than to send the children
down the street a couple of miles to a white school that had
space. The Hebrew school was going to cost over $180,000. To
staff it and supply it with books and equipment would cost
$100,000 more a year. To send the children into available
seats in nearby white classrooms (no new teachers needed)
would have cost $40,000 to $60,000 for the year. The school department was willing to spend as much as an extra $24,000 in
order to put the Negro children into another segregated school.

As it happened, the school committee debated the issue in so
many directions that most of the school year passed before anything of a final nature was decided. Meanwhile, the children in
the Endicott classrooms had lost another year from their lives.

In my own school there was another bad situation in the third
of the three fourth grades. This class had been subjected for most
of the year to a highly unstable teacher—a man of good will and

mild disposition, who, however, had been dismissed from another position within the Boston system after serious trouble of a psychiatric nature. It was readily apparent that he was in no emotional condition to handle the problems posed by a crowded ghetto class. Beginning in October and continuing through March, his teaching had brought little to the children besides unending noise and chaos. Yet all the complaints of the bewildered Negro parents and even the stated dissatisfaction of the principal had not been able to effect a change.

At last in early April, after about six months of agony, the man was leaving. But the school administration did not have the competence or insight to assign a better-qualified person in his place. Instead of a confident or experienced instructor, a bashful and quite terrified young lady took over the class, and then, after her departure, a string of substitute teachers, who seemed at times truly to have been grabbed off the street at seven thirty, knocked over the head, handed a twenty-dollar bill, and shipped over to our schoolhouse in a taxi. Some of them were nice people, but few had any kind of real qualifications.

One fellow, I remember, did not even get there until about ten thirty because he had been out driving a cab the night before, and he announced within about forty-five minutes that he would certainly not be coming back. The consequence of all this in academic terms was an overall retardation of almost the entire class.

A chart on the wall gave some measure of the situation by keeping a record of math and spelling grades. The math average of the class for weeks had remained, almost without exception, below the point of failing—for certain stretches of time, as much as 30 points below. The spelling and writing had fluctuated around the third-grade level. Reading levels were a year, and often two years, beneath the national norm. All of these subject failures were major tragedies because in many respects and for a number of the children the stunting of their learning at such an early age was likely to prove almost irreversible.

But the setbacks in math and spelling and writing were not as serious for them as the lack of continuity in their work in social studies. For at least in the basic subjects, no matter how poorly they were doing, the children had had some continuity of material. In geography and history, there had been no continuity, but rather a frantic shifting of focus almost every day.

One morning a substitute teacher, groping for a way to kill an hour, would have the children read aloud to him about India. The next day, another teacher, not knowing what had been done before and having a special fondness for another country, Holland perhaps, would tell the class to flip back a hundred pages and read about dikes and wooden shoes. Then someone would appear long enough to get some help from one of the full-time teachers, and the children would get two or three abortive sessions on the desert, but the day after that they would be doing India over again; then off to Lima, Peru; suddenly to American cotton production, or the corn belt, or coal production—or then, with the arrival of a new teacher, back to dikes and wooden shoes. It is not surprising that with a crazy arrangement of this sort, the children would frequently start out by lying to a new substitute and would do their best to break him down. Nor is it surprising that their sense of place and time soon grew to be disastrously confused. They could make no distinction, even in the most tentative and general manner, between a city, town, state, or country, or even between a continent or island. Words like Yangtze River, hemisphere, Himalayas, pyramid were all mixed up in their minds. A question about what one could get from rushing streams in Switzerland might elicit such an answer as "population" or "migration," and a question about what "self-evident" meant, or "created equal," would easily bring back from the class such answers as "Red Coats," "transportation," or "white coal."

Seven different teachers in the course of ten days became the final catastrophe of this classroom. The children grew wild, and the atmosphere from day to day grew more explosive. At this point, on the morning of the third of May, the principal called me into her office and asked me if I would agree to take the class for the remainder of the year. With the assurance that my own students would not be getting a string of substitutes, I agreed to make the transfer.

Consider what it is like to go into a new classroom and to see before you suddenly, and in a way you cannot avoid recognizing, the dreadful consequences of a year's wastage of so many lives. You walk into a narrow and old wood-smelling classroom and see thirty-five curious, cautious, and untrusting children, aged nine to thirteen, of whom about two-thirds are Negro. Lifetime records of seven of them are missing, symptomatic and emblematic at once of the chaos of the teacher changes. On the first math test the class average is 36. The children tell you with embarrassment that it has been like that since fall.

You check around the classroom. Of forty desks, five have tops with no hinges. You lift a desktop to fetch a paper, and you find the top has fallen off. There are three windows; one can't be opened. A sign on it written in the messy scribble of some custodial person warns: "Do Not Unlock This Window. It Is Broken." The general look of the room is that of a bleak-light photograph of a mental hospital. Above the one poor blackboard, gray rather than really black, and hard to write on, hangs from one tack, lopsided, a motto attributed to Benjamin Franklin: "Well begun is half done." So much within this classroom seems to be a mockery of itself.

Into this grim scenario, drawing on your own pleasures and memories, you do what you can to bring some kind of life. You bring in some cheerful and colorful paintings by Joan Miró and Paul Klee. While the paintings by Miró do not arouse much interest, the ones by Klee become an instantaneous success. One picture in particular, entitled *Bird Garden*, catches the imagination of the entire class. You slip it out of the book and tack it on the wall beside the doorway, and it creates a traffic jam every time the children have to file in or file out. You discuss with your students some of the reasons why Klee may have painted the way he did, and you talk about the things that can be accomplished in a painting which cannot be done in a photograph. None of this seems to be above the children's heads. Despite this you are advised flatly by the art teacher that your naïveté has gotten the best of you, and that the children cannot possibly appreciate these drawings.

For poetry, instead of the materials recommended by the course of study, you decide to introduce a poem of William Butler Yeats. The poem that you select is "The Lake Isle of Innisfree." The children do not go crazy about it at first, but a number of them seem to like it as much as you do, and you tell them how once, two years before, you were living in England and you helped a

man in the country to make his home from wattles and clay.
Many of them grow more curious than they appeared at first.
Here again, however, you are advised by older teachers that you
are making a mistake: Yeats is too difficult for children. They
can't enjoy it, won't appreciate it, wouldn't like it.

On a number of other occasions, the situation is repeated. The
children are offered something new and lively. They respond to
it energetically, and their attention doesn't waver. For the first
time in a long while, perhaps, there is actually some real excitement and some growing and some thinking going on within that
room. In each case, however, you are advised sooner or later that
you are making a mistake. Your mistake, in fact, is to have im-
pinged upon the standardized condescension upon which the
entire administration of the school is based. To hand Paul Klee's
pictures to the children of a ghetto classroom, particularly in a
twenty-dollar volume, constitutes a threat to the school system.
The threat is handled by a continual underrating of the children.
In this way many students are unjustifiably held back from a great
many experiences that they might come to value, and are pinned
down instead to books the teacher knows, and tastes that she can
handle easily.

My own feeling was that it was precisely the familiar material
that had so deadened the previous three years of schooling and
that had been so closely identified with the misery and chaos
and intellectual aridity of this most recent year. To attempt to
revive or reawaken a child's curiosity long gone dead or long
sedated by use of the same poison that had laid him low seemed
futile. Only by introducing new and totally fresh materials did
there seem a chance to make a difference. Although the poems
and pictures I brought in did not appeal to every student, there
is no doubt at all of the degree to which the will to learn, as well
as the most simple will to laugh or speak or smile or joke, reap-
peared among the children.

The change in attitude carried over, curiously, into utterly
unrelated areas. One teacher of an older grade, who had little
fondness for me, felt impelled, nevertheless, to come upstairs and
offer me a compliment. "Everyone has been so impressed," she
said, "by the way your children have been filing in the stairways."
In an odd way, I felt pleased by what she had told me. I couldn't

have cared less how my pupils were filing in the stairways, but it was a source of satisfaction to me to think that they were doing something which, within the context of this school, was so much to their advantage.

A more serious measure of the impact of these changes came to light when I started testing the class on the intensive work we had been doing in math and English. In less than a month, the math average went up to a median well above grade level. Test score averages over the course of three weeks began at 36, rose to 60, and leveled off at 79.

There was no unusual expertise at work within the classroom. There was, in fact, total professional naïveté as well as considerable technical incompetence. One thing *was* present, however, and this was the personal motivation of the children. It was there, unused and wholly unawakened, but very much in evidence as soon as it was looked for and believed in. To care about their work, the children asked only a few grains of faith and expectation, a small degree of fun, a mood of relaxation, and an open understanding between their teacher and themselves that the things that had been going on that year were not their fault.

A great deal has been written in recent years about the purported lack of motivation in the children of the Negro ghettos. Little in my experience supports this, yet the phrase has been repeated endlessly, and the blame in almost all cases is placed somewhere outside the classroom. Boston's former deputy superintendent, in putting forward the aims of the compensatory program, presented it in this way:

It is our hope through this program to raise the achievement of these pupils closer to their potentials, which have for too long been submerged by parental lack of values.

Such language belies a sense of failure on the part of those who run these schools. The suggestion is made that the child will be offered a certain amount of compassion, just so long as it is made absolutely clear ahead of time that the heart of the problem is the lack of values of his family. Unquestionably, there are Negro children whose school careers give testimony to the problems that plague their parents' lives. Both Stephen's original and foster parents are pertinent examples. But the greater number of Negro parents whom I have known in Boston do not lead lives lacking in real values. Faced with the particular nature of the deputy superintendent's rhetoric, we have to ask whose values we are talking about—and deprived in the eyes of whom. To say that Negroes in Boston are deprived of rights would be an honest statement. It would also be honest to say that they are deprived of good schools, and at least to that degree, of a fair chance for democracy, for opportunity, and all the things these words are supposed to mean. But to say that they are deprived culturally, in the face of the present school administration and in the face of the profound callousness and cynicism of the entire system, seems to me meaningless.

Glimmerings of a personal understanding of these points and of the ironies involved in them can sometimes be perceived among the teachers. I recall a conversation I had with an unusually frank red-neck teacher in my school. "They talk about the Negroes being culturally deprived," he said with an unembarrassed smile, "I'm the one who's been goddamn culturally deprived, and I don't need anyone to tell me. I haven't learned a thing, read a thing that I wished I'd read or learned since the day I entered high school, and I've known it for years, and I tried to hide it from myself, and now I wish I could do something about it, but I'm afraid it's just too late."

The same teacher confided to me on another occasion that he had been beaten around and treated rough and whipped by his parents and by his Yankee schoolmasters when he was a child. To him, this seemed to clear the field for beating others around today. The attitude of many people in Boston and other cities has been consistent with this view: "We had a hard time of it, so why shouldn't they?" This less than gentle attitude seems characteristic of a less than gentle society, in which the prevailing viewpoint of those who are moderately successful is too likely to be that they got theirs, and the others can damn well wait a while before they get the same.

There has been so much recent talk of progress in the areas of curriculum innovation and the textbook revision that few people outside the field of teaching understand how bad most of our elementary school materials still are. In isolated suburban school districts children play ingenious Monopoly games revised to impart an immediate and first-person understanding of economic problems in the colonial period. In private schools, kindergarten children begin to learn about numbers with brightly colored sticks known as cuisenaire rods, and second-grade children are introduced to mathematics through the ingenuity of a package of odd-shaped figures known as Attribute Games. But in the majority of schools in Roxbury and Harlem and dozens of other slum districts stretching west across the country, teaching techniques, textbooks, and other teaching aids are hopelessly antique, largely obsolete, and often insulting or psychologically oppressive for many thousands of Negro and other minority schoolchildren.

I once made a check of all books in my fourth-grade classroom. Of the slightly more than six hundred books, almost one quarter had been published prior to the bombing of Hiroshima; 60 percent were either ten years old or older. Of thirty-two different book series standing in rows within the cupboard, only six were published as recently as five years ago, and seven series were twenty to thirty-five years old. These figures put into perspective some of the lofty considerations and expensive research projects sponsored by even the best of the curriculum development organizations, for they suggest that educational progress and innovation are reaching chiefly the children of rich people rather than the children of the urban poor.

Obsolescence, however, was not the only problem in our textbooks. Direct and indirect forms of discrimination were another. The geography book given to my pupils, first published eighteen years ago and only modestly updated since, traced a cross-country journey in which there was not one mention, hint, or image of a dark-skinned face. The chapter on the South described an idyllic landscape in the heart of Dixie: pastoral home of hardworking white citizens, contented white children, and untroubled white adults.

While the history book mentioned Negroes—in its discussion of slavery and the Civil War—the tone of these sections was ambiguous. "Men treasure freedom above all else," the narrative conceded at one point, but it also pointed out that slavery was not an altogether dreadful institution: "Most Southern people treated their slaves kindly," it related, and then quoted a stereotyped plantation owner as saying: "Our slaves have good homes and plenty to eat. When they are sick, we take care of them. . . ."

While the author favored emancipation, he found it necessary to grant to arguments on the other side a patriotic legitimacy: "No one can truly say, 'The North was right' or 'The Southern cause was better.' Remember, each side fought for the ideals it believed in. For in Our America all of us have the right to our beliefs."

When my class had progressed to the cotton chapter in our geography book, I decided to alter the scheduled reading. Since I was required to make use of the textbook, and since its use, I believed, was certain to be damaging, I decided to supply the class with extra material in the form of a mimeographed sheet. I did not propose to tell the children any tales about lynchings, beatings, or the Ku Klux Klan. I merely wanted to add to the study of cotton-growing some information about the connection between the discovery of Eli Whitney's cotton gin and the greater growth of slavery.

I had to submit this material to my immediate superior in the school, a lady whom I will call the Reading Teacher. The Reading Teacher was a well-intentioned woman who had spent several years in ghetto classrooms, but who, like many other teachers, had some curiously ambivalent attitudes toward the children she was teaching. I recall the moment after I had handed her that sheet of paper. Looking over the page, she agreed with me immediately that it was accurate. Nobody, she said, was going to quibble with the idea that cotton, the cotton gin, and slavery were all intertwined. But it was the question of the "advisability of any mention of slavery to the children at this time," which, she said, she was presently turning over in her mind. "Would it," she asked me frankly, "truly serve the advantage of the children at this stage to confuse and complicate the study of simple geography with socioeconomic factors?" Why expose the children, she was asking essentially, to unpleasant facts about their heritage?

Then, with an expression of the most honest and intense affection for the children in the class, she added: "I don't want these children to have to think back on this year later on and to remember that we were the ones who told them they were Negro." This remark seemed to take one step further the attitude of the text-book writers. Behind the statement lay the unspoken assumption that to be Negro was a shameful condition. The longer this knowl-edge could be kept from the innocent young, the better off they would be.

After the journey across America, the class was to study the life of the desert Arab. Before we began, the Reading Teacher urged upon me a book which she said she had used with her own classes for a great many years. It was not the same book the children had. She told me she preferred it, but that it was too old to be in regular use.

I took the book home that night and opened it up to a section on the Arabs:

The Bedouin father is tall and straight. He wears a robe that falls to his ankles and his bare feet are shod in sandals of camel's leather. . . . Behind the Bedouin father walk his wife and his children. . . .

These people are fine looking. Their black eyes are bright and intel-ligent. Their features are much like our own, and, although their skin is brown, they belong to the white race, as we do. It is scorching desert sun that has tanned the skin of the Arabs to such a dark brown color.

Turning to a section on Europe, I read the following de-scription:

Two Swiss children live in a farmhouse on the edge of town. . . . These children are handsome. Their eyes are blue. Their hair is golden yellow. Their white skins are clear, and their cheeks are as red as ripe, red apples.

Curious after this to see how the African Negroes would be treated, I turned to a section on the Congo Valley:

The black people who live on this great continent of Africa were afraid of the first white men who came to explore their land. They ran and hid from them in the dark jungle. They shot poisoned arrows from behind the thick bushes. They were savage and uncivilized. . . .

Yumbo and Minko are a black boy and a black girl who live in this jungle village. Their skins are of so dark a color that they look almost black. Their noses are large and flat. Their lips are thick. Their eyes are black and shining, and their hair is so curly that it seems like wool. They are Negroes and belong to the black race.

Perhaps without being conscious of it, the Reading Teacher had her own way of telling the children what it meant to be Negro.

Not all books used in a school system, merely by the law of averages, are going to be consistently and blatantly poor. A large number of the books we had in Boston were only mildly distorted or else devastatingly bad only in one part. One such book, not used in my school but at the junior high level, was entitled *Our World Today*. Right and wrong, good and bad alternate in this book from sentence to sentence and from page to page:

The people of the British Isles are, like our own, a mixed people. Their ancestors were the sturdy races of northern Europe, such as Celts, Angles, Saxons, Danes and Normans, whose energy and abilities still appear in their descendants. With such a splendid inheritance what could be more natural than that the British should explore and settle many parts of the world and in time build up the world's greatest colonial empire? . . .

The people of South Africa have one of the most democratic governments now in existence in any country. . . .

Africa needs more capitalists. . . . White managers are needed . . . to show the Negroes how to work and to manage their plantations. . . .

In our study of the nations of the world, we should try to understand the people and their problems from their point of view. We ought to have a sympathetic attitude towards them, rather than condemn them through ignorance because they do not happen always to have our ways. . . .

The Negro is very quick to imitate and follow the white man's way of living and dressing. . . .

The white man may remain for short periods and direct the work, but he cannot . . . do the work himself. He must depend on the natives to do the work. . . .

The white men who have entered Africa are teaching the natives how to live. . . .

Sooner or later, books like these will be put to pasture. Either that, or they will be carefully doctored and rewritten. But the problem they represent is not going to be resolved in any important way by their removal or revision. Too many teachers admire and depend on such textbooks, and prefer to teach from them. The attitudes of these teachers are likely to remain long after the books have been replaced.

Plenty of good books are available, of course, that give an honest picture of the lives of black Americans. The tutorial programs in Boston have been using them, and so have many of the more enlightened private schools. In the public schools of this city, however, it is difficult to make use of books that depart from the prescribed curriculum. When I made a tentative effort to introduce such materials into my classroom, I encountered firm resistance.

Earlier in the year I had brought to school a book of poetry by the Negro author Langston Hughes. I had not used it in the classroom, but it did at least make its way onto a display board in the auditorium as part of an exhibit on important American Negroes, set up to pay lip service to "Negro History Week."

To put a book by a Negro poet on display is one thing. To open the book and attempt to read something from it is quite another. In the last weeks of the spring I discovered the difference when I began to read a few of the poems to the children in my class. It was during a period in which I also was reading them some poems of John Crowe Ransom, Robert Frost, and W. B. Yeats.

Hughes, I have come to learn, holds an extraordinary appeal for many children. I knew this from some earlier experiences in other classes, and I remembered, in particular, the reaction of a group of young teen-agers in a junior high the first time I ever had brought his work into a public school. On the book's cover, the children could see the picture of the dark-skinned author, and they did not fail to comment. Their comments concentrated on that single, obvious, overriding fact:

"*Look—that man's colored.*"

The same reaction was evident here, too, among my fourth-grade students: the same gratification and the same very vivid sense of recognition. It seemed a revelation to them that a man could have black skin and be a famous author.

Of all the poems of Langston Hughes that we read, the one the children liked the best was a poem entitled "Ballad of the Landlord." The reason, I think, that this piece of writing had so much meaning for them was not only that it seemed moving in an obvious and immediate human way, but also that it *found* its emotion in something ordinary. It is a poem which allows both heroism and pathos to poor people, sees strength in awkwardness, and attributes to a poor person standing on the stoop of his slum house every bit as much significance as William Wordsworth saw in daffodils, waterfalls, and clouds. At the request of the children, I mimeographed some copies of that poem, and although nobody in the classroom was asked to do this, several of the children took it home and memorized it on their own. I did not assign it for memory, because I do not think that memorizing a poem has any special value. Some of the children just came in and asked if they could recite it. Before long, almost every child in the room had asked to have a turn.

One day a week later, shortly before lunchtime, I was standing in front of my class playing a record of French children's songs I had brought in. A message-signal on the wall began to buzz. I left the room and hurried to the principal's office. A white man whom I had never seen before was sitting by her desk. This man, bristling and clearly hostile to me, as was the principal, instantly attacked me for having read to my class and distributed at their wish the poem entitled "Ballad of the Landlord." It turned out that he was the father of one of the few white boys in the class. He was also a police officer.

The mimeograph of the poem, in my handwriting, was waved before my eyes. The principal demanded to know what right I had to allow such a poem—not in the official course of study—to be read and memorized by children. I said I had not asked anyone to memorize it, but that I would defend the poem and its use on the basis that it was a good poem. The principal became incensed with my answer and blurted out that she did not consider it a work of art.

The parent was angry as well, it turned out, about a book having to do with the United Nations. I had brought a book to class, one of sixty or more volumes, that told about the UN and its Human Rights Commission. The man, I believe, had mistaken "human rights" for "civil rights" and was consequently in a patriotic rage. The principal, in fairness, made the point that she did not think there was anything wrong with the United Nations, although in the report later filed on the matter, she denied this, and said, instead, "I then spoke and said that I felt there was no need for this material in the classroom." The principal's report went on to say that she assured the parent, after I had left the room, that "there was not another teacher in the district who would have used this poem or any material like it. I assured him that his children would be very safe from such incidents."

I returned to my class, as requested, and a little before two o'clock the principal called me back to tell me I was fired. She forbade me to say good-bye to the children in the class or to indicate in any way that I was leaving. She said that I was to close up my records, leave the school, and report to School Department headquarters the next morning.

The next day an official who had charge of my case at the School Department took a much harder line on curriculum innovation than I had ever heard before. No literature, she said, which is not in the course of study could *ever* be read by a Boston teacher without permission of someone higher up. She said further that no poem by any Negro author could be considered permissible if it involved suffering. I asked her whether there would be many good poems left to read by such a standard. Wouldn't it rule out almost all great Negro literature? Her answer evaded the issue. No poetry that described suffering was felt to be suitable. The only Negro poetry that could be read in the Boston schools, she indicated, must fit a certain kind of standard. The kind of poem she meant, she said by way of example, might be a poem that "accentuates the positive" or "describes nature" or "tells of something hopeful."

The same official went on a few minutes later to tell me that any complaint from a parent meant automatic dismissal. "You're out," she said. "You cannot teach in the Boston schools again. If you want to teach, why don't you try a private school someday?"

Other Boston officials backed up these assertions in statements released during the following hectic days. The deputy superintendent, who wielded considerable authority over these matters, pointed out that although Langston Hughes "has written much beautiful poetry, we cannot give directives to the teacher to use literature written in native dialects." She explained: "We are trying to break the speech patterns of these children, trying to get them to speak properly. This poem does not present correct

grammatical expression and would just entrench the speech patterns we want to break."

A couple of weeks later, winding up an investigation into the
matter, School Committee member Thomas Eisenstadt concluded
that school officials had handled things correctly. Explaining in
his statement that teachers are dismissed frequently when found
lacking in either "training, personality or character," he went on
to say that "Mr. Kozol, or anyone else who lacks the personal
discipline to abide by rules and regulations, as we all must in our
civilized society, is obviously unsuited for the highly responsible
profession of teaching."

In thinking back upon my year within the Boston system, I am
often reminded of a kind of sad-keyed epilogue that the Reading
Teacher used to bring forward sometimes at the end of a discussion: "Things are changing," she used to say with feeling; "I am
changing too—but everything cannot happen just like that."

Perhaps by the time another generation comes around a certain
modest number of these things will have begun to be corrected.
But if I were the parent of a Negro child, I know that I would not
willingly accept a calendar of improvements scaled so slowly. The
anger of the mother whose child's years in elementary school have
been squandered may seem inexplicable to a person like the
Reading Teacher. To that mother, it is the complacency and
hypocrisy of a society that could sustain and foster so many thousands of people like the Reading Teacher that seem extraordinary.
The comfortable people who don't know and don't see the ghettos
deliberate in their committee rooms. Meanwhile, the children
whose lives their decisions are either going to save or ruin are
expected to sit quietly, fold their hands patiently, recite their
lessons, draw their margins, bite their tongues, swallow their
dignities, and smile and wait.

6 FAILURE STRATEGIES AND TEACHERS OF THE DISADVANTAGED

SHEILA SCHWARTZ

A recent *New York Times* report on the interaction between young male dope addicts and their mothers emphasized certain recurring neurotic patterns. Basically, the mothers of these boys do not want them to be cured. They want them to remain addicted, immature, and dependent, because this gives the mother ego gratification and a *raison d'être*. A symbiosis is created, and mother and son find themselves locked in a destructive relationship which neither wants consciously but which both need subconsciously.

The same unconscious need often exists between a teacher and his disadvantaged students. The slum teacher in many cases needs failure, and through various strategies guides his students to achieve this destructive goal.

Of course, this pattern does not exist *only* in slum schools nor with disadvantaged students. Jersild describes a young teacher who encouraged her students to be dependent on her and derived great satisfaction from their tears when they left her on the last day of school. After she was encouraged to examine her motivations, her behavior began to change. She was able to ask herself if she was "perhaps encouraging dependence to gratify her own need for power or her need to be assured of her own adequacy. She decided that her reasons for fostering dependence had been devious and she also came to think that she really did not need this kind of assurance." [1]

Negative patterns do not exist only in slum schools. Teachers who would prefer to destroy rather than to create can be found

Sheila Schwartz, "Failure Strategies and Teachers of the Disadvantaged," *Teachers College Record* (February 1967), pp. 380–393. Reprinted by permission of the author and publisher.

anywhere. However, it is far easier to get away with student failure in slum schools. For one thing, the parents, failures themselves, are less likely to protest. Any teacher in an upper-class suburban school who produced 100% non-readers year after year would soon find himself out of a job.

Modes of Ego Gratification

The subject of this paper is not the cruelty often practiced by teachers against students or the tendency of the stronger to exploit the weaker. The misuse of teacher power has been well documented. For example, George Orwell, James Joyce, Piet Bakker, and Charles Dickens have written about the ability of certain teachers to terrify their charges. The subject of this paper is not personality or temperament, but ways in which teachers obtain ego gratification. Whether the temperament is sweet or bad-tempered is irrelevant.

Let us hypothesize, for the present, the following: most teachers would prefer to achieve ego gratification from seeing their students clearly evidence growth in self-control, content-control, peer-relationships, and adult relationships. Most teachers would prefer to achieve ego gratification from viewing themselves as kind, sensitive people who are so skilled in content and human relations that they have few learning or discipline problems in their classrooms.

Let us further hypothesize that teachers who are unable to achieve ego gratification in the above ways, and who stay in teaching, are forced to find other sources of satisfaction. It is this writer's contention that these are often negative ways and that the lack of parental power in slum schools enables teachers to get away with much more of this than they could in schools with the natural checks and balances provided by parent involvement.

The Slum School Teacher

Who are the teachers who go to slum schools? Green has described a not unusual situation in which a prospective teacher with a mediocre student teaching and undergraduate record was being considered for a position in a large urban community. After her credentials were carefully evaluated she was offered a "probationary position in a school which had the highest Negro population, the highest dropout rate, and whose members ranked high in family disorganization, physical illness, and residential mobility." [2] She was told that if she performed well in this school during the probationary period, "she would be promoted to a higher prestige school within the system."

Ravitz reiterates this idea by describing depressed areas as "Siberias" to which teachers were sent as punishment . . . "without any real concern for these children and with the common stereotype of them as children of low ability. As a result . . . the children were not encouraged to learn very much; the teacher expended little energy on anything but maintaining order and bemoaning her lot, the children fulfilled the low expectation, which in turn reinforced the original assumption to prove that the teacher was right." [3]

It is highly probable that the beginning teacher described by Green has had no specific training to equip him for what he finds in depressed areas. "Unfortunately, we have been training our teachers for essentially a middle-class world of white students, and many of them do not grow up to work in such a world." Those beginning teachers who do go to work in depressed schools anticipate with fear the large classes, discipline problems, unattractive school surroundings, and a frightening and unfamiliar social milieu. "An absence of status, recognition, and esteem, complete the dreary outlook." [4] The possibilities that this beginning teacher will receive in-service guidance and support are indeed doubtful. He is more likely to encounter overcrowded classes, shortages of books and supplies, and administrators who are themselves so threatened that they resent teachers who need help.

The Supporting Principal

A recent *New Yorker* profile about Elliot Shapiro, an outstanding Harlem principal, makes the point that Shapiro is outstanding because he "cares." One of his teachers, describing his supportive function says: "In some schools, if you have a child in trouble, it's like *your* fault. The principal doesn't want to have anything to do with it." [5]

Despite the fact that in Dr. Shapiro's school there exist many of the same problems found in other schools, his teachers have been able to get ego gratification from the positive accomplishments of their pupils. Perhaps this is due, in part, to Dr. Shapiro's training in clinical psychology.

Dr. Shapiro is in constant interaction with his teachers and the children. One teacher, jubilantly reporting to Dr. Shapiro that thirteen of her students had just finished a reader, said, "That's when we get the rewards. You feel you're up against a blank wall, and suddenly one day light dawns, and the child unfolds. No wonder a teacher feels like shouting when that happens."

Positive ego gratification for teachers is also described in relation to the acceptance of one student from this school at Hunter College's Junior High School. Dr. Shapiro, recounting the bringing of the good news by a secretary, said: "Her hands were shaking and she could hardly talk. Then *my* hands began to shake. A wave of exultant hysteria spread among the teachers. They laughed and cried all at once. Even now, when I talk about it, I'm moved all over again."

Self-Defensive Abuse

Few teachers in depressed schools have the good fortune to be encouraged to do their best. A teacher in a suburban school in the New York City area, which is 85% Negro, told me: "You go downhill in a job like this. After a while you get to hate the kids because of their problems. Guidance is a joke. All they do is sit in their offices and make telephone calls to truants. Most of the teachers here are rejects from the other schools in the system, and the principal wants a quiet school. Everybody gets suspicious if you try to do anything unusual, like take a trip. Most of the teachers here are first generation college graduates. Their parents are butchers and truck drivers. They all have inferiority feelings. The only people they feel superior to are their Negro students and their parents."

His remarks may seem extreme, but the problems with colleagues faced by teachers who want to break the failure pattern have been documented elsewhere. Kornberg states that the teacher with commitment faces "the ridicule and cynicism of many colleagues. How can he be so brash as to really try to teach these children, and do what these other teachers have given up trying to do? Many of us have seen this withering, self-defensive abuse of the new teacher. . . ." [6]

This contrasts sharply with the following statement of a junior high school teacher in a wealthy Westchester community.

"I enjoy the children," he said.

He had taught at a fashionable prep school before going to Westchester, but in his present school he found even more intellectual challenge and stimulation than before.

"You get the feeling that you're involved in something really important here," he said. "Everything is going for you."

His salary was high, getting the job was in itself an achievement, he had more materials and supplies than he could use, and he was encouraged to recommend additional materials for purchasing.*

When this teacher attended conferences of national organizations (to which he was urged to go and for which his expenses were paid by the system), he felt a sense of pride when he mentioned his school system. It had received nationwide publicity, important visitors frequently went through his classes, and administrative personnel regularly rose to high educational positions in the state and in Washington, D.C. This teacher did not feel isolated from the mainstream of contemporary life.

The intellectual level of his students was challenging and he learned from their experiences. Conveniences such as a telephone in each classroom and a large well-furnished teacher's room in which he could quietly read and study, strengthened his self-image as a professional worker.

This teacher had no need to obtain ego gratification from feeling superior to his students. On the contrary, the fact that he was considered equal to the task by the school and wealthy, highly educated parent body, gave him a strong feeling of self-worth and accomplishment.

* In each room in an elementary school of this system I found the following equipment (K-3): terrarium, aquarium, slide projector, individual filmstrip previewers, filmstrip projector, listening station with six individual earphones, two sinks, paints, papers, bathroom, television, motion picture projector, tape recorder. The Parents Association, running out of ideas, had just given each class an electric ice-cream maker.

It is evident that teachers in depressed schools, holding conferences across radiators, who have received the same kind of training as the Westchester teacher, are destined to ultimate bitterness, disillusion, and warping.

The average teacher probably anticipates some discipline problems during his beginning years, and perhaps at the beginning of each school year, but the very fact that he enters teaching implies his belief that each school year will be easier than the preceding one because he will grow in ability to handle content, methods, and discipline. He expects satisfactions from his students as they demonstrate cognitive achievement, ability to develop self-control, improved peer-relationships, and ability to reinforce his own self-image.

Failure Patterns

When teachers are denied all of these satisfactions they are forced, for their own self-preservation, to join the self-fulfilling prophecy chorus. They are able to escape from the guilt of their own lack of achievement in the belief that nobody could teach such pupils. This is why, as was mentioned, the teacher who attempts to use unusual facilitating methods meets with group ostracism in many situations. He is interfering with the existing status quo.

Teachers caught in this failure pattern produce it throughout the year as the only means of saving face. "Some teachers establish low expectations, anticipate failure, and, true to the Mertonian self-fulfilling prophecy, find an increasing rate of failure." [7]

The self-fulfilling prophecy is the insidious base on which failure predictions are based. It serves as the essential rationale for teaching, which is not only non-facilitating but is more often boring, confusing, non-sequential, and non-essential.

Clark views the prophecy, along with IQ scores, class prejudice, and racial prejudice as essentially an "alibi for educational neglect, and in no way . . . a reflection of the educational process." [8] Assumptions about the above, whether "well-intentioned . . . (or) . . . the obvious reflection of prejudice and ignorance, contribute to the perpetuation of inferior education for lower-status children, whether their lower status is socio-economic or racial."

Depravity and Determinism

Glatt relates the self-fulfilling prophecy to "a religious concept called *depravity*" [9] and adds that "those who held this view believed that man was afflicted with a tendency toward sin and evil rather than righteousness. . . ." Although this concept had a strong influence on Americans for many decades, "in recent decades the doctrine of inherent depravity has been questioned; now we are not sure whether people are depraved or deprived." Nevertheless, if we act as if either depravity or deprivation is inevitable, we find ourselves in the grip of the self-fulfilling prophecy. In twentieth-century life it appears that the only area in which belief in determinism is still entrenched is in the education of slum children.

Acceptance of the self-fulfilling prophecy "leads to negation not only of the essential responsibility of the school but also of the actual and potential strengths of the children. Most important, it indicates an elaborate rationale for the further alienation of teachers from their primary function, teaching." [10]

Teachers perpetuate patterns of failure with many specific strategies of which they may or may not be aware. Among these is the language strategy. The obvious misuse of language in yelling and sarcasm is a familiar pattern; but the strategy involves even more subtle misuses of language.

Lowering the Language Level

Teachers in depressed schools often use obscenity and crude phrases which they would not use with middle-class children or with their colleagues. Instead of attempting to speak with clarity on a standard level, they sink to the slum level in the mistaken belief that this is the only way they can communicate, because this is what the students have previously known.

It is a truism that speaking down to a person implies contempt. The Nazis, masters of degradation strategies, were well aware of the role language could play:

Degradation was accentuated by the entire absence of civilized manners, as manifested in the language. Thus, in addressing the prisoners, the pronoun "du" (the familiar form of address) was always used, whereas it was compulsory for the prisoners to use "Sie" (the polite form) when they spoke to the SS. The sense of degradation was fostered by the show of respectfulness that prisoners were expected to observe toward the SS.[11]

It is not until children are spoken to in this way in school that they become aware of the role of language as a status determiner. Although this may have been the same language level to which they were previously exposed in their homes and in the streets, this was the language used by all and for all. The teacher's subtle shifts of usage to fit the listener make the students suddenly aware of an inferiority implicit in the way they are addressed.

Visitors to depressed schools have heard teachers speak of rape, pregnancy, dope addiction, prostitution, etc., in an open way they would fear to use with middle-class youngsters. Their speech and language imply an assumption that the children have been exposed to so much degradation there is no longer any need to protect them from conversation about these things.

Strategies in Use

The following incident occurred in an 85% Negro junior high school near New York City, where I had a student teacher. At the end of one day I was conferring with the cooperating teacher when three boys, of approximately seventeen, entered. Apparently they were on friendly terms with the teacher, who was affable and fairly intelligent.

They asked him if he could "drop them at the high school for track practice," and he explained that he could not because he had a meeting that afternoon at his school. At this point I volunteered to drop them since I would be passing the school.

At this, the teacher quipped, "I couldn't leave you alone with these three. They might rape you or take your purse. You know what these kids are like."

In all fairness it must be noted that this particular teacher is far kinder to his students than are most of the teachers in the school. Nevertheless, it is doubtful that a teacher could employ such images with middle-class students, even in jest.

Kenneth Clark reports this same language strategy in the case of Mrs. X. who told a visitor "in front of the class, that the parents of these children are not professionals and therefore do not have much background or interest in going ahead to college . . . She

discussed each child openly in front of the entire class and myself
. . . She spoke about the children in a belittling manner." [12]

The language strategy to put students down and perpetuate
failure is also extended to their parents. I observed an interesting
Role Playing session ** in which teachers improvised conversations with parents of Negro and white students. These were taped,
and it was a shock for the teachers involved to hear themselves
talking down to the Negro parents in quite a different way from
their customary mode with white parents. In one episode, for
example, a white teacher refused to believe that a Negro parent's
explanation of why her child would not be permitted to go on a
class trip was not a lie.

The language strategy is used negatively in cognitive as well as
in affective situations. For example, directions are given too
rapidly, too slowly, out of sequence, tangentially, and often
inaudibly. Confusion is compounded when teachers refuse to
repeat instructions in the mistaken belief that failure will induce
better listening in the future.

Essentially, language is used throughout the day, not as the
most astonishing creation of men, but as a weapon to keep people
in their places. Perhaps the best way of eliminating the language
strategy is to have teachers consistently tape and listen to their
teaching under the guidance of trained personnel, capable of
pointing out the ultimate results of this misuse of language.

The Fragmentation Strategy

The more deprived a student is, the more he needs guidance for
fitting separate bits and pieces of knowledge and experience into
a framework that makes sense. Good teachers effect connections
from past learnings to present and future ones, help students to
transfer ways of thinking, observing, and reporting, and de-
emphasize instantaneous recall of nonconcatenated facts.

The fragmentation strategy induces failure by establishing situation after situation in which students are frustrated by unrelated

** This Role Playing session was observed at one of the Desegregation
Institutes which were evaluated by the writer during the summer of 1965.
These Institutes were set up on college campuses under the Civil Rights Act
of 1964, to help teachers and supervisors in newly desegregated educational
situations.

facts and are not guided to make future or past connections. Teachers who use this strategy do not point out relationships, do not help students to recall similar situations, and do not give students increasing opportunities for making choices based on related experiences.

Below are listed some of the questions from the weekly examinations given to the *lowest* achieving class on the eighth grade level in the above mentioned 85% Negro junior high school. The teacher told me that he had found that students at this level couldn't learn anything but facts. But he was concerned because they were even doing badly on these factual examinations. I have listed some of the questions below in the teacher's sequence to illustrate the fragmentation strategy:

11. Who is the head of the AFL-CIO?
12. Why was it necessary for the Clayton Anti-Trust Act to be passed?
13. Give the meaning of "Open Range."
14. Name the act that attempted to stop unfair labor union practices.
15. Define "arbitration."
16. What helped to make cattle raising boom in the West?
17. How did an act of 1924 help Indians?
18. Why did workers begin to leave the Knights of Labor?
19. Explain the meaning of "Monopoly."
20. Describe the type of workers who joined the CIO.

Perhaps the best way to overcome the use of this strategy is to expose teachers to programmed learning and to logic.

The Disrespect Strategy

This is closely related to the language strategy but it has a separate category here because it is generally more blatant than the language strategy.

In one class I heard a teacher say to a student while the class listened uneasily: "I just got a new dog and it looks like you. That's why I'm going to call it Blackie." Shocking as this episode is, what is even more disturbing is the fact that the presence of a visitor in no way constrained or inhibited the teacher. Although only one child was addressed, the rest of the class tittered slightly and then waited to respond further, unsure about what they were supposed to do or feel. Each child was aware that if bells toll often enough, sooner or later it may be for him.

Once again, the ultimate result is that failure is perpetuated. "One may assume that if a child is not treated with the respect which is due him as a human being, and if those who are charged with the responsibility of teaching him believe that he cannot learn, then his motivation and ability to learn may become impaired." [13]

The Dishonest Praise Strategy

Dishonest praise does nothing to promote success. Even the slowest students can see through phoniness. If the teacher praises a student for something nonsensical, he is indicating his surprise that the student can achieve even these heights. I have heard teachers go into raptures about a big husky boy's ability to get the shades even, or about a class's ability to stand in a straight line. A child who is learning to read or to figure something out for himself feels an inner glow of accomplishment and does not need extrinsic praise.

A few years ago I supervised a student teacher of English on the twelfth-grade level in an all-girl high school in New York City. The class was all Negro, and at the lowest achievement level. Carol, the student teacher, was an exceptional person; and the girls, almost as old as she, loved her. She never patronized them, wasted time, or gave them dishonest praise. Her every effort was devoted to teaching. She almost willed understanding with her body. She was totally involved in the task of teaching.

"You can do this," she would say over and over; and by the time she finished explaining, showing, and willing understanding, the students could indeed do what she had predicted. After a while, experienced teachers started to drift in to watch.

Carol did not have to invent praise because her every movement was constructive. It was not really anything she did. Her teaching techniques and background were shaky, and none of her college courses had given her specific procedures for a class like this one. Her secret weapon was the way she felt about people.

No teacher really has to put into words the way he feels about students. Praise cannot cover a rough hand, a pursed mouth, badly concealed impatience, or an instinctive gesture of disgust. All of these communicate far better than words can.

Carol felt no revulsion for her students. They would crowd around her at the end of a period, touch her, wait for her smile, or put an arm across her shoulders. Her movements of approval and acceptance gave them the praise they so desperately needed.

When she left, one student, speaking for the class, said: "Other teachers say, 'We're not gonna waste time teaching you. You'll all end up scrubbing floors anyway.' But you're different."

The Inappropriate Content Strategy

The inappropriateness of much of the reading materials used for disadvantaged children has finally led to the publishing of books such as the Chandler and Holt, Rinehart series. But when the teacher closes the door of her room, regardless of which materials are available, the choice of which to use and how to use them is up to the individual teacher.

Twenty years ago there was no material available for teachers to use for Negro History Week, and so the New York City Teachers Union published a four-page information sheet in which many teachers for the first time came across names like Sojourner Truth and Crispus Attucks. Dedicated Teachers Union members went out of their way to obtain materials which would help them to work with minority groups.

In contrast, teachers willing to accept failure use materials which will achieve negative results. The teacher may be totally unaware of the meaning of her choices.

The Desegregation Institutes mentioned above, in many cases, had Practicums, in which experienced and specially selected teachers taught mixed groups of Negro and white students so that the teachers attending the Institutes could observe methods of working with mixed groups.

In one Practicum, on the sixth-grade level, the teacher based her lesson on the poem, "America for Me," by Henry Van Dyke. The poem is reprinted in its entirety:

'Tis fine to see the old world, and travel up and down
Among the famous places and cities of renown,

To admire the crumbly castles and statues of the kings—
But now I think I've had enough of antiquated things.

So it's home again, and home again, America for me!
My heart is turning home again, and there I long to be,
In the land of youth and freedom beyond the ocean bars,
Where the air is full of sunlight and the flag is full of stars.

Oh, London is a man's town, there's power in the air;
And Paris is a woman's town, with flowers in her hair;
And it's sweet to dream in Venice, and it's great to study Rome,
But when it comes to living, there is no place like home.

Oh, it's home again, and home again, America for me!
I want a ship that's westward bound to plow the rolling sea,
To the blessed Land of Room Enough beyond the ocean bars,
Where the air is full of sunlight, and the flag is full of stars.

When the teacher of this Practicum distributed this poem on
dittoed sheets, I thought possibly it was to be used as a jumping
off place for the exploration of ideas of American freedom, etc., in
a way that would point up the discrepancy for many people, but
would nevertheless leave them with something to work for.

Although the choice of the poem did not seem to be the best,
conceivably it could have been used to develop the ideas used by
Langston Hughes in the poem, "Let America Be America Again,"
the first stanza of which says:

> Let America be America again.
> Let it be the dream it used to be.
> Let it be the pioneer on the plain
> Seeking a home where he himself is free.
>
> (America never was America to me).

Instead, the poem was related to the song "Home, Sweet
Home," and the idea was developed that although America is not
perfect it is still the best place in the world and travelers feel
homesick if they stay away long enough.

It is significant that none of the Negro students participated in this discussion. What is even more significant is the fact that the teacher was Negro. This is how insidious failure strategies can become. Watching this lesson I was reminded of my childhood in an all-Jewish elementary school in Brooklyn in which the teachers were primarily Irish. Every Christmas, the school was decorated with mangers, trees, stockings, etc., and all of the little Jewish children felt vaguely inferior because they did not celebrate in their homes what seemed to be so tremendously important in the school. In the same way, the content of this lesson was likely to reinforce feelings of failure because the real and the ideal for the Negro students were so far apart. The students might well wonder why America is not "the land of youth and freedom" for them, and might, like the little Jewish children, feel that this lack was somehow their own fault.

The Pettiness and Guilt Strategies

The pettiness strategy is so frustrating that it can achieve failure even when many other strategies fail. It is one of the best ways for a teacher to totally avoid confrontation with teaching. The teacher who practices this is skilled at making obfuscating mountains out of specks of dust.

Big scenes can be caused by dozens of "crimes" such as chewing gum, sitting incorrectly, wearing long hair, wearing short skirts, losing or forgetting books or papers, failing to speak in complete sentences, failing to address the teacher properly, failing to use the proper forms of courtesy, answering without teacher recognition of a waved hand, laughing at a joke the teacher doesn't share, relating to other students instead of exclusively to the teacher, seeming to be enjoying oneself, asking a tangential question for which the teacher isn't prepared, initiating a question or subject area, asking questions for purposes of clarification, or failing to guess instantly what the teacher wants.

The guilt strategy is more destructive to the students if the teacher is seemingly pleasant. If the students feel outright hatred for the teacher, the guilt strategy serves no purpose. For strategy to work effectively and produce failure, the teacher must view everything egocentrically. Poor behavior and lack of achievement are evaluated in terms of the teacher's need. Over and over the teacher says, in effect, "I worked so hard, and despite my best efforts you have not learned."

Teachers who use this strategy prefer to think that students "won't" rather than "can't." They do not accept the idea that it is the teacher's responsibility "to put himself into contact with the intelligence of his students, wherever and whatever they may be. . . ." [14]

They place the burden of human contact on the shoulders of the students and berate them when they are unable to establish this contact on the teacher's level. The teacher, like a coach *in extremis*, exhorts the students to produce "for me," and their inability to do so becomes cause for further failure.

There are many other strategies for the destruction of people. For example: "the testing strategy" (tests are used as punishment, designed badly, etc.); "the run-on talk strategy" (teachers talk and talk, beg, cajole, promise, scold, nag, criticize, exhort, and finally the students tune out); "the reference to wayward family members strategy," and "the personal attack strategy" (you never were any good, etc.).

Gratification from Failure

Let us go back to the original hypothesis of this paper. Teachers who cannot get ego gratification from student accomplishment learn to get it from student failure, and therefore resort to strategies designed to perpetuate failure. It is easier for teachers to do these things where there are no checks and balances.

Part of our American mystique is the belief in the Horatio Alger hero. Of course, the Horatio Alger approach was always two-thirds wishful thinking, but even the most resourceful person would find it hard to rise above the multitude of handicaps suffered by children in depressed areas. A social worker, describing the frustrations which beset these students, said: "Some of these kids can be caught in time and given help. Even some of the ones who don't get help will live reasonably O.K. lives, except that they'll never realize anything like their full potential. And some, of course, are just plain doomed." [15]

The self-fulfilling prophecy is perhaps the most difficult of all the handicaps the depressed-area child faces. It is particularly difficult when the children sense that their teachers want them to fail. Because people can be led to behave in ways inimical to their own best interests, they start to fail and continue to fail, *in order to succeed.*

They resort to learning-avoidance behavior which complements teacher failure strategies. John Holt, describing the failure strategies of children, suggests that "what hampers their thinking, what drives them into these narrow and defensive strategies, is a feeling that they must please the grownups at all costs . . ."

Students quickly learn what is expected of them. This is why they appear to be unteachable in many depressed school situations. We need only contrast teacher procedures in Mississippi's Freedom Schools to see how quickly pupils started to behave in a desired way, even though they had many deep-seated racial taboos to overcome. The students who came to the Freedom Schools were accustomed to associate schools with the total white power structure, with "the police, the White Citizens' Council, the mayor or sheriff, and the governor of the state." To overcome this traditional association teachers had to proceed as follows:

In your 'class' your teacher sat with you in a circle, and soon you got the idea that you could say what you thought and that no one, least of all the teacher, would laugh at you or strike at you. Soon, too, you got the idea that you might disagree with your teacher, white or black, and get a respectful hearing, that your teacher was really interested in what *you* thought or felt. Soon you were forgetting about skin colors altogether and thinking about ideas or feelings, about people or events.[16]

There is no need in a situation such as the above one for students to fail in order to please or to appease the teacher. There is no need for these students to act like subject peoples who "both appease their rulers and satisfy some part of their desire for human dignity by putting on a mask, by acting much more stupid and incompetent than they really are, by denying their rulers the full use of their intelligence and ability. . . ."[17]

Remedies

What is the solution to this failure syndrome? The most obvious point is that teachers in slum schools need ego gratification which they cannot now get in constructive ways. Elliot Shapiro suggests that what teachers in depressed schools "really need are workshops in group dynamics and group therapy . . . which should last one or two years, under instructors who have had expert training in psychology."

Deutsch, while pointing out that the teacher cannot be the scapegoat in a generally poor scheme of things, suggests that the educator be helped to:

. . . develop a comprehensive consciousness of the psychological, as well as the learning difficulties of the disadvantaged child; the real potential for change; the specifics involved in training children, for example, to ask questions or to become aware of syntactical regularities, or to use autoinstructional materials; and the imperative need to maintain as high as possible the level of stimulation and relevancy in the classroom.[18]

Clark points out that "the day when teachers should be permitted, like psychiatrists, to alibi their results without any standards of judgment of their personal effectiveness, must come to an end." [19]

Haubrich suggests that beginning teachers "begin their professional careers in schools serving depressed areas, after doing their student teaching in these same schools . . . (so that) . . . prospective teachers . . . (are) . . . specifically prepared in schools where they will eventually teach." [20] Clark further suggests that problems which should be considered in the curricula of teacher training institutions should include:

. . . the meaning of intelligence and problems related to the IQ and its interpretation; the contemporary interpretation of racial and nationality differences in intelligence and academic achievement; the role of motivation, self-confidence and the self-image in the level of academic achievement; and general problems of the modifiability and resilience of the human being.[21]

This is a monumental problem and there are no easy answers. One simple idea which I would like to suggest is that fundamental changes will take place when societal expectations begin to change. For example, suppose we said, as do the Israelis, that it is a disgrace for any American child not to read, whether he be black or white. Suppose those teachers who achieved this goal were praised and feted and regarded as state heroes. We can see the differences in attitude and achievement even in Dr. Shapiro's school because of his desire for his students' success.

If there is ever to be any help for the deprived child, steps must be taken so that, as Kenneth Clark puts it, "teachers can no longer be permitted to get away with crude or sophisticated alibis for their failure to teach children, who, like all normal beings, are capable of learning."

NOTES

1. Jersild, Arthur T., "Behold the Beginner," unpublished paper read at New York Conference, National Commission on Teacher Education and Professional Standards, June 23, 1965.
2. Green, Robert Lee. "After School Integration—What? Problems in Social Learning," *Personnel and Guidance Journal*, March, 1966, p. 706.
3. Ravitz, Mel. "The Role of the School in the Urban Setting," in A. Harry Passow, Ed., *Education in Depressed Areas*. New York: Teachers College, 1963.
4. Strom, Robert D., *Teaching in the Slum School*. Columbus: Charles E. Merrill Books, Inc., 1965.
5. Hentoff, Nat. "The Principal," *The New Yorker*, May 7, 1966, p. 76. (Later published as *Our Children Are Dying*. New York: The Viking Press, 1966.)
6. Kornberg, Leonard. "Meaningful Teachers for Alienated Children," in A. H. Passow, Ed., *Education in Depressed Areas,* op. cit.
7. Deutsch, Martin. "Some Psychological Aspects of Learning in the Disadvantaged," *Integrated Education,* Issue 15, June–July, 1965, III, 3, p. 53.
8. Clark, Kenneth B., "Clash of Cultures in the Classroom," *Learning Together*. Chicago: Integrated Education Associates, 1964.
9. Glatt, Charles A., "Children in the Inner City." Paper read to New York State Association for Student Teaching Annual Conference, Buffalo, May, 1966.
10. Deutsch, Martin, *op. cit.*
11. Cohen, Elie A., *Human Behavior in the Concentration Camp*. New York: Grosset and Dunlap, 1953.
12. Clark, Kenneth B., "Educational Stimulation of Racially Disadvantaged Children," A. H. Passow, Ed., *op. cit.*
13. Clark, K. B., *ibid.*
14. Holt, John. *How Children Fail*. New York: Pitman Publishing Company, 1964.
15. Hentoff, Nat, *op. cit.,* p. 119.
16. Howe, Florence. "Mississippi's Freedom Schools: The Politics of Education," *Harvard Educational Review*, Spring, 1965, XXXV, 2, p. 144.
17. Holt, John, *op. cit.*

18. Deutsch, M., *op. cit.*, p. 55.
19. Clark, K. B., "Clash of Cultures in the Classroom," *op. cit.*
20. Haubrich, Vernon F., "Teachers for Big City Schools," in A. H. Passow, Ed., *op. cit.*
21. Clark, K. B., "Educational Stimulation of Racially Disadvantaged Children, *op. cit.*

7 THE CULT OF "CULTURAL DEPRIVATION"

KENNETH B. CLARK

Among the earliest explanations of the educational inferiority of Negro children was that the poor average performance was to be accounted for in terms of inherent racial inferiority. After the research findings of Otto Klineberg and others in the 1930s came a serious re-examination among social scientists of the racial inferiority explanation.

More recently, it has become fashionable to attempt to explain the persistent fact of the academic retardation of Negro children in terms of general environmental disabilities. Taking their lead from the Klineberg type of research, these explanations tend to emphasize the pattern of environmental conditions as the cause which depresses the ability of these children to learn—economic and job discrimination, substandard housing, poor nutrition, parental apathy. The most recent version of the environmentalistic approach comes under the general heading of "cultural deprivation." The literature on this topic has used a variety of synonyms for this concept. Among them are: culturally disadvantaged, the disadvantaged, minority groups, socially neglected, socially rejected, socially deprived, school retarded, educationally disadvantaged, lower socio-economic groups, socio-economically deprived, culturally impoverished, culturally different, rural disadvantaged, the deprived slum children.

The cultural deprivation approach is seductive. It is both reasonable and consistent with contemporary environmentalistic thought, which seems to dominate social science thinking. Indeed, it is presented as a rejection of the inherent racial inferiority theories of the nineteenth and early twentieth centuries. The recent rash of cultural deprivation theories, however, should be subjected to intensive scrutiny to see whether they do, in fact, account for the pervasive academic retardation of Negro children. Specifically, in what way does a low economic status or absence of books in the home or "cognitive deficit," referred to constantly by proponents of this point of view, actually interfere with the ability of a child to learn to read or to do arithmetic in the elementary grades?

What is meant by "cognitive deficit"? How remediable or unremediable is it? If it is remediable, how? Is it merely a jargon tautology which says only what everyone knows: that these children are not learning? In what way does it explain difficulties in learning to read? What are the implications of these cultural deprivation theories for educational prognosis and methods? What is the relationship between the methodology for educating these children suggested by proponents of these theories and the theories themselves? A rigorously objective study of these problems and attempts to answer these questions might provide answers which will not only increase our understanding of problems of education of lower status groups but might contribute to our understanding of problems of education in general—the teaching and learning phenomena. Cultural deprivation theories might also be crucial to the important problem of determining the reasonable expectations and limits of education.

To what extent are the contemporary social deprivation theories merely substituting notions of environmental immutability and fatalism for earlier notions of biologically determined educational unmodifiability? To what extent do these theories obscure more basic reasons for the educational retardation of lower-status children? To what extent do they offer acceptable and desired alibis for the educational default: the fact that these children, by and large, do not learn because they are not being taught effectively and they are not being taught because those who are charged with the responsibility of teaching them do not believe that they can learn, do not expect that they can learn, and do not act toward them in ways which help them to learn.

The answers to these and related questions cannot be found in rhetoric or continued speculative discourse. Speculation appears to reflect primarily the status of those who speculate. Just as those who proposed the earlier racial inferiority theories were invariably members of the dominant racial groups who presumed themselves and their groups to be superior, those who at present propose the cultural deprivation theory, are, in fact, members of the privileged group who inevitably associate their privileged status with their own innate intellect and its related educational success. Such association neither proves nor disproves the theory in itself, but the implicit caste and class factors in this controversy cannot and should not be ignored. Many of today's scholars and teachers came from "culturally deprived" backgrounds. Many of these same individuals, however, when confronted with students whose present economic and social predicament is not unlike their own was, tend to react negatively to them, possibly to escape the painful memory of their own prior low status. It is easy for one's own image of self to be reinforced and made total by the convenient device of a protective forgetting—a refusal to remember the specific educational factor, such as a sympathetic and understanding teacher or the tutorial supports which made academic success and upward mobility possible in spite of cultural deprivation. The role of empathy, the understanding and identification of a teacher with his students in eliciting maximum academic performance from them, is an important educational question which should be studied systematically. The problems of empathy and identification between Negro students and their teachers are complex in an essentially racist society. It is significant that this relationship, as a systematic examination of the cultural deprivation literature reveals, has been so far totally ignored.

Looked at one way, it seems the epitome of common sense— and certainly compassion—to be convinced that a child who never has had toys to play with, or books to read, who has never visited a museum or zoo or attended a concert, who has no room of his own, or even a pencil he can call his own, ought not to be expected to achieve in school on a level to match a more fortunate child. His image of himself is certain to be poor, his motivation weak, his vision of the world outside the ghetto distorted. But common sense and compassion may not tell the whole story. The evidence of the pilot projects in "deprived" schools—odd though it may appear to many—seems to indicate that a child who is expected by the school to learn does so; the child of whom little is expected produces little. Stimulation and teaching based upon positive expectation seem to play an even more important role in a child's performance in school than does the community environment from which he comes.

A key component of the deprivation which afflicts ghetto children is that generally their teachers do not expect them to learn. This is certainly one possible interpretation of the fact that ghetto children in Harlem *decline* in relative performance and in I.Q. the longer they are in school. Furthermore, other evidence supports this conclusion: Statistical studies of the relationship between social factors such as broken homes, crowded housing, low income with performance in Harlem schools show a very tenuous link between environment and performance.* Depth interviews and questionnaires with Harlem teachers and school supervisors sustain the same observation. There are some school personnel who feel that the learning potential of the children is adequate. Though the majority believed one-fourth or less had potential for college, they did believe the majority could finish high school. One suspects that the children's level of motivation is, to some extent, set by their teachers. One guidance counselor said: "The children have a poor self-image and unrealistic aspirations. If you ask them what they want to be, they will say 'a doctor,' or something like that." When asked, "What would you say to a child who wanted to be a doctor?" she replied, "I would present the situation to him as it really is; show him how little possibility he has for that. I would tell him about the related fields, technicians, etc." One suspects, from this type of guidance reinforced by poor teaching and academic retardation, that the poor motivation and absence of a dignified self-image stem from the negative influence of such teachers more than from the influence of home and community.

The majority of teachers and administrators interviewed, nevertheless, talked of lowering standards to meet what they considered the intellectual level of their students. Assistant principals, who expressed this view with particular frequency, are in a position to influence curriculum. If they view the ghetto students as unteachable, one could scarcely blame the teachers they supervise

* *Youth in the Ghetto: A Study of the Consequences of Powerlessness and a Blueprint for Change* (New York: Harlem Youth Opportunities Unlimited, Inc., 1964), pp. 239–240.

for adopting a similar skepticism. When schools do not have confidence in their job, they gradually shift their concept of their function from teaching to custodial care and discipline.

Defeatism in Ghetto Schools

As Haryou gathered data on the schools, it became increasingly clear that the attitude of the teachers toward their students was emerging as a most important factor in attemping to understand the massive retardation of these children. It was necessary to find out what they really felt, and so the schools were asked to recommend teachers to discuss the problems of teachers in slum schools. Interviews were held; group discussions were conducted; questionnaires were distributed. They tended to make clear what a crucial role the teachers really played in the success or failure of their students. The problems of identifying with children of different backgrounds—especially for persons from the white middle class—the problems of rejection of children deemed unappealing or alien, and the problems of achieving empathy are multiple. Courses in educational philosophy and psychology as presently taught do not prepare these teachers for the challenge of their job.

The pattern of teaching in Harlem is one of short tenure and inexperience. Many white teachers are afraid to work in Harlem; some Negroes consider a post outside of Harlem to be a sign of status. Discipline problems pervade a number of the schools, as students show contempt for teachers and principals they do not respect; and, in turn, the emphasis on "good discipline" displaces an emphasis on learning, both in evaluating a teacher's record and in a teacher's estimate of his own effectiveness. Apathy seems pervasive.

A pattern of violence expected from students and counterforce from the teachers creates a brutalizing atmosphere in which any learning would be hard. One teacher reported: "The children are not taught anything; they are just slapped around and nobody bothers to do anything about it."

Some teachers say or imply that Harlem children expect to be beaten:

When I came to school "X," I had never seen anything like that school. I cried, they behaved so badly. I soon learned that the boys like to be beaten; like to be spoken to in the way in which they are accustomed, and when I learned to say things to them that, to me, would be absolutely insulting and to hit them when they needed it, I got along all right and they began to like me. Somehow that made them feel that I liked them. I talked to them in the terms and in the way to which they are accustomed, and they like it.

Another white teacher said:

Here, both the Negro and white teachers feel completely free to beat up the children, and the principal knows it. They know he knows it and that nothing will be done about it. The principal is prejudiced. Because he knows he is prejudiced, he covers it by giving the Negro teachers the best classes. The Negro teachers are the best teachers because they are more stable. Some colored and white teachers ask for the worst classes because they don't want to work. In the worst classes they don't have to work because whatever happens, they can just say, "It is the children." The white teachers are largely inexperienced—the principal does not expect very much from the teachers. He often says, openly, "Why did they put me here?" The Board of Education should have put an experienced principal there. There is a lot of brutality—brutal beatings, and nobody cares—nothing is done about it. The parents, the principal and the teachers don't care.

One teacher told of a teacher who exploited his students:

The teacher should set a good example; not a teacher who comes to class to shave, clean his teeth, and sleep—as does one of the teachers in my school. Then, so that he will be free of responsibility, he tells one of the bullies of the class to strong-arm the class and keep order.

One teacher of some sensitivity commented on the reaction of Negro children to the often severe, even brutal punishment inflicted upon them:

A child won't respond to minor discipline and will more often only respond to a more brutal form of discipline. There is inconsistent discipline and a lot of brutality in the Harlem schools. Many children are immature and, therefore, are extremely hurt by being disciplined. I have had the experience of children running out of the room after they had been yelled at—there seems to be a very low frustration point at which they can take discipline.

It is only in a context of utter apathy that such behavior could be tolerated. If only *one* teacher could talk of children expecting to be beaten, this would be evidence of inhumanity. The fact is that in the ghetto schools many teachers believe that such discipline is necessary for children who come from ghetto homes. In such an atmosphere where the priority is not on superior teaching, it is not surprising to discover that nearly half of the school personnel report that they find their work in the ghetto "more demanding and less satisfying" than work in other parts of the city.

Negro teachers tended to feel that the Negroes in Harlem are better teachers than the whites, in part because they stayed longer and could keep better discipline. One Negro woman teacher said that a white male teacher constantly asked her to restore order in his classroom. Whites, in turn, often feel a Harlem post is a step down. A Negro teacher said Harlem schools are "a dumping ground for condemned white teachers." Some white teachers report that they feel uneasy with Negroes. One white teacher interviewed said, "When I walk through the streets here I feel conspicuous; I would like to be able to blend into the scenery." Yet there are a number of dedicated men and women for whom the job of teaching the many neglected children of Harlem brings satisfaction and reward.

White teachers who feel they are in hostile territory and Negro teachers who resent their presence can hardly be expected to work together without friction. Much of the feeling is repressed, however, and only emerges in depth interviews conducted in confidence. Negroes express the feeling that whites feel and act superior and "cold" even when they are less well educated. Many of the white teachers are Jewish; for some of them this fact brings a sense of identification with another oppressed minority; for others, an impatience with an ethnic group, unlike their own where the tradition of eager learning has not yet been firmly established. One Negro teacher expressed her view on the subject in these words:

I find that the Jewish people, in particular, will protect their own and are protected by their own. In our school, this young teacher says that the children "just can't be taught" and even when the method used to teach is not a good one, she blames the children for not having the mentality to learn.

Unless she is a lackey, the Negro teacher has a hard road to travel. Mostly, they are doing a good job, but I don't think that there are enough Negroes in the teaching field with the guts to fight against the things that should not be. Negro teachers are too often trying to placate and please the white teachers. Most of the white teachers are Jewish. They respect the Negro who will fight, but if they find that they will not fight, they will walk all over them.

Negro teachers generally prefer not to associate with white teachers. As one said:

I, by choice, try not to socialize with them because I get sick and tired of hearing how our children will never amount to anything, our children are ignorant, the homes they come from are so deprived, these children are nothing, and so forth, and so on. I get tired of hearing this conversation even though I realize there is a problem.

Another Negro implied that friendliness to white teachers was taboo, and would be frowned upon or punished by her Negro colleagues:

I am a person who has been around and I get tired of "Oh, you feel white today, you're eating with the white teachers." "Oh, ha, she's joining their gang, she's turning on us." I won't eat with any of them. You know what, I'd rather go down to the Harlem Embers and eat by myself.

The dominant and disturbing fact about the ghetto schools is that the teachers and the students regard each other as adversaries. Under these conditions the teachers are reluctant to teach and the students retaliate and resist learning.

Negroes seldom move up the ladder of promotion in urban school systems. There are only six Negroes out of more than 1,200 top-level administrators in New York City, and only three Negroes out of 800 are full principals. Practically all of the Negroes are to be found quite far down in the organizational hierarchy—a fact discouraging in the extreme to Negro teachers and indirectly damaging to the self-image of Negro children who rarely see Negroes in posts of authority.

In past attempts to obtain experienced and qualified teachers for the schools in deprived communities, the Board of Education of the City of New York has not used its statutory power to assign teachers to these schools. The implicit and explicit reasons for not doing so were based upon the assumption that, given the "teacher shortage," teachers would refuse to accept such assignments and would leave the New York City school system if the board insisted upon exercising its power to make such assignments. The board, therefore, sought "volunteers" for these schools and flirted with proposals for providing extra bonuses for teachers who sought assignments in them. These methods have not been successful. The Allen Report declared that:

A spurious "reward structure" exists within the staffing pattern of the New York schools. Through it, less experienced and less competent teachers are assigned to the least "desirable" yet professionally most demanding depressed area schools. As the teacher gains experience and demonstrates competence, his mobility upward usually means mobility away from the pupils with the greatest need for skilled help. The classrooms that most urgently need the best teachers are thus often deprived of them.

Schools in deprived communities have a disproportionately high number of substitute and unlicensed teachers. Some of the classes in these schools have as many as ten or more different teachers in a single school year. Although precise figures are unavailable, nearly half of the teachers answering a Haryou questionnaire said they had held their posts for three years or less—far more than the citywide average (20 percent in present post three years or less).

The persistent failure on the part of the New York Board of Education to solve the problem of the adequate staffing of these schools points to the need for a new approach to this problem. It is suggested that teachers be selected for assignment in these schools in terms of their special qualifications, training, and human understanding. Rather than seek to entice, cajole, or bribe teachers into serving in such "hardship or ghetto outposts," the board should set up rather rigorous standards and qualifications for the teachers who would be invited or accepted for this type of service. These teachers should be motivated and recognized as *master teachers* or individuals working toward such professional recognition. Realistic professional and financial incentives must be provided if this professional status is to be other than perfunctory or nominal. Extra pay should be specifically tied to superior skill and more challenging responsibilities. A high-level professional atmosphere of competent and understanding supervision, a system of accountability—objective appraisal of professional performance—and a general atmosphere conducive to high-quality teaching and clear standards for differentiation of inferior, mediocre, and superior teaching with appropriate corrections and rewards must be maintained.

Excellent teaching can be obtained and sustained only under conditions of excellent supervision. The roles of field assistant superintendents, principals, and assistant principals must be re-examined. Those individuals who are assigned to schools in deprived communities must be selected in terms of special competence and in terms of the highest professional and personal standards. It should be understood that they would be judged primarily, if not exclusively, in terms of objective evidence.

Part Two

HOW CAN TEACHERS OF
DISADVANTAGED YOUTH SUCCEED?

There is not much written at the level of actual practice of teaching the disadvantaged. This section combines theory with practice; it emphasizes that so-called "uneducables" are reachable and teachable, given the proper climate and materials and, above all, teachers who are competent and concerned. Although there are no pat strategies, the authors set forth concrete proposals that teachers may utilize or modify according to their own teaching styles and personalities.

Three articles are written by Allan C. Ornstein, with full awareness by the author that they are essentially subjective. First, writing when he was a ghetto-school teacher, he challenges the views of many educators who have criticized those who teach the disadvantaged. By presenting his own views, and those of his colleagues, he gives the critics cause to reassess their opinions. Ornstein's other two articles examine the importance of discipline, classroom management, and motivation.

Among recent authors who are ghetto-school teachers, Herbert Kohl is one of the few who seems successful. Kohl explains what he was able to do with 36 Harlem sixth-grade students. In his discussions of the actual work and progress of his students, he shows that disadvantaged youth can learn.

Walter J. Foley evaluates teacher-pupil interactions and factors that affect their behavior. With special reference to the disadvantaged, he discusses procedures to evaluate the attitudes and values of students and procedures for teachers to use to improve the behavior and learning patterns of their students.

For many disadvantaged children, standard English is a second, if not third language. Virginia F. Allen recommends a packet of procedures for teaching standard English to these children. She maintains that the teacher needs to respect and try to understand the language patterns of the disadvantaged, for one cannot teach a new language to a child whose language one scorns.

Gertrude Whipple argues that "equal opportunity" for the disadvantaged means that the schools must provide a "better than equal" curriculum. Her paper is organized around conditions for providing such a curriculum, with emphasis on reading instruction and reading materials that teachers can utilize.

Hilda Taba and Deborah Elkins give a comprehensive view of improving the teaching-learning process; materials, media, activities, and the role of the teachers and administrators are examined. They focus on the need to bring learning experiences in line with the values and life realities of the disadvantaged.

Irving R. Melbo and David W. Martin point out that the areas of greatest concern to administrators, as they view the role of teachers, frequently encompass a range of behavior that can be subsumed under the rubric *morale*. One of the factors, according to Melbo and Martin, that has contributed significantly to low morale in many depressed urban area schools involves the teachers' feelings that they are incapable of accomplishing their tasks. In order to build effective morale, the authors suggest several avenues that they believe will develop teacher morale and effectiveness.

Daniel U. Levine points out that although there are few studies dealing with the achievement of Negro pupils in integrated as compared with segregated schools, the small amount of available data tends to indicate that pupils in the former setting do better in school than do comparable pupils in the latter situation. However, he emphasizes that education can be significantly improved in the segregated slum schools. What we need to do, according to Levine, is to demonstrate that both integrated and compensatory education can be effective in improving the achievement of disadvantaged Negro youth.

Robert J. Havighurst affirms that to lay the entire blame for the failure of educating the disadvantaged on the teachers and schools is unjust and unwise. He believes the newspapers, journals, and educators are making wholesale generalizations about teachers and schools that are misleading and that have harmful consequences. He seeks a "moratorium on negative criticisms," implying that teachers need encouragement—not discouragement—to reach and teach the disadvantaged.

Anthony N. Baratta raises several pertinent questions concerning school decentralization. The most fundamental question that he discusses is whether school decentralization will be an impetus or dilemma for learning and teaching in our ghettos. He further points out that school decentralization of big-city school systems has recently emerged as an alternate avenue for improving the quality of education as a counter trend to school consolidation.

Raymond S. Klein suggests an alternative strategy for meeting the needs of our disadvantaged youth. If the programs offered by our schools are to succeed, the real needs of youth must be identified and followed up beyond what has been attempted in the past. The schools must equip the students with the necessary tools to achieve independence in our society. Traditional patterns can no longer operate in the midst of a changing environment.

8   36 CHILDREN

HERBERT KOHL

I remembered my barren classroom, no books, a battered piano, broken windows and desks, falling plaster, and an oppressive darkness.

I was handed a roll book with thirty-six names and thirty-six cumulative record cards, years of judgments already passed upon the children, their official personalities. I read through the names, twenty girls and sixteen boys, the 6-1 class. . . .

. . . The weight of Harlem and my whiteness and strangeness hung in the air as I droned on, lost in my righteous monologue. The uproar turned into sullen silence. A slow nervous drumming began at several desks; the atmosphere closed as intelligent faces lost their animation. Yet I didn't understand my mistake, the children's rejection of me and my ideas. Nothing worked, I tried to joke, command, play—the children remained joyless until the bell, then quietly left for lunch.

There was an hour to summon energy and prepare for the afternoon, yet it seemed futile. What good are plans, clever new methods and materials, when the children didn't—wouldn't—care or listen? Perhaps the best solution was to prepare for hostility and silence, become the cynical teacher, untaught by his pupils, ungiving himself, yet protected.

I tried for the next six weeks to use the books assigned and teach the official curriculum. It was hopeless. The class went through the readers perfunctorily, refused to hear about modern America, and were relieved to do arithmetic—mechanical, uncharged—as long as nothing new was introduced. For most of the day the atmosphere in the room was stifling. The children were bored and restless, and I felt burdened by the inappropriateness of what I tried to teach. It was so dull that I thought as little as the

Herbert Kohl, *36 Children* (New York: The New American Library, Inc., 1967), excerpts from pp. 3–180. Copyright © 1967. Reprinted by permission of the publisher.

children and began to despair. Listening to myself on the growth of urban society, realizing that no one else was listening, that though words were pronounced the book was going unread, I found myself vaguely wondering about the children.

One day Ralph cursed at Michael and unexpectedly things came together for me. Michael was reading and stumbled several times. Ralph scornfully called out, "What's the matter, psyches, going to pieces again?" The class broke up and I jumped on that word "psyches."

"Ralph, what does *psyches* mean?"

An embarrassed silence.

"Do you know how to spell it?"

Alvin volunteered. "S-i-k-e-s."

"Where do you think the word came from? Why did everybody laugh when you said it, Ralph?"

"You know, Mr. Kohl, it means, like crazy or something."

"Why? How do words get to mean what they do?"

Samuel looked up at me and said: "Mr. Kohl, now you're asking questions like Alvin. There aren't any answers, you know that."

"But there are. Sometimes by asking Alvin's kind of questions you discover the most unexpected thing. Look."

I wrote *Psyche*, then *Cupid*, on the blackboard.

"That's how *psyche* is spelled. It looks strange in English, but the word doesn't come from English. It's Greek. There's a letter in the Greek alphabet that comes out *psi* in English. This is the way *psyche* looks in Greek."

Some of the children spontaneously took out their notebooks and copied the Greek.

"The word *psyche* has a long history. Psyche means mind or soul for the Greeks, but it was also the name of a lovely woman who had the misfortune to fall in love with Cupid, the son of Venus, the jealous Greek goddess of love. . . ."

The children listened, enchanted by the myth, fascinated by the weaving of the meaning of *psyche* into the fabric of the story, and the character. Mind, playing tricks on itself, almost destroying its most valuable possessions through its perverse curiosity. Grace said in amazement:

"Mr. Kohl, they told the story and said things about the mind at the same time. What do you call that?"

"*Myth* is what the Greeks called it."

Sam was roused.

"Then what happened? What about the history of the word?"

"I don't know too much, but look at the words in English that come from *Cupid* and *Psyche*."

I cited *psychological, psychic, psychotic, psychodrama, psychosomatic, cupidity*—the children copied them unasked, demanded the meanings. They were obviously excited.

Leaping ahead, Alvin shouted: "You mean words change? People didn't always speak this way? Then how come the reader says there's a right way to talk and a wrong way?"

"There's a right way now, and that only means that's how most people would like to talk now, and how people write now."

Charles jumped out of his desk and spoke for the first time during the year.

"You mean one day the way we talk—you know, with words like *cool* and *dig* and *sound*—may be all right?"

"Uh huh. Language is alive, it's always changing, only sometimes it changes so slowly that we can't tell."

Neomia caught on.

"Mr. Kohl, is that why our reader sounds so old-fashioned?"

And Ralph.

"Mr. Kohl, when I called Michael *psyches*, was I creating something new?"

Someone spoke for the class.

"Mr. Kohl, can't we study the language we're talking about instead of spelling and grammar? They won't be any good when language changes anyway."

We could and did. That day we began what had to be called for my conservative plan book "vocabulary," and "an enrichment activity." Actually it was the study of language and myth, of the origins and history of words, of their changing uses and functions in human life. We began simply with the words *language* and *alphabet,* the former from the Latin for tongue and the latter from the first two letters of the Greek alphabet. Seeing the origin of *alphabet* and the relationship of *cupidity* to Cupid and *psychological* to Psyche had a particularly magical effect upon the children. They found it easy to master and acquire words that would have seemed senseless and tedious to memorize. Words like *psychic* and *psychosomatic* didn't seem arbitrary and impenetrable, capable of being learned only painfully by rote. Rather they existed in a context, through a striking tale that easily accrued associations and depth. After a week the children learned the new words, asked to be tested on them, and demanded more.

"Vocabulary" became a fixed point in each week's work as we went from Cupid and Psyche to Tantalus, the Sirens, and the Odyssey and the linguistic riches that it contains. We talked of Venus and Adonis and spent a week on first *Pan* and *panic, pan-American,* then *pandemonium,* and finally on *demonic* and *demons* and *devils.* We studied *logos, philos, anthropos, pathos,* and their derivatives. I spun the web of *mythos* about language and its origins. I went to German (*kindergarten*), Polynesian (*taboo*), or Arabic (*assassin*), showing what a motley open-ended fabric English (and for that matter any living language) is. The range of times and peoples that contributed to the growth of today's American English impressed me no less than it did the class. It drove me to research language and its origins; to re-explore myth and the dim origins of man's culture; and to invent ways of sharing my discoveries with the children.

The children took my words seriously and went a step further. Not content to be fed solely words that grew from sources that I, the teacher, presented, they asked for words that fitted unnamed and partially articulated concepts they had, or situations they couldn't adequately describe.

"Mr. Kohl, what do you call it when a person repeats the same thing over and over again and can't stop?"

"What is it called when something is funny and serious at the same time?"

"What do you call a person who brags and thinks he's big but is really weak inside?"

"Mr. Kohl, is there a word that says that something has more than one meaning?"

The class became word-hungry and concept-hungry, concerned with discovering the "right" word to use at a given time to express a specific thought. I was struck by the difference of this notion of rightness and "the right way" to speak and write from the way children are supposed to be taught in school. They are supposed to acquire correct usage, right grammar and spelling, the right meaning of a word, and the right way to write a sentence. Achievement and IQ tests give incomplete sentences and the child is instructed to fill in the "right" word. Many teachers correct children's writing on the basis of a canon of formal rightness without bothering to ask what the children's words mean. I did the same thing myself.

.   .   .   .

Later in the semester I taught the class a lesson on naming, a topic that seems deceptively simple yet minimally encompasses history, psychology, sociology, and anthropology. I put everybody's full name on the blackboard, including my own, and asked the class how people got names. The answer was, naturally, from their parents who made the choice—but not the full choice, it emerged, when Michael remembered that his parents' surnames came from their parents. Then how far back can you go? The children thought and Grace raised a delicate question. If the names go back through the generations how come her name wasn't African since her ancestors must have been? In answer I told the class about my own name—Kohl, changed from Cohen, changed from Okun, changed from something lost in the darkness of history; one change to identify the family as Jewish, one change to deny it. Then I returned to the question of slave names and the destruction of part of the children's African heritage that the withholding of African names implied.

Neomia said that she knew of someone who changed his name because he wanted to start a new life, and Sam told the class that his brother called himself John X because X meant unknown and his original African name was unknown. We talked of people who named their children after famous men and of others who gave exotic names. From there the discussion went on to the naming of animals—pets, wild animals, racehorses; things—boats, houses, dolls, and places. The class knew by that time in the school year that one doesn't talk of words in isolation from human lives and history, and by then I had begun to know what to teach.

The emphasis on language and words opened the children to

the whole process of verbal communication. Things that they had been struggling to express, or worse, had felt only they in their isolation thought about, became social, shareable. Speaking of things, of inferiority and ambiguity, or irony and obsession, brought relief, and perhaps for the first time gave the children a sense that there were meaningful human creations that one could discover in a classroom.

Yet not all concepts have been verbalized, and the children frequently talked of having feelings and desires that no words I gave them expressed adequately. They had to create new words, or develop new forms of expression to communicate, and that can neither be taught nor done upon command. We could go to the frontier, however, and speak about the blues, about being bad or hip or cool—about how certain ways of living or historical times created the need for new words. We talked about the nuclear age, the smallness of the modern world, the jargon of democracy and communism, integration and segregation. The children looked in awe at *Finnegans Wake* and Joyce's monumental attempt to forge a new language; they listened to Bob Dylan, recorded the words of soul songs and classical blues, read poetry. We started out talking about words and ended up with life itself. The children opened up and began to display a fearless curiosity about the world.

I sense that I've jumped ahead too quickly, for the whole thing happened slowly, almost imperceptibly. There were days of despair throughout the whole year, and I never learned how to line the class up at three o'clock. There were days when Alvin was a brilliant inspiring pupil at ten and the most unbearable, uncontrollable nuisance at eleven thirty; when after a good lesson some children would turn angry and hostile, or lose interest in everything. There were small fights and hostilities, adjustments and readjustments in the children's relationships to each other and to me. I had to enlarge my vision as a human being, learn that if the complex and contradictory nature of life is allowed to come forth in the classroom there are times when it will do so with a vengeance.

⋅   ⋅   ⋅   ⋅

I brought part of my library to school and temporarily substituted it for social studies. The children were curious about those

Greeks and Latins who contributed so many words and concepts to our language. I brought in books on Greek and Roman architecture and art, as well as Robert Graves' version of the *Iliad,* a paperback translation of Apuleius' *Cupid and Psyche,* the *Larousse Encyclopedia of Mythology,* and anything else that seemed relevant or interesting. I showed the books to the children and let them disappear into their desks. It was made clear that the books were to be read, the pages to be turned. If someone reads a book so intensely that the book is bruised it is flattering to the book.

For three-quarters of an hour a day the Pantheon circulated along with Floyd Patterson and J. D. Salinger, Partridge's dictionary of word origins made its way through the class with Langston Hughes and the Bobbsey twins. Anything I could get my hands on was brought to class—a great deal remained unread, and some books I hadn't read myself shocked and surprised the class. They were sexy and popular. Later that year my supervisor told me I was running a very effective individualized reading program. That may have been it, but the truth seemed simpler and less structured. I overwhelmed the class with books, many of which I loved, and let them discover for themselves what they liked. There were no reports to be written, no requirements about numbers of pages to be read. Some children hardly read at all, others devoured whatever was in the room. The same is true of my friends.

Robert Jackson grabbed a book on Greek architecture, copied floor plans and perspective drawings, and finally, leaping out of the book, created a reasonably accurate scale model of the Parthenon. Alvin and Michael built a clay volcano, asked for and got a chemistry book which showed them how to simulate an eruption. Sam, Thomas, and Dennis fought their way through war books; through the Navy, the Seabees, the Marines, and the Paratroops. The girls started with the Bobbsey twins and worked through to romantic novels and, in the case of a few, Thurber and O. Henry. I learned that there were no books to fear, and having been divested of my fear of idleness, I also wasn't worried if some children went through periods of being unable to do anything at all.

People entering my classroom during those forty-five minutes of "social" studies usually experienced an initial sense of disorder followed by surprise at the relative calm of the room. If they bothered to look more closely or ask, they would find that most of the children were working.

.   .   .   .

I asked the assistant principal for equipment for the kids, and he replied that the school hadn't received any. When I told that to the boys they laughed and said they knew where it was, only they'd never see it because their school was in Harlem. I was incredulous, but have since learned how often the children are acutely aware of what the staff attempts to conceal from them. Instead of becoming moralistic and telling the children that they couldn't possibly know about such things as hidden science materials, I challenged them and they led me into the hall and up to a locked supply closet. The next day I managed to get the key and found just what I'd been told, several years' untouched, packaged science supplies—batteries in sealed boxes dating as much as five years back, bells, buzzers, chemicals, aquariums, terrariums—enough for a whole elementary school.

It was useless trying to fight the administration over their irresponsibility. I had done that before in another public school in New York City, had been given thoroughly evasive answers, and found myself transferred to Harlem at the end of the year. The principal may have thought that was a deserving punishment for defiance. At any rate it sobered me—I wanted to teach, and after a few months did not want to leave Harlem and the kids. Grade 6-1 had become a part of me. So I learned to keep quiet, keep the door of my classroom shut, and make believe that the class and I functioned in a vacuum, that the school around us didn't exist. It was difficult not to feel the general chaos—to observe the classes without teachers, the children wandering aimlessly, sometimes wantonly through the halls, disrupting classes, intimidating, extorting, yet being courted by the administration: "Please don't make trouble, anything you want, but no trouble." I kept quiet that year anyway, and tried not to make trouble for them either. I wasn't a good enough teacher yet, or confident enough to accuse others of failing with the children when I wasn't sure of my own work. But I had to get that science equipment, so I volunteered to take care of science supplies for the school, mentioning casually that I noticed that there were some in the closet. The principal gave me the closet key with a smile that said, "Anytime you want to do more work, come to me. Who knows what you could find hidden in the other closets. . . ." Then he asked, truly puzzled, "Do you think those children will get anything out of it?"

We had the equipment, and that was the important thing at the moment. The boys went through many experiments, put together elaborate combinations of bells, buzzers, and lights, and contrived a burglar-alarm system for the classroom. They made a fire extinguisher and invisible ink. After a week they were joined by several girls who took over the equipment as the boys broke away to help Robert with the Parthenon. The groups formed and re-formed as projects developed and were abandoned. It was good to see the children, once so wild over a simple game of chess, move freely about the room, exploring socially and intellectually. Still there were moments of doubt and anxiety; it was difficult to see where this classroom of mine was going.

As usual, the children led me. I have found one of the most valuable qualities a teacher can have is the ability to perceive and build upon the needs his pupils struggle to articulate through their every reaction. For this he needs antennae and must constantly work upon attuning himself to the ambience of the classroom. To the mastery of observation of children must be added the more difficult skill of observing his own effect upon the class, something only partially done at best. But if the easy guides of a standard curriculum and authoritarian stance are to be discarded any clues arising from actual experience in the classroom are welcome.

.   .   .   .   .

Music became an integral part of the classroom. The children brought in their records; I responded with my own. One morning I put twenty-five records ranging from blues and Fats Waller through Thelonious Monk and Coltrane to Mozart and Beethoven on top of the phonograph. During the morning breaks the kids explored freely, and when the music began to interest some individuals enough, I brought in biographies of the composers, pictures of the musicians. We talked in small groups during social studies of chain gangs, field music, modern jazz, rock and roll, child prodigies, anything that came up. A dialogue between the children and myself was developing.

. . . One day I brought an orange cardboard binder filled with loose-leaf paper to school. It was for my observations on the vocabulary lessons. During free time that morning I became exasperated by the ease with which Robert yielded a book to Margie, who merely glanced at it and stuffed it in her desk. I wanted to say something to him, yet words were useless, would only cause further withdrawal. *Maybe I could give him something that he wouldn't surrender so easily* . . . the only thing on my desk was the notebook. An idea cautiously formed; I took the notebook to Robert and said that his interest in myths and history was so obvious, and his grasp of the discussions in class so full that I felt he might want to go beyond reading books and write and illustrate one himself.

He looked at me as I were mad.

"Me?"

"Why not you? Somebody writes books; anyone can try. That's the only way to discover how well you can do. Why don't you take this notebook and try. You don't have to show me or anybody else what you do if you don't want."

A sly triumphant look came over Robert's face as he snatched the notebook out of my hand. I retreated to my desk, afraid of spoiling the whole thing with unnecessary words.

It wasn't until a week later that I discovered that my attempt had worked. Maurice came up to my desk before class and asked me if Robert was the only one in class who could write a book. I said no and then Maurice asked me what Robert was writing about anyway. Robert, it seems, refused to tell him or even show him one page.

I explained that I didn't know either, and that Robert could be writing about anything, that the book was private unless he chose to show it to anybody, and that included me.

"What about me? Could I write a book?—even about myself, the truth, you know . . ."

"It's been done before. There's no reason why you can't do it."

I promised to bring Maurice a binder (having the symbol of being sanctioned to write privately and as one pleased was very important) and the next morning brought a dozen to school. I explained to the entire class that some children wanted to write their own books and that the binders were available for anybody who cared to write. I also explained that though I was available to help or to read their work for pleasure, still the books were their private property—the author's control over his work would be respected completely. There was no mention of grading or grammar as it never occurred to me then even to bother with a disclaimer.

The children were suspicious of my talk about privacy and wanted to know what kinds of things people write books about. Though they had seen some of the scope of literature in the books I brought to class, I think the children still believed there were only two kinds of books—the "good" books they read in school which were nice, boring, and unreal, and the "bad" books they sneaked to each other which were filthy, exciting, and unreal. It was hard to explain what people wrote about. Instead of trying, I spent the next week selecting from my library and reading to the children, asking them to attend to the subject and to the writer's voice as well. I read about love, hate, jealousy, fear; of war and religion, quest and loss. I read in voices that were ironic, cynical, joyous, and indifferent. The class and I talked of the writer's selection of his subject and the development of his voice; of the excitement of not knowing entirely where the book you set out to write will take you.

A few children dared at first, then more, until finally most of the children in the class attempted some written exploration. I put an assignment on the board before the children arrived in the morning and gave the class the choice of reading, writing, or doing what was on the board. At no time did any child have to write, and whenever possible I let the children write for as long as their momentum carried them. Time increasingly became the servant of substance in the classroom. At the beginning of the semester I had tried to use blocks of time in a predetermined, preplanned way—first reading, then social studies, arithmetic, and so forth. Then I broke the blocks by allowing free periods. This became confining and so I allowed the length of periods to vary according to the children's and my interest and concentration. Finally we reached a point where the class could pursue things without the burden of a required amount of work that had to be passed through every day. This meant that there were many things that the class didn't "cover"; that there were days without arithmetic and weeks without spelling or my dear "vocabulary." Many exciting and important things were missed as well as many dull things. But the children learned to explore and invent, to become obsessed by things that interested them and follow them through libraries and books back into life; they learned to believe in their own curiosity and value the intellectual and literary, perhaps even in a small way the human, quest without being overly burdened with a premature concern for results.

Not that some of the children in 6-1 weren't initially distressed by the freedom of the room and the increasingly experimental curriculum. They were and told me, and at times I almost wavered and returned to the crutches of standard preplanned material. But I believed in what was happening in class and bore the uncertainty and days of chaos until together we saw work emerge that none of us expected or believed possible.

Maurice was the first to show me his book.

As the year developed the class did a lot of writing. I discovered that if the children were allowed to write without being marked, and if they were challenged and tempted by the subject, they wrote with great pleasure. At first it was just a question of writing sentences using the vocabulary and spelling words. The children tested me to see how far they could go, but they really never went very far.

. . . .

Over the year the creation of myths was one of the children's favorite challenges. Initially we only spoke of Greek mythology, and the children's stores were peopled by their own versions of Cyclops, Psyche, Hades, and Zeus. Maurice and Michael changed that by introducing members of the League of Justice—Superman and Wonder Woman—and movie characters such as Dracula and the Frankenstein monster into their stories. I remember Michael's *Cyclops Meets Frankenstein* in which Cyclops and the Frankenstein monster battled over the lovely Psyche, whom Michael saved at the last minute from both of them. Maurice contributed adventures of the League of Justice in which the members of the League did not always triumph.

We talked about comic books in class, and about heroes and monsters. I brought in pictures of ancient monsters and told the class of the Minotaur and the Sphinx. From the children I learned about Gorgo and Godzilla. For a while some of the children would come up to the room before nine o'clock, and we would swap tales.

I asked the children if there were any neighborhood myths or legends, and though they were reluctant to talk about them at first they began to speak of heroic villains who were "upstate" in prison but unbroken by the police, of stories they heard about beautiful women and strong, bad men who lived down south and got away with fooling and defying the white man. I encouraged the children to talk and blend past and present, to let their imaginations create mythical worlds. I also encouraged them to write and share their fantasies. In the case of a few children, and most notably Robert Jackson, the creation of myths and heroic tales became almost an obsession.

As the writing accumulated in the class and the walls of the room flowered with the children's work, the uneasy pride and generous greed characteristic of many writers developed. The children wanted a larger audience; they wanted to share their work and at the same time receive the praise they felt it deserved and confront the criticism they feared it would evoke. Several children suggested independently that the class create a newspaper or magazine. I think it was in late November that I gathered all the journals and magazines in my apartment and brought them to class. For the first time the children saw *Time, Life, Dissent, i.e., etc.,* and after a while the class fell to discussing titles for their own magazines. There was no need to bother with a discussion on whether or not there would be one.

As I remember, the children were fascinated with the simplicity of magazine titles, something I hadn't thought of myself until the children pointed it out. The idea that abbreviations such as *i.e.* and *etc.* could be used made the process of finding titles easy. If *Life* could be used so could *Death; Look* led to *See, Find, Search; Time* easily led the children to suggest *Night, Work,* and *Second.*

Robert Jackson suggested *et al, Children,* and *Why.*

Alvin countered with *Because, Often,* and *Maybe.*

Barbara offered *And,* and the class dropped their other words and rhapsodized on its advantages.

"*And* could be used on posters, Robert could draw people and have them say '*And.*'"

The children created *And.* They chose an editorial board, chose the selections to be published, and put them on rexograph paper—going through at least a dozen master sheets for every page that passed their own scrutiny. Robert drew posters, enticing pictures of famous men declaiming . . . *And.* Dennis and Thomas commandeered the rexograph machine while Alvin and Leverne managed to slip copies of Robert's posters into teachers' mailboxes, under doors, even onto the principal's desk.

.   .   .   .

It was in April . . . that I talked to the class about my limitations within the educational system. Before that, however, I found myself telling them about the demands that the system made upon them. There were compulsory achievement, and at that time, IQ tests given halfway through the year, and it was on the results of those tests that the children's placement in junior high school would be based. Nothing else really counted; classes were formed on the basis of reading grades and my pupils *had* to do well. It was a matter of their whole future since in junior high school all but those few students put in the "top" classes (three out of fourteen in each grade) were considered "not college material" and treated with the scorn that they merited in their teachers' eyes.

The easiest way to bring this up in class was to tell the children exactly where they stood. I braced myself, and defying all precedent as well as my own misgivings, I performed the unforgivable act of showing the children what their reading and IQ scores were according to the record cards. I also taught a lesson on the definition of IQ and of achievement scores. The children were angry and shocked; no one had ever come right out and told them they were failing. It was always put so nicely and evasively that the children never knew where they stood. After seeing the IQ scores—only two of which were above 100, the majority being in the 80 to 90 range—and the reading scores, which with few exceptions were below grade level, the children were furious. I asked them what they wanted to do about it, and sadly they threw back at me:

"Mr. Kohl, what can we do about it?"

And I told them. Only I didn't say read more, or take remedial lessons, or spend another year in school, and you will be better off. I told them what middle-class teachers usually tell their pupils, what I heard myself while in public school in New York City, and what teachers in Harlem are usually too honest and scrupulous to tell their pupils. I said if you listen I will teach you how to take tests and how to get around them.

This scrupulosity of Harlem teachers and administrators with respect to tests is a curious psychological phenomenon, completely at variance with the irresponsibility they display in all other educational and disciplinary matters. Yet I think it is all too easily explicable. They feel their own failures with the children are vindicated if an objective test, objectively administered, shows the child to be a failure.

There were no sample tests available, to prepare the children beforehand. The assistant principal told me that if old tests were made available the children would have an unfair advantage over other children. I reminded him that keeping files of old tests was frequently standard procedure at middle-class schools, and that P.S. 6, a predominantly white school located less than a mile down Madison Avenue, even gave after-school voluntary classes in test preparation. He shrugged and told me that a rule was a rule. So I went to friends who taught in white schools and got copies of the old tests and sample questions that they used and went ahead with my plans. No one checked on what I was doing, and no one really cared as long as my class wasn't disruptive.

The first thing I had to do was familiarize the children with test instructions. I spent several weeks on practicing following directions as they were worded on the standard tests. The class asked me why such practice was necessary, and I explained that with all the fine writing they could produce, with all the words of praise and recommendation I could write, they would go nowhere in junior high school unless those grades on paper were up to the standards the Board of Education set. The kids didn't like that idea, I don't like it; but we had to get tough and face the fact that like it or not they *had* to do well. When I put it that way they were willing to try.

After going through the reading of directions, I broke down the types of questions that were asked on the various reading tests and tried to explain something of the psychology of the people who created the test. I frequently found that some of the children were deliberately choosing wrong answers because they had clever explanations for their choices. They had to be convinced that the people who created objective tests believed as an article of faith that all the questions they made up had one and only one correct answer. Over and over, it is striking how rigid teachers tend to be and how difficult it is for children who haven't been clued in on this rigidity to figure out what the teacher expects in the way of suppression of original and clever responses. The children agreed to be dull for the sake of their future.

After these exercises we simulated testing situations, and the children gradually learned to cease dreading and avoiding the testing situation. Their anxiety decreased to a manageable level, and therefore they were able to apply things they had discovered in their own thinking, reading, and writing to situations that arose in the test.

Unfortunately I had no say in determining when the tests were given. Both the reading and IQ tests had to be given before February for administrative reasons, and so the full benefit of the year's work did not show in those tests. The IQ test was close to a disaster. True, there were about ten children who came up over 100 and one—Grace—who scored 135, but the children were not yet able to cope with the test and didn't show themselves as well as they could. With the reading test it was different. The children were almost ready and in a few short months performed the seemingly impossible task of jumping from one to three years in reading. There were a few children on fifth-grade level, about twelve on sixth-grade level, another twelve on seventh-grade level, and eight who ranged from the eighth to the twelfth grades. I couldn't believe it myself. When I told the results to the children, they for once showed their pride in themselves unashamedly.

The children learned that they could do unpleasant but necessary work; they also knew that the test preparation was not all there was to education, that the substance of their work, the novels and stories, the poems and projects they created, were the essential thing no matter how the external world chose to judge them. They were proud of their work and themselves. I felt thrilled and privileged to teach them and witness them create. I offered what I could to them; they offered much in return. I am grateful that over the course of the year I could cease to be afraid and therefore respond to what the children had to teach me of myself, of themselves and the world they lived in and which we shared as human beings.

Not all of the children made it through the year; two moved, and one, John, was too much for me to control. He was tough and shook my confidence. It would take me another year before I could reach children like him. We never fought, he didn't disrupt the class; he just disappeared into the halls and then the streets. I have to admit that I made a very feeble and false effort to stop him; the rest of the class occupied me. The next year I had a class of Johns, and seeing how easily they responded to adult confidence and trust, I have always regretted my lack of effort with John. Yet I have to admit that I did not have the necessary confidence as a teacher and as a human being the year I taught the thirty-six children. It took the thirty-six children to give me that.

9 TECHNIQUES AND FUNDAMENTALS FOR TEACHING THE DISADVANTAGED

ALLAN C. ORNSTEIN

Introduction

We often read why disadvantaged children do not learn; we are familiar with the immense dimension of their problems. What we do not often read is how we should teach these children so that they will learn, so that they will get decent jobs, so that they will break their chains of deprivation. This paper will examine two major areas related to teaching the disadvantaged child; that is, *discipline and classroom management* and *motivation and student achievement*.

Discipline and Classroom Management

"Unruly" students are considered a norm among disadvantaged youngsters. Those who are given special help often return to the classroom as difficult as ever. The problem of discipline is acute, and in most ghetto schools is the teacher's number-one problem. Pat rules of discipline and teaching are discarded. Teachers resort to methods not prescribed or condoned by the book. Such methods are considered practical and more effective. Good teaching in many ghetto schools really means good discipline. Many disciplinarians are not good teachers, because they feel they have achieved what the next teacher cannot; and many good teachers are not good disciplinarians, because they worry more about teaching than enforcing order. A combination of both types is not frequent. Similarly, some teachers who successfully teach in ghetto schools could not successfully teach in a middle-class

Allan C. Ornstein, "Techniques and Fundamentals for Teaching the Disadvantaged," *Journal of Negro Education* (Spring 1967), pp. 136–145. Reprinted by permission of the publisher.

school, and some teachers who are ineffective in ghetto schools would be very effective elsewhere.

It should be noted that disadvantaged children are not naturally "bad" in class. They want to learn and can be taught, as long as the teacher does not lose his confidence or surrender his authority. With any group of children, a teacher's authority will be tested immediately, and possibly thereafter, depending on how he handles himself and the class. The students who are testing the teacher hope he will not find out what they are doing or hope he will not be able to cope with them, but at the same time if the teacher ignores them or indicates that he is helpless, they will feel insecure and lose their respect for him. By the same token, the other children in the class are watching and hoping that the teacher handles the situation properly. If he fails them, they, too, will reject and eventually turn against him. The tests will probably be more difficult and more frequent with disadvantaged children. But the teacher can ill afford to fail, because he will be more ineffective with these children than with other children.

The teacher, then, must learn to solve his own classroom problems. The dean or guidance counselor is usually too overburdened to mete out punishment or provide assistance for every "problem" child. The classroom is the teacher's fortress, and the students must be made to realize this all important fact. To what extent the teacher is successful will largely depend on his classroom management; that is, the rules and routine he establishes with his students. In middle-class schools it is possible to get along without good classroom management, but in ghetto schools it is not. While the failure to implement basic rules and routine often goes unnoticed in the middle-class school, failure to do so in a ghetto school does not go unnoticed, as evidenced by chaotic classroom situations and the plight of teachers in such classrooms.

On a one-to-one basis most disadvantaged children are very friendly, but in a class situation the relationship may radically change. They are restless and impulsive. They cannot tolerate waiting and have a voracious desire for excitement. They easily get disconcerted and "fly off the handle." The teacher, therefore, must set order and routine immediately (before he attempts to teach) so they know what to do and what is expected.

Disadvantaged children of junior high school are perhaps the most difficult to deal with. By then, many are rebellious and too retarded in basic skills to learn in a regular classroom situation. Many are strong enough to be a physical threat or sophisticated enough to probe a teacher's weak points. But they are not mature enough to reason with or old enough to be legally expelled if they really become a "problem." These children in particular demand a strict, structured, workable routine. They need and want a teacher who can assure them the stability they usually do not receive at home.

The child should understand the reasons for the rules and routine. They should be clear and have a definite purpose. One main objective is to remove hindrances to the teaching-learning process. They should be consistent with school policy and ordered around the viewpoint that the teacher and the class are working together—achieving team work so that learning can take place— and any discord is a breach of this mutual endeavor as well as a waste of time. Some of the rules to be examined seem almost too basic for explanation. Yet my experience is that they are far from rudimentary. Although they can apply to any group of students, they must be used with the disadvantaged, and only slightly varied according to the teacher's personality and teaching style. In short, what apparently works with the disadvantaged is nothing more than plain good rules and regulations. The following methods would also work in middle-class schools, but are necessary in ghetto schools.

1. *Train your students to enter the room in an orderly fashion.* Arrive on the scene before your students; many problems are avoided this way. Get the students to feel that they are entering your room to learn, not that they are visiting you to have fun. As soon as the children enter the room, they should know to open their notebooks, copy the assignment and get started on a specific task. Do not allow them to socialize or to walk around; the beginning of the lesson is delayed and disciplinary problems develop.

2. *Keep a clean and attractive room.* Never start and continue a lesson in a dirty atmosphere with wardrobes gaping and closet doors swinging wide or with paper and chairs flung about. It is in a sense condoning or ignoring an intolerable condition. The tone

of disorder is set. By the same token, there should be no extra props that the children might want to touch or could throw. Pictures and bulletin boards should not only be examined but also frequently changed. This caring on the part of the teacher pays off. The students realize that you are aware of and concerned with the total classroom situation.

3. *Be certain that you have everyone's attention before you start the lesson.* If you ignore the slightest infraction, the general tone of the class will steadily worsen. Stop work if you have to. Get the offender to order immediately; do not make the common mistake of waiting for the child to stop when he feels like stopping. If you require 100 per cent attention, you will get it.

4. *Be consistent with your class routine.* These children cannot cope with change. The place reserved on the blackboard for homework, the date, and aim of the lesson should not be changed. Any change should be gradual and not frequent.

5. *Get to know the students early in the term.* The quicker you know your students, the quicker they realize they cannot be shielded by anonymity. Learn the difficulties or failures of each individual student. A mutual understanding is established when the teacher knows the child by name and knows what his limitations are.

6. *Hold students accountable.* Challenge the student who comes late or does not do his homework. Make him an example, but never humiliate him. Make sure he understands that his grade is affected by everything he does in class. Do not let anything go unnoticed if you can possibly help it. The children will soon realize that they cannot get away with poor preparation or behavior.

7. *Speak softly.* A loud voice suggests that someone else is competing against the teacher. A low voice, but one that is distinct enough to be heard in all parts of the room, is pleasant and denotes a calm atmosphere. Do not shout. It is an admission that you have lost control. Try not to get excited. Not only is it fun for any class when the teacher loses control, but it also causes the children to lose control. A firm personality, quiet dignity tempered with common sense, will best maintain good daily discipline.

8. *Be clear with your instructions.* Give one instruction at a

time, or else you will confuse the children. Be sure your commands are understood and executed before posing another one. Be specific so you do not have to repeat yourself. Repetition weakens your control. Make only reasonable and necessary rules; be willing to explain the reasons for them, but rigidly enforce them. A weak disciplinarian should establish fewer rules; therefore, there will be fewer chances to break the routine and more opportunity to enforce the orders that are required.

9. *Aim to have full class participation.* By getting everyone in the class involved with the lesson, a teacher has better control. Train students to show respect to each other by listening to each other. Ask daydreamers to repeat what has previously been cited in class. Explain to the child that he has taken away valuable class time. End in a positive note, reminding him that he usually does good work. Keep your students attentive by walking around the room and through the aisles, and by asking questions at random.

10. *Be aware of undercurrents of behavior.* Reserve part of your attention while instructing to watch, look, and listen. Never become so absorbed in the lesson that you lose audience contact. Do not fix your eyes merely on the child who is reciting. Take note of everyone's work. Avoid trouble by anticipating trouble. Call on a disruptive child to answer questions or to go to the blackboard. Try not to turn your back to the class, especially for any great length of time. Have a student erase the board, or distribute and collect materials. When you write on the blackboard try to face or frequently turn to the class; or, if possible, have someone write on the board for you.

11. *Keep the pupils in their seats.* Limit the students from getting out of their seats, and most of your serious discipline problems will be reduced. Never permit indiscriminate walking or wandering about. Do not allow students to come to your desk to ask questions. Only permit one student to stand at one time. Keep a record of those who use the pass for any "emergency." Do not allow a student to regularly leave the classroom; otherwise, you will have a great many students demanding the pass.

12. *Depend on interest to maintain order.* Interest is the most effective way for maintaining good discipline. A bored class is potentially a "bad" class. Always keep the students engaged in a

meaningful activity. Plan your work ahead of time. Have all your materials on hand. Have optional and omittable items, and use them according to the amount of time left.

13. *Be friendly but maintain a proper distance.* Be willing to play the marginal role of entertainer. Be willing to ride waves; namely, take a joke, or else the children will try to make more waves. However, never become too friendly. The children will take advantage. Similarly, never get to their level. The children prefer to keep the teacher on a different plane.

14.ʲ *Be consistent with discipline.* Do not be lenient one day and strict the next. Inconsistency is bewildering for any child. All threatened punishments must be carried out. The minute the children discover you do not remember they will feel you always forget. Then, when you punish someone else, they will hold it against you for not reprimanding the student you forgot about. The second student will immediately claim favoritism, and he will have a good case against you.

15.ʲ *Be flexible.* Deviations from routine must be handled according to the individual and not as routine. Some children need guidance, not discipline; others need a strict approach. Some children can be dealt with right on the spot; others are too excitable and can only be dealt with after class.

16. *Always work with the individual offender.* Never punish the whole class when a few are responsible. It is a sign of weakness and indicates that you cannot cope with the situation. More important, it causes resentment and creates additional disciplinary problems. If you cannot distinguish the guilty ones, stop work and explain that a "few selfish children" are responsible for having to stop the lesson. Invoke peergroup disapproval without asking for names (urging children to inform on each other will only unite them against you), but watch to whom the children turn. Even if the offenders cannot be differentiated, this method should at least contain them.

17.ʲ *Handle all disciplinary cases yourself whenever possible.* When you call on someone else to maintain discipline in your class, you are in a sense surrendering your authority; in fact, you are admitting defeat. The problem must be serious for you to rely on a higher authority's help, because when you do you will probably never again have the same control.

18. *Do not threaten.* Doing without threatening is far more effective. Your point can be made by the way you touch the child, look at him, and handle yourself. If you do threaten, avoid the impossible. Once you are unable to carry out your warning you lose face.

19. *Never make the offense personal, never allow audience situations.* The child's breach in the classroom should never appear to be directed at the teacher, but at his classmates. Says the teacher, "John, you are ruining it for the class." Avoid public issues. Avoid giving any student a chance for an argument in front of the class; the child becomes a hero and the breach becomes obvious. Says the teacher, "John, I've been fair to you, but you're not being fair to me," or "John, let's talk after class."

20. *Be certain to dismiss the class.* The class works to the *end* of the period or until you want them to stop. They should not be allowed to start packing their books two minutes before the end of the period. The bell is a signal for the teacher, not them. Younger children can be dismissed or lined up by rows, but they should all be dismissed with no undue waiting. Students are in no mood to learn once the bell rings. By delaying them, you are overstepping your authority. A good gesture on the part of the teacher would be to wish the class a good day.

The above suggestions are by no means complete. If anything, they should indicate the extent of my frame of reference, what I consider effective discipline and classroom management which I work by in the classroom with the disadvantaged child. Similarly, they should indicate a cardinal rule; namely, it is much easier to avoid discipline problems than to handle them; prevention is far more important than cure. Let us go on.

Motivation and Student Achievement

Discipline and structured routine are essential for teaching the disadvantaged, but they should complement, not displace, emphasis on "good teaching." Probably a teacher's attitude is most crucial. A teacher who expects achievement will make his students achieve, but not without hard work and not without being a master of discipline and motivation. Disadvantaged children want to get away with as much as possible and do as little as possible, but at the same time they want to learn and like learning; and therefore, the teacher must see them as children who can learn. If a teacher conducts the lesson on their level, the students will be receptive and become deeply absorbed. If the youngsters feel a teacher cares, they will care. If a teacher sets reasonable academic standards and enforces them, the youngsters will meet those standards. If the students see a teacher means business, they will come to class on time and prepared. In short, only a highly motivated teacher can work with or effectively teach these children.

Disadvantaged children lack confidence in their ability to achieve and to perform. Many are too disillusioned and dispirited to care, and have second-class self-images of themselves. Many are so used to failing that they will not do any work or they have no desire to continue unless they have immediate success and evident reasons. The teacher must take these problems into consideration. He tries to reward his students daily; he encourages them; he prods them. He never embarrasses or criticizes them because of their inability. He makes his students realize that he accepts them; he stresses their strengths (they are all too well aware of their weaknesses), and uses their strengths to provide experiences that will help them cope with their deficiencies.

To enhance the learning process, the teacher should supplement the text or manual with intercultural lessons, and with the history and culture of minority groups which relate to his particular subject. It gives the children academic satisfaction, and builds up their image and feeling of self-worth and belonging in context of national life. This can be done in every subject, except perhaps in mathematics. Some elementary schools are now using "integrated" primers and spellers. Some secondary schools are now using social-studies and English books which are concerned with the roles of minorities. The trouble is, however, they have not been fully implemented in all schools, and will not be for a number of years. This means that the teacher should be willing to write material, preferably in story form, on the reading level of the children he is teaching. He should also write to popular magazines and digests for free reprints (most of the magazines and digests will cooperate if the reasons are stated) or for permission to rexograph feature articles about stories of Negro, Puerto Rican, and other minority groups.

As a general rule motivation should be thought in terms of a broad context, not specifically with individual lessons because it is always a problem when it is concerned with individual lessons scattered across the year's work to fill up time, keep the children quiet, or make the lesson appear interesting when it is really not. The fragmented existence and presentation of a stunt or gimmick used solely for the purpose of motivation, and not as a means for developing a lesson or for using it as a worthwhile procedure, usually lacks continuity, and at best engrosses the students for as long as it lasts—usually a few short moments—but as soon as the transition is attempted it leaves them not caring about the rest of the lesson or about the subject.

A teacher's enthusiasm for his subject and pupils is in itself a motivating force. Indeed, a working relationship founded on mutual rapport between the teacher and class is the key to interest these or any group of children to learn. The fact that the children feel the teacher cares, that he respects them, that he trusts them, that he encourages them, that he makes them feel important, that he is convinced they can learn, that he sets reasonable standards will accomplish something a teacher will never be able to do with a "stereophonic, three dimensional accoutrement." The teacher will have motivated these children, something few teachers—no matter how sincere they are—manage to do.

In short, motivation need not be imposed or falsely generated for a few moments. What the teacher should do is make proper use of the whole period and the whole day. Teaching must be practical, concrete, interesting, and oriented toward the child's level of learning. Similarly, there must be definite rapport between the teacher and the class. Of course, I am not so naïve as to think that what I suggest is easy to accomplish. But I am close enough to the classroom situation to realize that what I say is possible if the teacher is sincere and works hard.

A good policy is to start at the beginning of the period with a short educational exercise. A daily five, ten, or fifteen-minute reading drill on the lesson is worthwhile, because so many of these children are retarded in reading. To be sure, every teacher is a teacher of reading. Not only does this type of exercise reinforce past learning as well as provide for a transition for the new work, but it also sets a proper tone for the day. Disadvantaged children need a structured routine; the class knows the procedure upon entering is to open notebooks and do the activity on the black-board.

But whether or not some type of drill is used to begin the period, the teacher should try to assess correctly the instructional level of his children so that he can stay below the frustration level when he begins to develop the lesson. While this may be considered not to be a productive learning experience for the middle-class child or for a more sophisticated learner, possibly leading to boredom, for the disadvantaged this approach meets many of their needs. The youngsters have had few successful learning situations. If they are not able to function on the level at which the material is presented, they will face but one more frustration, one more area of failure, one more blow to a weakened self-image. Now they find themselves competent and successful. The teacher gains status and the students gain confidence; they feel tangible references for their success and learning. Similarly, success in the initial classroom period prepares the children for further learning; it also provides for added verbalization and questioning. Thus, an enigmatical class atmosphere can be illuminated in this manner; children are aroused, heads lift up, thoughts are ignited, hands begin to wave—the wheels of learning are set in motion.

Because the students' attention span is limited, the teacher must continuously change activities and vary the presentation of his lesson. Of course, it is not desirable to change activities too often. This would lead to confusion, which should be avoided with these children. If on the other hand, the students become restless or bored, the teacher should sense it and not continue his procedure by thinking that the children do not want to learn. Any transition should not be abrupt, since the disadvantaged cannot cope with a sudden change. Asking a student to demonstrate what has just been taught is effective. Supplementing the lesson with pictures, graphs, and other visual aids is advisable. These children are impressed and learn better when they see what they are being taught.

Since disadvantaged children are doers and do not think in concepts, the teacher should devise creative experiences so that they will actively be engaged and take part in the lesson. The teacher can have the students act the different roles of people or events they are studying. The Bill of Rights, for example, can be dramatized by short five-minute plays. The students can learn about geography with picture puzzles; they can study Vietnam by taking time to write to a pen-pal, an orphaned Vietnamese child; they can study bacteria or blood types by examining their own skin, hair follicles and blood through microscopes. Younger children can help construct a terrarium where they may study plants, the water cycle, condensation and evaporation, molecular action, rocks, soil, etc. They may help decide what will be needed in the terrarium, write a plan for a walk to get what is needed, read what they have written, execute their plans, observe results, and evaluate outcomes. Students should know what it feels like to be completely absorbed in a problem.

Learning should be meaningful, that is, related to the child's experience as well as to his past learning. This idea should be applied to the teaching of reading during the exercise in the beginning of the period. A student who is given dull material which is not associated with anything in his range of concern will not be interested in reading. On the other hand, almost any student, even a "slow" or "retarded" reader, will read if two things are present: enjoyable and meaningful experiences with which he can cope. The first factor is certainly more important. A child who is interested in what he is reading will try even if the work is above his reading level.

Based on my experience one solution is for the teacher to select daily one or two page excerpts from books that will interest the children (James Baldwin, Langston Hughes, Florence Means, Arna Bontemps, Joan Lexau, Hila Colman, etc.), and use an opaque projector to project the material before the class. Now the students are interested in reading. Perhaps they will even be motivated to make their first trip to the library and read the entire book on their own time. A reading list can be given to the class which covers a wide range of topics and types of reading. If the school library does not have the books, and in some cases it will not, arrangements can be made with a neighborhood library to collect those books from other branches and reserve them.

By the same token, a vocabulary lesson based on the reading can be developed. Learning new words can be fun if the students are asked to write each new word in a sentence with "hip" or "cool" words.

Learning through games also has special appeal for children, and especially for the disadvantaged. Whenever possible, games should be used to create interest as well as to teach something; they should be part of the lesson not separate from it. For example, in the intermediate grades children like riddles and will test their friends and classmates. Riddles can be used to develop careful listening and critical thinking.

Descriptive words often relate to one of the five senses. The teacher can write a list of nouns on the blackboard and have the class suggest one of the senses that is related to it. For each noun, the pupils are asked to describe what is named. In this way, a vocabulary and grammar lesson is developed. The children may describe the ocean as blue (sight) or as loud (hearing); they may describe a hamburger as tender (taste), as a pleasing, spicy scent (smell), as hot (touch).

For primary-grade children, a student or a number of students can make up a series of directions to be read to the class. Various members of the group are selected to perform the directions in correct sequence. Pupils will think of directions such as erase the blackboard, close the window, clean your desk, staple the picture on the bulletin board, return to your desk. By playing this game the children practice their reading and listening, and learn to follow directions so that they can improve in their ability to follow the teacher's own instructions.

It is important, too, that the teacher observe his students at work, display their work and comment on it. By doing this, he shows they must meet academic standards, and at the same time he indicates his interest. This familiarity with the students' work increases rapport; it also gives them a feeling that they will receive recognition for their work. If a student is unprepared, the teacher brings this to the attention of the class; but he terminates with confidence, confirming that the student can do good work when he tries. Similarly, if another student does the homework for the first time, the teacher acts interested. The class is reminded that this student can do the work, too. (In short, the teacher never ignores his pupils.)

When the teacher questions the students, he tries to give attention to all their individual problems. Many are verbally inhibited in the classroom. The teacher, consequently, calls upon non-volunteers; he never exploits bright students. With this in mind, he directs the questions to the class, not an individual, and allows sufficient time for deliberation, which most of these children need. He encourages pupils to ask questions of one another and make comments on what has been said. He invites further explanation and clarification and aids in the process of verbalization without inhibiting the uniqueness of their expression. The children often have faulty English-speaking habits, so he supplies the correction without stopping recitation unless the mistake is typical enough to justify special attention.*

With a difficult class, however, the teacher must ask less questions and give more reading and written exercises. This type of presentation is helpful because it reduces any personality clash that may exist between the teacher and the class. It lessens the need for discussion with the students who are unwilling to listen. It also allows the teacher to direct his attention at the trouble-makers while the class is working, instead of constantly having to stop the lesson and make the rest of the class wait, a situation where no one learns and which all the children dislike. When classwork is marked daily, the grade lowered for disorderly students—and returned the following day—coupled with frequent tests, which also tend to tone the atmosphere, even the most disruptive class learns to cooperate.

With a slow class, similarities rather than differences should be emphasized. A child who is a slow learner has many things in common with other children. Indeed, the teacher should give these students credit for knowing much more than their standard tests seem to indicate. Units of work should be short and simple; homework, class activities, new words, and all aspects of new work should be fully explained. Reviews, summaries, and drills should be frequent but widely spaced and varied so as to avoid boredom. A change of pace and a variety of procedures are needed during each lesson; work should be functional and centered around the children's needs, heroes, interests, and problems. In

* For a more detailed discussion on the techniques of classroom questioning see Allan C. Ornstein, "Do's and Dont's in Asking Questions," *Chicago Schools Journal* (February 1965), pp. 214–216.

particular, the teacher should discard grade and group standards in favor of individual achievement and growth in connection with present academic ability and potential. A scoring chart is valuable for having pupils watch their growth. Also, they enjoy engaging in contests and seeing their names in print, even if it is only on a bulletin board. The teacher must praise them when they work to capacity. The students want this recognition; in fact, most of them are sorely in need of it, and therefore are willing to work when they receive recognition. In discussing this point, even the worst paper has something in it that can be praised. A personal comment, but one that is positive, is effective and is appreciated by the child, even though he may not always show it. Alas, the teacher must not ignore the fact that the slow learner can and should work just as hard as other children, even though the total amount learned is less, and the pace is slower.

10   IN DEFENSE OF
SLUM-SCHOOL TEACHERS

ALLAN C. ORNSTEIN

Educators of many kinds have begun—of course, only with the best of intentions—voicing their opinions about the slum school. As a result, teachers have become an easy target for those concerned with the school's ineffectiveness, an ineffectiveness mainly due to shortcomings in society. "Most who work with underprivileged children today," wrote Frank Riessman,[1] "find this a most unattractive, unrewarding task. . . . Teachers much prefer to teach 'nice' children, in 'nice' schools, in 'nice' zones." According to Edgar Z. Friedenberg,[2] school personnel "dislike and distrust youngsters (from the lowest social class) more often than they like them." Elena Padilla[3] has suggested that among the factors causing dropouts among Puerto Rican children, "beatings by teachers and attacks on the part of other students push many out of school and into job-hunting." In A. Harry Passow's book,[4] it is stated that teachers assigned to slum schools have often been "people without any real concern for these children and with the common stereotype of them as children of low ability." Also ". . . many teachers in slum schools are bewildered and desperate; they feel they cannot reach these children. . . ." Patricia C. Sexton[5] has found among a great many teachers "a deficiency of the understanding and insight needed to solve the educational problems of lower-class students." Pointing to the difficulty of finding people who will willingly work with children who are often "dirty, sullen, violent, and disobedient," she believes that many of the teachers involved "grow to dislike their work and—even worse—their students." James B. Conant[6] commented several times on the high turnover of teachers in slum schools and the need to retrain teachers "engulfed with slum-area children

Allan C. Ornstein, "In Defense of Slum-School Teachers," *Teachers College Record* (May 1968), pp. 759–766. Reprinted by permission of the author and publisher.

whose values run directly counter" to theirs. And Kenneth B.
Clark [7] has several times stressed the fact that a "key component
of the deprivation which afflicts ghetto children is that generally
their teachers do not expect them to learn." His view is that such
teachers emphasize discipline rather than learning, that "apathy
seems pervasive," and that many classes in deprived communities "have a disproportionately high number of substitute and
unlicensed teachers."

Many of these judgments are distorted. They have been made
because teachers have at times expressed feelings of frustration
and futility. But these feelings, while typical of a minority of
teachers, have been construed to represent the majority. They
have been "interpreted" to support preconceived opinions based
largely on observations rather than actual involvement in slum-
school teaching. It seems to many teachers in the school system
that the educators who have commented so often might do well
to accept the challenge they talk about, apply for teaching
licenses, and begin teaching before venting their criticisms. There
are many vacancies in the slum schools, and there is a great need
for effective teachers.

The Challenge of the Slum School. Obviously, the writers mentioned are to some extent correct; but, if they had the fortitude
to work in slum schools, their pictures might not be so one-sided
and so dismal. The question that should be answered is: Does
anyone *want* to teach in a slum school? According to the authorities, no one apparently does; but, based on my own teaching
experiences, this is not the case. Using comments by some of my
colleagues in a New York City slum school (Sands Junior High
School in Brooklyn), I will show the reader a picture that is too
often ignored. My only reference will be my colleagues' own
statements. It is probably clear that no systematic data exist
on teachers' positive feelings concerning their work in such
schools.

I would begin by saying that many young teachers volunteer to
teach in a slum school because of the challenge involved. "The
majority of new teachers," says Mathematics teacher Spivak,
"come with honorable purpose. Therefore, they are often able to
overcome frustrating experiences associated with their lack of

experience." Probably no group of teachers is more sincere, more hopeful, or more energetic. Their inexperience is sometimes compensated for by the fact that, because of their youth, they can easily relate to the children. In a secondary school, a freshman teacher may well be of the same generation as his students and is sometimes more aware of their mores and values than an older person would be. "There seems," says Guidance Counselor Chimes, "to be a new breed of teachers—usually more sophisticated and better educated—lacking experience with disadvantaged children, but capable of adjusting to the task of teaching them." Frequently, the new teachers are sharper-witted than some of the old, more attractive and athletic-looking, providing potential models for children to emulate.

The challenge also exists for the veteran teacher, who often wants to teach in a slum school because he desires something sterner and more rigorous than is provided by another sort of teaching situation. Language Arts teacher Ransom, for instance, says: "Many teachers work in slum schools because they feel challenged. They do a good job; they are satisfied and not interested in leaving the school. . . ." No doubt such teachers have had their share of harassment from difficult students. Many, to be sure, have had vivid, unprintable language directed at them. Not all their students come to school to learn; and many feel hostile and alienated. But this is the challenge, the vital factor that inspires many teachers to work in slum areas.

The Matter of Dedication. Dedication is not merely a catchword, educational whoop-de-do. A large number of teachers are unquestionably dedicated to their profession—and to teaching poor children. They find it stimulating and rewarding; it is their way of helping children in particular need of support and interest. They know they are going to get little recognition and praise, except from their own colleagues. "Teachers are not adequately recognized or paid for their efforts, and the situation is more unjust for slum-school teachers." This is the view of Art teacher Upshur, who goes on to say that "instead of being praised for our work, we are constantly attacked and ridiculed." Physical Education teacher Epstein agrees: "The picture of the 'special service' school teacher is that of a disheartened and discontented individual who would rather be somewhere else. Those who have fostered this myth have either never had the experience or, if they did, never gave it a fair chance."

More slum-school teachers than can be counted spend free time and after-school hours on experimentation and guidance. Social Studies teacher Lewis puts it this way: "Many slum-school teachers are creative and dynamic, using all sorts of experiments and demonstrations. They devote extra time comparing and contrasting new media and materials . . . for meeting the needs and academic level of their students." Such teachers are not the "clock-watchers" too frequently described. They are committed enough to act on the realization that slum children sometimes need special consideration.

Most teachers in slum schools are there because they have been assigned to such schools, not because they had a choice; and some might well prefer to work in middle-class schools. "Teaching in a 'special service' school," says Language Arts teacher Bookman, "sometimes means I am unable to teach, and my ego is threatened. Although this is not an everyday occurrence, it happens often enough to constitute a major problem. However, I go on; for if I should give up, the children would give up too." The tendency is, even among the young teachers, to accept the responsibility gracefully. Art teacher Levy comments that "education is the only real way these children we call disadvantaged will ever escape from their poverty. Teachers—new and old alike— recognize the role and responsibility they have toward these children." French teacher Parnes puts the sense of obligation into eloquent words: "Having been assigned to a difficult school rather late in the term, I was given a position held previously by four different teachers. The circumstances were far from ideal, but I decided I would stay and do the best job I could (although it was possible to change schools), partly for the experience, but mainly because of my awareness of the shortage of teachers. . . . It was almost as if, were I to leave, I would be letting down both the other members of the faculty and the children."

It would be foolish not to admit that some teachers are counting the days until they can be transferred, and that some describe their school as a "battlefront" or "jungle," but this does not negate my thesis. "Some teachers," says Social Studies teacher Russo, "are frustrated and unable to teach or to see results. . . ."

This accounts for the turnover, he explains; but he goes on to insist that, until they are transferred, most teachers "still try their best."

The Joy of Teaching. There remain many teachers who experience a unique sense of satisfaction in the slum school. "Working in a slum school," says Physical Education teacher DeLuca, "can be very satisfying and worthwhile; it largely depends on whether the teacher can teach and 'get through' to his students." Language Arts teacher Nemoytin adds: "It seems we only hear the voices of embittered teachers. There are many teachers, however, who enjoy teaching disadvantaged children. They like their work, but do it without fanfare."

The teacher who enjoys working with slum children usually understands and responds to their positive qualities: their frankness and code of fair play; their vitality and sense of humor; their unique awareness and sophistication, despite their naïveté, in certain dimensions of life. He realizes that they are sensitive and defensive, but he sees that they are likely to be more grateful and apologetic than other children. They respect teachers who respect them; and they are capable of lively relationships with teachers who are able to relate to them. "Once the necessary rapport and mutual respect have been created," explains Guidance Counselor Cohen, "the teacher and his students jointly enter a realm of learning and shared experiences that can be found, at its best, only in a 'special service' school."

The effective teacher can strongly motivate and perform well with slum children. Empathy and understanding are important; but good rapport and discipline are essential. Language Arts teacher O'Rourke makes this clear: "Without good discipline there can never be any teaching. . . . Probably the greatest need for 'special service' schools is to staff them with tried and tested, strong, sympathetic teachers . . . men and women who have proven . . . that they are inwardly strong-minded, firmly dedicated to their profession, and genuinely concerned for disadvantaged children."

Because of lack of previous contact with slum children, few teachers start their careers with genuine empathy or clear understanding. "The picture of the 'blackboard jungle' still exists," says Social Studies teacher Bailey. "Many middle-class teachers come to slum schools full of fear and trepidation, with preconceived notions of all sorts of dire problems—gang fights, for example, shakedowns, assault against teachers. The problems exist mainly in their minds. . . . The overwhelming majority of pupils do not fit the 'blackboard jungle' pattern. Teachers who feel this way are merely covering up their own insecurities and irrational fears of children." Mathematics teacher Kafka asserts that many new-comers learn by trial and error: "Once teachers learn the dis-advantages of being disadvantaged, they can slowly but surely convert these liabilities into positive assets. These children want a sincere and understanding teacher, in touch with the realities of their lives."

Assistant Principal Greenberg stresses the fact that pupils repay a teacher who respects them and is courteous to them: "If he comes with just a little pedagogical knowledge and looks and acts like a teacher, he will find that he has a most appreciative audi-ence. It is surprising what a little bit of instruction disadvantaged children will settle for." On the other hand, good rapport and discipline are difficult to learn when a teacher's personality is not suited for teaching these children. What works for one teacher does not always work for another; personality is the key factor. Advanced degrees in psychology or education do help, but not unless the teacher has what it takes to teach slum children and is able to apply what he has learned.

Who has what it takes? What is the right personality? How do we know who is suited for teaching these children? Often by looking at and listening to someone, it is possible to get a good idea. The way a person combs his hair and knots his tie, or the way he speaks and walks may become factors to take into account in judging his potential effectiveness. This is because they reflect his total personality. "Personality," says Science teacher Andretta, "is the key to one's ability to maintain order in the classroom. It is true that a strong disciplinary control can be developed; but, unfortunately, as with 'potential,' one must possess certain mental and physical qualities, for example in voice and gesture, which when developed . . . will enable a person to control his classes and, in turn, effectively teach and gain satisfaction from his job."

The Easy-to-Teach Subjects. Disadvantaged children tend to like and do well in physical education, industrial arts, art, and music; and teachers of these subjects have less difficulty with their pedagogy than others and find their efforts frequently rewarded. This is because the learning styles of slum children are best utilized in these areas: teaching is visual, concrete, and practical; it is physically oriented; it involves movement, excitement, and freedom of expression. Physical Education teacher Koproski stresses the ease of teaching his subject: "Most of them find it hard to verbalize and communicate their ideas in the classroom. However, they can coordinate very well when performing a difficult task of tumbling, and can work with other children on a team. . . . Slum children need recognition and praise; they are used to defeat and despair. In physical education, the need for recognition and praise for a job well done is very often met. . . ." Industrial Arts teacher Giovannetti talks of the "high appeal" of his subject: "They can see and feel what they make for their projects, and it is natural for their young curiosity. The feel and smell of woods, paints, etc., and the knowledge of how to use a tool never seen before are the best rewards of all for the children; for the teacher, the reward comes when a pupil says, 'I never thought I could finish my project, but you always said I should listen and be patient. Thank you.'"

Similarly, as Art teacher Smith makes clear, disadvantaged children enjoy art classes, and the work they produce is "strong, vibrant, expressive, imaginative. They come to the classroom with all the energy and joy that I could ever help them channel into their art. They are timid at first, for fear of failure. I show them they have to express their feelings to achieve . . . and since every child has feelings, he can achieve in his own way in art." The difficulty arises when one tries to find ways of utilizing such approaches as springboards for conceptualization in the academic subject matter areas. Perhaps academic subject teachers should at least keep the learning styles discovered in the other areas in mind when they prepare and teach their lessons.

The Sameness of Children. Some teachers claim there is no difference between teaching slum children and other children, that color or poverty does not change the needs or interests of children. Science teacher Rifkin says that children "generally have the same interests and desires." Most teachers feel that supervisors, not students, determine whether a school is "good" or

"bad." Teachers might be helped, suggests Guidance Counselor
Rivatuso, "in fulfilling their desire to teach if supervisors would
give them the necessary assistance, and if the administration
would provide the controls necessary for encouraging good classroom behavior."

Other teachers conceive disadvantaged children to be handicapped by poverty and think, as Social Studies teacher Pine puts
it, that their background "induces alienation and hostility, which
are directed at the teacher, making it very difficult to teach. . . ."
Librarian Norton talks of the children's emotional handicaps and
says these "make it harder for them to learn, and harder for the
teacher to instruct them. Although they do respond to a personal,
individual approach, their presence in a regular class deprives the
other pupils of the individual attention . . . which is their right."
Few teachers will admit that they themselves are unqualified or
afraid. Nevertheless, both groups are sincere; and it is probably
necessary to take the view that slum children *do* have special
problems, but that they can learn with proper instruction. As Art
teacher Milberg sees it, "we must devise methods to reach these
children . . . for example, by revising curriculum and teaching
techniques. . . ."

Degrees of Teaching. Many teachers care more, work harder,
and do more teaching when they work with slum children than
they would do if they were working with others. "The approach
used," says Science teacher Foley, "must be adjusted so that a
given group, in this case the disadvantaged, can achieve the goals
of the lesson. The specialized planning required takes more
time and personal effort. If there seems to be little teaching, it
only means the lesson was carefully planned." Noting that disadvantaged youth are usually behind grade level in their academic work, Social Studies teacher Kanner says "a teacher usually
has to prepare his own materials, because materials are unavailable; and this demands a good deal of extra work." Language
Arts teacher Hirshhon adds that "slum-school teachers are not
only teaching their subject matter area. . . . Every teacher also
acts as a guidance counselor, minister, and substitute parent."

True, there is a small minority who choose to teach slum children mainly because they would rather not be bothered with
teaching at all; but it is simply not the case, as many critics con-

tend, that most teachers read their newspapers or do paper work and a multitude of trivial tasks, while assigning mere "busy work" to their classes. The critics do not point out (and perhaps do not realize) that most of the teachers who do little teaching are those who have given up and simply cannot cope with the classroom situation. As Guidance Counselor Rivatuso puts it: "When the teacher gets to the point where he cannot control his class and is working against odds compounded by a lack of direction from the administration and insufficient help from his supervisor, he deteriorates as a teacher, and little if any teaching takes place." But even those who do not teach would rather teach if they could. Industrial Arts teacher Watkins says: "Teachers want to teach. If they are solely blamed for the educational neglect of the disadvantaged child, it is 'passing the buck.' A good educational system depends on all involved knowing and assuming their responsibility." Critics of the schools would be more just if they distinguished between the teacher who does not teach because he does not want to and the one who does not because he cannot. As of now, they have not been discerning or sensitive enough to note the difference.

To Conclude. It is safe to say that a number of teachers are "marking time" in slum schools. It is also safe to say that more junior-high-school teachers are doing this. There are two reasons for this. First, by the time slum children reach junior high school, they are more rebellious and frustrated; consequently, the problems of discipline are more acute. Second, many junior-high teachers have intentions to teach in high school, but because of the lack of available positions they have been forced to wait for an appointment.

Whether a dissatisfied teacher cares enough to teach is questionable, and largely depends on the individual's maturity and devotion to his profession. But no matter what, the longer a teacher has to wait to be transferred from a school he does not want to have any part of, the more probable it is that he will lose interest and stop or just go through the motions of teaching.

The fact is, no teacher should be assigned to a school he does not want. The school is a trap to him, and the children are the ones who are really hurt. One solution would be to allot extra funds to pay qualified volunteers to teach in slum schools, to be selected by principals on the basis of performance. With this system, dissatisfaction would be minimal among slum-school teachers, and more effective teachers would be working in slum areas.

NOTES

1. Frank Riessman, *The Culturally Deprived Child*. New York: Harper and Row, 1962.
2. Edgar Z. Friedenberg, *The Vanishing Adolescent*. New York: Dell Publishing Company, Inc., 1962.
3. Elena Padilla, *Up From Puerto Rico*. New York: Columbia University Press, 1958.
4. A. Harry Passow, Ed., *Education in Depressed Areas*. New York: Columbia University Press, 1963.
5. Patricia C. Sexton, *Education and Income*. New York: The Viking Press, 1961.
6. James B. Conant, *Slums and Suburbs*. New York: McGraw-Hill Book Company, 1961.
7. Kenneth B. Clark, *Dark Ghetto*. New York: Harper and Row, 1965.

11   DISCIPLINE PRACTICES FOR TEACHING THE DISADVANTAGED

ALLAN C. ORNSTEIN

Introduction

I want to caution the reader that what I say in this paper fits most disadvantaged children, but not all, although some statements can apply to *all* youth. Many experts will not agree with all of my suggestions. This is only to be expected, for it is often difficult to agree on what approaches are most effective; furthermore, the success of any approach is essentially related to each teacher's style and personality. Similarly, many readers may not find comfort with my own recollection of teaching experiences. If anything, my anecdotes are personal and should indicate my teaching style, which guided my work in the classroom.

Although discipline is not the major task, but rather a necessary adjunct of teaching, it often becomes the main concern in ghetto schools, and observers usually judge the teacher's success in terms of the way he handles or disciplines a class. That a great many ghetto-school teachers "mark time" or request transfers indicates in part at least that they are unhappy with their disciplinary prowess and are unable to teach.

Unfortunately, the word *discipline* has negative connotations, because it so often refers to the amount of fear induced to keep students quiet or the proper balance of trickery, rewards, and punishments needed to manage a class. For this discussion, the word *discipline* refers to the degree of order and control established in a group. It is a process in which the teacher's understanding of his students and himself, and his ability to manage their surface behavior and his own behavior, go hand in hand. It also measures the teacher's ability to establish a positive relationship with his students, whereby they work toward an ultimate

Unpublished paper. Reprinted by permission of the author.

163

goal of self-discipline, based on a mentally healthy framework.

The paper is divided into four areas that should help teachers by:

1. Providing insight into the problems of the disadvantaged that specifically affect the classroom.

2. Providing insight into common behavior problems that often lead to emotional stress.

3. Providing insight into students' impulsive behavior and frustration tolerance.

4. Providing insight into their own behavior and teaching styles.

Problems of the Disadvantaged That Specifically Affect the Classroom

In order to develop and maintain discipline, the teacher must know his students and be aware of their problems. The teacher must recognize that his students have lives that go on outside school which affect the teaching-learning process. A few examples suffice.

Many disadvantaged children come to school with untreated physical ills. Often when they are supposed to wear glasses, they do not because of embarrassment. Lack of a well-balanced diet, coupled with their popular eating habits—coke and candy between meals, or instead of breakfast and lunch—is why many are undernourished and in great need of dental care. Nevertheless, when the school does arrange a clinic appointment, many children do not show up because no one is at home to see that they do go, or the family is too large for the mother to keep track of her older children.

A check with the school nurse or health records might amaze the teacher. There are students sitting in the back of the classroom who are reported to have severe cases of myopia but are not wearing glasses, never have worn them, and have not told the teacher. Some students, who are scheduled to visit the health clinic after school is dismissed, are playing basketball instead in the school center in the afternoon. Certainly a teacher can at least remind and check students to see that they keep their clinic appointments, seat children in the front who cannot see from the back of the room, and explain why glasses are important.

Many children come to school with poor health habits and with inadequate clothing. Although every teacher in every school should be a model of cleanliness and good health habits, it is even more important in teaching the disadvantaged. Good health habits should be stressed in the curriculum. Because of inadequate clothing, one child may stay at home on days that require white blouses or shirts; another, on days that require the student to have sneakers and gym suit. Rarely, if ever, will the child voice his economic plight. A teacher, therefore, should look for such patterns in examining class attendance. A tactful discussion and referral to the proper school agency can correct the situation. Indeed, a child may be absent for a number of other reasons, and for a long duration. A teacher who notices a great number of absences should have a class monitor make an extra set of notes (this job can be rotated daily) so that when absentees do return to school they can at least make up the work.

The disadvantaged child is often reared in a matriarchal family and feminine culture. When he enters elementary school, he finds that here, too, he is dominated by women, both teachers and administrators. Thus, the gang serves as a means for the male to prove himself as a man. Instead of passively permitting him to engage in antisocial activities, the teacher ought to encourage a youngster to assert his masculinity in positive ways—doing well on school athletic teams or in shop; and most important, the teacher should try to instill in him the idea that by getting a good education he will be able to get a good job and be able to support himself and, therefore, be a real man.

Some black children have newly gained confidence in their demands not merely for "civil rights" but for full equality. Some see themselves as leaders, and not as helpless, inferior youngsters. This new pride is evidenced by their tendency to challenge authority. The teacher should expect, encourage, and be able to cope with this energy and channel it toward constructive goals. Classroom discussions about this movement can be helpful for stimulating instruction and clearing the atmosphere of any tension that might exist.

An additional problem of classroom behavior is sometimes manifested by Spanish-speaking children. A knowing teacher investigates to see if these children are quiet or withdrawn because they do not understand English, and not because they are "dumb" or "slow." These children usually will not inform the teacher of their communication problem, because they are shy about their language barrier and because they are taught at home to be polite to teachers, and this is interpreted as not annoying their teachers with any personal problems. Hopefully, the school has a non-English-speaking class. However, if the school does not have such a class, the teacher can arrange a "buddy" system with the Spanish-speaking child and with a couple of bilingual students for the remaining academic year, to explain classroom and school routines, as well as to try to improve the language skills of the non-English-speaking child.

Along with understanding the disadvantaged child, the teacher needs to respect him. Having middle-class values, most teachers measure progress on a middle-class scale. They encourage the child to succeed on their terms, therefore teaching the child that his values are wrong. To win their favor and receive the rewards of school that come with middle-class conformity, the child must give up his individuality and style of life. He must change his language, dress, and manners; he must come to school clean, neat, and punctual; he must not fight. This much sacrifice cannot justify the loss of identity. Thus, teachers are seen as condescending caretakers, who lack understanding or insight into his problems, yet want to make him one of them. The clash between the expectations and life style of the disadvantaged and that of their middle-class teachers is reflected in terms of *us* and *them*, with the teachers siphoning off the "bright ones" from the group and preventing the rest of the group from expressing their values.

It does little good to try to change the teachers' middle-class values. Teachers need only to be made aware of the differences in cultural values without viewing one as right or better. Instead of trying to reshape the disadvantaged child, teachers should accept his life style and improve him within the scheme of his own values. Teachers should maintain their system of values, but, at the same time, respect and enhance the child's own values in order to reach him. Children want respect and the opportunity to develop their own thinking in context with their life style.

Often the disadvantaged child does not respond to the teacher and is labeled "lazy" or a daydreamer. This behavior usually indicates that his school work is too difficult or confusing, but, unfortunately, as long as the child remains "good" in class, teachers tend to give him little attention. As a defense, the child learns to procrastinate; this behavior confirms the teacher's original low opinion of him which he treats as a minor disturbance. Actually, the child's procrastination is a plea for help; he is informing the teacher that he cannot cope with the subject or with what he is being told to do. He may continuously hang around the doorway after the late bell sounds, ask for a pass to leave the room as soon as he enters, claim he left his notebook in another class, take five minutes to find and open his notebook, be unprepared, or have five pencils to sharpen.

Sometimes the disadvantaged child is unwanted at home so he ventures to the street, and a child who is brought up on the street is going to be governed by the laws of the street. He is going to resort to violence as the primary means of protecting himself from anything that seems threatening or makes him look fatuous. In school, where many provocations will arise early in his career, his normal pattern of behavior will be greeted with reprimands and limitations, adding to his confusion and frustration in the new, unfamiliar, and unfriendly surroundings. The child will soon feel that his teachers are unfair, single him out and take advantage of him, and therefore will be readily angered. Often the child's lack of maturity and emotional control will compound the problem. Little wonder, then, that so many ghetto-school teachers contend that they are burdened with hostile and angry youngsters. To make things worse, the teachers reject this behavior and in turn aggravate the behavior they wish to change.

Too often, a teacher creates a discipline problem by condemning a student before he tries to find the cause of his actions. This does not mean the teacher should condone the behavior in question, but that he should use the child's action as a point of departure for creating understanding. An aggressive child usually needs a friend, not a lecture. His teachers probably have given up on him. His misconduct, whether verbal or physical, is usually the only way he can reveal that he needs help. The teacher should distinguish between aggression that originates from immediate frustration and aggression that reflects hardened anger and contempt. The first kind can be handled by directing the child's energies into more challenging and interesting activities. The second requires a firmer approach, with suitable rules and routine, which will be discussed later. In particular, this type of student needs a teacher whom he can respect and who will set firm and consistent limits on his behavior. It is essential, however, that the teacher be liked by the student, as well as the group, or firmness will only harden the student's behavior. Teachers who are disliked by or lack rapport with students often increase resistance when they try to discipline, and the more they demand or threaten the greater the students' resistance.

The causes of immediate aggression can be many: failure to understand the subject or to see purpose in going to school, being asked to do something that is beyond one's capacity, conflicts in personality between the teacher and child, etc. Assuming that at least the rudiments of basic trust exist between the teacher and child, an effective approach is to try to help the child see his problems and the problem he is creating for his classmates. By recognizing the child's major reason for noncooperation, the teacher and child can work together, not against each other. Regardless of what the problem is, the teacher should be able to handle the full strength of the child's emotions when it arises, helping him to contend with and transfer his frustration and anger into more constructive purposes.

Socially maladjusted and emotionally disturbed children pose a special challenge, and there are many of them to deal with in ghetto schools, especially because their home conditions are likely to have had harmful effects on emotional stability. These children may suffer from many different psychological disturbances, and their school difficulty may be only one of its manifestations. Because they often cannot function in a regular classroom situation and because school seems a threat to them, their school problems snowball as they pass from grade to grade. Some are quiet and inhibited, passive and indifferent. They are too dispirited, lack self-confidence, and are afraid of the world around them. Some are easily provoked by minor frustrations. They lack self-control and cannot postpone gratification; their rage is immediately discharged. Some are demanding; their expectations are infantile and must immediately be satisfied. Some are alienated, extremely rebellious, and unwilling to do their work. These kinds of children are probably the most difficult to deal with, because for them the teacher represents authority, which they resent.

Because of their inability to get along, socially maladjusted and emotionally disturbed children usually are looked upon with suspicion and feel isolated from the rest of the class. They are school failures and are afraid of more failure, no matter what its nature. What they need is a sympathetic and understanding teacher who will coax and help them understand themselves and adjust to their peer group. They need to be given work that they can successfully complete. They need to feel that they belong in the class and in school; for example, by working with their classmates on class projects and by participating in class and in extracurricular activities. The fact is, they are sometimes interested in one or two fields to the extent of possibly becoming experts; it is for the teacher to find their proper field of interest by closely scrutinizing their class work and by talking to them privately. Their adjustment in life depends on this. Of course, the teacher has the right to call on the school counselor for assistance or referral to a specific socio-psychological agency.

When I was a freshman ghetto-school teacher, in accordance with the common practice for the initiation of new teachers into the system, I was assigned five difficult classes. Whether I was able to teach was of little importance to the administration. That I proudly kept the door open while my classes were in session— a sign in ghetto schools that the teacher has the situation under control and an open invitation to colleagues to look inside—was more than the administration ever expected.

One class, 7–16, consisted of 21 students in September, but only 5 or 6 remained in June; the exact number I cannot recall. The rest of the students were eventually sent either to Creedmore, a state psychiatric hospital, or various "600" schools for emotionally disturbed and maladjusted youth, or were transferred to different classes or neighboring schools for disciplinary reasons.

My goal was to survive, and according to the text that is the wrong attitude, but the text does not tell a novice how to teach in such a situation. I was on my own and found success in lining up my students before they entered the room and seating them three at a time, then running the class like a drill master. Midway through the term, I realized that my strategy, although it seemed to keep the students under control, was not the answer. I came to the conclusion that I was not really teaching, but merely holding down the fort. I realized that the students had little feeling of responsibility and were unaware of their misbehavior. Because of my "boot-camp" attitude, the students were growing to dislike me and felt they had the right to be "bad." Harsh discipline was not the proper approach; being a friend and a source of understanding was more effective. Even with my other classes, where only one or two students appeared to be emotionally disturbed, I began to make special allowances. The other students knew these children were different and accepted the fact that concessions had to be made. With this approach, I began to teach sometime in March. It was also at that time that I closed the door, for I no longer had time to say hello to my colleagues.

Common Behavior Problems That Often Lead to Emotional Stress

Disadvantaged children often deny their contribution to class incidents. When they are caught—they call it being "snagged"— many will play dumb, fake, or try to "con" their way out. They have a system of subtle excuses that the teacher should recognize and differentiate. "Who, me?" "What did you say?" For this reason, all disciplinary action should be taken immediately after the incident, or as soon as possible, and without argument. The child must understand the reasons for the punishment; otherwise, there is no reason for him to change his behavior. Punishing a child without making the reasons clear will worsen his general behavior and strengthen his hostility toward the teacher.

Many disadvantaged children do not take care of their possessions. They lose, destroy, misplace, and deface their school supplies and their personal belongings. To make matters worse, they often steal and hide things from each other—sometimes to obtain one of the many things they are denied, or sometimes just for plain delight. Therefore, the teacher should remind students that they are responsible for their actions, and must look after their own belongings and whatever items the school lends them. The group must be encouraged to work together and not against each other. Any theft or defacing of property must be accounted for— even if it means having to call a dean or supervisor—to stop a potentially intolerable condition, which can worsen if not checked.

Disadvantaged children are not accustomed to success at school or in society. Consequently, when they do succeed, many cannot cope with it. Some become aggressive or boisterous; some will goad others to copy them. Unless instantly curtailed, this will result in a verbal or physical confrontation. The teacher is required to be swift and capable of acting as a judge. He does not ignore the students' clash of interests or their daring one another, which they call "wolfing." These children need the teacher's advice, and if he is fair they will appreciate it, even though they will not readily admit it.

Many behavioral problems (which teachers often experience with these children) can be avoided—if good judgment is used. There are no basic rules. It depends mainly on the teacher's use of the right approach at the right time with the right child. Without stopping the lesson, a nod of the head, a snap of the finger, or a stern glance can sometimes be effective. Moving about the room and coming in close proximity with a student who is about to break the rules may be the thing that will alert the student and bring him back to the proper fold. Often the teacher can put his arm around the shoulder of a student (of the same sex) and get his point across. But he should know who cannot be touched. He should not impinge on a student he does not know, or go close to someone with whom he has little rapport—someone who is tense and sensitive about being imposed upon.

When a child threatens another student, the teacher should "talk him down." The child wants a face-saving way out. If a child verbally harasses another student, the teacher should not get upset or make the situation an issue. Most of these children are continuously exposed to abusive language, and cannot help using it when excited. An apology is sufficient. However, no matter how serious the problem is, it should not be aggravated by getting the child worked up to the point where he loses control. Similarly, the teacher should not react to the behavior of the child by expressing his own emotions or mood. A hostile or emotional teacher continues the cycle of frustration; moreover, students enjoy seeing their teacher lose control. In fact, violent outbursts occur when children or teachers try to preserve their dignity. The teacher should calm the student and take direct action.

He must make certain the class is aware that the child was dealt with, because this type of behavior is contagious if allowed to go unchecked. Also, the teacher must make the child realize that he is not rejecting him, but that he is rejecting the child's behavior and that he demands more respect.

The disadvantaged child learns at an early age to take no stock in promises. Promises are meaningless; they often have been in the past. A teacher who makes it a general rule not to make promises to these children will do better. Promises often involve adults, and adults represent authority. Adults whom he has known have sometimes lied to this child—why then should one with whom he has had no prior contact be obligated to tell him the truth? Promises have little influence over present acts—or for much time. They are considered signs of weakness. However, any promise that is made must be carried out. The teacher who does not fulfill his promise breaks a contract that these children will not forget. The teacher, too, cannot be trusted, they conclude.

The teacher should be equally ready to refuse what is undesirable or unreasonable. A refusal is made with quiet firmness and without apology. It is factual, reasonable, and brief. Lengthy explanations have a defensive ring as if the teacher were unsure or preaching, but the teacher may appeal to the common sense of the child: "Now you know you're trying to take advantage." "I've been fair to you, but you're not being fair to me or to the class." "If you do this, you know you'll be in trouble." He might suggest positive alternatives: "Wouldn't it be smarter if you do it this way?" "Your idea has merit, but let's see if there is another way to do it." If the child still needs to be disciplined, the teacher should try to use the child's own values, and not impose a different, middle-class set of values on him. A punitive climate is to be avoided, because it is damaging to class rapport. In the same vein, it is wrong to mistake fear for good discipline. The amount of force required to maintain order is related to the inappropriateness of the teacher's methods. It does not enhance cooperation, but increases alienation and forced conformity. Students stop caring, do not fight the teacher's efforts any more (or if they do fight the teacher, it becomes a group effort which is very difficult to cope with), and they grow to despise him and have no interest in the subject.

Disadvantaged children will continuously test the teacher until they are convinced of his worth as a person. The teacher should be aware of what is happening, and be capable of using such incidents to his advantage, or joke about the situation to show his sharpness of wit. For example, the teacher walks into the room and finds an unflattering picture of himself drawn on the blackboard in front of the class. Instead of getting upset, the teacher could say jokingly, "I see we have an artist among us." Without demanding the identity of the student he might add, "Would the artist like to sign his name?" Or he could use the picture as a part of his lesson. The science teacher could extend the arms of the picture and draw a test tube or Bunsen burner, then proceed with the actual demonstration. The social studies teacher could begin his lesson on "The Closing of the Frontier" by drawing a cowboy hat.

When the teacher is exposed to ridicule or looks foolish, he should admit it and laugh with the class, rather than deny or oppose it. False vanity and excessive pride cause more disciplinary problems. Similarly, when a teacher makes a mistake, he admits it. When the teacher has to account for something he did, the explanation is clear and brief. An effective procedure is to make clear the position of the teacher, and ask what the child would do if he were the teacher.

Sometimes the teacher will turn around to write on the blackboard, only to hear someone tapping his feet or to see a paper missile whizzing by. Many teachers make the mistake of placing blame on the entire class. It is not uncommon to hear a teacher assert, "If this happens again, all of you are going to stay after school" or, "If someone doesn't tell me who did that, the class will get an extra homework assignment." The teacher must learn to cope with and work with the individual offender; otherwise, he will lose the rapport of the group. One approach is for the teacher to maintain, "Sooner or later the individual is going to be caught and it will be assumed that he has been responsible for all the other incidents. That student will be in trouble." The teacher never traps himself by saying just what will happen to the offender. Often the students will focus their attention on the offender, and if the teacher is alert enough he will have a good idea at least of where the tapping or paper missile is coming from. To divert the class (if the situation does not improve), the teacher might ask for a volunteer to write on the blackboard.

In some instances, the teacher will be confronted by a student who thunders vivid or obscene language. "See me after class," is a sufficient response. If the child regains his composure and begins to work, the teacher should leave it at that for the time being. An audience situation was prevented and there is time to think of what action to take. Under pressure, it is wise to count to ten, one number at a time, before deciding on what to do, making sure not to react with anger or frustration, and not saying or doing things that will be regretted later.

If the child persists, the teacher must deal with him at that moment in order to maintain authority. I am reminded of a method that I used, which worked even with a defiant child. "Any further statement or action will be recorded, and it is going to be added to what you have already said." The lesson would continue, and apparently shocked, the class realized that no matter what the student said he would get himself into more trouble. The student also came to realize it, and eventually stopped. I used this method of controlling a child while I was teaching with great success. After class, I always got in touch with the parents by telephone or special-delivery letter. In either case, I first stressed the positive attributes of the child, then continued by describing the child's misbehavior and dialogue in class. I would conclude by offering to keep the parent informed about the child's work and behavior on a bimonthly basis; the mother or father was asked to sign the report for the child to return to me.

All parents are usually concerned about their children's education and are glad to work with the teacher. Obtaining reinforcement from home is more effective than taking one's problems to an overworked dean or assistant principal. If one decides to use the latter approach, he must follow up on another free period to see just what action has been taken or to remind the person to get to the child before the day ends.

The disadvantaged child easily becomes excited and disorderly when in groups. Because this behavior is contagious and can disrupt the entire class, the teacher should immediately stop the upset, provoked child or separate him from the class—even if it means asking other students for assistance or calling another teacher. When faced with a chaotic group that is yelling, running around the room, turning over chairs, etc., the teacher should not try to restore order by shouting. The group is too excited to listen, and he only adds to the noise. A good practice is for the teacher to use a loud or sharp signal to get the group's attention: blow a whistle, or crack a ruler or similar object against the desk. Another procedure is for the teacher to focus on someone who seems to be a leader. If the teacher can get him to quiet down the others will follow suit; they have probably already calmed down to watch. Unless the teacher has a very powerful appearance or a reputation of strength, and his presence alone will get these students under control, he should never try to deal with or discipline an entire group that is out of control.

It was mentioned earlier that the disadvantaged are usually inadequately dressed. When they can afford it, nevertheless, they spend large sums of money on clothing and go to great lengths to be well-dressed, in an effort to gain recognition and status among their group. Clothing becomes a means of communication; it connotes respectability, being "hip" or "with it"; it reinforces pride and identification among the group.

It is a good practice for the teacher to take notice and comment when students are smartly dressed and wearing new clothing, or what they call new "vines." The compliment should be made without fanfare, sometimes privately, to avoid being labeled as teacher's pets and to avoid hurting or unintentionally comparing other students. Even the most difficult student appreciates the recognition of his new pair of shoes or hair style. Not only does such recognition help foster rapport, but it also can mark the beginning of communication between the teacher and the student.

Of course, there are many students who wear sunglasses, hats, and long, black-leather coats in the school, especially when co-operation among teachers is minimal. Students must be made to conform to regulations, at least when they enter the classroom. In this case, the teacher is dealing with a subtle form of rebellion. He is being tested, too, and the class is anxiously awaiting the outcome. The teacher can mention the rules of the class, incorporate humor, or perhaps even compliment the student for having such good taste in clothing, but he should insist on the removal of the inappropriate items.

A note of caution is in order. The disadvantaged are very sensitive about their "shades," "brimmers," and "sacks." They are signs of status; the type of hat, for example, and the way it is worn indicates the youngster's peer group and what he thinks of himself. An explosive situation is likely to occur if the teacher removes the hat or even touches the student in order to coax him to remove it. The teacher should be equally discreet about other unpermissible items of clothing.

As a teacher, I was once confronted with a new student who walked into my homeroom class with a new, costly looking, black-leather coat and boldly declared that he was not going to remove it and put it in the students' closet because it might be stolen. The youngster had a good point, especially because other classes used the room and many articles of clothing had previously disappeared from the closet. On the other hand, I was worried about the gradual undoing of my rule that students hang their clothes in the closet, which might lead to other rules being challenged.

From the youngster's tone of voice and the pride he had in his coat, I realized he meant what he said. A confrontation was unavoidable if I enforced my regulation, so I effected an immediate compromise. For the day, the student would be allowed to hang his coat in my closet, and I would be personally responsible for it, because I had the only key. He was satisfied, and I told him to wear a less expensive coat from now on, for he would have to abide by the rule. No excuses would be accepted. Sensing that the other students might seek the same compromise, I made it clear to the class that an exception had to be made because the student was new to the class and unfamiliar with the rules. The rule was never challenged again.

This episode, besides illustrating the importance of clothing to the disadvantaged child, shows that when a teacher must rebuff a child's strong convictions a compromise is sometimes needed. Similarly, when the teacher must interfere with a student's activity, humor and compliments serve as a transition or cushion, reducing the possibility of a confrontation. No child should be rudely interrupted from an activity unless it is absolutely necessary. For example, the student who is about to shoot a water gun, roll dice, or let fly a paper clip, and who is abruptly told to stop will often continue, in an effort to maintain his dignity; he may even lose control of himself because of the threatening situation. The best procedure for the teacher is to gradually approach the student, while complimenting him, to joke about the student's being "snagged," and/or to point out the uses of the item he has in his hands, and then to ask him to surrender it, guaranteeing that at the end of the day the item will be returned.

Perhaps the best way to avoid trouble is to anticipate what is going to happen. This is a matter of common sense and sensitivity—the ability to predict how a child will think, act, and feel in a situation. This cannot be learned from books, only from having been in a similar situation, having done something wrong, realizing what happened, and trying not to make the same mistake next time. The teacher must continuously ask himself, "What is happening now and what is going to happen?" For example, on the first day of school six children might come to class unprepared—some accidentally and some intentionally. Of course, it is permissible for one child to borrow pencil and paper from a classmate, but when six children have to ask six others, and perhaps walk around the room to get what they need, with one child throwing a punch at someone just for fun, control is reduced. Anticipating the situation, the teacher could have paper and sharpened pencils on hand.

The better the teacher's ability to predict the children's behavior, the better he will get along with them and maintain discipline. Common sense and sensitivity to the students' behavior are necessary if one is to reinforce rules, routine, and rapport. Lack of common sense and sensitivity mean the teacher is unaware of unforeseen pitfalls, which will eventually lead to the continuous testing of his authority and a mixture of minor skirmishes and major battles. The method I used in handling the student who was reluctant to hang his coat in the closet indicates the effect common sense has with disadvantaged, sometimes hostile children.

Students' Impulsive Behavior and Frustration Tolerance

Ideally, the teacher has an understanding of the manifestations of his students' behavior, and has a working knowledge of how he can cope with their problems. He sets up safety measures for relieving classroom tensions and permits a measure of prudent restraint, but at the same time establishes limits of acceptable behavior. He accepts the students as they are, not as he wishes they were. He is tolerant of differences and respects each child for his individuality. The teacher accepts the fact that sometimes the child needs to hate him, that the child expresses anger easily, that he resents authority figures, and that his language is vivid and expressive. This does not mean that the teacher accepts *any* behavior, but that he expects hostility and does not become upset or feel that it is a sign of his own inadequacy, or that the child really wants to be at variance with him.

Victims of an environment that is hostile and damaging to them from their birth, the disadvantaged are extremely defensive and are accustomed to being rejected, sometimes even by their parents or guardian. Many are not acquainted with having an adult—for that matter an adult from the larger society—as a friend, but will enthusiastically welcome such a relationship once their initial apprehensions are proven groundless. In effect, this is an important step for establishing "psychological safety" and mutual trust and respect. Teacher and students feel secure with one another, which is essential for maximum teaching and learning. The teacher is confident enough to experiment without apprehension or losing control and to devote his full energies to teaching. The students are comfortable enough to express themselves without fear, and free to think and develop their ideas. The teacher is able to communicate and make contact with his students, while they look to him for advice and recognize him as a person of greater experience and understanding.

Early in the term rules and routine * are established for entering, moving about, and leaving the room, in order to keep unnecessary disturbance to a minimum. This not only facilitates the teacher's job, but it instills a sense of security and assurance that all children, especially the disadvantaged, need: they know what to do and when and how to do it. The ground rules are established with the idea that the students will eventually manage themselves. At first the efforts may be awkward and noisy, but they will improve. The students will appreciate the teacher's continued trust, and they will not lose control as long as the

* See Allan C. Ornstein, "Techniques and Fundamentals for Teaching the Disadvantaged," *Journal of Negro Education,* Spring 1967, pp. 136–145.

teacher maintains his control. In the end, the rules and routine will lessen the teacher's need to exert his authority, or even to be constantly present. The students will work together and take the responsibility for their own actions, and possibly they may reach the point where they can enter the classroom in an orderly way, start to work, and function as a cohesive group, performing their required duties and sometimes learning even without the presence of their teacher. The teacher might even come late to class or step out of the room for a moment; when he enters the room the students will be working. If he is absent for a couple of days, the substitute teacher (to his surprise) finds a group ready to tackle the lesson.

To be honest, when I was a ghetto-school teacher, I never had a substitute teacher tell me how well-behaved my classes were when I was absent, but I was able to come late or walk out for a moment, without fear of my students losing control or misbehaving. There was one exception. An impulsive 7-13 homeroom group used to post a guard by the doorway, and when he saw me in the distance, he would signal the group. When I entered the room everyone was in his seat, laughing or smiling, knowing that I knew they had been running around the room, playing tag, and verbally assaulting each other. The students were in their seats because they knew that they had to be orderly if they wanted to line up and be dismissed. Surprisingly, they were the first class to have lunch and leave at 3 o'clock. Most of them had lunch in school and appreciated being the first group in line, and they liked being the first group to stand outside after school and tease the classes that were still in the process of closing the windows and lining up. Most students, even teachers, prefer getting at the head of a snail-like lunch or clock line.

To help sustain a healthy classroom atmosphere, as well as his rules and routine, the teacher should learn how the students feel about themselves and each other as they perform in the classroom. Teachers can study their students as individuals and as members of the group. Cumulative records often perpetuate prejudiced viewpoints, based on low scores from culturally biased tests and remarks made by angry, often unsuccessful teachers. These records do not reveal the students' current feelings, anxieties, and problems, but observing does, or at least helps, if the teacher can learn to separate his middle-class values from the objective.

The teacher observes the students: whom they associate with, what they say, how they say it, what they do, how they do it, who assumes leadership, who follows, who is the buffoon, antagonist, braggart, etc. The teacher learns who influences whom, and in what way. These insights increase his sensitivity and ability to predict behavior. For example, his observations help him in assigning seats to the class and in organizing them in special work groups. By recognizing the leaders of the class, the teacher realizes which students to include in an activity in order to facilitate his teaching.

In the ghetto, leadership is often associated with physical prowess and power, especially among the adolescents. Often, the leaders in the classroom are aggressive and hostile, and used to asserting themselves. Observing the leaders early in the term, the sagacious teacher will not wait until problems develop, but will prevent them by establishing a positive or special relationship with those who have influence over others. This, of course, does not mean he should ignore the rest of the class; in fact, many of the others need special attention, but for "openers" the teacher should devote extra time with the leaders of the class.

Teachers often issue passes to "problem" children—to get them out of class so they can teach. Whenever I saw one of my students walking through the hallways with a pass, I would begin a conversation. I would talk about something that was of interest to the student: yesterday's ball game, tonight's school dance, tomorrow's talent show. The student would realize that I was taking an interest in him. I was communicating with him, pursuing a topic that he could talk about with insight and sophistication. At this moment, we were laughing, being frank, and verbally making contact. It was getting to know the student as I never could in class; this communication always paid high dividends in class.

A number of other methods can be utilized for learning about the feelings and judgments of children. Various sociometric approaches, for example, autobiographies, written reports on personal topics, class discussions, "gripe" sessions, and prearranged individual conferences can be used. Two books recently written by former ghetto-school teachers, Kohl's 36 *Children* and Herndon's *The Way It Spozed To Be,* illustrate the use of the first three methods, so I shall limit my discussions to the latter group, that is, discussions, "gripe" sessions, and prearranged individual conferences.

Many subjects can, but rarely do, provide for students to express themselves. The trouble is, most teachers talk too much, ask "what" instead of "why" and "how would you feel" questions, and are too worried about finishing the prescribed curriculum to allow free expression. Also, the teacher usually presents a "phony," irrelevant curriculum, which alienates the students and causes many to withdraw from discussion because of boredom. For example, there is no valid reason for ignoring the "civil rights" and black power movements. Omitting them from discussion, or teaching only safe subjects, implies a lack of respect for students. Teaching about these areas of conflict is an exercise in freedom and citizenship. Moreover, students are continuously exposed to many forms of mass media that report this black-white conflict. Here is the chance for the school to have real meaning for both the black and white child. Teaching the black revolution would improve the image and ego development of the black child and diminish some of the distortions, as well as the poverty of awareness, of the white child.

Students must be encouraged to voice their own opinions, and hear all sides before making a decision. They need to understand what color and race mean by learning about black heroes and black culture but without overcompensation. Students need to examine the principles and purposes of various black "civil rights" and black power organizations. They need to read about Marian Anderson, George Washington Carver, and Martin Luther King; they must also read about Le Roi Jones, Malcolm X, Stokely Carmichael, and H. Rap Brown, even if the discussion makes the white teacher feel uncomfortable or guilty. The black students need to realize their potential power, not only in the world but locally, as more black people migrate to the city. The reason for the riots should be investigated in order to teach black students how to take socially accepted, grass-roots action. Demonstrations, sit-ins, and marches should be discussed, perhaps organized, in relation to real-life experiences. The fusion of reality with learning is the best way of getting the students excited enough to express their anxieties, fears, and hopes. It will make school make sense, and develop their intrinsic motivation. This would make the task of discipline much easier.

Of course there is danger, but there is more danger in ignoring what is happening beyond the classroom as black youth develop their own strategy. The race riots testify to this fact. In this manner, teachers must find ways of really making contact with their students. The curriculum must be real and relevant. Teachers must allow their students to think for themselves, to act out and air their feelings. "Psychological safety" and trust must be established so that students can say "I believe," "I feel," "I dislike," "I prefer."

Exercises that utilize discussions and bring feelings to the surface are reports, dramatics, poetry, role playing, and "hip" language. All children and youth need the opportunity to discuss and express their feelings. Their emotions and anxieties are evident. "Mature, intelligent, middle-class," college students across the country from Berkeley to Columbia have exploded into violence in much the same way as "immature, slow, lower-class," potential dropouts who smash windows, flash knives, and frankly tell their teachers to get out of their way. Both groups are expressing feelings that were brewing for a long time and were not aired or "utilized" in a fruitful exchange.

Serious incidents do not just happen; anxieties collect and build up. A discerning teacher permits his students an outlet so they will not find another one that may lead to disciplinary problems. "Gripe" sessions or group discussions serve as a safety valve for students to let off steam, as well as for the teacher to obtain information about what is bothering them. During these sessions, the teacher can route the youngster's frustration into more positive efforts before his behavior becomes uncontrollable and before direct action is needed.

Rules must be established that permit one student to speak at a time, and discussions must be confined to specific problems, preferably one at a time; otherwise, the session may get out of control and increase the group's anger. As long as students think their feelings will be respected, they will express themselves. The feelings they express will vary depending upon their rapport with each other and their teacher.

Each student has to feel that he can contribute in the discussion, and should be encouraged to respect the values and opinions of others. The students must learn to reason for themselves, and arrive at their own decisions and accept the consequences. They should ask questions and comment about each other's work and behavior. They already know who the cut-ups are and what they want but they rarely have the opportunity to express their viewpoint.

If group values are utilized, the interaction will make for good rapport between the teacher and the class, and provide a healthy class atmosphere. The students should eventually learn to better understand themselves and cope with their personal and environmental problems. The disadvantaged child needs to understand his behavior and to accept himself in order to take part effectively in the learning process. He needs special help to distinguish right from wrong in our middle-class society, not because its values are better, but because this is still the world that he must enter if he is going to succeed. Similarly, he needs to learn to get along with authority, because he is always going to have someone above him who will enforce rules and tell him what to do, whether he likes it or not. Hopefully, the students will drain off their frustrations, see themselves more objectively, accept the learning situation and the role of the teacher, and accept their responsibilities in class.

At times, the teacher may provide a more definite structure by arranging for an individual conference with a student. He can talk to the child before school, after school, or during lunch or a free period. If the teacher devotes time to getting to the root of the problem, and the child's behavior, he shows the student that he cares. As long as the child believes he can trust the teacher and believes that his feelings will be accepted, he will most probably reveal his problems. The teacher must respect the student's opinions and avoid criticizing or embarrassing him. Rather than talk, the teacher must listen and sense the student's feelings. He might suggest the proper word or phrase in order to clarify an emotion or situation, but he should not speak for the child.

A primary concern is to help the child understand his behavior and the effect it is having on the rest of the class. For the child to be made aware of this problem, the teacher must draw out the student's own feelings and evaluations about his actions; the student should reach his own conclusions about what can be done. Sometimes the teacher can offer suggestions, but he should be careful not to pass judgment or use his middle-class values as a measuring rod.

Most important, the teacher should not feel he is ill-equipped to listen or to suggest approaches for solving problems. People have always confided in others and given advice to each other, and there is no reason an educated adult cannot help a child or youngster with the problems of growing up. The teacher should keep in mind that the worst problem child needs a friend, an adult to whom he can talk freely and frankly, and who will accept him. Praise and understanding are new to someone who is accustomed to failure and rejection. The teacher's interest pays off and usually earns the child's good will. The student who was the teacher's biggest problem in class can become his best friend.

Behavior and Teaching Styles

Teaching, then, involves more than just providing knowledge; it consists of a constant interaction between students and teacher. Every child responds differently to a teacher; the teacher's personality, and his anxieties, in some way affect his behavior and in turn his relationship with his students. It is this relationship that influences his students' feelings toward learning more than the subject matter.

The teacher's personality is a reflection of the sum of his physical and mental attributes. Not too many days of a school term elapse before the students size up their teacher and start to probe for sore spots. They will seize upon and react to any weaknesses or strengths the teacher displays, and most obvious (although probably not most significant) are the physical attributes of the teacher. For example, as previously mentioned, a large number of disadvantaged children exhibit a flair for and an appreciation of fashion. These children equate fashion and good taste in dress with knowledge or "being with it." Thus everything the teacher wears, and the way he wears it, is scrutinized by these children.

The mental make-up of the teacher is more significant, and in the end will essentially determine the teacher's success or failure.

Teachers have specific feelings toward their students, and the feelings discernibly affect their teaching and cannot be disguised or concealed from students as sensitive as the disadvantaged. Teachers prefer, dislike, stereotype, or are biased toward some students. These feelings largely stem from their own attitudes. To some teachers, the disadvantaged are "uneducable." To others, they are reachable and teachable. The teacher must be convinced that the disadvantaged can learn, because students who are not expected to learn will not learn, and will reinforce the original assumption. Similarly, it goes without saying that the person who is selected to teach disadvantaged students must not be racially or socially prejudiced and must want to teach these students. No matter how knowledgeable or strong the teacher may be professionally, his attitude must be one of wanting to help the students he teaches; otherwise, he will be no teacher at all. The teacher should be dedicated, or at least committed, to his role; otherwise, he will give up and become a cynic. The teacher must not lose confidence or express overt fear. Whatever teaching is accomplished in the classroom must not be canceled by the loss of his authority.

The teacher's emotions and problems also affect his behavior and relationship with his students. A teacher who comes to school with numerous anxieties carries them into the classroom and they affect his behavior. For example, a teacher with financial problems may be too overwhelmed or overworked in the evening to prepare his lessons, or to take an interest in the problems of his students. A teacher with a poor supervisory relationship may be so dissatisfied and demoralized that he no longer cares about teaching.

A teacher's behavior can be conscious or unconscious, obvious or subtle. The way a teacher talks, looks, or gestures communicates his feelings: anger, hostility, warmth, humor, etc. The fact that behavior is sometimes unconscious or subtle does not necessarily mean it is harmful. In fact, such patterns of behavior can sometimes make the difference between success or failure. Many times we hear that a teacher is effective in the classroom; yet, we are unable to explain the reasons, or if we do they are nebulous. Are not the seemingly unnoticed acts of behavior between the teacher and students one explanation for the teacher's success?

Some teachers resent or fear the disadvantaged because they are difficult to teach. Rather than feeling guilty for such sentiments, the teacher should realize that it is perfectly natural to have them, and that they arise when teachers, along with other people, feel threatened. Teachers who lose control in class or receive criticism tend to be more vulnerable and fearful of allowing their unconscious feelings and behavior to come to the surface. However, these teachers, more than others, need to confront and gain understanding of themselves. They need to develop a sense of security, not to take outbursts personally, not to expect students always to be "good" or "proper." If teachers learned to evaluate themselves and their students in both separate and interacting perspectives, they would be able to evaluate their own effect in the classroom and their relationships with individual students.

A teacher's self-awareness reflects his ability to understand his own behavior and to perceive what is going on around him. All teachers should possess this self-awareness, but the need is more crucial for those who teach the disadvantaged. A teacher's self-awareness somewhat measures his emotional maturity and willingness to confront himself and keep open the channels of criticism. It means the teacher understands his problems and prejudices; or, at least is consciously aware of them, and plans to adjust. It suggests that he is more likely to be objective and accepting of his students. By knowing himself, the teacher is more comfortable and feels less threatened by his students' behavior. In turn, he is less prone to react with hostility or criticism in a situation that calls for emotional control or humor.

In order to know himself, the teacher must be willing to assess his own weaknesses and strengths. This is important in order to adopt a realistic teaching style appropriate to his personality. Astute appraisers and knowing manipulators of their environment, the disadvantaged usually assess the teacher's worth as a person before they become at all interested in him as a teacher. They know what will upset teachers often better than their teachers know, readily learn the behavioral patterns of their teachers, sense what will get their teachers angry or make them lose control, realize that threats are ineffectual, and that the teachers' authority is limited. In this connection, they quickly learn the educational clichés about themselves and are able to behave in the manner expected of them.

A teacher who unrealistically evaluates his strengths and limitations is greatly handicapped with these children and youth, and eventually makes a number of mistakes; in turn, this weakens his authority. For example, a teacher may tell a student, "You're staying in after school so I can talk to you," but expects the student to come on his own. However, the student fails to show up. Another teacher will threaten, "If you don't keep quiet, I'm going to send you to the dean." If the student continues to chatter, the teacher may write a pass for the student to take to the dean, only to have the student refuse to budge from his seat.

One teacher may be strong enough to look at a disruptive child and make him stop whatever he is doing. Another teacher realizes his limitations, and gets results with a different approach —perhaps, simply reminding the child that he is disturbing his classmates. But no matter what approach is used, the teacher must be himself, straightforward. He cannot fake himself. The realities of life have made these children quite sophisticated in recognizing the phonies right away, and they take offense to such deceit. Also, there is nothing more dangerous than trying to adopt a teaching style that does not fit one's personality. The teacher will never really be at ease, because what he is attempting to do is false.

All teachers must realize that they will have difficult students in their classes. If the situation becomes uncontrollable (and this is not uncommon with teachers of the disadvantaged), the teacher may feel a sense of despair and failure. It may take months, or even the entire school year, before any of the students can get psychological help. Even then, there is no guarantee that the students will change or be "better" in class. The teacher is forced to keep the students in the class, though the teacher and other students suffer. For a colleague to merely inform the teacher that the class is difficult and that he understands why the teacher is unable to teach is not enough. Instructing the teacher that there are no pat answers, but to keep on trying anyway, is discouraging, too.

Conclusion

Teachers need immediate and long-range help with their class-room problems. Textbooks and course work are too remote and cannot be realistically consolidated with the classroom situation. Suggestions for coping with these problems are linked with the transference and mental health of the teacher and are listed below.

1. Teachers need counselors or consultants who can help them evaluate their personal and classroom problems. The armed forces and industry have counseling services for their employees. Surely teachers, whose work depends almost entirely on inter-action with children, deserve help. Change can only come if a teacher is aware of his biases, fears, and anxieties. A qualified counselor can present a more objective view, help make teachers aware of their behavior, and support a healthy approach to discipline.

2. All teachers, especially those who teach the disadvantaged, need the support and encouragement of their supervisors and administrators if they are to maintain their equilibrium and function at peak effectiveness. We need leaders who will protect teachers against unfair criticism and outside pressure. Many educators and parents have let loose a barrage of criticism against ghetto-school teachers. The unfortunate results of these attacks have alienated many teachers and convinced others that the accusations are correct. Morale, confidence, and teaching standards have suffered. Panicky school administrators have proposed hasty and ill-conceived schemes to placate attackers without determining the validity of the criticisms.

Support of education by the parents and community is needed, not criticism for the sake of criticism. The black poor, who identify the school with the larger society that has been unkind and unjust to them, are prone to vent their frustrations on the school and teachers. Without the fear of sounding illiberal, the demand for more black administrators in big cities without regard for merit or examination scores but for the sake of black pride and power, although understandable and psychologically justified for black children, negatively affects the morale of white teachers who work with these children. We need supervisors and adminis-trators—black and white—who will be effective and not bend to critics and pressure groups when their demands are flagrant or unjust, but will explain carefully the objectives of the school to the different groups.

3. All teachers need recognition, especially ghetto-school teachers because they are continuously accused of poor teaching. Teachers need to be reassured that their work is appreciated by those working with them and above them, and by those who live in the community. Teachers', administrators', and parents' groups should publicly recognize effective teachers. This way a better teacher-administrator-parent relationship could develop, one that is badly needed in many cities. At the time of this writing, almost all the news about ghetto-school teachers in the newspapers and magazines is news of how many teachers are threatened, attacked, or departing. We can only guess how great has been the recent decline in morale in such schools.

4. Once teachers gain tenure their supervisors usually limit their observations to an annual or semiannual basis; there is little cognizance of their ability—or of improvement. Even worse, beginning teachers are often unable to stand up alone against the cultural shock and initial years of teaching the disadvantaged. Left alone, they make many blunders, often never adjust, and sometimes drop out of the profession. To be sure, teachers are forced to face their classroom problems alone. Only when discipline problems snowball and mental stability dwindles does someone take notice and provide help, and then only on some emergency basis.

Teachers need to work together, learn from one another, and share ideas and insights. Time should be set aside during some administrative periods for teachers to observe one another in order to see many varied teaching styles, some of which will agree with their own personalities and which they can adapt and use. Because the observers are not involved in the teacher-student relationship, they should be able to provide objective feedback, as well as clarify the teacher's behavior patterns and approaches, and perhaps some of their own, in discussion groups. As long as supervisors are absent from the observations and feedback periods, these sessions should not be hazardous or threatening to the teachers.

5. Although T-groups have no present agenda or rules by which

they must operate, teachers should be given the task of evaluating their own problems, performance, and progress among themselves; moreover, to discuss discipline and mental-health pressures, as well as teaching styles. Teachers can learn in T-groups to evaluate their own feelings and attitudes. They are confronted with unexpected feelings on the part of others, in reaction to behavior or relationships. They focus on facing up to themselves, evaluate their weaknesses and strengths, and adapt realistic approaches to discipline and mental health. What works for one teacher does not necessarily work for another; an individual's personality makes the difference. Although approaches to some classroom problems are basic, and should be subjoined to the individual's style of teaching, the methods of implementing them vary, depending on the teacher's personality. Hopefully, the T-groups will give teachers the opportunity to develop appropriate, effective methods.

6. Teachers need predictive understanding of their students, especially teachers of the disadvantaged, whose values and life styles usually differ from their students'. Predictive understanding is essential for maintaining discipline and a mentally healthy atmosphere, and teacher-training institutions ought to find ways of developing and using it in their programs. But the ability to predict a child's behavior is based on more than just understanding the child, although this helps. Being able to recognize what a child will do is related to sensitivity and common sense, an awareness of one's environment, a sharp-witted, responsive attitude. None of these attributes can be learned by studying, but perhaps they can be developed when an individual is put into novel and challenging situations that demand that he cope with and react to the forces of his environment.

A part of teacher training should prepare teachers for the range of roles, pressures, and problems with which teachers are confronted in the classroom. For example, trainees might assume and change roles of teacher and students, and enact classroom incidents. Videotape could be used to help in the feedback process.

7. Teachers should be given the opportunity to see themselves perform and see what they look like in front of their classes. By listening to and watching one another's films, they should become aware of teacher-student behavior patterns. Movement, manner-

isms, and methods are explored. Classroom problems and strategies are measured in terms of progress. Approaches to discipline and mental health are compared—and changes are made according to personalities. Teachers explain why they did what was filmed and feedback provides alternative ways of doing what they have been previously doing wrong.

8. Teachers usually complain that course work in college is impractical. These criticisms have also been made about NDEA Institutes for Teachers of Disadvantaged Youth.* We need more mental-health workshops and training programs, for they combine a wide range of teaching practices and procedures, relate discipline approaches, teaching behavior and teacher-student relationships, and help teachers face themselves. In this connection, all method courses and student teaching should be taught from the viewpoint of mental health, and combine classroom procedures with mental-health principles.

Teachers also need regional educational clinics where they can telephone or register for help at any time, where they can express their anxieties and emotions, and ask questions and gain insights into their feelings. No matter how naturally self-aware they seem, they can always use more help to understand themselves. For others, it may make the difference between gaining facility in coping with classroom problems or dropping out of the profession.

9. Knowledge and understanding are not enough. What counts is what the teacher does with them. Some teachers just cannot teach the disadvantaged, though they might be very successful with other students. Perhaps some day we can look forward to new techniques that will help in the selection of more adequate teachers for the disadvantaged.

The armed forces and industry have had interviews and personality tests devised in order to determine the aptitude of men and women for various fields of endeavor. Education is the largest industry in the United States. Surely it can benefit from following this lead. It then becomes the problem of those experts in the field of psychological testing to devise suitable and expedient methods to measure aptitudes. The emphasis on pre-service training should be on selecting prospects most likely to

* See Gordon J. Klopf and Garda W. Bowman, *Teacher Education in a Social Context.* New York: Mental Health Materials Center, 1966.

become effective teachers of the disadvantaged. It could be said, then, that education had done its best to find the best personnel for educating the disadvantaged population.

NOTES

1. Almy, Millie, *Ways of Studying Children*. New York: Teachers College, Columbia University, 1959.
2. Blackhman, Garth J., *The Deviant Child in the Classroom*. Belmont, California: Wadsworth Publishing Company, 1967.
3. Driscoll, Gertrude P., *Child Guidance in the Classroom*. New York: Teachers College, Columbia University, 1955.
4. Dunn, Joan, *Retreat from Learning*. New York: David McKay, 1955.
5. Fantini, Mario D. and Weinstein, Gerald, *The Disadvantaged: Challenge to Education*. New York: Harper & Row, 1968.
6. Gallagher, J. Roswell and Harris, Herbert I., *Emotional Problems of Adolescents*. New York: Oxford University Press, 1964.
7. Gray, Jennie, *The Teacher's Survival Guide*. Palo Alto, California: Fearon Publishers, 1966.
8. Hunt, David E., "A Model for Analyzing the Training of Training Agents," *Merrill-Palmer Quarterly* (April 1966), pp. 137–156.
9. Jersild, Arthur J., *In Search of Self*. New York: Teachers College, Columbia University, 1952.
10. Lichter, Solomon O., *et al.*, *The Dropouts*. Glencoe, Illinois: Free Press, 1962.
11. Long, Nicholas J. and Newman, Ruth G., "The Teacher and His Mental Health," *The Teacher's Handling of Children in Conflict*, Bulletin of School of Education, Indiana University (July 1961), pp. 5–26.
12. McSwain, E. T. and Haskew, L. D., "Mental Health in Teacher Education," *National Society for the Study of Education*, Part II. Chicago: University of Chicago Press, 1955, pp. 334–353.
13. Ornstein, Allan C., "Basic Understanding for Teaching the Disadvantaged," *Kappa Delta Pi Record* (December 1967), pp. 35–39.
14. Ornstein, Allan C., "Guidance Practice for Teaching the Disadvantaged," *Selected Articles for Elementary School Principals*. Washington, D.C.: National Education Association, 1968, pp. 169–175.
15. Ornstein, Allan C., "Preparing and Recruiting Teachers for Slum Schools," *Journal of Secondary Education* (December 1967), pp. 368–374.
16. Ornstein, Allan C., "Reaching the Disadvantaged," *School and Society* (March 30, 1968), pp. 214–216.
17. Ornstein, Allan C., "Selecting Teachers for the Disadvantaged," *Negro Educational Review* (January 1968), pp. 29–40.
18. Ornstein, Allan C., "Teaching the Disadvantaged," *Educational Forum* (January 1967), pp. 215–223.
19. Ornstein, Allan C. and Rosenfeld, Stanley S., "Environmental and Other

Factors Which Mitigate Against Disadvantaged Youngsters in School," *Contemporary Education* (January 1968), pp. 156–160.

20. O'Rourke, Patrick J., "The Ideal Teacher for Low-Income Children," Unpublished.

21. Rankin, Paul T., "Fostering Teacher Growth," *National Society for the Study of Education,* Part II. Chicago: University of Chicago Press, 1955, pp. 354–374.

22. Redl, Fritz and Wineman, David, *Children Who Hate.* Glencoe, Illinois: Free Press, 1951.

23. Redl, Fritz and Wineman, David, *Controls From Within.* Glencoe, Illinois: Free Press, 1952.

24. Riessman, Frank, "Teachers of the Poor: A Five-Point Plan," *Journal of Teacher Education* (Fall 1967), pp. 326–336.

25. Trout, Lawana, "Involvement Through Slanted Language," in Peter G. Kontos and James J. Murphy (eds.), *Teaching Urban Youth: A Source Book for Urban Teachers.* New York: John Wiley & Sons, 1967, pp. 23–44.

12 TEACHING DISADVANTAGED PUPILS

WALTER J. FOLEY

Educators have reviewed attempted solutions to the educational problems presented by the disadvantaged student. Their discussions show the wide variation in the scope and diversity of the various programs. In essence, they have been conducted on the thesis that an expansion of, and improvements in, the services which have proven effective in the past was the way to attack the problems presented by pupils enrolled in culturally disadvantaged schools. In short, more of the best known practices.

These procedures have led to degrees of saturation in the areas of social work, psychological testing, curriculum enrichment, guidance services, remedial programs, counseling and direct encouragement of pupils and their parents. Typically, the approach has been *total*. That is, there was an increased concentration of all available services.

Present Status

To date, the information and program evaluation coming out of these efforts has been more normative than specific. There is little factual information in the form of actual practices for the teacher who must face the problems of the classroom. Why has there been little research evidence from these extensive programs designed to support alterations in classroom practice? The possible answers include: (1) It may be that the *total* approach was the determining factor. So many services and aids were added simultaneously that the influence of any one factor became obscure and impossible to distinguish. While the general feeling was that pupils benefited from the total program, there was no way to tell which service helped most, or how much any one factor contributed to the overall program. (2) Also, the lack of any clear-cut evidence supporting certain classroom practices over others and the resulting lack of a listing of procedures common to any successful classroom in depressed areas was based on the absence of a behavior model against which to evaluate the programs.

At this time, the writer favors the second explanation. There is a growing lack of confidence in the *more of the same* method. In part, this distrust is based on the conflicting results of the research on teaching. By working through the maze of teaching research, with its false starts and blind alleys, we will better understand the shortcomings of the attempted solutions to our present problems.

Research on Teaching: A Source of Confusion

Some of the more obvious early fallacies were caused by investigators examining a single facet of the classroom and thus isolating it from the total teaching context. Results of these early studies have become so entrenched that they are now stereotypes in the educational literature. To summarize, autocratic teachers were identified, they were then made democratic; teacher-centered classrooms were identified, they were shifted to pupil-centered; the grouping of pupils was investigated and found to be heterogeneous, homogeneous grouping was attempted. This is not to mention the many lists of teacher personality characteristics developed to determine and evaluate the *good* teacher.

With time and sophistication, the single factor attacks were put together and the research model became more complex. By combining the various possibilities, relationships and interactions were found. A general conclusion from the newer more complex model was that each variable must be studied only in relation to all other variables before the contributions could be understood. To help grasp the implications of this generalization, consider that a democratic male teacher in a pupil-centered classroom grouped heterogeneously has a different *effect* on the learning process than a democratic female teacher in a pupil-centered classroom grouped heterogeneously. There are hundreds of possible combinations, as can readily be seen, to confuse our understanding of the pupil-teacher relationship.

The outcome or effect of teaching was also investigated. A better understanding of the many possible outcomes added a new dimension that had to be included to complete the model of "research on teaching." A revaluation of the various teacher-pupil combinations had to be made on the basis of the defined outcomes of teaching. An autocratic teacher might be better able to communicate facts while a democratic teacher might better influence classroom atmosphere. Add to the top of the three dimensional teacher-pupil-outcome model the overriding variable of social class, parental attitude, organizational pattern of the school and the community . . . and the complexity (or perplexity) of this method of research comes into bold relief!

Typical Teacher Attitudes

Taking a moment to look at what might be considered typical practice in teacher behavior and attitude in culturally disadvantaged areas will help to understand a teacher's problems in this situation. Becker, who interviewed teachers in Chicago, found that typically those who were first assigned to culturally disadvantaged schools left for a more desirable school as soon as possible.[1] This transfer pattern is generalizable and consistent with teacher behavior in other metropolitan areas. Generally, the reason for the decision to leave the first assignment is related to the negative evaluation placed on teaching in depressed area schools by veteran teachers as well as to the more obvious explanations such as old buildings, poor support, low pupil motivations, etc. Young teachers are influenced by the attitudes of the older teachers.

The sequence of events leading to the decision to transfer follows a pattern. A teacher assumes, when he begins, that students will know how to behave as students, that they will exhibit and value behaviors the teacher feels are typical of students. Further, our new teacher assumes that pupils will know what is expected of a teacher. In other words, the teacher and the pupils will know their roles. They will each show the behaviors expected of teachers and pupils.

These role assumptions carry with them many behaviors, many expectations, that cannot be assumed for pupils in culturally disadvantaged schools. The characteristics of the pupils are such that the expectancies of the new teacher will not be realized. The resulting disappointment often causes a confirmation of the negative evaluation of the teaching situation in disadvantaged areas conveyed to the new teacher by others in and out of the profession. His attitudes change from optimism to pessimism.

The new teacher then expects the worst of his pupils and finds it. A self-fulfilling prophecy is established. The new teacher loses his motivation to improve instruction given to culturally disadvantaged children and the cycle is complete. Working with these children becomes *doing time* until a transfer can be secured. The teacher is eventually replaced by another newly assigned teacher and a new cycle is begun.

Proposals for Changing Teacher Attitude

Attempts have been made to change this situation and to alter the attitudes teachers have about assignments to schools in deprived areas. Experts and laymen have proposed a variety of methods which have met with varying degrees of success. Special service pay, shorter teaching hours, team teaching, smaller classes and appeals to the moral obligations of teaching have been included as possible alternatives.

One of the most unique plans was a peace corps-type program tried in New York City by Haubrich.[2] He appealed to student-teachers to take assignments in difficult schools and worked extensively with those who volunteered. His efforts have met with a relative degree of success and have been highly publicized. But, the number of new teachers involved in the program has been small and the approach has to be considered inadequate on the basis of sheer number of student-teachers willing to participate in the program.

A New Look at the Problem

A more pragmatic effort would not focus on obtaining missionary-type volunteers, but upon the changing of the attitudes and evaluations of teachers concerning teaching assignments to deprived area schools. This approach would involve the systematic teaching of specific methods of changing the behaviors of pupils. It would allow teachers to enter the classroom situation with methods and techniques designed to alter pupil behavior and thus reinstate the sense of order necessary for the teacher to experience accomplishment.

The Teaching Situation

There are two questions involved in the teaching situation. The first is concerned with what must be taught while the second focuses on the methods of teaching. These two questions will be treated as they relate to the social learning that must be a part of the education of disadvantaged pupils.

The decision the teacher makes as to how and what to teach in the cognitive area has been well defined. The course of study, tests of achievement, previous grades, and day to day evaluation of pupils all contribute to the decision. Courses in education are designed to assist in making these decisions, but the difference between the theoretical and the actual is considerable.

The Culturally Disadvantaged Pupil

Consider the research on the culturally disadvantaged child. For over a decade, we have been bombarded with psychological, sociological, and cultural-anthropological analyses of the *why* of his behavior. The mores of his culture have been investigated. The marital patterns of his parents have been followed. The female domination of his household has been detailed. The lack of a proper male identification figure has been hypothesized. But, as in the case of the research on teaching, few recommendations in the form of specific practices to alter the attitudes, values, and beliefs of these children have come to the fore. While the *why* is necessary for a better understanding of a problem, the *how* is necessary for the planning of change!

Pupil Behaviors

We have already discussed the expectations of the typical teacher in our teacher-pupil discussion. Now, the typical pupil will be described. While this procedure is fraught with the difficulties of overgeneralization and stereotyping, it does furnish a set of behaviors against which the principles of social learning can be outlined.

The term culturally disadvantaged child is used here in a broad sense to include the many different groups of disadvantaged. When used in this general way, it refers to children living in depressed areas of the cities. In the schools, disadvantaged pupils present problems of academic retardation, discipline, truancy, transiency, and, with older pupils, dropout. They are insecure, not highly motivated for the tasks of the school; their health is poor, they are often malnourished and in many cases unclean. They can be classified as the lowest socioeconomic group.

Culturally disadvantaged children are also present-oriented, value motor skills, physical strength, manual skills, and are concerned with immediate gratification. They are typically behind in grade level in school, have a negative self-evaluation, have experienced a restricted social environment and do not expect things taught in school to have any influence on their adult lives. Along the same line, their future typically holds reading retardation, learning disability, and increasingly poor discrimination of verbal directions.

A Proposal

This proposal makes only the following assumptions: (1) that teacher characteristics and behaviors do, and should be expected to, vary; (2) that pupil behaviors and characteristics also vary both within and among classrooms; (3) that teaching is a process of interaction between the teacher and the pupils; (4) that teachers and pupils must learn to exhibit the behaviors that are necessary to facilitate the process; and (5) that teachers and pupils desire to improve their classroom relationships.

It is a truism that the teacher is assigned a central role in the learning process. Learning theory provided the research evidence that established this truism. But, the learning theory was based on the nonemotional or cognitive processes. Most of what has been written about teaching methods was also influenced by the same body of evidence and concerned itself with the teacher's role in cognitive learning. Until recently, there has been little systematic investigation of the role of the teacher in the emotional, or affective, learning process. Affective learning is concerned with attitudes and valuations.

Recognition of the teacher's role in the learning of social behaviors is slowly coming out of the research findings in several areas. This new social learning theory has certain postulates that are directly transferable to the classroom. In terms of the teaching process, the principles may be stated as: (1) teaching is a directive process which follows lawful predictable learning principles, and (2) the factors which affect classroom relationships involve reinforcement, modeling, manipulation, shaping, exhortation, vicarious learning, and control. Each factor contributes to both the cognitive and affective learning process and is used throughout the remainder of the discussion. Each factor will be briefly defined.

Reinforcement. The effects of behavior have the power to either strengthen or weaken the behavior. As behavior becomes more complex, the pupil is constantly watching the effect on others of each of his behaviors that make up his total act. This knowledge of results is described as *feedback* and allows the pupil to alter his course of behavior during an act, thus allowing change in the final act. Changes are based upon the observation of the effects of the preliminary steps.

Modeling. This term describes the behavior of the teacher and/or pupil who demonstrates behaviors and the outcomes of behaviors. Modeling is done intentionally or unintentionally. The teacher is acting as a model when he disciplines his pupils as well as when he demonstrates the solutions to an arithmetic problem. In a broad sense, an individual is modeling whenever his behavior is being observed by others.

Manipulation. The person who controls the reinforcements in the classroom is in a position to manipulate the behavior of others. In this sense, the term has much in common with teaching. An attempt to alter the response potential of pupils by controlling the reinforcement is defined as manipulation. The devices a teacher employs to manipulate the responses of pupils include among others: grades, awards, praise and reproof, isolation, and pleasant and unpleasant facial expressions. When a teacher manipulates, he attempts to alter pupils' responses or to institute new behavior responses judged desirable. To date, emphasis has centered on the manipulation of pupils' cognitive behaviors through reinforcement.

Shaping. Shaping refers to rewarding in a sequential manner behaviors that approximate the desired behavior. This is usually done by demanding that the pupil make closer approximations of the desired response with each successive attempt. Verbal behavior serves as a prime example of the shaping of response by successive approximation. An infant utters "Nana" in the presence of the grandmother. This response is reinforced positively by attention, praise, and physical contact on the part of the grandmother. The grandparent models the response by repeating it for the infant. Over time, finer and finer approximations are demanded before the infant is given reinforcement. This, "Nana" becomes "Nama," "Gama," and, finally, "Grandma." In the classroom, the expectancy of a closer and closer duplication of the model in writing, reading, and speaking is demanded by the teacher.

Exhortation. This more general term refers to the urging, advising, warning, admonishing, sermonizing, and pleading that goes on in the classroom. Exhortation is the most common method of attempting to control the behavior of pupils. It would be fair to say that most remedial efforts undertaken by parents and teachers in the area of pupil social behavior can be classified as exhortation.

Vicarious Learning. While most learning occurs by watching the behavior of a model, cognitive learning theory pays little attention to the implications of this method in the learning process. Research on affective learning has demonstrated that the act of observing a sequence of behaviors performed by another leads to the learning of the proper or rewarded behavior by the observer.[3] It has also been shown that observing a model punished for exhibiting undesired behaviors leads to the inhibition and suppression of the punished behaviors in the observer.[4] In the classroom setting, the teacher reinforces many pupil behaviors on an individual basis. The class observes the sequence of events leading to the reward or punishment of a fellow student and in this manner learns many expected classroom behaviors.

Control. The prime requisite to the classroom situation is control. The teacher uses all the variables here defined to maintain control of his class. Factors which contribute to teacher control include his physical size, education, age, possession of the rein-forcement system, and social expectations of the pupil. We shall concentrate on the application of these variables which are common to, and controllable in, every classroom setting.

Attitude Evaluation

We have described the tools a teacher employs to alter the behavior of his students. Now, we will present a model for evaluating the attitudes and valuations of students. With this model, a teacher can evaluate the degree to which the "typical" disadvantaged pupil so often described approximates the "actual" pupils in his classroom. This evaluation should be an ongoing process as well as an initial measure of the class.

The teacher, to better understand his role in the process of influencing attitudes, can now look to several theoretical frameworks. Each model describes attitude formation and attitude change. Heider, Newcomb, Osgood-Tannenbaum, and Festinger have all contributed positions that are similar and can be summarized under the more general rubric of *Consistency Theory*.[5]

The Attitude Model. Social learning as a part of classroom learning can be clarified by understanding one of the consistency theories. For our discussion, Osgood-Tannenbaum furnish a method they define as *Congruity Theory* for evaluating an effect-laden situation. In congruity theory, there are three variables in an interpersonal situation. The variables viewed through the eyes of the person to be influenced by the situation are the perceptions of the learner. Since we assign the observing, or vicarious learning, role to the pupil, his perception of the source of a communication, the object of a communication, and the tone of a communication represent the three variables in the theory. To make this clear, let us assume that a teacher is attempting to motivate his class by telling them how doing well in English will help them when they grow up.

The congruity principle states that when the observer associates one object or person with another, by an assertion, the evaluation of the two objects, ideas, or persons involved is always given the same degree of value. This value can be in the same direction or in an opposite direction for each of the two, but the amount will be equal. An example will help clarify this principle.

An Example of the Model. An interpersonal situation, as seen by the observer, is shown in Figure 1. In the figure, the middle line represents the line of zero evaluation. The plus direction represents the positive evaluation of an object, person, or concept. The space below the base line represents the strength of feeling or the degree of polarization. The person making the evaluation is not represented on the grid, but the placement of the three elements represents the observer's evaluation of the situation.

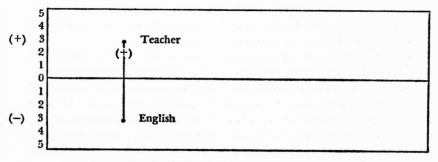

Figure 1. The Evaluation of Teacher Assertions.

In our example, we assume that the teacher is positively valued by the pupil. This assumption is in part based on the age, training, role, and other characteristics of the teacher. Furthermore, English is assumed to be negatively evaluated by the pupil. The reason being that the pupil feels there is no immediate gratification from studying English. The line of teacher assertion is marked as positive since the teacher has told her class the value of English in life. The situation is summarized as a positive teacher making a positive assertion about a negative concept.

Elements and Congruity. From the point of view of the observer, two elements (persons, ideas, or objects) of an interpersonal situation joined by an assertion are either compatible or they are not compatible.[6] When congruity exists, there is no tendency for change in the evaluation of any of the elements. Congruity would exist if a negatively evaluated teacher made a positive assertion about a negative concept. Going back to our example, had the pupil positively valued both the teacher and English, he would have expected the teacher to express favorable comments about English. Also, had the pupil negatively valued the teacher and English, he would expect to disagree with the teacher's favorable comments about English. The teacher's positive assertion regarding English constitutes a confirmation of the pupil's negative evaluation of both elements. In either of the above congruous conditions, there is little tendency for the pupil to alter his evaluation of either his teacher or English. Restated, congruity theory postulates that an observer feels comfortable in a situation when two of the three elements are negative or when all are positive.

Elements and Incongruity. Incongruity or incompatibility exists when two of the three evaluated elements are positive while the other is negative. Our example, Figure 1, is incongruous. This condition causes a tendency toward change. The three combinations of elements in our example that would be incongruous and cause discomfort are: (1) a positively evaluated teacher making a positive assertion about a negatively evaluated concept; (2) a negatively evaluated teacher making a positive assertion about a positively held concept; and (3) a positively evaluated teacher making a negative assertion about a positively evaluated concept.

Possible Solutions to Incongruity. The various consistency theories also describe the possible solutions open to the pupil when faced with an incongruous situation. This unique aspect, that of presenting all possible solutions, is central to understanding the role of consistency theory in social learning.[7] A pupil who is faced with a situation which he sees as incongruous or inconsistent has three courses of action. He can: (1) leave the field; by this we mean that either figuratively or literally a pupil can remove himself from the situation; (2) change his valuation of one of the elements; in our example, he could solve the dilemma by either changing his judgment of the teacher or English; or (3) reinterpret the meaning of the assertion made by the teacher about English. If this solution was chosen, the pupil would in effect reinterpret the teacher's assertion about the English assignment.

Usefulness in Culturally Disadvantaged Schools. If we are willing to make the assumption that teachers do care for their profession, then the conflicting teacher-pupil expectancy pattern described earlier as the basis of teachers leaving culturally disadvantaged schools can be altered. To accomplish this end, it will be necessary for the teacher to consider himself a social reinforcer. The teacher must define himself as a model with a social stimulus value and systematically present affective learning situations. His social stimulus value is, of course, based on superior age, education, dress, and manner. Primarily though, a teacher's positive stimulus value is gained from his role as the controller and dispenser of reinforcement. The teacher who would implement the social learning model presented must remember that his first task is to teach systematically the necessary social learnings. The reward for this effort comes in providing the proper classroom climate for cognitive learning.

Teaching and Social Learning

The remainder of this paper is devoted to specific ways a teacher can change the social behavior of his pupils. After changing pupils' social behaviors, it is assumed that altered academic behavior will follow. This assumption is based on the belief that a pupil must understand and appreciate the social context of education before the values and attitudes reinforced in cognitive learning situations will have meaning.

After all, gold stars and other educational rewards have little meaning in and of themselves. They are secondary rewards. Their secondary value is gained from association with things that do have value such as praise, attention, and verbal associations. It would be consistent with social learning to concentrate on the learning how to learn aspects of classroom behaviors in the early grades and slowly make the transition to systematic development of positive academic attitudes as the age of the pupils increases.

Consider the first day of school. It is, by definition, in some respects new and novel for each pupil. The responses shown by the pupils are based on past experiences that approximate the experiences of this first day. In situations that are new and ambiguous, pupils look to their peers as models and exhibit affiliatory behavior. Rather than be disappointed that pupils do not know how to *behave* the teacher should consider the first day of school as an ideal situation to step in and demonstrate the proper social behaviors for the class.

Let us say that a fourth grade teacher wishes his class to be favorably inclined toward homework assignments. On the first day, or perhaps the first several days, he would present to his new class pupils from the previous class to demonstrate homework assignment procedures. The teacher would structure the type of work turned in, the method of collection, the rewards given, and have the older models show their feelings of pleasure and satisfaction with the system. This "programing" of the mechanics would also demonstrate student expected behavior and reward satisfaction. For teacher feedback and also to teach delayed gratification, the demonstrations would be followed by an assignment due the following day. To insure that pupils could accomplish the new "homework behaviors," an assignment that could be completed on paper received in class would be assigned first. The possibilities and examples are endless.

The unique factor of this method centers on the teacher considering each task assigned and each project undertaken as an opportunity to teach social behavior as well as cognitive behavior. Also, it is important to remember that grade level will affect the emphasis placed. The two main divisions of teacher concern would be the acquiring of new social behaviors and the altering of existing behaviors.

Imitation Learning

In the area of cognitive learning the potency of imitation is often neglected. It is forgotten that "to teach" literally translated means "to show." Much of what is learned by pupils in classrooms is acquired by imitation. Again, the use of a model is the basic ingredient for imitative learning and requires that someone do the showing.

Earlier in our history, it was not uncommon for a child to accompany the parent during the working hours and acquire the skills and attitudes that accompanied the parent's craft. Today, it is more common for a child to acquire much of his skill learning through the imitation of symbolic, in contrast to actual, models. These take the form of filmstrips, movies, written directions, verbal instruction, demonstrations and various combinations of these. While the efficiency in teaching cognitive skills has become very sophisticated, the teaching profession has systematically neglected the utilization of the socialization potency of its role. Teaching in culturally disadvantaged areas demands that the prime importance be placed on the affective learning that forms the pre-learning or co-learning experiences.

Teaching How to Be a Student

Culturally disadvantaged children do not expect the things taught in school to have an influence on their adult lives.[8] It then follows that emphasizing the future as a reward for present learning has little value. Since this is the case, and the evidence supports this position, then the teacher must first teach his pupils to value the goal or point toward more meaningful goals.

When we say that we are trying to "raise the level of aspiration" of pupils in culturally disadvantaged areas, are we not saying that these pupils do not value the existing reinforcements of the educational system? Are we not saying that pupil values and attitudes are such that they do not care about the rewards and punishments we have so painstakingly developed in education?

Literally, these pupils must *learn to learn.* The typical culturally disadvantaged pupil does not know how to be a student in the existing educational system. He does not place a value on the controls and rewards traditionally assumed adequate for the learning process. If we are to change the level of aspiration of pupils, it becomes the teacher's task to first teach the necessary social behavior before he can expect that pupils will exhibit and conform to this behavior. Further, this social behavior must be taught, for it forms the basis of cognitive learning in our present educational system.

Methods in Social Learning

Reinforcement and *nonreinforcement* are the two terms that define the methods best able to establish new behavior and stop the occurrence of undesired behaviors. The operation of these more general concepts is simply one-to-one. Reinforced behavior becomes established while nonreinforced behavior is not established, or is extinguished. The method, or schedule, of reinforcement is more the complex of the two and has been shown to be the determining factor in the establishment of new behaviors and the altering of undesired behaviors.

Learning theory defines three ways to administer reinforcement. It can: (1) be continuous, (2) vary with frequency of occurrence, and (3) vary with time elapsed. Reinforcement can contain elements of all three of the above schedules.[9]

We must remember that the learning of new behavior and the alteration of existing behavior is an entirely separate process from the judgment of the desirability or undesirability of the behavior. Reinforcement is consistent in the learning process and is not related to any judgment of the social value of the behavior. Again it should be pointed out that the pupil can receive reinforcement vicariously and need not be directly involved in the reinforcement process.[10]

Establishing New Behavior

In learning new behavior, the most satisfactory method or schedule of reinforcement for teacher use contains elements of both continuous and intermittent reinforcement. First, new behaviors should be reinforced as soon as possible after they occur. This establishes the new behavior. Then, the newly established behavior should be rewarded intermittently to insure the continued use of the new response. A gradually lengthened schedule would be appropriate in most cases.[11]

When a teacher desires that his pupils learn a behavior which does not have the opportunity to occur in the classroom, he should structure a situation in which it will occur, model the situation, reward the occurrence of the behavior and then, on the basis of time, provide for the reoccurrence of the situation and reward the desired behaviors.

Stopping Undesired Behaviors

Behavior that is judged undesirable can be stopped or extinguished by not reinforcing the behavior when it appears.[12] This is not a simple process as the behavior the teacher judges deviant may not be positively reinforced by the teacher. The other pupils or someone completely outside the classroom setting may be the source of reinforcement for the pupil. In any case, research shows that the nonreward of behavior judged undesirable frequently causes an immediate increase in both the rate and intensity of response.[13] A good instance involving the problems related to ignoring undesirable behavior can be found in attention-seeking behaviors. The sequence which follows is applicable in instances of either an approval or disapproval response on the part of the teacher to the pupil's behavior.

A pupil wants the attention of the teacher and/or the class and attempts to gain it by behaving in a way the teacher judges as undesirable. When the teacher ignores the behavior, the pupil then increases both the intensity and frequency of the response. By using the technique of ignoring the behavior, the teacher has actually increased the probability of the occurrence of the behavior immediately after the nonreward sequence.

Although this increase in response is predictable on the basis of learning theory, frequently it causes an increase in anxiety in the teacher. He then deviates from the *ignoring* schedule, pays attention to the pupil and reinforces the occurrence of an increase in intensity of response when the earlier response is ignored. From the point of view of the child, the siutation becomes one of increasing the intensity and frequency of response when behaviors of lesser degree are ignored.

Even when the teacher does not make the mistake of finally giving in or paying attention to the pupil when response intensity increases, he may still become discouraged when nonreinforced behaviors reappear. It is easy to forget that this is the normal process in eliminating undesired behaviors. Research has shown that behavior presumed extinguished will periodically reappear as time passes.[14] Typically, the recurrence of the undesirable behavior will be less intense each time it recurs once the initial extinguishment period is over.

Also the teacher can help speed up the process of extinguishing undesirable behavior by providing alternatives for these responses. He is then providing opportunities for the pupils to learn new and more appropriate responses while eliminating older more undesirable behaviors.

Pupils from culturally disadvantaged areas should be expected to show behaviors that are judged undesirable in the classroom. In many instances, the behaviors that teachers judge deviant are behaviors necessary for the pupils to function in the world in which they live. Education, for these pupils, must provide the opportunity to learn and practice the fine discriminations in response necessary to succeed in both the world in which they live and the world in which they learn.

Reinforcement encompasses the rewards and punishments that are at the control of the teacher. Consider that it is the teacher who determines which pupil sits where, who recites, who gets to play, who takes notes to the office, who passes out papers. He gives out the gold stars, the grades, the compliments, the attention. The teacher smiles, frowns, nods, approaches, repeats, paraphrases. In fact, the teacher even controls the medium of expression in the classroom.

Timing in Punishment

Since a paper like this would be incomplete without a mention of punishment, the following represents the author's best understanding of its usefulness in teaching. The term *punishment* has the meaning of inflicting a noxious stimulus to stop an undesired response. It inhibits the occurrence of the response. It does not eliminate the response. In education, punishment is usually verbal. It takes the form of scolding, reprimanding and coercion.

Since a deviant, or undesired, pupil act constitutes a culmination of a series of behaviors, it would help most if a teacher knew the best time to administer a punishment. Research supports the position that early punishment is most effective. That is, punishment administered early in the sequence of events that make up the act judged undesirable. For example, a teacher who wishes to avoid the act of paper-wad shooting would be most effective if he punished those playing with rubber bands.

Conclusion

All that has been written in this paper has been an attempt to refocus attention on the dual learnings of education. Pupils leave our classrooms supplied not only with subject matter competence; they have also acquired a set of fine social discriminations as a by-product. This was an effort to reemphasize the importance of social learning in education.

The ability to make discriminations is probably the most

important characteristic of human intelligence. Behavior that shows fine discrimination in response is what is observed in most higher order learning situations. In the context of social learning, discrimination takes the form of altering the response and expectancy of response as the situation alters. This social learning is also a product of education. In fact, a case might be made for its central importance in a democracy. Pupils from socially deprived areas have the right to expect that they too will be taught the social discriminations necessary for achievement in our society.

NOTES

1. Howard Becker, "The Career of the Chicago Public School Teacher," *American Social Review*, 17 (7) (July 1952), pp. 470–476.
2. Vernon F. Haubrich, "Teachers for Big-City Schools," in Passow, A. H., (Ed.) *Education in Depressed Areas* (New York, Bureau of Publications, Teachers College, Columbia University, 1963).
3. Albert Bandura and Richard H. Walters, *Social Learning and Personality Development* (New York, Holt, Rinehart and Winston, Inc., 1963); R. H. Walters and L. Demkow, "Studies of Reinforcement of Aggression, II. Transfer of Resistance to Temptation," *Child Development*, 34 (1963), pp. 207–214.
4. P. A. Cowan and R. H. Walters, "Studies of Reinforcement of Aggression, I. Effects of Scheduling," *Child Development*, 1963.
5. F. Heider, *The Psychology of Interpersonal Relations* (New York, Wiley, 1958); T. M. Newcomb, "Individual Systems of Orientation," in S. Kotch (Ed.) *Psychology: A Study of A Science*, Vol. 2 (New York, McGraw-Hill, 1959); pp. 384–422; C. E. Osgood, G. J. Suce, and P. Tannenbaum, *The Measure of Meaning* (Urbana, University of Illinois Press, 1957); L. Festinger, *A Theory of Cognitive Dissonance* (Evanston, Row, Peterson, 1957).
6. T. M. Newcomb, pp. 384–422; F. Heider.
7. R. Zajonc, "The Concepts of Balance, Congruity, and Dissonance," *Public Opinion Quarterly*, 24 (1960), pp. 290–296
8. David R. Miller and Gug G. Swanson, *Inner Conflict and Defense* (New York, Henry Holt, 1960); Frank Riessman, *The Culturally Deprived Child* (New York, Harper, 1962).
9. A. W. Staats (Ed.), *Human Learning* (New York, Holt, Rinehart and Winston, 1964); B. F. Skinner, *Verbal Behavior* (New York, Appleton-Century-Crofts, 1957).
10. P. A. Cowan and R. H. Walters; R. H. Walters and L. Demhow, *op. cit.*, pp. 207–214.
11. B. F. Skinner, *Science and Human Behavior* (New York, Macmillan, 1953); A. W. Staats and C. K. Staats, *Complex Human Behavior*

(New York, Holt, Rinehart and Winston, 1963); Albert Bandura and R. H. Walters, *op. cit.*

12. B. F. Kinner, R. H. Walters, and L. Demkow, *op. cit.*, pp. 207–214.
13. *Ibid.*
14. Albert Bandura and R. H. Walters, *op. cit,* R. A. Cowan and R. H. Walters, *op. cit.*, B. F. Skinner, *op. cit.*, R. H. Walters and L. Demkow, *op. cit.*, pp. 207–214.

13   TEACHING STANDARD ENGLISH AS A SECOND DIALECT

VIRGINIA F. ALLEN

Few people today need to be told that standard English is virtually a "second language" for millions. Almost every teacher knows students who cannot speak, read or write the sort of English that educated persons consider standard, even though some variety of English may be the student's mother tongue. Not only is the problem prevalent, of course, it is also old. It dates back past the days of Huck Finn and Topsy to the eighteenth century, and beyond.

Yet two facts do appear to come as news—good news.[1] One is that some teachers are developing a fresh and clearer view of what is involved in learning a standard dialect of English in school when some other dialect is spoken in the home. A second newsworthy fact, and an even more cheering one, is that these fresh insights have suggested some practical classroom procedures which are being tried with encouraging results. Some of those promising procedures will be described in this paper.

Standard English

First, however, it would be wise to show what the term *standard English* will mean in the context of this discussion. For our present purposes, standard American English is the kind of English habitually used by most of the *educated* English-speaking persons in the United States.

Thus "He doesn't want any" would qualify as a sample of standard English—not because some "authority" has certified it as being "correct," but because evidence suggests that educated speakers habitually *say* "He doesn't want any" in situations where less educated speakers might say "He don't want none."

Virginia F. Allen, "Teaching Standard English as a Second Dialect," *Teachers College Record* (February 1967), pp. 355–370. Reprinted by permission of the author and publisher.

It is important to note the emphasis on *habitually* and *educated* in this definition of standard English. A teacher who undertakes to familiarize her students with the standard dialect of English as here defined is careful to focus attention upon grammatical forms which educated speakers are in the *habit* of using. For instance, even though some grammar books decree that the "comparative" form *more* "should" be used in place of the "superlative" form *most* when only two are being compared, an enlightened teacher today would be undismayed if a student said, "Both Pete and Bill get good grades in school, but I think Pete really has the most sense." Habitual usage among educated speakers is what counts—whether or not that usage obeys some grammarian's rule.

On the other hand, the stress on the word *educated* in this definition is significant, too. What is being advocated here is emphatically *not* an "anything goes" approach to English usage. Standard English, as defined here, is the variety of English generally used by the *educated* members of the American speech community. Statistically speaking, one has reason to suspect that the number of Americans who say "you was" exceeds the number who say "you were." This fact does not establish "you was" as standard usage, however. Standard English is what the majority of *educated* speakers habitually use.

Teachers who start with this definition then go on to link it up with their student's experience and observation. They point out that the kind of English they have in mind is the sort used on radio and television by announcers, sportscasters, civil rights leaders, and news commentators, as well as by practically all TV heroes, including Batman, Superman and Flash Gordon. It is the English heard in the public statements of astronauts, bankers, congressmen, and movie stars. It has been called "the language of educated ease," because it is used by people who *know* they sound "educated" and so do not have to think about their use of language.

When the target language is defined in these terms, even young children know what the teacher means by "standard English." Martin Joos, who has made a special study of people's attitudes toward language, says:

Long before any teacher began to correct his English, the child has learned all he needs to know, at his age, about people and their places; he has developed considerable skill in judging adults by their speech . . .[2]

Morality and Comprehensibility

Class time invested in discussing standard English along such lines is time well spent. For one thing, such discussions remind both teacher and students that the presence or absence of standard forms in a person's speech is not a moral or ethical issue; among announcers, congressmen and movie stars there are some who are moral, honest and upright and some who are not; yet both kinds are speakers of standard English.

Then, too, such discussions give the teacher an opportunity to grant that people who speak standard English do not always and invariably communicate any more clearly or forcefully than speakers of non-standard dialects do. Since the students themselves will doubtless have observed this fact, they will appreciate the candor of teachers who acknowledge that a person's grammatical usage has little effect—for better or for worse—upon the clarity and vigor of his message. Too often, teachers try to convey the opposite impression by feigning incomprehension when a student says something like "I don't have no pencil"—a statement whose import is perfectly clear, as the student well knows. The reason for learning to say "I don't have any pencil" has little to do with comprehensibility; when teachers imply that the standard English way is better because it is clearer, students can hardly be blamed for regarding English teachers as "phonies" or, more charitably, as living in an unreal world.

There is a further advantage to be gained from discussing standard English in terms of professional groups who characteristically use it. Such discussions help to dispel the impression that what the class is being urged to learn is a language spoken chiefly by teachers, by *English* teachers, at that. As a motivating force, such an impression has very low potential.

A Scale of Importance

Moreover, a definition which identifies the target of instruction as "the kind of English habitually used by educated speakers" gives teachers a useful scale for weighing the relative importance of various items found on English tests and in English textbooks. Textbook "rules" which would teach the class usages no longer habitual among most educated Americans can be passed over lightly or omitted altogether, and time thus saved can be more profitably spent in a study of usages that actually do distinguish the standard dialect from other varieties.

Thus far we have been concerned with identifying the kind of English that teachers should be helping their students learn to use. We have stressed the need for frankness and realism. It is good strategy to acknowledge that this standard dialect, this variety of language habitually spoken by educated Americans, has no inherent virtue of its own, unpossessed by other dialects. It was not divinely bequeathed to some Moses on tablets of stone. Furthermore, language problems are very different from arithmetic problems, though for centuries this difference has traditionally been ignored. Standard English is not a set of "right" answers, like the answers found at the back of an arithmetic textbook. (The right answer to "two plus two" is "four"; any other is, has always been, and doubtless always will be, wrong. Yet one cannot in the same sense assert that it would be "wrong" for a slum child in a rat-ridden flat to say to his mother, "That landlord, he *mean*. Ain't nobody no meaner'n him.") Hence, in good programs for students of standard English as a second dialect, the terms *right* and *wrong* are not often used. When they are, right means "appropriate to the situation," and wrong means "likely to put the speaker at a disadvantage," much as one might say it is "wrong" to chew gum while being interviewed for a job.

Standard vs Non-Standard

There is another truth that teachers in modern programs publicly acknowledge. Students whose families speak some variety of English other than the standard dialect appreciate being told that several features of their home language were once characteristic of standard speech. In seventeenth century England there would have been nothing non-standard about a sentence like "My brother and his family, they live in Atlanta." After all, the authors of the King James version of the Bible wrote "Thy rod and Thy staff, they comfort me." Double negatives, too, were features of standard English for hundreds of years: Chaucer and Shakespeare often used them. For that matter, double negatives are regularly used in Spanish even to this day.

Teachers who share this sort of information with their students earn a reputation for honesty and reasonableness that stands them in good stead when the hard work of learning the standard dialect begins. For of course the standard dialect must be taught, and it should be learned. Even though there is nothing inherently "wrong" or "bad" about using a non-standard dialect, there are times when it can harm the person who uses it. No matter how tastefully he may dress, no matter how impeccable his grooming may be, the applicant for white collar employment does not enhance his chances by saying, "I come because I seen your ad."

"Front Door" English

Undemocratic and unfair as it may seem, the fact is that standard English is "front door" English. And American schools are committed to the task of making it possible for every citizen to enter by the front door if he wishes to do so.

Just as candor and a clear view of the facts are essential in defining what standard English is, so also one needs to be factual and frank in saying why the standard dialect ought to be learned. The student needs to understand that a command of standard English is vital to any American (particularly any "minority-group" American) who aims to associate with speakers of the standard dialect on anything like an equal footing.

Note the phrase: "A *command* of standard English." To command something is not merely to have a vague notion of it, but rather to be able to *summon it up at will.* The student must be given the ability to summon up the standard dialect whenever he himself wants to use it, in any situation where fluency in that dialect would be to his advantage.*

Often, in the development of such fluency, the school can

* Of course there are other reasons for teaching standard English—reasons more palatable to those who dislike treating language as a status symbol (which, in America, it is). Quite apart from the fact that non-standard English makes a poor impression, there is the obvious fact that the standard dialect is the medium for imparting information and ideas in print and on the air.

count on little help from the environment outside. In urban "gray areas," for example, and in the rural South, a non-standard dialect is generally the medium of communication for most members of the student's immediate community, standard English being used only by members of the school staff. It is then entirely up to the school to teach young people how to use the standard dialect with ease and self-confidence when occasions demand.

Teachers are well aware of this responsibility, and they have worked at the task, year in and year out, but often with little success. Why? Partly because many a teacher antagonizes the very people she is trying to help. She makes her students feel that their natural way of talking is a shameful thing, marred by "errors" that need to be rooted out. She seems determined to wrest the students' familiar dialect from them, leaving in its place a language that may well estrange them from homefolks and lifelong friends. Small wonder that many students resist!

Towards Linguistic Versatility

Nowadays, luckily, there *are* teachers who recognize that other varieties of English have validity for many communication situations profoundly important to their students. Such teachers offer standard English as a second—or additional—dialect without demanding that it *supplant* the students' home language.

In Europe, such a view of the standard dialect would be taken as a matter of course. In France, for example, it is taken for granted that a citizen will learn to use a standard dialect of the national language for communication in relatively formal situations involving educated speakers, and in conversations with persons from regions other than his own. It is not expected, however, that the standard dialect will replace for all time and for all occasions the dialect the individual learned at home. He retains his local dialect and uses it when he goes back to his home community, switching from one language-track to the other as he moves from scene to scene. This two-track versatility in language usage seems to be characteristic of most societies, especially the older ones. It is unfortunate that the possibility of achieving such versatility has been given so little systematic attention in the United States. To the traditional teacher in America, any and all non-standard utterances have seemed like evil tendencies, to be stamped out with Calvinistic zeal.

In earlier times, this may have been because so many teachers in American public schools were themselves members of immigrant families, to whom the learning of English had meant an unremitting struggle. Frequently, by dint of prodigious effort and some pain, these teachers had cut their ties with families whose "broken English" posed a threat to the teachers' own hard-won status as new members of an American middle class. One can understand how the experience could have accounted for a teacher's inability to tolerate the thought that a non-standard dialect might have a right to live on in some of the relationships her students held dear.

One of the new things to be said about the teaching of standard English is that some teachers now feel secure enough in their own middle-class status to view the school's language-teaching responsibility in a somewhat different light. Such teachers try not to treat non-standard forms with abhorrence and disdain. At the same time, they press vigorously toward the goal of developing in every student the *ability* to use the standard dialect in any situation that *requires* its use. When this is the teacher's policy, many students eventually do stop using non-standard varieties of English altogether. They find themselves moving over to the standard dialect in a widening range of situations as they develop fluency and confidence in handling the standard modes. In time, many are willing to risk speaking standard English with family and friends. But even if a student continues to use the home dialect with his family and peer-group associates, the teacher need not feel that the language program has failed. The test of success is the student's readiness to "turn on" the standard dialect in situations where his standing as a person will be judged in part by his speech.

Instructional Strategy

Sometimes, however, even when the teacher has managed to avoid arousing hostility through her attitude toward the home dialect, results have fallen short of success. A realistic, understanding attitude is not enough: one must also take stock of tactics and techniques.

Just what must be done by anyone who tries to become fluent in standard English when his home dialect is something else? His problem is much like that of someone learning a foreign language in school. Of course there are differences, too. On the debit side, the learning of a second dialect is harder to motivate than the learning of a language entirely foreign and new. And on the other hand, the non-standard dialect speaker has at least the advantage of knowing far more of the *meanings* of the target language than the foreign learner knows.

Still, despite these differences, the needs of second-dialect students and second-language students are alike in one important respect: in both cases the learner needs to develop a new set of language *habits*. He needs new habits that will enable him to utter appropriate responses instantaneously, whenever the need arises, without having to stop and think.

A student who has to stop and think whether to say "I done it" or "I did it" in a standard English speech situation has not *mastered* the target dialect. A person who has mastered a language or a dialect is no more conscious of making such decisions than he is conscious of deciding how to tie his shoes. The problem for teachers, then, is how to lead students to develop a repertoire of routine habits in connection with the forms and arrangements that make up the grammar of the standard dialect.

Clues from Foreign Language Teaching

Teachers of foreign languages give much thought to this matter of "automatic control over the patterns of the language" as it is often called. Hence some of the foreign language teacher's procedures will suggest useful strategy to teachers of standard English as a second dialect.

The first element in the foreign language teacher's strategy is *selection*. Even the most skillful teacher cannot give a student a thorough mastery of every individual linguistic feature. The teacher (or the textbook writer) tries to select the smallest possible number of really essential items to be learned. The students concentrate on these, item by item, until they are able to "produce" each essential type of utterance without hesitation. After that, if time remains, attention is turned to finer points, minor patterns, alternate forms of expression. And once the student has been given a substantial start through the development of control over the major patterns of the language, he is able to fill in the remaining gaps on his own, through observation and analogy.

What does this mean for teaching English as a second dialect? It suggests that teachers and students need to concentrate their energies on features that truly do distinguish standard English from non-standard usage. These need to be taught before items that do not conspicuously characterize one dialect or the other—items which are prescribed or proscribed by some grammar books, but which are used in much the same way by speakers of both standard and non-standard dialects.

Some concrete illustrations may be needed in order to clarify this point. In the list below, certain sentences contain obvious examples of non-standard usage. Any novelist who put those sentences into the mouths of his bankers, stock brokers, optometrists, head nurses or airline hostesses would be accused of having a poor ear for talk. Other sentences in the list would seem quite at home in the discourse of educated Americans. Let us sort out the fifteen sentences, noting which ones would sound out of place in the "language of educated ease"—and which ones would not.

1. Cartwright don't want nobody to help him.
2. They give the burglar five dollar, which was all they had.
3. The man die after he had drank the poison.
4. This author explain why everything cost more now.
5. They always trying to find a way to get rich, no matter how it hurt other people.
6. Their children has went to Washington to spend six week with Mrs. Green sister.
7. I hope William and his family, they going to be more happier now.
8. In my opinion, neither Adams nor Reeves are really qualified for the job.
9. In each of these novels, the hero has to choose between riches, fame and happiness.
10. Somehow this hotel looks different than it did the last time we stayed here.
11. Both Detroit and Denver have possibilities, but I believe Denver would be the best for our conference.

12. But who could Patty stay with if we went abroad without her?

13. Even though I try not to be over-protective, I can't help but worry every time the children are away from home.

14. Carson is efficient, but Peters is certainly easier to work with.

15. Don't look so startled, Janice; it's only me!

Every one of the fifteen sentences contains something that violates some "rule" in grammar books still extant in American schools, but that fact is beside the point here. What has significance to the teacher of standard English as a second dialect is that only seven of the fifteen sentences would sound out of place in conversations among educated Americans. Those are sentences one through seven. The patterns represented by those sentences are the ones that need to be given intensive study by students who are trying to master the standard dialect. If the class has not yet learned to use these high-priority features of standard English, it will be pointless to spend valuable time on grammar-book rules which are "violated" by sentences like the last eight above—rules which condemn usages like "different than" and "neither are." It will be futile and foolish to dwell upon rules governing *between* and *among* and *who* and *whom.* It is sad to think how much precious energy is being squandered on such esoteric distinctions in courses for students who need all the help they can get in mastering the basic hallmarks of standard speech.

In essence, then, the strategy of teaching a second dialect (as in teaching a foreign language) amounts to teaching the smallest possible number of vitally significant items—and *teaching each of them hard.*

Teaching vs Scolding

What does a teacher do about a language pattern when she really wants students to learn it? Above all, she gets the students to *use* the pattern, to say sentences illustrating the pattern, again and again, until that mode of speech begins to sound natural to the students themselves. The skillful teacher of a second dialect does not simply remark in class, "Stanley should have said 'I saw it,' not 'I seen it.' You remember that, Stanley, don't you? All right then, let's go on."

Yet this is the sort of "teaching" that often takes place, and it has not been of much help to children from non-standard dialect homes. Year after year they have brushed briefly up against the same features of standard English; they have been "corrected" for the same "mistakes" from grade to grade in the same reproachful but off-hand way.

Now to get back to Stanley, a hypothetical child in perhaps the third or fourth grade. Supposing he has just said, "I seen it on my way to school this morning." Supposing the teacher has murmured, "You *saw* it, Stanley. You know that, don't you?" and Stanley has mumbled, "Yeah."

As a matter of fact, Stanley probably does "know it"—in a way. That is, he has heard something about *I seen* as opposed to *I saw* a number of times before. The trouble is, no one has ever made him settle down on this bit of the standard dialect long enough to learn to use it. He has never been given a chance to *command* the form "I saw." Naturally, then, even in situations where he would be willing to use standard English—if only to mollify the teacher—the standard form is just not *in* him to be summoned up. If the teacher wants Stanley to *focus* on this bit of language, the very least she can do is ask him to repeat the sentence after her: "I saw it on my way to school this morning." (And she waits while Stanley repeats the sentence.) If several of the students share Stanley's problem, and she wants the class to master this use of *saw*, something like the following has to take place:

TEACHER: *Let's practice using* saw *in some standard English sentences. Let's start by saying Stanley's sentence: I saw it on my way to school this morning. Class!*

CLASS (*in unison*): *I saw it on my way to school this morning.*

TEACHER (*to Thomas*): *Thomas,* when *did Stanley see it? Use* saw *in your answer.*

THOMAS: *He saw it on his way to school this morning.*

TEACHER: *Right! Gloria,* who *saw it on his way to school? Use* saw *in your answer.*

GLORIA: Stanley *saw it.*

TEACHER: *Yes! Now let's all mention things we saw on our way*

	to school this morning. I saw a fire engine. What about you, Paul?
PAUL:	I saw a garbage truck on my way to school.
TEACHER:	Good! Laura, tell us what Paul saw, and then tell us something you saw.
LAURA:	Paul saw a garbage truck on his way to school. I saw a . . . a . . . I saw a black kitten in front of the supermarket.
TEACHER:	Fine! Anthony, what did Laura see?
ANTHONY:	She seen . . .
TEACHER:	She saw. Please say, "She saw . . ."
ANTHONY:	She saw a kitten
TEACHER:	Yes. And what did you see?
ANTHONY:	I seen . . . I saw a . . . a motorcycle.
TEACHER:	Good. Class, what did Anthony say he saw? Use saw in your answer.
CLASS:	He saw a motorcycle.
TEACHER:	Right! Now, then, let's play the game in a different way. Did anyone see a taxi or a jeep on the way to school today? Gregory, did you see a taxi or a jeep?
GREGORY:	I didn't see a jeep, but I saw a taxi.
TEACHER:	Good. Daphne, did you see any dogs or horses on your way to school?
DAPHNE:	I seen—saw some dogs, but I didn't see no horse.
TEACHER:	I didn't see any horses. That's the standard English way to say it. Say: "I didn't see any horses."
DAPHNE:	I didn't see any horses.
TEACHER:	Fine! George, what did Daphne see, and what didn't she see?
GEORGE:	She . . . she . . . (silence)
TEACHER:	Daphne, tell George what you saw and what you didn't see.
DAPHNE:	I saw some dogs, but I didn't see no . . . I didn't see any horses.
TEACHER:	Good for you, Daphne! You did it the standard English way without any help. Say it again.
DAPHNE:	I saw some dogs, but I didn't see any horses.
TEACHER:	Fine! George, what did she tell us?
GEORGE:	She saw some dogs, but she didn't see any horses.

(And so on, with contributions from all who need to gain command over this feature of the standard dialect. The last to speak is Stanley, who is asked to say what various classmates saw on their way to school.)

This is the kind of drill—disguised as a conversation—that has become important in foreign language teaching. Its aim is to make a language pattern begin to sound natural, feel right, through repeated uses in sentences that have some interest and meaning for the speaker and his listeners. It belongs, in fact, to the species of drill that is often called "pattern practice" or "substitution practice." For several years it has been widely used in courses for students of English as a Foreign Language (or Second Language); and it is used when people teach foreign languages along "audio-lingual" lines today.

True, it takes time to teach patterns of speech in this way. The easier way is merely to mention the student's "error"—or to give him a workbook exercise that he can do at home—though he probably won't. But to deal thus with a language habit is not to deal with it at all. Next year Stanley and the rest will still be using the same non-standard forms on occasions that call for the standard dialect, and next year's teacher will still deplore and nag, rather than teach. True, too, the list of items to be learned is long (particularly if the student's home dialect differs greatly from the standard) but the number of really crucial items is finite: these *could* be mastered during the many years English teachers are given for the task. In no other subject do teachers in all grades try to work on everything at once. Why can't English teachers divide up the list of linguistic habits to be learned? If the fourth grade teacher could make her students fluent with regard to a specified few of the items on the list, the fifth grade teacher could go on from there, and so on up through the grades.*

* Below grade four, the teacher's most essential task is to help children learn how to read and write the English they already know. They need to learn how letters and combinations of letters are used for representing sounds and combinations of sounds that are already familiar. They need to hear stories of the sort the children of educated Americans hear their parents read aloud. They need games that call their attention to rhymes, games that make them notice words. Above all they need to be listened to, and they need help in learning to use their minds. Activities directed toward these ends should be central to the language curriculum for grades one through three.

Some Sources of Help

As yet little has been written about the possibilities of this kind of "fluency practice" for students of standard English as a second dialect, but three helpful studies will be mentioned here. One is Marjorie Barrows' *Good English Through Practice*,[3] which shows how to use a set of cleverly devised games for getting junior high school students to use many troublesome standard English forms over and over again while taking part in entertaining, creative language activities.

A second helpful text is Ruth Golden's *Improving Patterns of Language Usage*,[4] in which the problems and attitudes of students learning the standard dialect are analyzed, and many language-learning activities are suggested, including games, stories and role-playing skits.

There is irony in the fact that both *Good English Through Practice* and *Improving Patterns of Language Usage* perpetuate in their titles the older, unhelpful policy of condemning non-standard dialects as intrinsically "worse" than the standard dialect and needing to be "improved." Fortunately, however, the attitudes reflected in the texts themselves are more harmonious with the spirit of modern courses in this field.

A third, and particularly fruitful, source of help for teachers is San-su C. Lin's report on a three-year research project financed by the U. S. Office of Education, in which Dr. Lin and her associates experimented with pattern-practice techniques as a means of helping students in South Carolina master standard English.[5]

The setting for the Lin program was Claflin College, a small, church-supported school serving mainly Southern Negroes from rural communities. The speech of many freshmen at Claflin included patterns like these: *three apple; nine childrens; I arrive here last week; Claflin have a new dormitory; They looks after theirselves; He don't want nothing; She's more prettier; She sang beautiful; I had wrote it; My uncle, he work in Richmond.* It was evident that the efforts of students and staff would need to be concentrated upon the mastery of basic grammar patterns distinguishing the standard dialect (in writing and in speech) from non-standard varieties. Consequently, problems of pronunciation were not permitted to occupy the center of attention in the Claflin

project. However, a few pronunciation problems (such as difficulties in adding the -s and -ed endings) did come within the
scope of the project because these interfered with the mastery of
grammatical forms.

Early in 1961, when the Claflin Project was conceived, there
were few guidelines for teachers of a second dialect. Dr. Lin's
1965 report tells an absorbing story of trials, false starts, frustrations, accomplishments, and—above all—cumulative learnings on
the part of both students and staff. The report tells of questions
to which answers were found. First there was the need to understand why the problem existed:

What makes a college freshman from a culturally deprived Negro community persist in the use of a non-standard dialect in spite of many
years of English instruction through high school and elementary
school? The dialect, no matter how other people may judge it, has
evidently proved socially and psychologically satisfactory to the individual who uses it. It is the language of his family—a symbol of security
and love. It is the language of his initiation into life—from the dawn
of awareness through successive steps in which he learned to adjust to
different groups and to establish rapport with the world around him.[6]

Next came the questions of approach, growing out of the staff's
analysis of the human aspects of the problem. Certain fundamentals had to be established:

First of all, the teacher must become aware, and help the student
become aware, of the infinite variations that exist in the many dialects
of American English, both regional and social. Both teacher and student must also understand the social implications of these variations.
If any change is desirable, the decision to change must come from the
individual himself. The teacher, with sympathetic understanding, can
help speed the process of change by supplying the necessary methods
and materials.[7]

In their search for procedures that could help these students
achieve proficiency in the use of standard English, the Claflin staff
turned to the field of foreign language teaching, particularly to
the teaching of English as a foreign language, in which Dr. Lin
had had training and experience. As the report points out:

. . . there has been little recognition among English teachers of the
need for a program basically different from the English program

catering to those who speak standard English at home. Not only are these linguistically different young people more sensitive to intolerance and tactless criticism, they also differ from standard speakers in being faced with the task of establishing a new set of language habits. In other words, if they are learning a second language to be added to their indigenous dialect, they must be taught with methods and procedures that are used in learning a second language.[8]

However, after a few weeks' experience with the "repeat-after-me" type of practice material found in most language-learning laboratories, the Claflin staff realized that major adaptations had to be made, since English was, after all, not a foreign language to these American students. Quite apart from the psychological resistance to having one's national language treated like a foreign tongue, there were difficulties arising from the fact that standard English and a non-standard dialect of English are so closely related that, as San-su Lin puts it, "the socially significant differences may be over-shadowed by the similarities and fail to present a real challenge to the students." Moreover, much as the students themselves wished to acquire skill in using standard English, they naturally resented having their entire Freshman English course devoted to drill on grammar patterns: they wanted to learn about literature, composition, stylistics, and other matters that they considered appropriate to a college course.

Thus the Claflin staff was faced with the task of devising procedures and materials that would give the students the kind and amount of drill they needed for mastery of the standard patterns, while at the same time satisfying the students' natural desire for "college level" instruction. Since much this same task is faced everywhere by teachers whose students are already fluent in some variety of English, Dr. Lin's report on solutions to the problem offers much practical advice. The Claflin staff learned to avoid the use of example sentences and drill sentences that merely illustrated a grammar pattern without offering information or ideas. They learned to construct practice exercises that gave these students information about science, etiquette and job-hunting techniques. They learned to design drills that increased a student's vocabulary, or improved his spelling and punctuation, while simultaneously strengthening his control over standard grammar forms.

For example, noting that the students needed to acquire the habit of using the -*s* ending for the third person singular form of verbs, the staff prepared an exercise which required each student to use third-person singular forms again and again while discussing "college level" vocabulary words that he knew he needed to learn to pronounce and spell.

The exercise was conducted about as follows: The teacher mentioned a polysyllabic word, such as *curriculum*. A student was then directed to analyze the word, using this sequence of sentences:

The word *curriculum* begins with the letter *c*.
It ends with the letter *m*.
It contains two *r*'s.
It has four syllables.
The accent falls on the second syllable.

A second student would then analyze another word (e.g. *accommodation*) using the same set of sentences:

The word *accommodation* begins with the letter *a*.
It ends with the letter *n*.
It contains two *c*'s and two *m*'s.
It has five syllables.
The accent falls on the fourth syllable.

The exercise would continue in the same way, until most members of the class had had an opportunity to construct sentences in this mold, each sentence containing at least one word with an -*s* ending. If any student said, "It *end* with . . . ," or "The accent *fall* . . ." he was asked to repeat the sentence, using the -*s* ending appropriately. In this way, for the first time, the -*s* ending began to "sound natural" and "feel right" to these students, because they had said and heard it over and over again. Moreover, they had accepted the drill as being appropriate to their level of educational maturity because it sounded like "college English."

Conducting Meaningful Drills

Exercises of this sort are not nearly as easy to construct as they may seem. First the teacher must know precisely what grammatical point it is that the students need to have illustrated and repeated again and again; and then the teacher must elicit many repetitions of the pattern from the students in the course of a discussion that is more than a mere mechanical drill.

In the Claflin project, the staff realized that just one drill on the -s ending would not be enough to ensure the ready use of this feature of standard English when next the student found himself in a situation calling for fluent, effortless use of the standard dialect. There were many other exercises leading to the same goal by different routes. For example, on one occasion the class discussed reading techniques, within the framework of "Five Things a Good Reader Does." Each student offered his own five sentences, based on a discussion of reading in the essay anthology. Sentences constructed by the class included the following:

A good reader keeps his mind on his work.
A good reader looks for answer to certain questions in his mind.
A good reader distinguishes between main ideas and details.
A good reader summarizes the writer's ideas from time to time.

(Note that this exercise would have lost its effectiveness so far as practice on the third-person -s ending was concerned if the students had been permitted to alternate between "a good reader" and "good readers." What they needed was to say and to hear a singular subject plus the -s form of the verb again and again, in order to forge a link between the form of the subject and the form of the verb.)

In similar fashion, the Claflin project students practiced the -ed ending for verbs within the context of a discussion of a chapel program, in which, they said, "The president introduced the guest speaker. The speaker talked for twenty minutes. He described . . . and explained that . . . , etc." Once again the strategy called for an oral account, with contributions from all members of the class, carefully elicited by the teacher so as to ensure many repetitions of the standard English form (in this case, the -ed ending) over which the students needed to develop control.

Role Playing

In addition to these "structured discussions" or "fluency drills," the Claflin staff experimented with skits and other role-playing activities. The most successful skits were those that simulated life situations in which standard English would obviously be the appropriate dialect to use. Some dialogs illustrated forms of etiquette relevant to job interviews, employer-secretary conferences, and the like. After the students had taken part in skits written by the project staff, the students themselves—working in small groups—wrote a number of role-playing exercises. Each student practiced his part with the aid of a taped standard English recording of it in the language laboratory. The best skit in each class was chosen for performance in a chapel program. The students found the experience interesting and helpful: among a few students, the speech patterns changed dramatically as a result.

Although the Claflin project extended from 1961 to 1964, a different Freshman class participated during each of the three years. Thus no student was enrolled in the program for more than one academic year. As the final reported pointed out, it would be wrong to claim (in San-su Lin's words) that "any method can, in nine months, give the student a full command of the standard dialect when it is psychologically and socially difficult for him to use anything but the non-standard dialect in his daily life, even on a college campus."

Even so, some very encouraging results emerged. From the taped interviews which formed part of the evaluation data, it was evident that the students had become more self-confident and more determined to develop dialectal versatility. Their enunciation had become clearer, they found it easier to communicate, and they appeared more ready to correct themselves after using non-standard forms. On the locally prepared grammar test, the project students proved to be more successful than the control group in identifying non-standard patterns and "translating" them into standard modes. In addition to items that were indisputably non-standard, the test also included items like "Everyone was supposed to bring their lunch," and "This color is different than that"—usages decried by grammar books but often heard in the speech of educated persons. Since such items had been given little attention in the experimental program, most of them were "missed" by project students on the final test. However, in terms of the conspicuous hallmarks of standard English (as contrasted with the non-standard dialect) the experimental students demonstrated significant improvement.

Reading and Writing

Nor were the gains at Claflin limited to matters of speech and social dialect. Somewhat to the surprise of the staff, scores on the Cooperative English Test revealed that the experimental group made greater gains in *reading* after a year of grammar pattern practice than did the members of the control group (which had engaged in free conversation in place of the structured grammar drills). What made this result the more striking was that the control group (the group not employing the experimental techniques) had given more attention to reading, as such, and to discussions of the material read. The Lin report points out that apparently "the use of pattern practice techniques can sharpen students' awareness of structural matters in such a way as to improve their comprehension of material that they read. After a year of working systematically and intensively with various patterns of English, the experimental students were apparently better equipped to read passages which required an alert attention to structural signals."

Another skill which benefited from the application of second-language teaching techniques in the Claflin project was *written*. At the end of the second year of the program, the director reported [9] that the compositions written by students in the project were "not only more free of errors, but more purposeful and more interesting" than any she had previously read during seven years' experience at the same institution.

Above all, what has been proved by the Claflin project (and by similar programs) is that speakers of non-standard dialects can make significant progress toward the mastery of standard English, even in a program of very short duration. (It should be remembered that no Claflin student was involved in the project for more than nine months.) How much could be accomplished if teachers at all levels of the instructional ladder were to apply the lessons learned from such experiments!

Target Language

Fortunately, more and more teachers are coming to realize that attitudes, approaches and procedures germane to the teaching of foreign languages have relevance to the teaching of standard English as a second dialect. More and more teachers are defining the target language as "the kind of English habitually spoken by most of the educated members of the American speech community." Guided by this definition, classes for non-standard speakers are concentrating upon language usages which indisputably characterize "the language of educated ease." Teachers are thus freeing class time for practice upon these crucial features of the target dialect by passing lightly over esoteric distinctions that carry little or no weight outside some grammar textbooks.

In their classrooms, these teachers guard against treating the students' home dialect as something faulty, flawed and inferior. They are willing to grant that the home dialect may even be the "right" one for a student to use in some interpersonal relationships deeply important to him. At the same time, they help their students achieve fluency in standard English by patiently guiding the class through practice exercises based on second-language teaching techniques, but adapted to second-dialect purposes with artistry and tact.

In programs conducted along these lines, there is much hope for students striving to command the dialect that is required for advancement in our national life—for entering fully into American affairs, through the front door.

NOTES

1. For front page news in the literal sense, see for example *The Wall Street Journal*, January 19, 1966, which featured an account of several current programs and approaches in standard English as a second dialect.
2. Joos, Martin. "Language and the School Child," *Word Study*, Vol. XI, No. 2, December, 1964.
3. Barrows, Marjorie Wescott. *Good English Through Practice*. New York: Henry Holt, 1956.
4. Golden, Ruth I., *Improving Patterns of Language Usage*. Detroit: Wayne University Press, 1960. See also her report on *Effectiveness of Instructional Tapes for Changing Regional Speech Patterns*, Detroit Public Schools, 1962.
5. Lin, San-su C., *Pattern Practice in the Teaching of Standard English to Students with a Non-Standard Dialect*. New York: Teachers College Press, 1965.

6. Lin, *ibid.*
7. Lin, *ibid.*
8. Lin, *ibid.*
9. Lin, San-su C. "An Experiment in Changing Dialect Patterns: The Claflin Project," *College English,* May, 1963, pp. 644–647.

14 CURRICULUM FOR THE DISADVANTAGED

GERTRUDE WHIPPLE

Disadvantaged children need a "better than equal" curriculum. This means discrimination in favor of the disadvantaged at all levels from the nursery school through the secondary school. An immensely superior curriculum is the only lever that will enable the children to make a good start in life.

The curriculum, as I shall use the term, consists of the experiences that the child has through the initiative of the school. The teacher is the key person in determining the curriculum. For given the same facilities, equipment, materials, and curriculum guides, any two teachers will provide vastly different curriculums, because teachers vary in attitudes, abilities, and insights.

For many years, most teachers and school officials have considered deprived children as inferior and unable to learn to cope with urban life. Today the view is being increasingly accepted that their backwardness does not necessarily result from low native capacity, but rather from impoverished environments. It is well substantiated that the children respond to instruction when their curriculums are unequal, in the sense of being far, far better and more costly than usual. This, one must hope and believe, if he is to help construct a satisfactory curriculum for the severely deprived youngsters pouring into our urban schools.

Teacher Education. Therefore, the first step to be taken is that of convincing and equipping the teachers through in-service education. The education must be tailored to meet their needs. One of the best approaches is on-the-job education. At regular periods, perhaps a day or a half-day each week or every two weeks, released time is built into their schedule. If this is not feasible, the teachers are compensated for attendance during out-of-school

Gertrude Whipple, "Curriculum for the Disadvantaged," Harvey Goldman (ed.), *Education and the Disadvantaged* (Milwaukee: School of Education, University of Wisconsin, Milwaukee, August 1967), pp. 91–105.

hours. In meeting with local supervisors or other leaders, they are introduced to the problems the children face, the types of experiences needed, and the effective new methods, materials and equipment. Best are special workshops held for teachers at different school levels.

Principals often confess that they know little about the basic school subjects, particularly the teaching of reading. Principals, too, must increase their knowledge if they are to guide a team of teachers working together to attain continuity in a sound program.

Through a variety of in-service helps, everyone concerned comes to see what is needed for the disadvantaged children—a general reconstruction, radical improvement and total reform of the curriculum.

Standards of Excellence. The goals and the standards of achievement must be every bit as high as those of curriculums for middle-class children. Before the disadvantaged enter the secondary school, the majority should have come abreast with the middle class in many respects including motivation to learn, oral vocabulary, firsthand experiences, basic concepts, and persistence in study.

To this end, the schools for deprived youngsters must have a larger proportion of superior teachers than do other schools. Their schools must have several times the financial investment for more fortunate children, a lower teacher-pupil ratio, more carefully chosen reading materials and more of them, much better everything. For to catch up with others, the disadvantaged child must learn much more in a shorter time.

Conditions Essential to an Effective Curriculum

More Flexible School Organization. Disadvantaged children are in special need of a continuous program from preschool through high school. The traditional organization of separate and distinct grades tends to create gaps in their schooling. A non-graded plan would seem better, first because this plan facilitates adaptation of instruction to the child's rate of progress, and second because it permits every child to proceed without experiencing non-promotion. In a primary unit, young children seem to benefit by having the same teacher during their first few years in school. In an intermediate unit, this sustained relationship helps the teacher to keep the tasks the child is expected to perform within his capacities at all times.

Smaller Classes. All the way through the elementary and secondary school, classes for instruction in the basic subjects should be much smaller than their present size. Even if the school budget is not sufficient to reduce class size, efforts can be made in this direction.

Eve Malmquist of Sweden describes the procedure used in his country to cut the size of beginning classes in half.

One half meets, for instance, with the teacher the first two hours of the day. The second half comes to school for the next two-hour period, during which the first half is free to play or engage in other activities. By this means the teacher has no more than 13 pupils at a time, for half of the time the pupils are at school.[1]

In our large cities, where there is heavy traffic and young children cannot be permitted to go to and from school at odd hours, this plan requires some modification. With one additional teacher or one qualified lay person, half of several classes can play in the gymnasium or on the school playground, while the other pupils receive instruction in a basic subject. This permits the teachers to give each child more individual attention.

This plan is even easier to administer in the middle grades. Here half the pupils of several classes can go to a school auditorium to receive TV instruction or enrichment programs such as viewing movies or enjoying plays, art, or music, or to a gymnasium for physical education.

Well-Organized Classrooms. In order to develop the good personal and social attitudes that have not been demonstrated in the home, the teacher gives particular attention to the classroom environment. For example, at the beginning of the primary unit, instruction in the care of personal and public property is begun. The teacher creates an orderly and well-structured classroom environment; he has a place for everything. Gradually, he gives over the care of some of the cupboards to the class. The teacher calls the children's attention to the neat arrangement, reads aloud the simple labels on the shelves, and discusses a few rules for the care of the material. The idea is suggested that no one will suffer when everything belonging in the cupboard is put away carefully. Likewise, the teacher shows the children how to arrange their own storage spaces, and checks them frequently.

Throughout the school, to prevent vandalism from developing, the teacher motivates the children to conserve personal and public property. Whenever the class receives a new set of books, the teacher develops habits of opening the book correctly, using a book mark instead of turning down pages, and never marking in the book. In the later-elementary unit, where conservation is ordinarily taught, the subject is begun with the theme of protecting one's home and neighborhood from loss, waste, and harm, rather than with the strange and remote concept of the life and death of the land.

A well-organized classroom is also necessary in teaching obedience, self-discipline, and willingness to work for more distant rewards.

High Aspirations

The successive units of an effective curriculum aim to develop a good self-image together with higher aspirations and self-confidence. This is accomplished chiefly through giving the learner tasks in which he can succeed. The teacher breaks every process into its components, develops each part carefully, provides practice under his supervision, encourages the child to carry on further practice independently, and creates situations in which the new learning is put to immediate use. Each work pattern is repeated often until mastery has been attained. Then the teacher shows the child his progress, using some concrete means such as a pictorial graph.

With a backlog of success and positive experiences as well as the teacher's frequent commendation, the child begins to develop self-confidence. His desire to achieve is enhanced. He acquires reasonable aspirations, not only academic but also life aspirations.

Life aspirations are encouraged through the content of the books he reads. In the primary unit, the books on the classroom library shelves include stories in pictures and text about various occupations, and in higher units, success stories of persons of the child's own background who have risen economically and socially.

The Language Arts

Among the deprived children, the predominating fatal handicap is retarded development of standard English. Before entering school, the children experience emotional encounters that repress their language. They lack vocal stimulation. They are deficient in listening power and suffer from limited language to express their ideas. They discuss fewer topics and use immature sentence forms. Therefore, the new curriculum must focus upon accelerating language development.

According to research findings, children's language power increases with an increase in adult contacts. For example, the fewer the children in the family, the more mature is their language. This finding indicates the value of grouping children around adults for conversation and discussion.

But talking calls for something worthwhile to talk about. At all school levels an effective curriculum exposes children to new worlds to make them curious, observing, and talkative. Let the children be taken here and there on walks and on buses, trains and airplanes. Encourage young children to note the effects of changing seasons and landscapes other than their own. Let students see men at work in different industries. Let them observe how boats and airplanes operate and ways of making a living in different areas. Such means enable disadvantaged children to relate verbal discussions to reality. The more the child sees, hears and experiences, the more ideas he will have to express.

It is vital that the curriculum afford the child an infinite number of opportunities to listen to good oral expression so that he will acquire an "ear" for standard English. Listening to recordings of stories and of fascinating information can give him models to follow.

Heavy emphasis on the language-experience approach is especially good since the teacher rephrases the child's contributions in standard English. This approach also develops concern for language as meaning. The teacher stimulates discussion, helps the children express finer shades of meaning, and records the ideas on the chalkboard. For young children, the teacher-class composition serves as reading material; for older children, it illustrates how to work out a good written paragraph or a successful letter of application for a job or it may summarize useful conclusions on managing time, managing money, improving personal appearance, or dealing with tensions, frustrations and disappointments.

Reading

Broadening experiences and interesting conversation and discussion make the child want to discover the unknown by reading. Reading is of great importance to him for success in the world of work. He must learn to read well so that he can secure immediate success in his chosen work. Later, when confronted with technological changes, he must be able to use reading as a means of gaining new information and skills.

Present efforts to strengthen reading abilities and skills are concerned chiefly with the establishment of remedial-reading centers. Indeed, 52 per cent of the current Title I reading programs focus upon remediation. The programs are designed for children who have suffered reading failure and have deep-seated reading difficulties.

Surely it is important for children who have not benefited by the reading instruction given them to be singled out for diagnosis and then provided with specialized professional help. But a strong reading program diminishes the risk of failure. It makes haste slowly and insures mastery at each level. Our No. 1 responsibility is to develop effective reading programs.

In 1964 Benjamin S. Bloom [2] summarized the findings of about 1,000 longitudinal studies in which the same persons were repeatedly measured or observed at different points in their development. One of Bloom's chief findings is that the environment in which the individual develops will have its greatest effect on his characteristics in the most rapid period of change and its least effect in the least rapid period of change. Bloom's study showed also that when the child enters first grade he has already gone through the period of life in which development seems to be most rapid. In fact, Bloom estimated that at least one third of the individual's development at age eighteen has taken place prior to his entrance into first grade.

Pre-reading Instruction. In view of Bloom's findings, a fundamental program takes the children at three or four and improves their opportunities and accomplishments long before reading instruction is begun. Classes are very small, no more than fifteen children to one teacher and two teacher aides. The children's special needs are met such as care of health, nutrition, and psychological and emotional disturbances, which ghetto conditions produce with such high frequency.

The curriculum is fitted to the individual children. It provides the experiences suited to their age that they have missed. Examples are: playing with toys; examining, discussing and eating common fruits and vegetables; caring for pets; using art materials; talking informally with a sympathetic adult who answers their questions; participating in games that build vocabulary and give practice in using proper word order in sentences; listening to stories such as folk tales with definite sequence; being read to and encouraged to talk about pictures, books, and their experiences; taking walking trips and bus trips; and sharing in role playing and dramatic representation. Rest periods are often used for music enrichment. Since the young children are not accustomed to having space inside a building, they are allowed to play in a large indoor space such as a gymnasium.

To develop ideas of good family life, the children are encouraged to talk about their families, and the teacher uses children's literature to illustrate the idea of a family and how the members help one another. To increase interest and attention span, the children are invited at the end of the day to review what they have learned that day.

In such a curriculum, the child hears a new style of language before he is introduced to printed text. After two or three years of hearing good spoken language, he will use more elaborate language himself—more exact words to fit a situation, a greater number of different words, and more sentences as opposed to phrases. Thus he is far, far better equipped for beginning reading instruction.

In the young children lies the main hope of curing inner-city reading problems. The heavily subsidized programs of remediation correct some of the reading difficulties created by substandard curriculums—substandard in the sense of being totally unsuited to the deprived child. What must be done, regardless of the effort and financial outlay needed, is to prevent reading failure. Any expense and sacrifice of time and effort is justified to this end.

No One Approach to Beginning Reading. During the last few decades controversies have raged concerning the best method of teaching beginning reading. A greater variety of methods has been proposed than ever before—programed reading, the electric typewriter, the linguistic methods, Words in Color, augmented alphabets, various phonic methods, individualized reading, et cetera. However, change to a new method is not necessarily progress; and research does not offer unanimous support for the use of any one approach. A best method of introducing children to reading does not exist. Every desirable reading program for disadvantaged children uses several methods in trying to give the individual the kind of guidance he needs.

Diagnostic Teaching. From the first day of school, the teacher makes an on-going diagnosis for those children who are incipient cases of reading retardation. Immediately the teacher gives special help before the child is advanced to more difficult tasks.

Today there are many ways for the teacher to detect a beginning illness in reading. He can observe lack of interest, inability to concentrate upon the reading activity, lack of persistence, signs of poor visual perception, low educational level of parents, and lack of emotional adjustment. He can test reading readiness, memory span, visual letter perception, auditory perception, accuracy in oral reading, comprehension in silent reading, spelling ability and phonetic knowledge. If class size is kept small, if enough good reading materials are available, and if teachers are provided with well-trained aides, at critical points a qualified teacher can reinforce the child's abilities and halt his failure.

But teachers will need plenty of time to work with the pupils. They should not be assigned lunch or other duties that can be performed by lay aides. An aide can do clerical work, operate audiovisual equipment, read aloud to children, and work with children on skills after they are introduced.

A resource teacher in the school can give help with the more difficult problems and share good ideas with regular teachers. A resource teacher is a dedicated, gifted person who over a period of years has sifted the helpful approaches from many methods and has consolidated them into effect procedures. Every school system has a limited number of these "artist" teachers who should be sought out for work with the disadvantaged.

Since the responsiveness of disadvantaged children is in direct proportion to the amount of individual attention and guidance children receive, they must be provided also with extended school services if their problems are to be alleviated. School libraries should be made available after school and during the summer months. The school should be an around-the-clock neighborhood and recreational center.

The provision of health services is imperative since poor nutrition, uncorrected physical handicaps and lack of personal care drain the child's energy and self-esteem. The children require the services of doctors, dentists, speech correctionists, nurses, etc. Breakfast and lunch should be given to the child who comes to school hungry.

A Skill Program. Many of the deprived youngsters who are in fourth grade and above have not mastered the simplest basic reading skills. Because of poor language development, they find reading a very abstract activity, and also have inadequate listening skills. They remember some of what they read but usually recall only facts or unimportant details.

Such children need to be given definite, demonstrable reading tasks that they can complete in a short time by using concrete materials. To illustrate, one such activity relates to a single skill in critical reading—arranging ideas in proper sequence. After the children have read a short story, at their reading level, they may each be given a duplicated sheet that lists five or six statements giving the main events in random order. The children may be asked to number these in the proper order, cut apart the sentence strips, and paste them in correct order on another sheet of paper. Later in a discussion period, the class may evaluate the results and recall the details surrounding each event. Later this skill may be applied to expository material where the child must grasp the steps in a process. Later still he can be led to develop other skills needed in critical reading such as evaluating information as being of primary or secondary importance or summarizing ideas. In all such tasks the child needs to work with concrete materials, to have short-range goals, to know that he has succeeded, and to have some tangible reward. Teachers who are aware of these needs are usually ingenious in meeting them and should have opportunities to share their ideas with one another.

Team Work. There is no school subject more in need of team work on the part of teachers than that of reading. A teacher in an intermediate unit must continue where the teacher in the primary unit left off. He must continue in each phase of reading, in word recognition, word meanings, oral reading, comprehension, and interpretation, rate of reading, and use of books and libraries. Furthermore, he must know that continuity in developing reading skills does not mean continuity for an entire class but for an individual child.

The teachers in each school need a breakdown of the specific skills to be taught from the lowest to the highest grade so that each one will know which skills were introduced earlier and should be maintained and what is a desirable order of introducing the new skills.

In order to increase reading abilities and skills, even the best teacher needs the assistance of reading materials that are excellent in quality and quantity.

Reading Materials

Until recently both schoolbooks and children's literature represented an all-white world. United States histories were insensitive to the contributions and achievements of Negroes. Basic readers for the primary grades were unquestionably white suburban. As Nancy Larrick [3] has said, 6,340,000 nonwhite children across the country were learning to read and understand the American way of life in books which omitted them entirely or scarcely mentioned them.

Recently authors and publishers have begun to break the color bars in the all-white world of children's books. Dual editions of basic readers have appeared that differ chiefly in the portrayal of Negroes. One edition, apparently designed for the disadvantaged, depicts Negroes in every book whereas the other edition depicts no Negroes at all. Of two series from another publishing house one called a regular series is predominately white, the other, a multi-ethnic series, uses stylized art which makes it hard to conjecture the race of the nonwhites portrayed. In still other series that are revisions of earlier editions, the reader sees an occasional picture of a Negro but the books focus on an all-white world. In the main, basic readers do not yet clearly reflect an integrated society.

Book selecting committees would do well to remind their members that change in schoolbooks is not necessarily equivalent to improvement. There must be a steady process of searching available books, trying them out in the classroom, and objective standards in evaluating and comparing their merits. As examples of standards to apply in the selection of readers for disadvantaged primary children, I submit the following basic questions:

1. Are the readers integrated so that the Negro child can identify with the characters or do the readers show built-in discrimination (e.g., showing Negroes only as bystanders and naming white characters only; putting the stories of Negroes at the back of the book; including stereotypes such as a Negro porter carrying a suitcase and omitting Negro characters of higher status)?

2. Do the beginning readers offer a concrete approach that lends itself to role-playing? The deprived child is dismayed by an impersonal, abstract approach.

3. To what extent will the content of the readers and the activities described in the teachers' manuals be useful in accelerating the child's language development? Stories that are a source of joy and excitement or give intriguing information stimulate the communication of ideas.

4. Do the stories include a large proportion that are boy-oriented? Since more boys than girls are likely to have reading problems, the books must make a special appeal to boys. The all-white suburban series with its two girls and one boy character is not suited to disadvantaged children who so often come from one-parent homes.

5. Are the story plots such that the child will follow them with interest or is there no effective plan of action (e.g., no climax that rewards the reader)? Disadvantaged children whose parents have found no pleasure in reading are especially in need of narrative interest appeal. The books should make reading more fun with surprise, humor and a dose of mystery.

6. Are the earliest books short enough to give the children a definite feeling of accomplishment?

7. Do the teachers' manuals provide direction for teachers in skill development and social learnings?

8. Do the books present enough suitable content to facilitate attainment of these objectives? This cannot be taken for granted since, for instance, tabulations show that one series particularly constructed for the disadvantaged has a heavier vocabulary load than other series and offers less reading material.

This discussion has stressed that a sound curriculum for the seriously deprived (1) is not "watered down"; (2) requires a wisely structured classroom and school environment; (3) stresses social as well as skill objectives; (4) promotes a good self-image on the part of the child; (5) emphasizes mastery rather than makes a "flying start"; (6) stimulates language development; and (7) gives the child success and satisfaction. By beginning early enough in the life of the child, the need for remediation can be reduced immeasurably.

NOTES

1. Malmquist, Eve, "Teaching of Reading: A World-Wide Concern," *Reading and Inquiry*, p. 18. International Reading Association Conference Proceedings, Vol. 10. Newark, Delaware: International Reading Association, 1965.

2. Bloom, Benjamin S., *Stability and Change in Human Characteristics* (New York: John Wiley & Sons, 1964).

3. Larrick, Nancy, "The All-White World of Children's Books," *Saturday Review*, September 11, 1965, pp. 63–65, 84–85.

15 CREATING CONDITIONS FOR LEARNING

HILDA TABA AND DEBORAH ELKINS

. . . In commenting on the role of Project Head Start, Hechinger (1965) expresses concern about the way of weaving the content and experience of the Head Start program into the fabric of American education.

Dr. Kenneth Clark, professor of Psychology at the City College, along with Dr. Deutsch, one of the pioneers of educational experimentation, has warned consistently that compensatory education for children of deprived minorities is no substitute for changes in the structure of education itself. Merely giving such children an opportunity to begin slightly ahead of the class is of little use if the regular schooling is not, at the same time, made relevant to them. There is little to be gained from surrounding these youngsters with loving and understanding adults in their pre-school taste of learning, if they subsequently are exposed to teachers who approach them with preconceived notions of limited potential. . . . The evidence of prior research, unrelated to the Head Start experiment, shows conclusively that early compensatory education is of very limited short-term benefit unless there is consistent follow-up. Children's pre-school gains have been shown to be spectacular as they entered first grade, but are quick to erode in the next four years unless they are constantly reinforced. If there is a gap between pre-school education and kindergarten or first grade, the gains are minimal. . . .

Perhaps the school can be an island that compensates for or offsets what is lacking outside, a key that unlocks individuals who have been closed to learning. But what are the conditions that would make this possible? These conditions could perhaps be spelled out by commenting on the role of the four chief instruments of the school: the teacher, the curriculum, the way of teaching, and the administrative organization of the school.

The Teacher

What kind of teachers are needed; what must they be and know? First of all, students need to see that the teacher cares, that she is a human being who is interested in them personally and cares about what happens to them. Such a teacher finds ways to make a student feel "good about himself." Sometimes these ways amount only to a word of praise for something well done. It can be a small remark such as "Aren't you the handsome one today," as the teacher greets the students in the morning. It can be a written note of praise that goes home to let his parents know how much the student is learning. But above all, the fact that the teacher cares is demonstrated by the effort she makes to shape a program to awaken the students, to help them with their problems of learning, and to share with them their triumphs of achievement, however small they may be.

But often "caring" involves more than that. It means helping students through some crisis. Schools often give children tasks that are utterly impossible for them to face, tasks set by an unknown outside force for a reason they do not understand. In such cases the teacher needs to be ready to "hold the student's hand" through these tasks. City-wide tests are an example of unreasonable demands, and their consequences are described by a teacher who tried desperately to help one student to "hold on."

During the midterm test I had to sit and hold that child's hand throughout the whole two days of testing. Otherwise, he just wouldn't take them. There's nothing wrong with his intelligence. He's afraid. He looks at the paper and he gasps. And he screams, "Ten papers! I can't do it!" Then he starts to cry. I took him out of class in my free period, and in three quarters of an hour he did four hours worth of testing. We read it together and he did beautifully. But when it came to the math examination, I didn't have time for him. So he didn't do it, and he got a zero. In science I couldn't help him, because I didn't know the answers myself. The topic sentences were incredibly ambiguous so that any answers seemed valid.

The teacher needs also to build self-respect and trust. The teacher has, at least in part, the power to build an atmosphere in the classroom in which individuals have an opportunity to play a role that is self-fulfilling and that develops a sense of worth. She demonstrates overtly her respect for every child; eventually the students begin to do the same for each other. One such instance is illustrated by a young teacher:

When he is reading the book that he chose for our reading program, it's his book; he feels that it is. I ask his permission every time. "Can we read the book that you're reading?" When I work with him alone, and he doesn't want to read then, he has enough gumption now to say, "No, I'm not in the mood." Fine, OK. Yesterday we read a chapter and he said, "No more." . . . But he's always being kicked out of classrooms. I walk by in the hall, and he knows that I'm going to talk to him. We talk and then he says, "All right, I can go in now."

This teacher accepts feelings as facts: the need to possess a book, the importance of the freedom to say, "I've had it!" She asks a child's permission to use "his" book as she would ask an adult whose possessions she wishes to borrow. She thus demonstrates to the entire class that her respect is real. Perhaps most important of all, she respects the "mood" of the youngster, the need to withdraw. She talks with a student ejected from class until he feels he can return to the classroom and function. However, it is the student, not the teacher, who makes that decision. Giving students a chance to make decisions about things that concern them is one way for teachers to demonstrate respect.

Trust develops also from evidence of sharing feelings. One teacher read *Happiness Is a Warm Puppy* (Schulz, 1962) to the class.

They loved it! It's a beautiful little book. I'd say, "Do you remember this?" and I'd tell them my experience, and then we'd start sharing experiences . . . to the part where he is learning to tie his shoe, and I said, "Well, I can remember learning to tie my shoe"; and then this one would say, "Me, too! Oh, I remember too!" Then they wrote about the things that mean happiness to *them*. And really what they wrote is just amazing.

The result of such experiences is that the teacher and the students have feelings in common—things that make them happy and things that hurt. There is reluctance at first to express feelings, because the students don't trust either teachers or peers. This trust must be developed.

Helping Students to Help Each Other

Another young teacher found her own ways of achieving a system of self-help in a group with a wide range of ability. At first she had many problems in managing the class, especially the six students of whom she speaks below. What had been achieved a few months later demonstrates that she learned much about these students and about the ways in which they can learn skills and content as well as respect for each other.

Some write as well as my first class, but on the other end are those six kids. . . . They collaborated on the worksheets for *Squanto*. . . . Beautiful! I let them. . . . They can help each other because one has a little bit more ability to read the question, another has the answer or knows how to write it. And they all sign names to the sheet.

This self-help can extend to understanding and controlling interpersonal conflict, one aspect of which is the ability to put oneself in the other person's shoes. Name-calling is one frequent cause of fights. How explosive this practice is can be seen in the description of one first-year teacher:

Another thing that sets the kids off in name-calling. I have one kid who is very sensitive and they call her "a black idiot" so she begins to fight and then they wind up with "Your mother. . . ." She doesn't have a mother; her mother is dead. Then she says, "I know who my mother is" and then they get onto "Your father" and then they begin to go to blows. When you go over to them when they are just about ready to start a fist fight, the rest of the kids start to scream and hoot. Finally you settle the two kids down, and you have the rest of the maniacs running around the room. My other class isn't that way. They aren't as volatile. They don't do as much fighting.

When teachers learn which situations are explosive, what to do to prevent them, and how to help children to examine the ingredients of the situation and the feelings that result, they can cultivate in their students an interest in finding out more about themselves as human beings with feelings. Which feelings are the same? Which are different? What makes them so? How does the same situation look from the opposite side?

During a siege of name-calling, one teacher planned role-playing sessions in which children portrayed how victims feel about aggressors and what the consequences of aggression are. The students tried to help each other become aware that both parties are ultimately losers in explosive interpersonal conflicts.

Teachers' feelings about the potentialities of their students were deeply divided. There were bitter arguments about the state of being and becoming of these unsuccessful learners. One side of the argument tended to fix the becoming according to the current performance—somewhat in line with the following teacher comment:

How can we raise the aspirational levels of these kids? They're not even average! Is it fair to them to raise their aspirational levels to heights they can never achieve? We used to have bull sessions when they wouldn't learn anything else. Robert said he wanted a lot of money, because then he wouldn't have to worry about reading and writing. Because he knew he couldn't read and write, he figured, well, if he had the money, then it wouldn't matter whether he could read or write.

A different point is expressed by another teacher:

When you open up some new idea to them . . . this in itself makes them want to move on to know more things, and in this sense you are raising the aspiration level.

This teacher had learned that since the attention span is short, it is difficult to talk at length and still hold the class. Teaching by talking must be kept to a minimum, for these students do not learn much merely by listening. One first-year teacher found this out the hard way. She also noted that her students became happier and truancy less frequent once she had learned new teaching procedures:

Believe it or not, when I had so few kids in my room yesterday, I gave one book to each two kids—those interesting easy paperbacks like *Down the Mississippi* [Bulla, 1954] and *White Sails to China* [Bulla, 1955]. They read to each other. It was beautiful. I didn't have to try to make them listen to me, and I could help the kids who weren't able to read at all, or who didn't want to read. . . . They feel you are trying to help each one individually and that we are all working together and that I am *with* them. . . . Next day more chil-

dren came to school. They heard about the new books and about the
tape recorder. Then we began to make up plays from the new books
and more truants appeared next day. . . . This kept them going for
over two weeks because their success sustained them. Cartooning had
the same effect. It worked with every single class. They made cartoons
about the sequences of events in the books they read, making sure that
they were put in a proper sequence just as they happened. The cartoons were good, and we rexographed all of them. . . . I had to do
the first one before they could try it. I did it right on the chalk board.
The best thing was that they had a sustained discussion about each
one and no monkey business either. They love to see what others in
their class can do, to talk about their own, about what they meant to
portray, and why these events were important. . . . They got into
arguments about the importance of each, but it was a positive intellectual argument. I never expected this of them. Usually they get into
a fist fight if someone disagrees.

Teachers are divided also on the question of upholding standards. Usually the questions regarding standards are framed in such
a way as to becloud the issue. "Are we lowering standards when
we accept from our youngsters something that would not be acceptable from the children in the higher academic classes?" It
takes a good bit of self-confidence on the part of the teacher
to maintain a position that in order to raise standards students
must first have some kind of positive self-image. Better still, the
two need to be built simultaneously: increasing the ability to
learn raises the self-image; this in turn releases the ability to
learn. When "standards" are individualized, achievement becomes possible. As the student experiences the thrill of achievement, he begins to regard himself in a new light. When this
happens over and over again, he gains the emotional strength to
raise his own "standard." The teacher who is insightful enough
to know this will perform his functions in such a way that the
student will eventually become self-propelling.

However, when the path to achievement is blocked by multiple
hurdles, it is difficult even to make a start. One cannot, for example, send students with meager reading skills to the library
and expect them to find suitable books. The hurdles of having to
go to a library and having to select a book are piled on top of the
obstacles of learning to read and of learning to want to read.

Students with continued experience of failure will not even make an attempt to jump these hurdles.

The idea that the teacher may need to provide or even to produce resource materials with which students can work is foreign to many junior high and upper elementary school teachers. Instead, the problem of reading levels and of the responsibility of using the texts is debated interminably. Yet, when teachers attempt to produce appropriate learning sequences and materials with which to implement them, such as were described in the preceding chapters, the results are often rewarding to teachers and students alike. A member of one such team summarized the insights he and his colleagues had gained as a result of the team planning and the tryouts of the new learning sequences and materials:

. . . This looked like miserable stuff to teach, but now it's interesting because it's—it's like putting cauliflower into a machine and then having it come out gold because of the wonderful results with the children.

Of course, to do all this, it is helpful to have a number of understanding adults present in the classroom. For example, student teachers in the classroom provide a second adult who can sit down with a student and help him before an unendurable amount of frustration sets in. He can talk with another student who is in such an emotional state than he cannot contain himself. He can walk the corridors with a third child who cannot bear to "stay in the room with all those dumb kids." He is another adult to whom a student can relate. The presence of additional adults cuts down the burden upon the one teacher who is constantly besieged for attention by a roomful of children who can get it nowhere else. This second person need not be a student teacher; he may be an aide who is compatible with the teacher. A first-year teacher who felt herself to be one of "the fortunate ones" to have had the additional help of a student teacher explains:

In that class the fact that there are two people made it possible for one to just sit down and talk with a student in trouble while other things are going on in the room. As long as he was there the lesson would go. But with him gone, that class is chaotic at times. . . .

In the absence of additional adult help, teachers have arranged to send to another teacher temporarily the students who cannot contain themselves in a particular classroom. Calhoun was one such child, sent to a colleague who was slated for a preparation period and therefore had no class.

I was alone. He wouldn't stay with me, and he went out of the room. My kids were in another class, and this was a free period for me. So I went outside and said, "Calhoun, would you like to help me? I'd really appreciate that." When he didn't answer I said, "Either say 'yes' or 'no.'" He still didn't answer me, so I said, "All right," turned my back, and started to walk into the room. Then Calhoun said, "I didn't say 'yes' or 'no.'" So I said, "Well-l-l?" and he replied, "Yes, I want to help you." He came in and helped me. He washed the blackboard and I gave him a commendation card. He was good all period.

Other teachers threw up their hands and cried, "Commendation card? Why? He was bad! Why should he get a reward? He'll only be worse. He'll want to get out again and he'll know this is how you do it. The other kids will begin to act up too. You're only inviting trouble." Somehow, teachers need to be helped to see that the others do not necessarily need the "relief" this child required; that they will not necessarily imitate his behavior; that they can be taken into a teacher's confidence enough to become aware that individuals are different and need to be handled differently.

It should be understood, however, that this type of relief is a temporary makeshift, and that, in classes with disturbed youngsters, there should be adults on hand to forestall impending "danger," to "read the signs" before a student "blows," and to help him reach the point where he can begin to function again in a positive way and "under his own steam."

What can happen when sufficient help is available was demonstrated in a summer workshop. This workshop was composed of a class of would-be teachers in their first professional course, a group of rather disturbed sixth- and seventh-graders from the classes described in this book, and a group of three-year-olds from the same neighborhood. The task of the sixth-graders was to read to the three-year-olds and to collect data about them so that the teachers would understand them better. The task of the

CREATING CONDITIONS FOR LEARNING

potential teachers was to help the sixth-graders in their "teaching" and to observe how they learned. In a way, this was a two-way "each one teach one" system.

There was one potential teacher for every adolescent and an adolescent for every young child. When the sixth-grade "teachers" were called together to discuss the problems they were having in reading to the young children or in helping them understand something, their "very own teachers" sat by their side, encouraging them, helping them write, helping them phrase a response, giving them a quiet word of praise, interpreting them when others could not understand. Each sixth-grader gained faith in his "own teacher" very early in the game. He knew that she was "on his side" no matter what happened, and there was no danger that still another adult would discover his inferior performance. If he wished, he could "test out" his "lesson" on his own teacher before exposing it to the judgment of the group.

What can happen under these conditions is illustrated by two incidents. One of the adolescents, a failing sixth-grader, met the coordinator of the workshop during the first month of the school and announced proudly, "You know, I passed!" "That's wonderful! How do you feel you are doing?" "Well, OK, I guess, but you know, I think I could use a little more help in reading." In other words, a two-week workshop conducted in a nonthreatening atmosphere enabled this student to begin to learn to read; he felt the thrill of knowing he could learn and now was willing to admit that he needed and wanted more help, a sign of increasing self-confidence and motivation. Conditions that permit these students to feel free to learn will raise their aspirations and thereby increase their potentiality to learn.

The same workshop revealed the hidden intellectual capacity of another highly disturbed and academically unsuccessful student. In school Mark was classified as a "nonwriter" and "very disturbed."

Mark produced a barrage of questions when, in connection with a series of science demonstrations, he was told that the warmth of the hen is responsible for the process of an egg becoming a chicken and when he observed the fetus of a shark in formaldehyde.

1. How does the egg become a chicken?

2. Well, if I eat an egg, and it goes into my stomach where it is warm, why can't a chicken grow in there?

3. Why is the baby shark dead?

4. Why did they kill the mother?

5. Why can't the baby shark live even though the mother was killed?

6. Why couldn't the baby shark be born before the mother dies?

7. If it's just an egg, how do the eyes, nose, ears, and mouth develop?

8. What makes some people grow tall, others short?

9. Then, why don't midgets grow? Why don't their bones grow too, like our bones, grow bigger and bigger?

10. Why do we have dwarfs?

11. Are rats poisonous? If not, why do babies die that have been bitten by them?

12. How does the child get food from the mother inside?

13. What would happen if I dropped a rock on a turtle's back and broke it? Would he die? Is there a turtle doctor to fix it and make him well? Who would be able to help the turtle get well?

Later, back on the campus, the potential teacher remarked, "I'll never forget . . . how he just poured out all these questions . . . how the teacher has to be prepared for anything. I wasn't and he just floored me."

Planning Learning Sequences

It is not easy to plan adequate learning sequences. It requires a fairly thorough knowledge of what students know and can do in order to break the learning down into bite-size pieces appropriate to the student's capacity to master them. Teachers must know how to select these sequences, how to plan for long- and short-range activities, how to translate what they know about children into motivational devices, and, above all, how to make abstractions concrete. Nor is deciding what is concrete or abstract a simple matter, especially when dealing with students with unexpected gaps and deviations in experience and learning.

The errors that can be committed in the name of "making

things concrete" are illustrated by a story of a teacher of a class in the first group with fairly high potential who was trying to "put over" the concept of government and its branches.

We were talking about the state government and I was trying to make them realize the reason we need government. We started talking about clubs, but only one person had anything to say, though a lot had been in clubs. That was my motivation—bring it down to the club level and why in clubs you need government. . . . One teacher told me that's not enough motivation, because maybe they don't belong to clubs at all, but I asked them to raise their hand. When I asked, "What do you do in your club?", they did nothing. And I even tried to use visual materials. I had the tree of government on the bulletin, and I tried to show them checks and balances and I had a scale to show them they had to be balanced evenly.

This well-intentioned, hard-working, and earnest teacher failed to understand many things about her students. First, very few of them belonged to clubs. In the whole school only 30 came to an after-school recreational program. Second, she did not sense that these students would raise their hands and say "yes" if that was what they thought the teacher wanted, especially if they liked her. Consequently, she was unable to detect the relationship between the fact that they said they did nothing in clubs and the fact that since they had no experience with them, they did not know what happens in clubs. Nor did she realize that a "tree of government" is a metaphor and an abstraction which means something only after experiences leading up to the concept of the branches of government, rather than as an introduction to it. Her well-intended use of the scale is in the same category. These students knew scales as something to weigh objects with, but had no preparation whatsoever for the concept of a scale as a symbol for balance. She was further unaware of the fact that it was she who did the talking and the thinking. As her record said, "only one student had anything to say." This difficulty followed her throughout the whole lesson. She was in the driver's seat: she did the talking, invented the clubs, asked the questions, and brought in a scale. There was nothing for the students to do, and therefore no involvement. Since students had no comprehension of the role of the three things to be balanced that grew on trees, the teacher offered them three "unknowns" and confounded them still further.

Since the success of the whole sequence on government and laws depended upon this introductory session, the failure to activate the students brought about the failure of the lesson.

This lack of meaning applies also to teaching skills per se, apart from the context in which they are to be used, under the mistaken assumption that drill in isolated skills is what the retarded students need. Actually, learning a skill apart from the context and the purpose of using it is both more abstract and less interesting. Since, in addition, the motivation of such students for learning per se is weak, it is practically impossible for them to master the skills taught in this fashion. The careers of many retarded students in disadvantaged areas have fully demonstrated this fact: by the time they reach the sixth or seventh grade they have been "taught" to read and to spell over and over again, but they can neither read nor spell. Evidently a revision of the whole approach to learning skills is needed, and repetitive practice of the same skill in new context is one promising possibility.

One of the most difficult skills for teachers to learn is how to conduct discussions that are in effect conversations. This involves the art of asking questions that permit a variety of levels of response. This is difficult to learn, especially for teachers who have long defined teaching as telling and practiced it as such. To conduct such discussions productively, teachers need to know when to talk and when to let students talk. Usually teachers also ask questions which require a single right answer or interpretation. Once the right answer is obtained from one student, it is assumed that the conversation on that topic ends, because the emphasis is on obtaining the right answer rather than on enabling many students to cope with the question in their own way. As the excerpt below illustrates, the result is a staccato and discontinuous discussion.

TEACHER: What do you think is the most important thing that happened in the story?

WAYLAND: That the water was clean.

TEACHER: Why was it hard to get water in those days?

LOLA: It might freeze.

TEACHER: Why did the boy and girl like to go to the well?

MALCOLM: Like the boy said, "She's lovely."

TEACHER: And what did the girl like?

DENISE: She liked he said, "Can I take water for you?" That's what she liked.

TEACHER: Did she like anything else?

MICHAEL: She likes to look at her face in the water.

It is easy to see the aimlessness and the lack of focus of this type of questioning. To build continuity and interaction in discussion requires a sequential and inductive question strategy that is not easy to develop. Many a consultant has discovered that converting teachers from answer-giving creatures into question-asking ones is one of the most difficult training tasks. Teachers need to learn not only to ask open-ended questions but also to ask them on issues of sufficient latitude. They need to help students listen to each other in order to make possible a productive exchange among them. They need to learn to pick up cues in student remarks and to make them available for the consideration of the entire class. They must find ways of lifting thinking from one level to another by asking questions that induce analysis, such as "Why did Jerry not appear when the woman was leaving?" as one teacher did at a point when the students were going around in circles either accusing Jerry of lying or criticizing the woman for not adopting him. Fiction offers good initial experiences in developing such skills, because it provides concrete and feeling-oriented incidents to stimulate perceptions on which concepts can be built.

Further, when teaching focuses on the development of concepts, especially when disadvantaged students are the learners, it is necessary to allow each student to find his own way to the concept. For example, when students study the growth of cities, and the problems and advantages of cities, there are common concepts to examine, but the specifics that students use to get at these concepts should be different. Each student may read on his own level and gain command of something he can contribute. Both the gaining of command and contributing are of utmost importance, because involvement in what is being learned is absolutely necessary to keep the class going. Participation and contribution are part and parcel of that involvement.

This implies a new concept of individualization: that of diversifying the approach to learning and the materials used while concentrating on a common focus.

A common fear in using such diversified materials is that "if you give them an easy book they won't learn anything." This may be true if students are to read for no purpose other than to remember the content. If used to supply material for discussion, even the simplest books can be used to contribute to fairly sophisticated generalizations, especially when combined with materials from many books read by different students. The same is true of vocabulary. Books are not the sole source of learning vocabulary, and, further, vocabulary without meaning is not worth learning. One must not forget the simple fact that if a student can only read on the second-grade level, he will learn from a book only if it is at that level. He should be permitted to stay on that level till he feels safe enough to step up. Usually, however, when books are used as aids rather than as sole sources of learning—if, for example, the ideas are discussed and clarified first and the questions to answer through reading are clear—half the battle of reading difficulty is won. Students who can read only on the second-grade level without this help may be able to read something more difficult.

Diversification of the sources of learning must go further than just having students read books of varied difficulty. Teachers need to learn to produce and to invent a variety of other materials. Observations on what different types of people do with their hands is a perfectly good source for comparing and contrasting, as is the interviewing of adults on aspirations or making scale maps and drawings of their apartments.

Using differentiated materials requires the use of new teaching strategies. For example, when each student reads a different book on the same topic, the discussion must be so structured as to permit their varied contributions to be made without creating confusion, e.g., by asking a student to explain how his book clarifies the idea under discussion. In such a structure, individual students serve as resource persons while the class and the teacher extend points they make and relate these points to what preceded. Such a procedure also creates motivation: only an unusually unresponsive student will resist the pull of his peers needing what he has to give and, perhaps, even being proud of it.

In modifying the teaching strategy, teachers must also be prepared to deal with certain unusual problems, some of which arise out of habits and expectations built by previous practices. One teacher, in developing a sequence on "Houses Around the World," had diligently marked for herself and the students the pages in several texts on the geographic factors that influence the types of houses that are built in various parts of the world. She had listed these pages on the board, but the students refused to skip any pages, asking how could they understand what came later if they did not read what came before?

The Need for a Variety of Activities

If one interprets activities as something to initiate the search for making abstractions concrete, to hold on to while struggling with difficulties, then activities are not frills and a waste of time, but a deliberate way of cultivating readiness and upgrading learning. Students with meager background and experience, with short attention span and poor work habits, need to engage in a great variety of overt activities. Making booklets, drawing hands, and pasting advertisements may seem like useless play. But if these activities help hold attention, provide appropriate starting points, and create a sense of accomplishment, they have a place in the program. Pairing students to read with each other extends the reading practice for students who will not read unless someone listens, and, in addition, they read much more frequently than they would if they had to wait for the teacher to listen to them. This arrangement also gives students routine tasks to work at as soon as they enter the room, which prevents them from engaging in disruptive activities at the beginning of classes. . . . Reading to each other also stimulates them to move faster in the reading because partners usually become interested in each other's books. As a result they also tend to read more and to cultivate such useful habits as using context clues to figure out the meaning of new words. Furthermore, if the students are paired sociometrically, they are likely to accept criticism from their partners without reacting as negatively to criticism as they usually do.

The use of technological aids is another method of providing "holding" activity. For example, for those students who cannot handle any book independently, there is the tape recorder into which stories can be dictated, a book, and a pair of earphones. They read as they listen, and they can do it as often as they need without disturbing anyone else, including the teacher. For students with long experience of frustration with books and with correcting teachers, this experience is a perfect antidote: It cuts out all previous blocks that stand between them and books and gives them a chance to start anew. Besides, for some students, being alone with the sound of the recorder is perhaps their first experience in privacy. Their ears, eyes, and hands are occupied and all distractions are eliminated. Often a student would sit and listen to a story, then repeat the experience, while reading and even writing. New readers seemed to learn to read in a shorter time, probably by seeing and hearing at the same time. Under these conditions, students may get the meaning from reading for the first time in their lives.

Of course the recorder was also used for many other purposes. In some classes sociodrama sequences were recorded to listen to later. In other classes they were used to record the practice of plays for others to listen to when their assigned work was finished. Readings of poetry were recorded for the same purpose. Often teachers played recorded stories so the whole class could read and listen at the same time.

Evidently the tape recorder is useful even for creating an atmosphere of disciplined behavior, as is illustrated in the record of one teacher:

The children came into the room that day, very noisy as usual, not out of bounds, but very noisy. The moment that tape recorder went on, every child sat at attention and the class was absolutely silent. This, by the way, was not their first introduction to the tape recorder. This technique is good only for certain occasions; it cannot be a regular diet. However, it is one way of using the tape recorder in the classroom.

On this day the children, after listening to the full tape which took about 25 minutes, went up to the tray, row by row, and obtained their books. As they were reading the books, I distributed a mimeographed reading chart. When they had had time to browse and see if they liked their book, I introduced the progress charts and explained how they were to be used.

On that first day an interesting thing happened. There were only a few copies of *Caddie Woodlawn* [Brink, 1935], and the students knew who was supposed to try and read it. With no suggestions from me, all moved toward the area in the room where there was sufficient space for five or so to gather together and read to each other. There were no instructions from me to do this. They were reading to each other and enjoying it. I just considered it a natural thing and no comments were made about it. On the second day they came in again noisily. However, as the tape began to talk and ask them to go up—this row first, that row next—they immediately got their books and sat down to read. Again, the children did the same thing, gradually moved to those people who happened to have the same book and gathered in little groups around one of the desks, in the front of the room, or around the teacher's desk—it didn't matter where, and read in this way. No one asked for help. This was the beginning of the training of the children to come into the room, get their book, and sit down to read. As I went around I asked the students who were reading their own books to read to me. If the student was having difficulty, I read a portion of the chapter, and then left him at a point where he felt he might be able to go on alone.

Apparently playing music on the tape recorder during art work, modeling, cutting and pasting, also has a calming effect on students. One teacher commented that this changed tigers into lambs. However, it is hard to "sell" this practice to administrators. One commented, "The teachers will think I'm crazy." A second was concerned about parental reaction. A third objected on the grounds that "there's enough noise already. We don't need to fabricate any." Still another wanted to know, "Am I running a school or an afternoon recreation center?" Most asked the standard question, "Where do you think we're going to get all those tape recorders?"

The Role of the Administrator

It is no easier for teachers to learn new things than it is for children. They need support from teamwork with other teachers and help from administrators as well. Regular team planning, first with a consultant or administrator, and then with other teachers, provides a source of strength. Teachers learn not only that two heads are better than one, but also that sharing ideas reduces the amount of research, and dividing the work on production of materials and devices reduces the "chorework": one makes a bibliography, another duplicates a story, and the third makes the preliminary visit to plan for a class trip. For new teachers who have not yet collected appropriate materials, team planning is necessary for survival.

Teamwork also helps teachers to be supportive of each other. Sharing a new process while it is being attempted builds confidence. Further, teamwork reduces fear of failure, for it demonstrates that other teachers also have problems. However, teamwork cannot flourish without administrative support. It requires appropriate scheduling for free periods and appropriate distribution of materials.

Perhaps the greatest contribution administrators can make is to support experimentation. Experimentation always involves some risks and hazards—the risk of making errors, the hazard of replacing "tried and true" skills with new ones. Administrators need to support teachers in such periods of transition, and to allow for the relatively slow pace that it takes to perfect new strategies of learning and teaching. Most teachers, as well as administrators, expect too much too soon and give up before the new practice has had time to ripen and to become fully productive.

Experimentation also involves creating flexible work teams instead of depending on the usual "standing committees" to invent and install innovations. It requires establishing new channels of face-to-face communication, ways of discovering leadership, and new ways of using existing leadership in the school. There is psychological resistance to considering teachers as experts to help other teachers, and to arranging free time for this purpose.

Finally, any innovation requires some outside consultant help, if for no other purpose than to articulate problems that are difficult for insiders to see or to express. Outside consultants also can gather more differences in points of view, perceive more problems and view them more objectively, than can those who have lived with the situation for a long time. An especially useful consultant function is that of establishing a methodological sequence in planning and testing new programs, such as having a careful diagnosis precede plans, and planning precede action.

BIBLIOGRAPHY

Brink, Carol, *Caddie Woodlawn* (New York: Macmillan Co., 1935).

Bulla, Clyde Robert, *Down the Mississippi* (New York: Thomas Y. Crowell Co., 1954).

———, *White Sails to China* (New York: Thomas Y. Crowell Co., 1955).

Hechinger, F. N., "Head Start to Where," *Saturday Review* (December 18, 1965), pp. 48–59.

Schulz, Charles, *Happiness Is a Warm Puppy* (San Francisco: Determined Publications, 1962).

16 BUILDING MORALE IN TEACHERS OF THE DEPRIVED

IRVING R. MELBO AND DAVID W. MARTIN

The areas of greatest concern to administrators, as they view the role of teachers, frequently encompass a range of behavior that can be subsumed under the rubric, *morale*. This is especially true when they work with teachers in depressed urban areas, and most observers have stressed the presence of low morale among these teachers:

They [the teachers] are bewildered and desperate; they feel they cannot reach these children. . . .[1]

. . . a more subtle teachers' strike, nation-wide in scope, has been going on for years. It cannot be ended by a court injunction, for it consists of the refusal of experienced teachers to remain in difficult schools and of new teachers to accept appointments to them.[2]

Added to the educational importance of slum schools is the demoralization of many teachers who staff them.[3]

Principals continually report that it is difficult to keep good teachers in the schools in the poorer areas of the city.[4]

. . . one of the great concerns consistently voiced by principals of difficult schools is their inability to keep teachers.[5]

Although the existence of low morale among teachers in depressed urban areas is recognized, studies of the nature and extent of morale are few. Without such studies, efforts to improve teacher morale will be difficult and will remain fragmented. Fragmentation is too often characteristic of current approaches to the education of slum children.

The conceptual model which was chosen for this study, derived from the work of Guba and Bidwell,[6] has been modified as a result of ongoing research at the University of Southern California.

Irving R. Melbo and David W. Martin, "Building Morale in Teachers of the Deprived," *The Educationally Retarded and Disadvantaged* (Sixty-sixth Yearbook of the National Society for the Study of Education, Part I), pp. 328–349. Reprinted by permission of the publisher.

Factors Involved in Morale

Essentially, there are four basic factors involved in any morale situation:

1. *Rationality* (R). Role expectations must be perceived by institutional members as a sensible means for attaining the goals of the institution.

2. *Commitment* (C_1). These goals must be perceived by institutional members as those which conform to their own personal needs.

3. *Acceptance* (A). Each institutional member must feel his acceptance by other institutional members, and this acceptance must be clearly communicated.

4. *Coaptation* (C_2). Institutional members must perceive prescriptions as being consonant with their capabilities; concomitantly, the institutional prescriptions must be sufficiently flexible to accommodate each individual.

Morale, then, is a function of four factors (R, C_1, A, and C_2) which can be expressed algebraically as $M = f(R \cdot C_1 \cdot A \cdot C_2)$.

Operational Definition of Morale

Morale within an institution may be operationally determined by the total attrition rate of its members (how long individuals and groups of individuals remain in it). Urban schools in lower-class areas have long been noted for high turnover rates in personnel:

. . . the "difficult," the "special services," the "project" schools reveal the highest turnover rates. . . .[7]

A study of the career patterns of Chicago public school teachers documents the fact that teachers normally begin their careers in lower-class neighborhoods and transfer out as soon as they can.[8]

When low morale is found in teachers, it is usually found in students too. Thus, low income in any community may affect the morale of both teachers and students. Data collected by the Bureau of Census suggest that 70 per cent of all dropouts come from families whose income is below $5,000.00 a year.[9]

Besides attrition rates, other indices of low teacher morale can be found in these schools: greater utilization of faculty sick-leave;

tardiness of and early departure by teachers; and unwillingness to participate in activities other than assigned duties.

The attrition rate itself can be readily demonstrated by data on resignations, dismissals, transfers, and the like. Sometimes, however, transfer and other policies may make it difficult or impossible to accurately gauge these factors.

Even if teacher-transfer policies are liberal, there often are variables which make transfers or requests for transfers inadequate indices of morale; for example, the proximity of the school to the teacher's residence and apathy.

One promising lead for measuring morale is found in military studies in which the factor of fear is stressed.

Fear is the major reason why many young teachers do not accept appointments to city schools. They are afraid they will be trapped in a "blackboard jungle"; they are afraid of physical attack; they are afraid that they cannot deal with the situations they will meet in the schools; and they are afraid they will have to spend their days being policemen rather than teachers.[10]

In a significant study of military morale during World War II, a key question was one which asked for an estimate from front-line troops as to the number of days a soldier could be expected to carry on at the front without a loss in efficiency.[11] We might similarly ask teachers: How long do you think the average teacher can teach in this school with maximum efficiency? Preliminary studies conducted at the University of Southern California indicate that these estimates may provide an excellent measure of general morale.

Morale indices may reflect the general atmosphere of the school which gives a clue to one source of either high or low morale. Morale indices are analogous to a thermometer which measures a symptom of ill-health; for the specific cause, one must turn to another source of information—behavior. Of course, for the etiology of poor morale, one must consider factors other than attrition.

The Factor of Rationality

Every institution, being goal-directed, has evolved behavioral expectations designed to achieve its goals. It is obvious that, for high morale to exist, the factor of rationality (R) must include a clear understanding of the goals of the institution and the means of achieving them.

Schools in depressed urban areas have often been characterized by low morale because confusion has affected both their goals and their means of achieving them. When the question, "educate for what?" is asked, ambiguities follow. Traditionally, schools have been middle-class institutions, staffed by personnel with middle-class perspectives, and populated chiefly by students of the middle classes; hence, the goals of the school have been determined by the value structure of that middle class.

With the growth of universal secondary education, our schools enrolled increasingly large numbers of students who represented divergent value structures. Since that time there has been disagreement as to the goals of the schools, particularly of those in depressed areas.

Some believe that it is wrong to emphasize a middle-class way of life since no one can demonstrate that this way is necessarily better than a lower-class way. It is true that many teachers observe that lower-class neighborhoods often contain unpainted homes, weed- and trash-filled yards, while at the same time a shiny new car may be parked by many of the houses. These teachers are critical of what they see, but those who take the relativity-of-value position may state, "Sure, so what? Who is to say that going in debt for a new car is any worse than going in debt for a new house in the suburbs? Who is to say that spending your weekend polishing the car is less desirable than spending the weekend manicuring the front lawn?"

The aim of teachers who look askance at the dilapidated house and yard with the new car in front may be to turn the schools into vehicles to get students to nice, neat homes in the suburbs.

Although these positions are extremes, they nevertheless represent prevailing attitudes. Neither is consonant with an overarching value of "free choice," for what we desire in a pluralistic society is the freedom of individuals to operate within a spectrum of value systems. In that case, students may look at houses in the suburbs along with the privileges and limitations of a middle-class way of life and choose this way of life; or they may look at the slum houses and the privileges and limitations of the lower-class way and choose them.

Before a student decides on one of these ways of life, he should have the skills to cope with his choice. The usual response of a middle-class person to this observation is: "What do you mean? It is the middle-class way of life that requires all the skills; it doesn't take any skill to be poor!"

It may not take much skill to become poor, but it certainly takes skill and knowledge to survive in the culture of poverty. Concerning the Negro who, in America, has lived longer in poverty than the Caucasian, Harrington quotes a Los Angeles welfare worker's remarks:

"Negroes live better on relief than whites. The whites will spend a major portion of their budgets on a roast and then live on spaghetti, macaroni, or potatoes. The Negroes, as members of the poorer group, have a much more balanced diet of cheap food, even if it is fatback and greens. The result is that whites are much more prone to the classic health problems of poverty (overweight, anemia, and cardiac diseases) than Negroes." [12]

It takes skill in learning the ins and outs of getting welfare; it takes skill in learning to extract every penny out of your environment: where to get second-hand clothes and day-old bread; how to avoid bill collectors. All that it would take to convince middle-class teachers of how much skill is needed to survive in a culture of poverty would be to thrust them in it and to let them attempt to eke out an existence with the money available to a typical slum-dweller. Such experiments with other professional people, such as social workers and ministers, have been tried in slum areas of New York and Los Angeles with dramatic results.

For instance, were we to have a situation in which, at the magical age of twenty-one, one-fifth of our children—with no choice in the matter—would be randomly selected to live in the slums, we would count on our schools offering a course in "slum living," which would be neither short nor easy. But the fact is that one-fifth of our children already live in slum areas, and they are getting the course at home. These children need a school course in middle-class living, one which is not forced upon them but which will help them become middle class if they later decide to do so.

Granted, teaching this course may have the effect of inducing students to choose a middle-class existence, but this is not necessarily so; studies indicate that even though people *are* aware of differences between groups, they do not consequently adopt the views of outsiders, even when the others are believed to be better off.

What would be some of the ingredients of the course in middle-class living? Obviously they would include all of the necessary tool subjects, such as the three R's (for middle-class people have more than minimal competence in these); speech therapy (to allow these children to produce *at will* middle-class speech); material on middle-class dress, behavior, and the like; and knowledge of vocational opportunities—in short, all the requisites these children would need in order to function within a middle-class world, *should they choose* to do so. We cannot wait until *they* make the choice because, first of all, they may need the course to make the choice and, secondly, certain physiological and psychological developments may make the course too difficult to teach them at older ages. For example, learned reproduction of middle-class speech patterns, like a foreign language, is best acquired early in life.

It is here that we can discover the utility of separating rationality as a morale factor from the other factors involved; for morale to be high in this respect, the individual *need not* accept the goals of the institution but should understand what they are and accept as rational what the institution does to attain them. The role of the teacher, then, is to make clear the goals of the school and, where they may diverge from the individual's goals, make clear that what the school requires makes sense in terms of the school's goals. Accordingly:

The successful teacher . . . sets clearly defined limits for his pupils and will brook few transgressions. He is aware that, unlike middle-class children, they rarely respond to exhortations intended to control behavior through invoking feelings of guilt and shame. He, therefore, sets the rules, fixes the boundaries, establishes the routines with a minimum of discussion. Here he is impersonal, undeviating, strict, but never punitive.[13]

Exhortations involving guilt and shame are sometimes effective with middle-class children because they are committed to the goals of the school; lower-class children are not necessarily so committed, and, with them, what must be appealed to is the sensibleness of structure and limits.

Similarly, teachers should be brought to realize that "the teacher is a member of a bureaucratic system in which the basic content which he teaches, the norms of behavior of students and teachers, the goals of teaching, and the evaluation of students are established for all to follow." [14]

Morale, however, will fall in a situation in which the goals are not made clear and the means for achieving them are not seen as attainable.

Equally important to seeing the rationality of the means is the provision of adequate measures for its attainment. This has not been especially important in middle-class schools where the reinforcement of home learning has made steady school achievement obvious to the teacher, even in some cases concealing handicapping school practices. In lower-class schools, it is the home and community that are usually responsible for handicapping the child, and we must devise instruments to measure the efficacy of school practices.

Also, where new means are introduced, teachers must be shown concretely the operation and the importance of these new procedures. Concreteness involves the actual observation of successful operation of the procedure. In Compton (California), where a highly successful communication-skills project has been developed, substitutes are hired so that teachers can be freed to observe other teachers in the project as well as their own students having a successful experience.

Industrial research also casts doubt on the effectiveness of procedures by which groups are permitted or encouraged to set goals for themselves without having information relative to what is actually possible. Morale can be quite high in such a group, but production quite low.[15]

In summary, rationality requires: (a) an understanding of what the goals of the school are; (b) an understanding of what the means of achieving these goals are; and (c) an evaluation as to the effectiveness of these means.

Measurement of the factor of rationality within a school or school system can be accomplished by instruments measuring the congruence of understanding between the evaluations by superordinates and subordinates.

The Factor of Commitment

Corresponding in importance to the goals of the institution are the needs of individuals, and morale on the commitment factor (C) is related to the degree of congruence between institutional goals and individual needs.

Individuals vary extensively in their need-structures, and no institution can be expected to accommodate completely to the needs of the individual within it. Obviously, the differing need-structures of individuals imply that some individuals will have more and some will have fewer needs satisfied within any given institution; therefore, personal need-satisfaction within the institution determines each individual's commitment.

Means of Increasing Commitment of Personnel

An institution can increase the commitment of its personnel in at least six important ways: (a) *Goal profusion*—the quantity of goals can be increased, thereby making it possible for more individuals to meet their needs. (b) *Goal extension*—goals can be widened to increase the likelihood of more individuals satisfying their needs. (c) *Goal specialization*—individuals within the institution can be allowed to spend more time on those activities which meet their needs and less on those which do not. (d) *Personnel selection*—institutions can select individuals whose need-structures already fit institutional goals. (e) *Personnel indoctrination*—institutions can modify the existing needs of individuals to coincide more closely with institutional goals. (f) *Personnel education*—institutions can assist individuals to perceive how their need-structures can be met by institutional goals.

Goal Profusion.—Goal profusion, especially for the students, must take place within schools in depressed urban areas simply because other institutions, particularly the family and the community, often fail to provide the need-satisfactions. For example, when children come from environments which fail to provide the basic background needed for beginning reading, the schools must start before kindergarten to develop the conceptual structures needed by these children; when children come from emotionally deprived homes, the schools must provide them with mental health services or, at the least, with warm acceptance by the school personnel; when children come from disorganized environments, the school must supply structure, regularity, and predictability. In instances in which children come from environments where basic physical needs are inadequately met, the school must assist in feeding and clothing them. Although the role of the teacher is to expedite such goal profusion within the classroom, it is quite clear that those teachers whose personal needs are chiefly for intellectual gratification are not particularly suitable for these children. As one teacher put it, "There are teachers who want to teach *history* to children, and there are others who want to teach *children* history. It is the latter who do the most meaningful job with deprived children or, for that matter, with any kind of handicapped child." [16]

Within the classrooms of teachers whose primary needs are for intellectual gratification, morale (as related to commitment) is usually quite low for both the teachers and their students.

Goal Extension.—Goals may be conceived as either narrow or wide. One important area for goal extension, particularly for teachers in slum schools, is found in opportunities to achieve status both within and without the institution. As Margaret Mead points out, one way to increase the status of teachers in a society, which is so unique that one value can be equated with any other value through the medium of money, is to increase the monetary reward for their services, since the evidence is quite clear that the work is much more difficult in depressed urban schools than in any others.

School systems can follow the lead either of Detroit, which made it possible for slum-area teachers to obtain university credit for workshop participation, or of systems in which individuals indicating their commitment by Saturday or summer participation are paid more. If neither of these alternatives is possible, still another resides in released time.

Still further opportunity for increasing teacher status is through promotion, and one avenue to promotion is team teaching. As Rivlin points out:

Team teaching may enable urban schools to retain experienced classroom teachers by opening avenues of promotion that do not lead them away from the classroom. There is motivational value, too, in letting experienced teachers see that the insight and skill they have gained are being recognized by the assignment of inexperienced teachers to work with them and learn from them.[17]

Another important goal extension for both teachers and students would be their sharing in determining their institution's goals. If we seriously consider making teachers expert in understanding children, we must treat these teachers as experts and free them to innovate, experiment, and modify programs within their classrooms. In the past we have followed a trickle-down practice in educational innovation. Research was initiated in upper- and middle-class schools, and seldom did the results filter through the system to lower-class schools. Moreover, teachers in lower-class schools did not have the status of their counterparts in the middle-class schools. What we now need is a change in this practice; research and innovation should take place in the lower-class schools, and the results should move upward, too. Prestige and status should be given teachers in lower-class schools.

In instances in which goal extensions have been encouraged through active participation by teachers and students, significant increase in commitment (and hence morale) of personnel has occurred.

Goal Specialization.—Some needs are obviously more important than others to an individual; therefore, to increase commitment, the institution should provide differential opportunities for its personnel. For example, most teachers resent clerical duties; and since teachers in many depressed-area schools frequently encounter disciplinary and other time-consuming problems, help in the resented routine responsibilities might well be provided. The hiring of teacher-aides also reduces the load, and the teacher is freed to concentrate on educational goals.

Also, if the educational experiences of the students in lower-class schools are enriched to compensate for conspicuous lacks, the teaching load of teachers should be significantly reduced. It is unwise to expect the teacher of thirty-five elementary students in a depressed-area school to do what a teacher is doing for a similar number of children in a middle-class school.

Personnel Selection.—Commitment is more readily achieved when the institution is able to select personnel whose needs are congruent with institutional goals. As Haubrich points out, not all teachers we train have goals that are consonant with teaching in depressed-area schools.

> . . . the traditional view of teacher preparation has an appeal to certain kinds of students with certain kinds of goals and ambitions. The student who is looking for a type of security, who wishes a relatively easy road to professional status, who has family and home pressures to get "something practical" from college, and the student who may feel that teaching is a second or subsidiary choice among occupational goals—all of these may enter teaching.[18]

What is especially needed now are suitable instruments for measuring a teacher's effectiveness with the students in depressed areas; however, it is to be noted that in industry paper-and-pencil tests are much less adequate or effective than techniques which measure personnel effectiveness in actual situations. A most useful technique, as demonstrated in a Hunter College program, is to choose volunteers who have a firsthand acquaintance with the situation for which they are volunteering and later to train and evaluate them on the job.

In the past, a kind of student selection operated (and still does in some areas) which drove out students whose needs did not seem to be congruent with school goals. In a democratic society, which sets as an all-encompassing goal the education of *all* its people, such a solution to the morale problem is becoming less tenable. We must, therefore, rely on other means.

Personnel Indoctrination.—One way for an institution to achieve congruence between its goals and the needs of its personnel is simply to attempt to force modification in the needs of individuals. Such practices, which predominate in such institutions as hospitals or prisons, have been used in some depressed-area schools. However, such coercive practices are antithetical to the goals of our society.

There are situations in depressed-area schools in which indoctrination is prescribed (for example, when individuals violate norms that seriously restrict the rights of others to be educated). This holds both for students and teachers; in the latter case, indoctrination may be attempted with tenured teachers who cannot be transferred and whose violations are not serious enough to warrant their dismissal.

Personnel Education.—The method of achieving congruence between institutional goals and individual needs that is the most compatible with our cultural and societal values is to help individuals perceive how institutional goals can assist them in meeting their basic needs.

Such help is especially desirable for children in depressed-area schools. As the Research Conference on Education and Cultural Deprivation points out:

> . . . the culturally deprived child has difficulty in learning for its own sake and in learning for the approval of an adult. He values things and activities which are concrete and which have immediate and tangible rewards. He has difficulty in seeing the relevance of much of school learning since he is unable to comprehend fully or accept the deferred and symbolic gratification that the middle-class child has come to accept.[19]

This does not mean that the teacher operates solely within the value structure of the child; instead, it means that the teacher has to start where the child is. We agree with the comment of Ravitz:

> It is absurd, too, for a middle-class teacher to set these children down each day to try to focus their attention on ancient history or on the multiplication tables or on nouns or verbs, when simple good sense demands a concern with situations and circumstances under which these children live. . . .[20]

If the middle-class values of teachers in these schools stand in the way of their students' learning, the teachers must be brought to a personal confrontation with values—not to change them, but to be made aware of them and the points at which they conflict with other value systems.

Commitment within the institution can be determined by a variety of measures. The time which an individual spends *voluntarily* within the institution or on any specific activity is a rough measure of his commitment to the institution or to that particular activity. Assuming the institution does not mandatorily burden personnel with work which necessitates overtime, the number of people engaged in working after regulation hours provides a rough index of commitment.

When schools make their facilities available during evenings and on weekends for voluntary participation in their programs, the relative amounts of use of these facilities provide another commitment index.

A more exacting measure of commitment is being studied at the University of Southern California by using a Q-sort technique to measure the congruence between institutional goal hierarchies as determined by superordinates and as determined by subordinates. Also, techniques utilizing both questionnaires and observation are being developed to measure relative teacher effectiveness.

Acceptance as a Factor in Morale

Within the school there must be a feeling of mutual respect on the part of all of the people within it. In schools in depressed urban areas the lack of respect by many teachers for their students has been repeatedly noted as a major source of problems:

. . . this author has frequently heard teachers say in private that the "others," usually children from lower-income groups, aren't worth bothering much about and that the best you can do is keep them quiet and busy.[21]

. . . among many of the teachers who are required to teach children from culturally deprived backgrounds there exists a pervasive negative attitude toward these children. These teachers say repeatedly, and appear to believe, that it is not possible to teach these children. They offer, in support of their conclusion, the belief that these children cannot learn because of "poor heredity," "poor home background," "cultural deprivation," and "low I.Q." [22]

Lack of acceptance goes beyond failure to accept for any specific cause. Sometimes it involves a rather complete rejection of the student's many-sided nature.

Davidson and Lang found that some teachers were unfavorably inclined toward deprived children even when their school achievements were good. Furthermore, those investigators observed that the underprivileged children perceived the teachers' rejection of them.[23]

Achieving Greater Acceptance

Student morale under such conditions is low, indeed. Now the question is, what can be done about it? First of all, the school can initiate a program of in-service training designed to modify the teachers' perceptions of and attitudes toward these students. Second, after the school has accurately evaluated the results of this in-service program, it can proceed to dismiss or to transfer to another cultural milieu those teachers who are incapable of accepting these students. It has become clear that the presence of such teachers will insidiously sabotage school programs and seriously lower morale.

Programs and Practices.—In-service training programs designed to foster acceptance of lower-class children should not rely on the traditional method of utilizing a visiting expert functioning in a typical lecture or classroom situation. It should focus, instead, on the personal involvement of teachers in the community.

At the University of Southern California, we are experimenting with a program which has been labeled "The Image and Sound of Society and the Schools." Teachers and teacher-interns are provided with cameras and tape recorders and, in cooperation with local community agencies, are sent into depressed areas to record in documentary fashion what they think they see. Their initial report provides an excellent projective measure of their attitudes toward the community. Since taking a picture always involves a choice, unconscious negative attitudes toward the community are often revealed by their choices. The analysis and structuring of their perceptions are thus made easier.

From this beginning, the program moves to an experience which is research-oriented. The staff works on projects of an action-research nature in cooperation with either the school or a community agency. This experience is designed to induce an attitude toward the school and the community which is more objective than the attitude that these persons have customarily shown.

This experience is based on the assumption that "like the anthropologist, the successful teacher views the alien culture of his pupils, not as a judge, but as a student. He understands the backgrounds from which the children come, the values placed on various achievements, the kind of work and life to which they aspire." [24]

In-service training programs which are designed to foster acceptance in teachers, while concentrating on modification of the attitudes of rejecting teachers, should not neglect two other types of teachers who maintain attitudes which inhibit acceptance: (a) the teacher who believes acceptance can be attained by becoming "one of the boys," and (b) the overtly patronizing teacher.

We have recognized for some time that, regardless of the cultural milieu, the ineffective teacher is often one who attempts to establish an equality relationship with students. Leadership studies show that effective leaders must maintain a certain distance between themselves and their followers. This is particularly true when the group is formally involved in their tasks. Also, studies of such widely divergent groups as basketball teams and surveying parties indicate that the most successful groups chose leaders who were relatively distant and reserved.[25]

If the middle-class teacher who establishes a peer relationship with middle-class students is ineffectual, the middle-class teacher who attempts to establish the same relationship with lower-class students is often ludicrous. Such a teacher is misled into believing that he is highly accepted by students because the students laugh and seem to enjoy his company: their reserve seems to disappear when he is about, and he feels he is among friends. Actually he is sometimes accepted for his entertainment value, and lower-class students may display attitudes toward him similar to those that the upper class shows toward the *nouveau riche*.

An informal study of student attitudes toward teaching personnel in a local junior high school recently uncovered such an attitude toward a vice-principal who made a fetish of using "jive" talk while affecting a "buddy-buddy" attitude toward students. To the superficial observer, he actually seemed to be well-liked as he traveled through the school. Students, however, actually developed an active dislike for him or regarded him as a clown. Unfortunately, he is an active proselyter for his approach, and he attempts to convince other personnel that his brand of "understanding" is the way to reach students.

The patronizing teacher, too, is ineffectual with lower-class students. The individual who comes into a low-class environment with an attitude of dispensing largesse to the "natives" will meet with failure because the students recognize that such an attitude indicates that he believes they are inferior and unworthy.

In spite of what many people believe, the phrase "not charity, but a chance" has real meaning for these students. Goodman points out what happens when we substitute charity for the chance:

Consider the following by the Executive Director of the New York City Mission Society: "We have experimented for two summers with employment of 100 to 150 teenagers from high delinquency areas. . . . Our $10-per-week employees all stayed out of trouble. . . . [But] on the occasions we tried what were essentially "make work" jobs, the young people understood this immediately and lost all interest.[26]

Teachers should realize that unless students recognize that they are respected by their teachers, little acceptance will occur. It is not enough that teachers feel respect for these students; teachers must communicate their feeling to them. The necessity for such communication is made clear by studies of both military and family morale. In a military study, the one distinguishing feature of high-morale combat units was the feeling of the enlisted men that their officers cared about them; in a family study, members of high-morale families were also characterized by caring for each other; however, many members of low-morale families also cared for each other, but they were differentiated from the high-morale families by *their failure to communicate their feelings to each other.*

In making teachers aware of the necessity for communicating acceptance, it is also necessary to stress the nonverbal, informal aspects of behavior. Teachers usually come from highly verbal environments; teachers are trained in institutions that are almost completely verbal; and, hence, teachers come to rely almost entirely upon verbalization as a means of communication.

This reliance probably contributes to the gulf that separates teachers in depressed urban schools from their students. Teachers must be taught to observe their own and their students' nonverbal behavior and to respond to and use this form of communication successfully.

Another aspect of acceptance important to school personnel is the deliberate fostering of a "we-feeling" that extends beyond the boundaries of the individual classrooms into the community. As the Educational Policies Commission puts it:

> . . . a community of interest between teacher and parents can in some cases do more to improve a child's school work or behavior than all the remedial and punitive measures at the school's command. This community of interest can be developed when parents sense that the school is genuinely interested in the welfare of their children, that meeting with school people can be pleasant and useful, and that respect for all human beings is, in fact, the hallmark of the public school.[27]

Teachers must get out of the classroom and into the community; the community cannot be expected to make the first move. For extra duty, however, teachers should either be released from school duties or should receive extra compensation.

Also, in depressed-area schools, special extracurricular student activities should be encouraged. Studies of the quantity of extracurricular activities indicate that fewer take place in lower-class than in middle-class areas. It is in the former areas that these activities are probably more crucial in fostering acceptance.

Teachers, too, should be encouraged to participate in informal staff activities, although, owing to residential patterns, this is often difficult; middle-class teachers usually do not live in the lower-class areas in which they teach. Faculty dispersion occurs much more in depressed urban-area schools than in others. Industrial morale studies indicate that the social integration of management and workers is best generated and sustained outside the work situation.

Measuring Student and Staff Acceptance

Measuring the factor of student and staff acceptance within the school can be accomplished by the use of several instruments. Within the classroom, standard sociometric devices are effective. In making such sociometric studies of their staffs, administrators, by utilizing committee assignments, can have staff personnel indicate personal preferences.

If various minorities are represented in a school, prejudice within the student body toward racial and ethnic groups can be studied by modifications of the *Bogardus Social Distance Scale.*

The records of the quantity and quality of attendance at extra-curricular functions on the part of the students, as well as of informal gatherings of the faculty, also are sources of information.

When the community is brought into the school, periodic checks by means of personal interviews can provide information as to shifts in the quality of community acceptance.

It is important to realize that because acceptance in a group is high, it does not necessarily follow that morale *from the institution's viewpoint* is high. Acceptance can rise and be extremely high in a situation in which a group is organized *in opposition* to the institution.

Coaptation in Relation to Morale

A factor that has contributed significantly to low morale in many depressed urban-area schools involves, on the one hand, the personnel's feeling that they are incapable of accomplishing their tasks, and, on the other hand, the institution's failure to appraise realistically what its personnel are capable of doing.

Teaching in a middle-class school is a world apart from teaching in a lower-class school, and teachers simply have not been adequately prepared for the undertaking; they often feel incapable and, hence, insecure. As Haubrich states:

The incoming teacher probably rejects the situation because of an inability to comprehend, understand, *and cope with* the multiple problems of language, development, varying social norms, habits not accepted by the teacher, behavior which is often not success-oriented, lack of student "cooperation," and achievement levels well below expectancies. . . .[28]

The problem is further complicated by the fact that well-trained and qualified teachers are not employed frequently in these schools. In Sexton's study of a major urban-area school system, it was found that "Almost one out of every ten teachers in the lowest-income high school is an emergency substitute working on a regular assignment."[29]

If teachers feel insecure, it is often because the school's administration has failed to adequately recognize that the goal of teaching these children requires a revised set of role prescriptions.

Until recently, if one desired to visit an educational museum, the nearest depressed-area school would probably have served adequately for the visit: the relic would include the building, its lighting, equipment, textbooks, and—most tragically—the teaching techniques.

But the lack of coaptation is not only confined to teachers; students in these schools are often made to feel inadequate and unworthy, not necessarily because they are inferior to their middle-class counterparts, but because they must function in an institution that furnishes them with alien materials, an institution that treats them as aliens—and inferior aliens at that.

When an institution operates as if its students are inferior, a lowering of academic standards often results; this is reflected by a decrease in student aspiration, which, in turn, is mirrored by a further decrease in standards, and so on in an ever descending spiral.

Another effect of the lowering of academic standards is the accumulation in these schools of teachers who because of inferior ability, laziness, or apathy—or any combination of these—find a haven for their inferiority, since all that may be required in such a school is a person who maintains a minimum of order and creates no administrative problems; continuous progress by students is not really anticipated by either the teachers or the school's administrators. For these teachers, morale within the factor of coaptation can be high: they perceive institutional prescriptions as being entirely consonant with their capabilities, and where few institutional prescriptions exist, great flexibility is often present.

To insure a high level of morale with regard to coaptation, an assessment of two items is necessary: (a) the role requirements for personnel within the institution must be determined; and (b) the abilities of personnel to fulfill these requirements must be assessed. To alter coaptation, then, either the role requirements must be changed or the abilities of the personnel must be upgraded, or both of these must be done.

With regard to the determination of role requirements for school personnel, little has been accomplished, particularly for teachers. This task is still to be finished, although the Teacher Education and Media (TEAM) Project of the American Association of Colleges of Teacher Education has made some progress in this direction through its attempts to restructure teacher education. Neither have valid ways to assess teacher abilities been devised, nor can they be until after the role-requirement analysis has been completed.

One need not, however, wait until role determinations and ability assessments are validly made to make some gains. Currently we know enough to state unequivocally that the tasks of teachers in depressed urban-area schools are substantially more difficult and complex than in middle-class areas and that the ability of teachers in these schools needs marked upgrading.

First of all, we know that the students who are in these schools suffer substantially from a host of academically handicapping problems arising from the cultural milieu in which they live: conceptual and, hence, language-formation difficulties; autistic behavior at one extreme and restlessness at another; emotional instability; and deficiencies in such basic needs as sleep, diet, and the like.

It is unrealistic to assume that any teacher can handle all of these problems alone. Depressed-area schools must operate, then, with much more role specialization than middle-class schools. Schools in New York, for example, have reading-improvement teachers, teachers for non-English-speaking children, junior guidance teachers who work with children of normal intelligence who have emotional problems, teacher specialists for the mentally retarded, and substitute auxiliary teachers to link the school with the home. In addition, there is access to psychologists, psychiatrists, medical doctors and nurses, and student tutors.[30]

In contrast, the California educational system is handicapped by an unrealistic state law which ties the number of elementary-school personnel to a teacher-student classroom ratio. Hence, instead of being able to increase role specialization, the elementary schools have, in some cases, been forced to eliminate special music and art teachers from their staffs.

Where role specialization exists, teachers can concentrate on using their special competencies instead of attempting to be all things to their students. It is naïve to assume, however, that placing specialists in a school will necessarily result in teacher-utilization of their services. Teachers must be trained to use these services. Much additional training is needed to break down the prevailing attitude that a referral to a specialist is a reflection on a teacher's competency.

Teachers also have to be trained to spot situations which call for a particular specialist. For example, teachers traditionally have received much more training in psychology than in sociology or anthropology. This has resulted in their perceiving students' behavior problems as being "psychological." Actually, the problems are much more often a product of social conditions and call for the services of specialists other than psychologists. This is particularly true in depressed-area schools.

Role specialization need not, however, rely on the introduction of specialists. Schools can take advantage of the unique abilities and talents of their present personnel and employ various forms of team teaching. Also, closed-circuit television can be used to introduce the specialists.

Before worthwhile in-service training of teachers can occur, reliance upon lectures given by experts to groups of tired teachers must go. Instead of listening to lectures, teachers must personally observe other teachers experience success with the same kind of students they teach, even, if possible, with the same students they teach. Among other values, this may lead teachers to realize that the inability of their students to learn often resides, not in the students, but in their own incompetencies.

The precise measurement of the morale factor of coaptation, as suggested previously, requires first the operational definition of role requirements and of personnel abilities. Such is not possible at present. However, rough instruments for the evaluation of personnel can be constructed, or existing ones can be employed with reservations. For example, superordinates can make use of an instrument first, and then subordinates can be asked to evaluate themselves with the same form. The congruence between the two evaluations can provide a rough measure of coaptation. A lack of congruence will furnish a basis for the discussion of problems. Similarly, in the classroom, a comparison of grades given by teachers compared with pupil estimates of their grades tends to perform a similar function.

The complex task of building morale in teachers will require a number of approaches. Some of these have been identified or are being recognized; some are being effectively used in situations that permit their use.

NOTES

1. Leonard Kornberg, "Meaningful Teachers for Alienated Children," *Education in Depressed Areas*, p. 265. Edited by A. Harry Passow. New York: Bureau of Publications, Teachers College, Columbia University, 1962.

2. Harry N. Rivlin, *Teachers for Our Big City Schools*, p. 3. New York: Anti-Defamation League of B'nai B'rith.

3. Clemmont E. Vontress, "Our Demoralizing Slum Schools," *The Schools and the Urban Crisis*, p. 61. Edited by August Kerber and Barbara Bommarito. New York: Holt, Rinehart & Winston, 1965.

4. Frank Riessman, *The Culturally Deprived Child*, p. 17. New York: Harper & Bros., 1962.

5. Miriam L. Goldberg, "Factors Affecting Educational Attainment in Depressed Urban Areas," *Education in Depressed Areas, op. cit.,* p. 79.

6. Egon G. Guba and Charles E. Bidwell, *Administrative Relationships: Teacher Effectiveness, Teacher Satisfaction, and Administrative Behavior*. University of Chicago, Midwest Administration Center Studies in Educational Administration, No. 4. Chicago: the Center, 1957.

7. "Teachers for Depressed Areas," *Education in Depressed Areas, op. cit.,* p. 237.

8. Richard A. Cloward and James A. Jones, "Social Class: Educational Attitudes and Participation," *Education in Depressed Areas, op. cit.,* p. 191.

9. S. M. Miller, "Dropouts—A Political Problem," *The School Dropout*, p. 12. Edited by Daniel Schreiber. Washington: Project: School Dropouts, National Education Association, 1964.

10. Rivlin, *op. cit.,* p. 9.

11. *Panic and Morale*, pp. 296–98. Conference Transactions, the New York Academy of Medicine and the Josiah Macy Jr. Foundation. Edited by Iago Galdston. New York: International Universities Press, 1958.

12. Michael Harrington, *The Other America: Poverty in the United States*, p. 67. New York: Macmillan Co., 1962.

13. Miriam L. Goldberg, "Teachers for Disadvantaged Children," *The Schools and the Urban Crisis, op. cit.,* pp. 234–35.

14. Sloan R. Wayland, "Old Problems, New Faces, and New Standards," *Education in Depressed Areas, op. cit.,* p. 57.

15. *Panic and Morale, op. cit.,* pp. 293–94.

16. Riessman, *op. cit.,* pp. 86–87.

17. Rivlin, *op. cit.,* p. 14.

18. Vernon F. Haubrich, "Teachers for Big-City Schools," *Education in Depressed Areas, op. cit.,* p. 248.

19. Benjamin S. Bloom, Allison Davis, and Robert Hess, *Compensatory Edu-*

cation for Cultural Deprivation, p. 21. New York: Holt, Rinehart & Winston, Inc., 1965.

20. Mel Ravitz, "The Role of the School in the Urban Setting," *Education in Depressed Areas, op. cit.,* p. 16.

21. Patricia Cayo Sexton, *Education and Income,* p. 7. New York: Viking Press, Inc., 1961.

22. Kenneth B. Clark, "Educational Stimulation of Racially Disadvantaged Children," *Education in Depressed Areas, op. cit.,* p. 149.

23. Riessman, *op. cit.,* p. 18.

24. Goldberg, "Teachers for Disadvantaged Children," *op. cit.,* p. 232.

25. Fred Fiedler, "Interpersonal Perception and Group Effectiveness," *Person Perception and Interpersonal Behavior,* pp. 247–49. Edited by Renato Tagiuri and Luigi Pettrullo. Stanford, California: Stanford University Press, 1958.

26. Paul Goodman, *Growing Up Absurd: Problems of Youth in the Organized System,* p. 205. New York: Random House, 1960.

27. *Education and the Disadvantaged American,* p. 29. Washington, D.C.: Educational Policies Commission, National Education Association, 1962.

28. Haubrich, *op. cit.,* p. 246.

29. Sexton, *op. cit.,* p. 212.

30. A. Harry Passow, "Education in Depressed Areas," *Education in Depressed Areas, op. cit.,* p. 346.

17 THE INTEGRATION–
COMPENSATORY EDUCATION
CONTROVERSY

DANIEL U. LEVINE

During the past few years the most important thrust in American education has centered in the need to provide better education for the hundreds of thousands of Negro youngsters who attend segregated schools in low-income neighborhoods in our large cities. First catapulted to national attention by James B. Conant's reference to the "social dynamite" which was accumulating in the urban centers in the early 1960's, disadvantaged youth who participated in widespread disorders in Watts, Chicago, Hough, and elsewhere have since proven that Conant's descriptive phrase was too mild: rather than "social dynamite," the urban centers are facing the equivalent of social "atom bombs." Educators and lay leaders cognizant of the urgency of the situation have responded by pushing to eliminate the segregated patterns of schooling and by organizing special remedial programs that might compensate for the learning handicaps associated with a background of deprivation and poverty.

As both these drives gained momentum in the sixties, it became clear that in some respects they embodied contradictory plans of action which inevitably would create a good deal of controversy. This has happened, and unless we somehow resolve the controversy by placing the whole problem in the perspective of a larger synthesis, the heat generated will limit effectiveness in working to achieve either integration or compensatory education.

To understand why this is so, it is only necessary to review the arguments and examine the implications for action of each position. Many vigorous advocates of integration, on the one hand, begin with the Supreme Court's 1954 generalization that separate

Daniel U. Levine, "Integration-Compensatory Education Controversy," *Educational Forum* (March 1968), pp. 323–332. Reprinted by permission of the author and publisher.

schools can never provide equal educational opportunities for minority group students, if only because the very lack of choice involved in a minority student's *de jure* or *de facto* attendance at a segregated school teaches him that he is not considered "fit" or good enough to participate fully in society. Relying on a solid body of knowledge in psychology and sociology, this position emphasizes the likelihood that an individual whom society has taught to doubt his own worth will not perform as efficiently as the individual with self confidence. The overriding importance of the student's assessment of his own capabilities in nourishing or crippling his performance in the classroom has been explicated as follows:

Of all the forces operating in a school the energy of the learner is the greatest. If it is 'turned on' at full voltage—and directed straight into the task at hand—it is almost irresistible. Even if teaching is mediocre and material resources are meager, the youngster will some-how move ahead. But if it is 'turned off'—or diverted from the task or opposed to it—nothing else matters very much.

That flow of energy is controlled by the learner's perceptions. . . . If a full charge of energy is to be delivered to any learning task, two conditions must prevail: The learner must see the task with clear eyes and sense that it is relevant to his private goals; and he must have faith that he is worthy to tackle it, that he is the kind of person who ought to do this sort of thing and who can do it if he stretches.[1]

If the disadvantaged Negro child is to overcome the debilitating mental effects of nonvoluntary segregation, concludes the strong advocate of integration, it is necessary to end the exclusion that implicitly calls into question his worthiness to claim an equal chance in life. In its implications for practical action, this position suggests that the primary effort in helping the disadvantaged Negro child must be to place him in an integrated school, even though doing so might put him in classes composed mostly of children without serious learning handicaps and would thereby make it very difficult or even impossible to provide special instructional experiences designed to overcome his particular academic deficiencies.

Advocates of compensatory education, conversely, tend to concern themselves not so much with the disadvantaged Negro child's possible sense of exclusion and alienation from the wider society as with the probability that his mental development has been inhibited, if not crippled, by the environment in which he grows up. Recognizing the undeniable fact that our educational system generally has had neither the will nor the knowledge to work effectively with the slow-learning youngster who does not respond very well to standard techniques and programs, they believe that steps must be taken to overcome the pupil's learning handicaps before he is placed in a more or less standard educational environment where he could only be made to feel more inadequate and inferior. The obvious conclusion is that integration could or should be de-emphasized, if not actually postponed, until the pupil has been prepared to function satisfactorily in competition with youngsters who are not handicapped by a disadvantaged background.

Despite the clarity of the difference between the two positions, a number of complications in the argument have emerged. Many advocates of both positions, after all, are sincerely desirous of supporting the program that will be most advantageous for the child, and this means that they cannot completely ignore the apparent logic of opposing points of view. In addition, the logic of each position, if pushed far enough, begins to work against itself in a most curious way. For example, the advocate of integration who argues that quality education is seldom, if ever, attained in an all-Negro school is interpreted as implying that this means there really is something "wrong" or inferior about Negroes. To counteract this conclusion, he may search out examples where educators such as Dr. Samuel Shephard in St. Louis appear to have made great strides in raising the performance of disadvantaged Negro pupils, in order to show that his line of reasoning assumes no inherent inferiority among Negro students. But in so doing he greatly weakens his case. Even if he then argues that integrated education is prerequisite as much or more for social and moral development as for academic understanding (an argument which has much to commend it), his general posture is still much weaker than it would be if he continued to insist on the unequivocal necessity of integration for improved academic achievement.

The advocate of compensatory education, if he is open-minded, is also forced eventually to acknowledge an element of validity in the central position of his opponent. His commitment to the wel-

fare of the disadvantaged Negro child, for one thing, should pre-
dispose him to lend at least some credence to the arguments of
many of those leaders in the Negro community who push vigorously for integration. Even more important, however, is the fact
that as he starts to wrestle with the classroom aspects of a program of compensatory education, he immediately confronts the
fact that the self-concept does play an exceedingly important role
in determining how a student responds to a particular set of learning experiences. Once he does so, it is but a short step to recognizing some validity in his opponent's insistence that a Negro
child can hardly have an adequate self-concept unless given an
opportunity to participate in the affairs of the larger society.

Without a fully developed set of priorities to order the con-
volutions of these two positions, the situation—to say the least—is
confused, and it becomes still more confused as one reviews the
small amount of research that bears on the outcomes of integrated
and of compensatory education. In essence this research con-
founds the critics on each side by suggesting that either compensatory programs or racially integrated school settings *can* result
in academic gains among disadvantaged Negro youth.

With regard to compensatory education, most technically acceptable studies dealing with compensatory programs have failed
to find significant and lasting improvements in experimental
groups as compared with comparable nonexperimental groups
in regular instructional programs (e.g., the final report on the
Higher Horizons Project). The results, in fact, have been discouraging so often as to justify Ivor Kraft's recent capsule history
of the typical compensatory program for an inner-city Negro
school as one that ". . . begins with a fanfare of slogans, proceeds
to a bustle of committees, advances to a much publicized and
photographed new school and smartened-up curriculum, blossoms
into a series of weekly newspaper testimonials, and culminates
after two or three years in a typical inner-city slum school which
has been sucked back into the inner-city slum environment and
forgotten." [2] Emphasizing the failure of so many compensatory
programs, Kraft goes on to conclude that

We are going to have to integrate the schools. There is no other
solution. We are going to have to bring rich and poor, black and white

together under the same roof. . . . Given the contemporary political and social reality of urban American life . . . there is no compensatory device, no neighborhood concept, no idealistic notions of community centers that will keep those schools from being centers of inferiority and backwardness.[3]

Despite the failure of most compensatory projects, however, the available evidence supports an interpretation which is more sanguine than Kraft's. Here and there, that is to say, studies can be found which show compensatory interventions yielding results better than would be predicted on the basis of the previous performance of a group of disadvantaged youth or the performance of similar pupils in a control group, particularly when the students involved have been in the upper fifty percent of their classes (on measures of achievement or motivation) and/or have been in the primary grades or in pre-school classes.[4] Even though they prove the exception rather than the rule, such studies do support the conclusion that compensatory programs can have positive results providing that sufficient attention and resources are devoted to making them effective.

There are few studies dealing with the achievement of Negro pupils in integrated as compared with segregated schools, but the small amount of data which are available tend to indicate that pupils in the former situation do better in school than do comparable pupils in the latter setting.[5] Despite the admittedly incomplete nature of this research, the results are consistent enough to justify the conclusion that integration is more likely to result in improved academic performance on the part of the disadvantaged Negro child than is a compensatory education program, though either approach can have some positive effect, providing it is well implemented.

As regards the relative merits of the two approaches, by far the most important and relevant findings are described in the section on "Comparative Effects of Compensatory Programs and Desegregation" in the invaluable study on *Racial Isolation in the Public Schools,* which the United States Commission on Civil Rights released on February 20, 1967. After first reviewing the results of large-scale compensatory programs in St. Louis, New York, and elsewhere, the Commission emphasized the failure of most such programs in pointing out that

Because the data often were incomplete and the period in which the programs had been in operation was too short, it is not possible to draw absolute conclusions about the relative success or failure of these programs. In most cases, however, the data did not show significant gains in achievement.[6]

In order to assess the relative potency of compensatory as against integrated education, the Commission then proceeded to review programs in four cities (Syracuse, Berkeley, Seattle, and Philadelphia) in which sufficient data had been collected on comparable groups of pupils in each condition to allow for valid comparison. The results were clear cut, and the Commission concluded that while the data do not ". . . suggest that compensatory education is incapable of remedying the effects of poverty on . . . academic achievement . . . [the fact remains] that none of the compensatory programs appear to have raised significantly the achievement of participating pupils . . . ;" disadvantaged Negro youth in the integrated schools in these four cities, on the other hand, appeared to have progressed more rapidly in academic achievement than did comparable pupils in *de facto* segregated schools in each city.[7]

What, then, are we to conclude about the claims of those who primarily favor integrated education or compensatory education? On the one hand, the failure of so many compensatory education projects indicates that it is inordinately difficult to implement such a program successfully, probably because, as the Civil Rights Commission went on to point out, compensatory programs do not in themselves ". . . wholly compensate for the depressing effect which racial and social class isolation have upon the aspirations and self-esteem of Negro students . . . the evidence reviewed here suggests that efforts to improve a child's self-esteem cannot be wholly productive in a student environment which seems to deny his worth." [8] The success of a few compensatory programs such as those referred to above, however, does suggest that the disadvantaged child's particular learning deficits can be remedied sufficiently well to lead to significant gains. When this happens, it must be assumed that even in segregated situations, disadvantaged youth somehow gained greater confidence in their own capabilities, and that strengthened self-image played an important mediating role in making it possible for them to do better in school. Nevertheless, no one has yet succeeded in delineating in any significant detail the particular components or dynamics that are responsible for the success of those compensatory programs that apparently have had some positive impact.

Although our understanding of the dynamic forces at work in the integrated school is hardly more satisfactory than our understanding of the compensatory classroom, the study of equal opportunity conducted and published by the U.S. Office of Education shed much light on the factors that operate to make integrated education a potentially effective means to improve the performance of the disadvantaged Negro child.[9] In brief, the evidence showed that Negro youngsters who had experienced integration tended to have a slightly less positive *academic* self-image than did comparable students receiving their education in all-Negro schools, which apparently push students less hard and are less competitive than the integrated school. The effects of this small difference, however, were more than overbalanced by the fact that the Negro youngsters in integrated schools appeared to possess a stronger *general* self-image in terms of feeling more power over their future and the world around them than did the sample who had experienced only the sense of powerlessness seemingly generated from nonvoluntary segregation. In addition to clarifying the psychological effects of integration, moreover, the study of equal opportunity reported relatively direct evidence supporting the conclusion that integrated education can be a potent force in improving the academic performance of disadvantaged Negro youth. Summarizing this part of their study, the authors conclude that in the many cases in which integration involves the placement of some low-income youth in schools with less disadvantaged students, the achievement of the former group improves with no detriment to the achievement of the latter:

If a minority pupil from a home without much educational strength is put with schoolmates with strong educational backgrounds, his achievement is likely to increase . . . the principal way in which the school environments of Negroes and whites differ is in the composition of their student bodies, and it turns out that the composition of the student bodies has a strong relationship to the achievement of Negro and other minority pupils.[10]

These findings of the equal opportunity study, incidentally, call attention to an important problem which has not been much discussed and which may become a matter of controversy as educators refine their thinking about integrated and compensatory approaches and begin to identify the best tactics for achieving one or the other or both. As indicated in the preceding paragraph, one reason why integrated education can be a promising way to help disadvantaged Negro youth is that integration *per se* appears to exercise a salubrious effect in counteracting a student's sense of exclusion from society. At the same time, however, the equal opportunity study as well as other studies [11] indicate that it is the opportunity to watch and learn from more privileged pupils that is responsible for much of the improved performance often noted among disadvantaged Negro youth placed in integrated classrooms. Thus the evidence presently available suggests that the socioeconomic mixing which usually accompanies integration as well as the racial mixing itself can exert a positive effect on the performance of the low-income minority child. If so, the possibility immediately suggests itself that disadvantaged Negro youth whom it proved impossible to place in integrated classrooms might be helped by a calculated effort to place them in schools with appreciable numbers of middle-income Negro pupils. It is perhaps unlikely that middle-income Negro parents could be persuaded to agree to such a plan, especially since many such parents already are enrolling their youngsters in private and parochial schools precisely in order to remove them from the influence of their disadvantaged peers. It may be confidently predicted, moreover, that few middle-class Negro parents will even listen to such a proposal unless they are convinced that it is part of a sincere and massive effort to desegregate white schools serving pupils of all income levels.

Although the general implications of the varied research studies dealing with integrated education and with compensatory education projects should now be evident, it is important to spell them out as forcefully as possible in order to minimize the possibility that unnecessary energy will be consumed in continuing what now appears to be a spurious and wasteful argument between schools of thought that turn out to complement each other as much as they contradict or detract from one another. Perhaps the best way to summarize the situation is to call attention to some preliminary findings in one school district which is making a vigorous effort to reduce *de facto* segregation at the same time that it is providing intensive remedial and developmental services for those disadvantaged Negro students who remain in segregated school settings. Describing the initial results of both the newly integrated arrangements brought about by redrawing of school boundaries and other desegregation efforts in White Plains, New York, and of the Project Able Compensatory Program, Superintendent Carroll F. Johnson recently stated that the academic performance of disadvantaged Negro students had improved over previous rates of growth in each situation.[12] Noting that it cost considerably less money to bring about more integration than to conduct expensive compensatory programs, Dr. Johnson regretted the fact that it had not been possible to assign every Negro child to an integrated school. The fact that both approaches were proving beneficial for the disadvantaged minority child, however, is most encouraging, and is in line with the conclusions argued in the preceding pages.

The study of equal opportunity provided massive evidence that convincingly supported a proposition perceptive educators had long recognized, namely, that family and neighborhood generally have been much more influential than the school in determining how well students perform there.[13] Aries, in his scholarly history of the family in Western society since the Middle Ages, has explained how it came about that the school and the inward-looking, nuclear middle-class family begin to reinforce each other's work in developing a child's intellectual potential, but the school never succeeded very well in finding ways to counteract the depressing influence of the low-income environment in which family life remained disorganized.[14] When we add to the weight of family and neighborhood influence the psychological effects of exclusion in a *de facto* segregated setting, it is not hard to understand why most projects to improve the education of the disadvantaged Negro child have not succeeded.

More particularly, it would be a tragic mistake to interpret the considerable evidence that most compensatory programs do not work as indicating that compensatory education cannot work. For one thing, it is unlikely that all or even most disadvantaged

Negro youngsters now in school can be placed in integrated class-rooms, no matter how vigorously federal and state officials and local educators might work together to end *de facto* segregation; to reject the possibility that we can learn to conduct more ade-quate compensatory programs, without complete certainty that such a development is impossible, might be tantamount to giving up on the future of hundreds of thousands of young people. Second, the philosophy underlying compensatory education often makes a good deal of sense, as can be seen, for example, in a program which brings the severely disadvantaged together and keeps them together in classes of ten or twelve in which they re-ceive help from professional speech therapists or other highly specialized personnel. Third, and equally important, just as com-pensatory programs are severely handicapped when conducted in a largely segregated school system which implicitly teaches Negro youth that there must be something inferior about themselves that will forever cause them to be "kept in their place," so the potency of integrated education in improving their performance may be severely limited by a social context which also subverts their self-concept because it is based on the explicit belief that they can never learn unless exposed to the influence of other racial groups in an integrated school. On the one hand, it can hardly be expected that youngsters severely handicapped by a disadvan-taged, segregated background will live up to their inborn poten-tial unless they have concrete reason to believe that the social barriers which signify their exclusion are really beginning to give way. By the same token, demonstrations that education can be significantly improved in the segregated slum school—that "black power," so to speak, can be a concept denoting pride and not defensiveness—will prove invaluable in dissolving the psycho-logical bonds which keep many disadvantaged Negro youth mired in a state of bitter hopelessness. What we need to do, then, is to demonstrate—and seek out demonstrations—that both integrated education and compensatory education can be effective in im-proving the achievement of disadvantaged Negro youth.

If for ideological or other reasons we look for examples where either integration or compensatory programs have failed to result in improved academic performance among low-income Negro youth, such examples will be easy enough to find. But if we truly wish to help these children of poverty and despair, we will mark those instances which credit rather than discredit either approach. For, given the almost unimaginably difficult task we thereby set for ourselves, progress must be made simultaneously along each front.

It would be easy to misinterpret the implications of the equal opportunity report, or of any other report that highlights how ineffective our schools still are in overcoming the deleterious effects of environments which are not conducive to good performance in the classroom. Soon after the report was issued, for example, Joseph Alsop argued in a syndicated column that if even those inner-city schools which now have the best facilities and most expensive programs are not very effective in overcoming the influence of the slums, it is more constructive to conclude that we need still better and more massive compensatory projects than to conclude, as some have, that education can make no difference. Even Alsop's conclusion, however, is still inadequate, for it ignores the complementary potential of integrated education as a key factor in the battle to defuse the social dynamite resulting from the failures of educational and other social institutions in the big cities.

Keeping in mind the evidence that integrated education benefits the disadvantaged Negro student academically by reducing his feeling of powerlessness and isolation, vigorous initiative to implement plans to reduce *de facto* segregation is indeed a legitimate professional response to the *educational* problems associated with disadvantaged and minority status. Even those who work primarily in the area of compensatory education should lend every effort to reducing segregation whenever and wherever practicable. While it may be unrealistic to expect that most Negro students in the big cities can be placed in integrated schools during the next few years, it would be a serious mistake to do other than redouble our efforts to provide integrated education for as many disadvantaged Negro youth as possible. If this can be done for at least enough Negro students so that integrated education is a visible fact of community life, it may then be possible to convince even those students still in segregated schools that equal opportunity for themselves and eventually for their children is indeed becoming a reality rather than an empty slogan. Let us not underestimate the perceptivity of disadvantaged Negro youth, for their intuitive understanding of the attitudinal and behavioral orientations which underlie American society is often far superior to that of sophisticated adults. Provided that educators and concerned laymen really make a dedicated effort, despite intense obstacles, to pursue every possible path toward desegregated education and are successful in significantly reversing the continuing trends toward *de facto* segregation, we may counteract much of the sense of powerlessness, exclusion, despair, and inferiority that militates against all our most profound efforts to implement meaningful compensatory programs. If and when this happens, integrated education and compensatory education will no longer be seen as embodying mutually exclusive answers to the challenge of improving the education of disadvantaged minority youth with all the means at our command in American education.

NOTES

1. Fred T. Wilhelms and Paul B. Diederich, "The Fruits of Freedom," in Fred Wilhelms (ed.), *Evaluation as Feedback and Guide* (Washington, D.C.: Association for Supervision and Curriculum Development, 1967), pp. 234–235.

2. Ivor Kraft, "Integration, Not 'Compensation,'" *The Educational Forum*, Vol. 31, No. 2 (Jan. 1967), p. 212.

3. *Ibid.*, p. 213.

4. For example, see official board reports on "The More Effective Schools Program in New York City," the "Special Summer Schools Program in Chicago," and the "Lincoln Plus Program in Kansas City."

5. For example, see Kenneth E. Anderson, Walter K. Beggs, and Herbert W. Schooling, *A Report to the Board of Education of the Kansas City, Kansas, School District* (November 1966), pp. 85, 86, 97.

6. *Racial Isolation in the Public Schools*, Vol. I (Washington, D.C.: U.S. Government Printing Office, 1967), p. 127.

7. *Ibid.*, pp. 128–138.

8. *Ibid.*, p. 138.

9. James S. Coleman *et al.*, *Equality of Educational Opportunity* (Washington, D.C.: U.S. Government Printing Office, 1966).

10. *Ibid.*, p. 22.

11. Alan B. Wilson, "Residential Segregation of Social Classes and Aspirations for High School Boys," *American Sociological Review*, Vol. 24, pp. 836–845.

12. Carroll F. Johnson, "Importance of Integrated Education to the Com-

munity," speech delivered at the Mid-America Conference on Integrated Education, Kansas City, Missouri, January 28, 1967.

13. For example, the British sociologist F. Musgrove began his retrospective examination on research dealing with education and the family with the flat statement that "Schools in general are remarkably ineffective in moderating the influence of family background, when such moderating influences are necessary. Our contemporary problem is less to buttress the influence of parents than to limit it." *The Family, Education and Society* (London: Routledge & Kegan Paul, 1966), p. 1.

14. Phillipe Aries, *Centuries of Childhood: A Social History of Family Life* (New York: Alfred A. Knopf, 1965).

18 TIME FOR A MORATORIUM ON NEGATIVE CRITICISMS OF THE SCHOOLS

ROBERT J. HAVIGHURST

On last November 2, the New York City School Board reported the results of school achievement tests that had been given last April to pupils in the second and fifth grades. The *New York Times* headline read, "City Pupils Losing Ground in Reading and Arithmetic." Let us examine some of the test results.

The national average reading scores for these two grades in April were 2.7 and 5.7 respectively. New York City school children averaged definitely below these levels, and there was some evidence that the New York City average was lower than it had been the year before.

The *New York Times did not* point out the fact that almost 300 of the 650 elementary schools had reading averages for their second grades of 3.0 or higher—that is, three-tenths of a year above the national mean. Nor did the *Times* report that 44 elementary schools had reading scores for their fifth grades averaging 7.0 or more—1.3 of a year above the national average.

During that same month of November, the New York State Board of Regents called for "a concerted effort to reform urban education." The "Bundy Report" of the Mayor's Advisory Panel on Decentralization of the New York City Schools, which was published on November 9, commences with the statement, "The New York City school system, which once ranked at the summit of American public education, is caught in a spiral of decline." The *New York Times* on that day in an editorial referred to what it called "the deterioration of New York's gigantic school system."

This paper was first presented at the annual John Mosler Lecture at Fordham University's School of Education, January 26, 1968. Reprinted by permission of the author.

The *Saturday Review* for November 18 carried the following two headlines on its front cover—"Requiem for the Urban School" and "Education in Washington: National Monument to Failure."

The unwary middle-income parent, with several school-age children, is very likely to read these pieces in *responsible* newspapers and journals, and to decide to move to the suburbs, where he is assured by the same press that the schools are good. This person may live in Queens District 27, where 20 out of 27 schools are well above average in reading achievement, or in Queens District 26, where every one of the 24 elementary schools averaged at least .4 of a year above the national average at the second grade, and at least one year above the national average at the fifth grade. But if he follows the *responsible* press, unless he explores the fine print, he is misled to suppose that he cannot find "good" public schools in the city.

Although these examples are taken from New York City, they can be duplicated in every large city. In some areas of the city, where the people of average and above-average income live, the school achievement is above the national average, and about the same as it is in the "better" suburbs. In the low-income areas, school achievement is low.

It has been known for 40 years that school achievement is related to the socioeconomic status of the families whose children are in the school. Dozens of careful studies have shown that the correlation coefficient of school achievement and family socioeconomic status ranges from .2 to .4. If a social scientist with a knowledge of these studies was presented with the facts about the changing socioeconomic status of parents in the central cities of our large metropolitan areas, he would confidently and correctly predict that the school achievement level of the central cities would go down as the proportion of low-income people in the central city increases, and that the school achievement levels within the central cities would vary with the socioeconomic status of the various areas within the city. What he would *not* do is infer that the schools are failing.

This is the error that is made by a group of *nonresponsible* writers who appear at this moment to have easy access to print in the responsible newspapers and journals. These nonresponsibles

include Robert Coles, John Holt, Herbert Kohl, Edgar Friedenberg, Jonathan Kozol, and Paul Goodman, to name the most visible
current members. These are not *irresponsible* people. On the contrary, they feel a tremendous responsibility to report their perceptions of the schools, and their hypotheses concerning the
school children and the school teachers. This writer is grateful
to them for their moral concern about the ways in which various
groups of children are treated in our society, and for their moral
indignation at what seems to them to be wrong.

However, perhaps because they have such a great sense of
moral responsibility for the ills of our society, they have been
making nonresponsible statements that may be doing more harm
than good. A nonresponsible statement is one that is probably
not true and in any case is easily misunderstood and misinter-
preted by many readers.

For instance, take the following statement from Edgar Friedenberg's piece entitled "Requiem for the Urban School" and published by the *Saturday Review*. After summarizing the observations made by a number of writers about conditions in "slum
schools," Friedenberg writes, "What Kohl, Kozol, Schrag, Greene
and Ryan, among others, have established beyond question is that
the dreadful conditions they describe are quite general. They are
not peculiar to any one school or city." What does the phrase "are
quite general" mean? Does it mean that the conditions described
by the writers are to be found in one percent or in ten percent
of the schools in *all* big cities, and are general in that sense? Or
does it mean that these conditions are present in 90 percent of
schools in big cities? Or does it mean that these conditions are
present in 90 percent of the classrooms in slum schools? Any one
of these interpretations might reasonably be made of the phrase
"are quite general."

When this writer directed a survey of the public schools of
Chicago, he found evidence of conditions like those referred to
by Friedenberg and described by the authors listed. He made a
serious attempt to separate the schools into four types, and to
describe the conditions in each type. In one of the four types
the conditions were somewhat like those described by the several
writers mentioned above. These schools were all located in slum

areas, but not all slum schools were of this type. One might say from this study, that the conditions were "general" in most of the slum schools, but not in all of them, and not in the other areas of the city.

Another nonresponsible statement is made by Edgar Friedenberg which he attributes to the books by Kozol and Kohl that report their experiences and perceptions as they taught in slum schools in Boston and New York. He says,

A second implication of these books—or, rather, of the conditions described in them—is also very obvious, thought it will be so repugnant to the liberal, intellectual tradition that it is hard to come right out and write it: The urban slum schools are run by awful people.

The worst categories of school personnel are brought together and reinforce each other here: tyrants whom the parents of higher-status children would not tolerate; silly and malicious teachers who would be shriveled by the sophistication with which middle-class parents would dismiss them as case studies in abnormal psychology; and timid and vulnerable beginners who are assigned to the slum schools because their own professional status is so low that the authorities assume— albeit, as these books show, with some risk—they will not dare criticize them. It seems to me important for the sake of clarity, that a moral judgment be made. These people are not going to be improved by instruction or therapy; they do not have good intentions; and so long as they dominate the schools, the schools are not going to be improved from within. But they may possibly be improved by coercion from without. We are dealing here with people who have a lot of faith in punishment, manipulation, and taking orders from above—and remedies do usually work with people who have faith in them, even when they are useless or harmful to others.

This is such a direct and positive statement that there can hardly be any question about its meaning. It means that urban slum school principals are bad people, generally tyrants; and classroom teachers are either silly and malicious, if they are experienced teachers, or they are timid and vulnerable beginners. This is a nonresponsible statement.

This writer does not argue against the publication of these books and articles. They are important pieces of what should be a very complex picture of a complex situation. Edgar Friedenberg presents his opinions with an effective and beautiful style. Jonathan Kozol writes subjectively as a young man pioneering and reacting personally to some disturbing facts of his new experience. Herbert Kohl gives a vivid picture of the reactions of middle-grade Harlem pupils to life and to school when they are taught by a creative and freedom-loving teacher. Thus the readers get little pieces of reality, without seeing the whole complex reality. And Friedenberg's conclusion about the character of teachers in slum schools is certainly not proven by these bits of experience. The statement quoted above goes beyond nonresponsibility and perhaps is irresponsible.

The responsible editors and publications may properly be expected to present a more responsible picture of the schools in the big cities. If they publish nonresponsible books and articles, they should at least balance their productions with writing that is more responsible, so that a reasonably careful reader may get a balanced picture. Take, for example, the review written by Herbert Kohl of John Holt's book entitled *How Children Learn* and published in the *New York Review of Books* under the caption *How Teachers Fail*. I recommend this review as an example of a nonresponsible writer reviewing a book by a nonresponsible writer. Why did not the editors of the *New York Review* seek a reviewer competent to deal with the question of how children learn in a balanced and objective manner, rather than a reviewer who holds the same prejudices and has the same limited scholarship as the author of the book he reviews?

The concerned and thoughtful reader will have the following two questions coming more and more forcibly to his attention as he reads the current publications about the schools.

Are urban schools as good as they were twenty or forty years ago?

What is wrong with inner-city or slum schools?

I shall try to answer these questions.

City Schools Are Better than They Were in the Past

I do not believe that big city schools have deteriorated. In fact, I believe big city schools are doing a better job than ever before of educating the kind of children who come to school ready and eager to learn.

I submit that the average interested and reasonably well-informed parent or citizen is *misled* by editorials and news articles in the *New York Times,* the *Washington Post,* the *Saturday Review* and other liberal media, to believe:

1. The public schools in the big cities are teaching less skillfully than the public schools in the suburbs.

2. The public schools of the big cities are teaching less skillfully than they were 20 or 40 years ago.

There is no basis of fact for these two propositions, but the parent or citizen, hearing and reading them repeatedly, naturally concludes that (a) he should move to the suburbs or put his children into a private school, and (b) he should support political and social action that would change the leadership and structure of the public schools.

What the educational publications *do not* make clear are the following propositions which are supported by facts. Compared with public schools in the big cities in 1920, 1940, and 1960, the big city schools today:

1. Are better in terms of textbooks and curriculum.

2. Are better equipped with school libraries, laboratories, visual aids, gymnasiums and swimming pools.

3. Are staffed by teachers with more years of college preparation.

4. Have smaller classes.

5. Have more special classes and courses for pupils with special talents and disabilities.

6. Do a better job of setting children and youth free to learn on their own initiative.

If a panel of judges (including the writers named above) were to visit a cross-section of city schools today, and to compare them with a reproduction of schools of 20 or 40 years ago, I have no doubt that they would unanimously agree with these propositions. They would also, I hope, point out that there is much room for further improvement.

The Main Trouble with the Slum School Is the Family Factor

Many of the vocal critics of big city schools have a naive faith in what the school can accomplish when it is not aided by the family. Yet substantial studies of school achievement in relation to family socioeconomic status show that the family environment is more important than the school in determining a child's educational achievement. Fundamental recent studies have shown that the family environment in the preschool years has more control over the child's later school achievement than any other element in the child's postnatal life. This is due to the fact that the most important steps of mental development are learned before school age from the language the child learns in the family, the examples he sees of parents and older brothers and sisters reading and conversing, and the way his own questions and attempts at conversation are treated.

The preparation given a child by his family for success in school is, on the average, poorer for families with low incomes than for families with middle and high incomes. Middle-income families move away from the center of the city to its edges and to the suburbs, and their places are taken by low-income families. The metropolitan area, consisting of the central city and its suburbs, does not change in its average scores on school achievement tests, but the central city falls below the suburbs because a higher proportion of low-income people live in the central city than in the suburbs.

Those who know these facts divide into two groups. One group says there will always be such a difference between the haves and the have-nots in our society, and we must be content to live with the situation. The other group says that we must find ways of *compensating* socially disadvantaged children for their low family factor, and the schools must work at this task.

The second group is quite varied. The writers whom I have named critically are in this group, as I am, and as most of the responsible educational leaders are. We seek ways to help disadvantaged children learn more effectively the things they need to learn in order to become competent citizens, workers, and parents of a modern democracy.

We have invested much money in the effort to help socially disadvantaged children, but we have not had much success, so far. A few creative teachers have had some success, and the best results are in the preschool classes. Still, people like Kozol and Kohl have had a limited success as long as their brief enthusiasm for the job has lasted. A few others, mainly seasoned school principals and teachers, have a modest and continuing success.

We need ideas and suggestions on how to do the job better. The "minischool" idea put forth by Paul Goodman is worth support on an experimental basis. A variety of programs for preschool classes are worth support on an expanding basis, having already proved themselves valuable.

What we do not need are nonresponsible statements that the fault is with the teachers and the school administrators, and if they would only work harder, or with more faith, their pupils would measure up to the children of the suburbs on these tests.

The only result from this kind of criticism of the big city school staff is one that we already see. The teachers' organizations become angry and defensive. They ask whether their critics have ever taught in a public school. They claim that parents and citizens are unfair to them, the hard-working teachers. They recognize that they are being made a collective scapegoat for the troubles of the city. They respond by criticizing the administration of the schools and the civic organizations that are concerned about the schools, and they demand a greater share in making decisions about the schools. As for the administrators of a school system, they tend to become apathetic when they see scanty results from their best efforts on the one hand, and get ill-founded criticism on the other hand.

We want to maximize the contribution of the public schools to the solution of the problems of the big city. We believe that public schools can contribute more than they now do. We do not know just what they can do. Therefore we must experiment and innovate with careful evaluation.

The public schools are probably doing as well, in their sphere, as are local government, police, traffic departments, church federations, recreation agencies, real estate boards, chambers of commerce, welfare departments, and public libraries. All must do better.

The tendency of some critics of the schools to lay the whole burden on the schools, and the whole blame for the plight of disadvantaged youth on the schools is unfair, unrealistic, and can only lead to more difficulties for the schools and for the cities.

It is time for a moratorium on purely negative criticisms of the public schools.

19 SCHOOL DECENTRALIZATION: IMPETUS OR DILEMMA FOR LEARNING AND TEACHING

ANTHONY N. BARATTA

Interest has increased in decentralization in big city school systems during the last year or two. However, various views about decentralization have been advanced within the last decade. This paper presents varying points of view regarding the need and purposes of decentralization; it will attempt to: (1) show that the movement is in an incipient stage of possibly reversing a school system organization trend; (2) focus briefly on the urban school system climate; (3) discuss several common concepts of big city school structure; (4) examine decentralization as an impetus or dilemma for teaching and learning; and (5) look at the prospects of the movement.

School decentralization is a relatively recent reversal in school governance in several large city systems in the United States. Decentralization plans, at varying embryonic stages, are reported in cities such as Chicago, Cleveland, Detroit, San Francisco, and Washington, D.C. However, in New York City, school decentralization has indeed become a controversial issue during the 1967–1968 school year. Yet, in the most recent yearbook of the National Society for the Study of Education, *Metropolitanism: Its Challenge to Education,* scant mention was given to the topic of decentralization.[1] In fact, the fundamental proposition of this yearbook focused on metropolitan school planning. It is interesting to note that almost 80,000 school districts have been consolidated through redistricting in the last twenty years. In 1949, there were approxi-

Unpublished paper. This paper was originally presented at the Twenty-first Annual Meeting of the National Conference of Professors of Educational Administration, at the University of Arizona, Tucson, Arizona on August 22, 1967. The material has been up-dated and modified for publication. Reprinted by permission of the author.

mately 100,000 [2] school districts and in 1967 the number of total operating school districts decreased to 20,195.[3]

Because of the cited trends, several pertinent questions come to the mind of the author: Why school decentralization in the United States today? What weaknesses exist in city school districts that need modification? Does school decentralization offer a substantive remedy for the present day problems of urban education? And the most crucial question: Is school decentralization an impetus or dilemma for learning and teaching for the schools' constituents?

The battle against bigness in city schools is part of a larger social phenomenon in our country against institutional bigness, i.e., business, church, government, and university. The outgrowth of this social phenomenon is a bureaucratic structure that alienates the common man and ignores the "grass roots," which in essence is tantamount to cutting the arteries of American democracy. Inherent in "bureaucracy" are such concepts as hierarchical structure, government encroachment, centralization of power, control by the few, and depersonalization of the functionaries. Yet, despite these criticisms, the author recognizes the merits of business mergers and the establishment of superagencies by government. The consolidation of resources has many advantages that warrant serious consideration.

School decentralization is one example of the counter trend to bigness in our society. Simply said, it can be explained in terms of giving control of the schools to the citizens of the community. Because the social milieu is the product of tremendously potent forces—seemingly simple and clear cut advantages and values favoring decentralization become involved in the midst of the multitude of problems of America today. For example, the dispute at Ocean Hill-Brownsville decentralization demonstration district in Brooklyn, in May, 1968, resulted in controversies ranging from the school issues to racial and ethnic discrimination and due process of law. Consequently, the conflict was broadened beyond the decentralization issue and further complicated the pending legislation in Albany. The advocates for the demonstration district strongly voiced sentiments that they wanted to control the destiny of the education of their children in the district. On the other hand, opponents of decentralization in New York City indicated that the Ocean Hill-Brownsville dispute gave notice of what would happen when control was gained of schools by the "black militants."

Teaching Climate in Urban America

There was a day when the big city was the envy and showcase of innovation in education. The big cities led the nation in teacher salaries and professional opportunities. In contrast, Commissioner Howe pointed out that large cities are becoming the ghettos of the very rich and the very poor. He indicated that the schools alone cannot solve problems that are not educational but civic. Urban education is more expensive than suburban and rural education because costs are higher for teachers, land, buildings and other resources. Howe also commented that the education of slum children must, in addition to doing the job of the school, make up for the neglect of the home.[4]

Serious misconceptions exist about the public schools in the big cities. Wide variations in the quality of these public schools can be easily observed. The author believes that socioeconomic factors are the significant influence on school programs. This proposition is equally true of the types of public schools in the cities. So we have in a large city such as New York, outstanding specialized high schools and advanced elementary school programs. However, unfortunately "schools-in-chaos" also exist in the big cities, in which the most negative and ineffective teaching and learning environments prevail. Critics of urban education often sensationalize these "negatives" and the "establishment" is blamed for virtually every problem of the inner city. On the other hand, the "establishment" has often been less than candid about "their" shortcomings. To illustrate this point, the author has selected two contrasting views that have been expressed on this subject. One is Jack Shepherd, an editor for one of America's large popular magazines, who did a special feature on city schools. The other is Robert J. Havighurst, a renowned social scientist, who has been a serious student of the socio-educational problems in our country, and who recently spoke out against the non-responsible critics of city schools.

Shepherd, in an article entitled, "Cities the Word on Schools," discussed the serious problems confronting urban education.

America's public education is a biracial system under which 90 per cent of the children attend segregated schools. He reported that New York, Chicago, Washington, Cleveland, Detroit, Boston, Philadelphia and St. Louis all have a majority of Negroes in their public elementary schools. Yet, even while the budget for New York City schools was more than doubled, the enrollment increased by only one-fifth; pupil achievement, however, has not kept pace with the communities' expectations. Approximately one out of three children is a year or more behind national norms in reading and arithmetic. Only one-third of those in schools are given preparation qualifying them for college. Another one-third give up before finishing high school.[5]

Havighurst, addressing a faculty seminar at Fordham University, asserted that urban schools have improved, not worsened, and the "nonresponsible" critics are giving the impression that a good education cannot be obtained in the big cities. He said:

I do not believe that big-city schools have deteriorated. In fact, I believe that big-city schools are doing a better job than ever before of educating the kind of children who come to school ready and eager to learn. . . . Public schools are probably doing as well, in their sphere, as are local government, police and traffic departments, welfare departments, church federation and other civic and municipal groups. But, the tendency of some critics to lay the whole burden on the schools, and the whole blame for the plight of disadvantaged youth on the schools is unfair, unrealistic and can only lead to more difficulties for the schools and for the cities.[6]

The city today is the modern frontier of tomorrow's living. City schools are where the action is. They are the battleground for the most crucial social problems of our day such as civil rights, crime, integration, housing and poverty. The National Advisory Commission on Civil Disorder Report painted a pessimistic picture of inner city school programs. They concluded that teachers and administrators were not measuring up to the demands of the new urban citizen. The urban schoolman has little sympathy for the life styles for these new immigrants. Large school systems were viewed as unresponsive and have compromised the accountability of the local schools to the communities they serve and are difficult to be reached by parents. The Commission reported that the ghetto schools are unresponsive to the community and parents are distrustful of officials responsible for developing educational policy. They warned that the consequences of such a negative milieu are grave. The parental hostility to the schools is reflected in the perceptions, attitudes and behavior of the ghetto child— with the result that the precious school experience of these boys and girls is lost.[7]

Ghetto schools must be revitalized. Highly competent teachers and administrators, relevant programs, and necessary resources are the *sine qua non* for good schools.

A necessary dimension for greater community support and harmony between the ghetto community and the ghetto school is needed. Will school decentralization help to promote this positive parent-school-community relationship?

Big City School Systems

Big city school systems are large complex organizations. For example, data for the New York City Public Schools in 1966–1967 show that the Board of Education operates over a billion-dollar enterprise ($1,022,674,215), employs about 65,000 professional persons and about 27,000 in noneducational positions, and educates over a million students (1,084,845).[8] Quite an organization!

Russell Baker, a witty observer of the contemporary scene for a large metropolitan newspaper, offered a view that in a humorous vein appears to be applicable to the subject of big city school system organization:

. . . What do we call the three organizations, Archer, that are to blame for the way the world is?
The Establishment, the power élite and the white power structure.
And what kind of democracy do these organizations militate against?
Participatory democracy. Through highly structured institutional patterns reinforced by an uncommitted technological bureaucracy and a depersonalized hierarchical management system, they deny all men a voice in making the decisions that control their lives.[9]

Comprehensive systems analysis of the present form of big city school organizations is necessary to make some proper judgments about school decentralization. This type of serious study is difficult, at best fragmentary, and to date used for specific limited purposes in few districts. It would be accurate to generalize that "systems analysis inputs" have not been utilized in any of the major studies for school decentralization. The force of public, prestigious, vested and political opinion had the major impact upon school decentralization decisions. The author selected three commentaries about the pros and cons of the bureaucratic type of school system. They were selected because two were reported in a serious professional research journal and one in a social science journal.

Philip Katz, a Chicago principal, offers various suggestions for the reform of the urban school systems structure. He noted that the present centralized, hierarchical structure is a deterrent to contemporary school systems. Because of the nature of the centralized structure, he believed modifications are difficult, and a school system structure cannot respond quickly and sensitively to the exigencies of the community.[10]

Thelen, in a rebuttal to Katz, agreed in part that the unresponsiveness of the urban school system might tend to be more marked in centralized than in the decentralized organization. He opted that would be because a centralized organization is more compact, more intracommunicative, and therefore can more easily become institutionalized. He elaborated on this concept stating, "It is the degree of 'institutionalization' (fossilization, routine efficiency, rigidity, technical-legal-proceduralness . . .) that Mr. Katz is objecting to, not centralization per se." The lack of contact, according to Thelen, between decentralized smaller units would keep them out of step enough to maintain conflict and vitality—which could either build or wreck the system.[11]

Kristol's article supports the bureaucratic form of organization. He indicated that it is an accidental fact, but an important one, that our large and cumbersome bureaucracies in such fields as education, welfare, and the civil service play a crucial role in integrating large numbers of middle-class Negroes into American society. He believes that bureaucracies are, in truth, the best-integrated sectors of American society. Decentralization of these bureaucracies will almost certainly mean disintegrating them. We shall end up with only Negro teachers in Negro schools, only Negro police in Negro neighborhoods, only Negro social workers handling Negro clients.[12] Moynihan also criticized school decentralization as likely to lead to "segregated bureaucracies." [13]

Accepting the analysis that big city school systems are centralized bureaucracies, what guiding administration principles promoted this type of organization? Realizing the impetus for reorganization of school districts into larger units was recommended in the more rural context, yet the general principles advanced by various educational administration experts has had impact on city systems. Two major reasons cited for reorganizing larger school districts were: (1) to help equalize tax support for public schools, and (2) to improve the educational programs. In small districts it was observed that good teachers were hard to find and harder to keep; the quality of administrative leadership was often considered inadequate; and that special programs, facilities, resources, and services were often lacking. A concluding view by strong reorganization proponents was that these deficiencies can be overcome in larger school districts.[14]

Big city school systems are also naturally vast organizations because of the size of the city. It is important to emphasize, however, that bureaucracy is a means of organizing work that places a value on specialization of talent and effort. This specialization requires authority systems, coordination of work, systems of standards and records, and personnel policies based on merit. These principles of organization seem congruent with American values for getting the job done. However, these guidelines may not necessarily meet the changing needs of the ghetto. The old established "systems for institutional functions" are no longer accepted at face value. A new look at the old order is required.

Purposes of School Decentralization

The purpose of school decentralization is to diffuse the loci of control, governance, and operations of a school system. Several fundamental purposes of school decentralization may be synthesized through an examination of recent reports, editorials, research studies, and legislation.

On March 30, 1967, a law passed by the New York State Senate mandated action on school decentralization in New York City. An excerpt from the State's law follows:

Increased community awareness and participation in the educational process is essential to the furtherance of educational innovation and excellence in the public school system within the city of New York. The legislature hereby finds and declares that the creation of educational policy units within the city school district of New York for the formulation of educational policy for the public schools within such districts will afford members of the community an opportunity to take a more active and meaningful role in the development of educational policy closely related to the diverse needs and aspirations of the community.[15]

This law also charged the Mayor of New York City to present a proposal for decentralization by December 1, 1967. This resulted in the document commonly called the Bundy Report, which is discussed subsequently in this paper.

On April 19, 1967, the New York City Board of Education adopted a statement of policy on decentralization. Excerpts from the statement of policy are presented:

All members of our Board are committed to the principle of decentralization of operations. In a city as large and varied as New York we believe it is essential to have much flexibility and authority at the local level.[16]

This statement of policy also served as the foundation for the establishment of several decentralization demonstration projects such as the I.S. 201 Complex in East Harlem and the Ocean Hill-Brownsville demonstration district in Brooklyn.

On November 9, 1967, the Mayor's Advisory Panel on Decentralization of the New York City Schools Report was presented to Mayor John V. Lindsay. This panel announced on April 30, 1967, included: McGeorge Bundy, President of the Ford Foundation, Chairman; Alfred A. Giardino, President of the Board of Education of New York City; Francis Keppel, President and Chairman of the Board, General Learning Corporation; Mrs. Antonia Pantoja, President of the Puerto Rican Forum; Mitchel Sviridoff, Administrator, Human Resources Administration for the City of New York; Bennetta E. Washington, Director, Women's Training Centers, Job Corps; and Mario D. Fantini, Executive Secretary of the Panel.

The Bundy Report was an extensive document containing many

facets on decentralization including Part I, Problems and Principles; Part II, A Framework for Change; Part III, Personnel Policy; Part IV, Fiscal Aspects of Decentralization; Part V, Concerns; and Part VI, Draft Legislation.

The report raises many controversial questions and recommendations that need to be explored. How people interpret these findings and recommendations naturally depends upon many factors that affect their perceptions and actions. Many serious answers are derived from the Bundy Report that focus on the purposes of school decentralization in New York City.

Specifically, the Bundy Report offers the following regarding the purposes of school decentralization:

In order to . . .

increase community awareness and participation in the development of educational policy closely related to the diverse needs and aspirations of the city's population,

open new channels and incentives to educational innovation and excellence,

achieve greater flexibility in the administration of the schools,

afford the children, parents, teachers, other educators, and the city at large a single school system that combines the advantages of big-city education with the opportunities of the finest small-city and suburban educational system and

strengthen the individual school as an urban institution that enhances a sense of community and encourages close coordination and cooperation with other governmental and private efforts to advance the well-being of children and all others,

all with the central purpose of advancing the educational achievement and opportunities of the children of the public schools of New York City.[17]

The Bundy Report became the focal point of discussion by the supporters and opponents of school decentralization in New York City. By the end of March, 1968, various supporting views and plans were offered by the Mayor, the Board of Regents of the University of the State of New York, special interest groups. For example, strong endorsement was given the Bundy Report with modifications, by Mayor Lindsay. He indicated that decentralization is not a panacea. He stressed that decentralization will not solve the problem caused by shortage of funds. He affirmed that public education is central to the life of New York City and that the establishment of a community school system is the necessary first step to reviving the strength of the schools.[18] *The New York Times* endorsed school decentralization and supported the Bundy Report. An editorial that appeared on this subject follows:

Decentralization of the city school system is no longer a subject for debate. Even prior to the Bundy report, the Board of Education had based its own reform plans on a policy of decentralization. But the Bundy panel has translated vague goals into a precise challenge.

We strongly endorse the panel's call for a federation of community school boards, with extensive local powers and responsibilities. Some of the report's specific proposals, however, require modifications or clarification.[19]

The United Federation of Teachers, the Board of Education of New York City, and several professional and parent associations criticized the Bundy-Lindsay school decentralization proposals. For example Alfred A. Giardino, president of the board, indicated that under the Mayor's plan, the board proposes and the Mayor disposes money for school operation, so that he, in effect, determines educational policies. Frederick C. McLaughlin, director of the Public Education Association, warned that to grant the Mayor great power for school district funding would be a backward step.[20] The United Federation of Teachers vigorously opposed the Bundy Report and prepared the UFT Proposals for school decentralization. In the summary of the critical analysis of the Bundy Report the UFT position was forcefully stated:

The United Federation of Teachers believes that the adoption of the Bundy proposals would irreparably harm the educational system. The Bundy model is based upon a glorification of the old-time rural school structure and is unfit for the greatest urban center in the world. The Bundy model is not decentralization; it is Balkanization. It runs counter to the current trend of enlarging school districts in order to provide both for greater efficiency and reinforce segregation. Finally, the Bundy report ignores the new power and integrity of the professional teacher who will not continue to teach in any school or district where professional decisions are made by laymen.[21]

In May, 1968, as the New York State Legislature was preparing for adjournment, of the various proposals for decentralization it appeared that the Senator John J. Marchi school decentralization plan (which in essence simply would postpone action for another year), would be enacted. Then, on May 9, the governing board of the Ocean-Hill Brownsville demonstration district in Brooklyn, summarily announced it had terminated the services of 13 teachers and 6 supervisors. Sydney Schanberg reported that the decentralization issue festered below the surface for months, with most legislators desiring not to act this year. When it came out in the legislature, one of the reasons for its emergence was the reason why most legislators wanted to keep it dormant in the first place—the neighborhood conflict over the demonstration schools. Social and political implications became more visible in the school decentralization matter with the troubles in the Ocean Hill-Brownsville district. Proponents for a strong decentralization law warned that if the Legislature were to pass a weak plan, the frustrations of the city's slums could explode.[22]

The matter of school decentralization in the nation's largest city is no longer merely a school matter. On May 24, the New York State Legislature passed a plan that would enlarge the present Board of Education from its present nine members to thirteen. This would allow Mayor Lindsay, who favors drastic reforms, to appoint four new prodecentralization members—they will be charged with designing a new proposal for next year.

Impetus for Learning and Teaching

School decentralization is a plan of organization and governance that aims to make the public school more public. A community has the kind of schools or government that it deserves, is an axiom that is pertinent to this topic. From the formal statements regarding the value of school decentralization, several of the following principles are identified as providing positive impetus for learning and teaching: (1) increased community awareness and participation in the educational process; (2) more meaningful role for community involvement in educational policy; (3) greater decentralization of operations to promote flexibility and authority at the local level; (4) strengthening and broadening the relationships of the community to the schools; and (5) improvement of coordination and cooperation between the school and other governmental and private efforts to advance the education of children.

The Bundy Report's reference to the learning process was through the reconnection theme of the proposal. The idea of rebridging people and the school for the benefit of the education of the children was the heart of the proposal. Several of the key propositions listed in that document elaborated on the desired impetus:

The children of the city of New York need a public school system that will liberate the talents, energies, and interests of parents, students, teachers, and others to make common cause toward the goal of educational excellence.

It should insist on the value of education for individual growth and provide young people entering a complex technological society with the skills they need to achieve economic opportunity and personal dignity.

It should restore the capacity of both lay and professional leadership to lead.

It should encourage initiative, in each school and locality as well as in the center.

In every school and in every neighborhood it should seek to make the school a true community institution, in which all are concerned and all can take pride.

It should encourage each school to develop a deeper understanding of the needs of the varied communities it is serving.

It should be responsive to the needs and sensitive to the desires of groups that are in a minority in a particular locality.

It should permit the flowering of a variety of curricula, school arrangements, and instructional strategies.

It should encourage constructive competition among schools and among localities—competition in effective educational ideas and practices, not in social or economic status.

It should distribute financial resources objectively and equitably, taking into account the higher costs of achieving educational quality in neighborhoods with economic and environmental handicaps.

It should guarantee a free flow of information, so that parents and the community at large are informed about the activities and performance of the school system and so that no part is isolated from the whole.

It should insure all pupils and all localities the benefits of the numerous and variegated facilities and services that major urban school systems can offer—ranging from special high schools to costly research, technical services, and logistic support.

It should couple the advantages of urban bigness with the intimacy, flexibility, and accessibility associated with innovative suburban school systems.

It should insure that progressive citywide policies, such as greater racial integration in the public schools, are advanced as far as practicable.

It should contain the seeds of self-renewal, so that the system does not again evolve into a web of negatives which immobilizes educators and citizens and defeats the purpose of public education.[23]

Dilemma for Learning and Teaching

Not all groups are optimistic about school decentralization as proposed in the Bundy Report. Often they are labeled as people representing the vested interests, the establishment, or the status quo. What are their messages?

Theodore Sizer, though not generally classified as an opponent to decentralization, in his analysis of the Bundy Report, had this to say:

If new and massive resources could be found, however, the problems would not be solved, even if the Panel's recommendation were carried out to the letter. . . . Factors outside of classrooms have profound effects only few schools are compensating for today. As the cliché goes, education is more than schooling, and if there is going to be a profound "reconnection for learning," a plan for working in a powerful and co-ordinated way with families, gangs, schools, and employers, among others will be needed.[24]

Some proponents of school decentralization privately admit that in that process some community controlled schools will experience temporary failures. They recognize that the quality of teachers and administrators may not necessarily be better than the present personnel though they quickly add that the climate, pupil achievement, and professional performance can hardly become worse.

On the other hand, opponents of the various decentralization plans question some of the assumptions advanced in the various decentralization proposals. In this regard, Sandra Feldman cited some dangers:

> . . . the disadvantages are heavy. For example, a careless redistribution of power could decrease efficiency by creating a number of little bureaucracies. More important, we need to re-examine the argument that heightened feelings of self-worth in children depend solely upon increased parent power and involvement.[25]

John King discussed various ways for overcoming problems of bigness in a large city school system. He indicated that the greatest defense against bigness is in the learning process itself. In the final analysis, King emphasized, regardless of the size of the school system, learning takes place in a very small, highly personalized setting. If a new plan for decentralization does not bear an immediate relationship to what happens to the teacher and learner in the classroom, it will have little impact on real educational quality.[26]

It is axiomatic that the pupils are the chief beneficiaries of a school system. And the basic assumption of the various proposals has been that school decentralization will improve the learning and teaching process in big city systems. Nevertheless, what will happen to the teaching and administrative personnel in the inner city schools through decentralization is at the moment controversial, unclear, and problematical.

Prospects of School Decentralization

In restrospect to what has been said by various proponents and opponents of school decentralization, there is little doubt that the urgent problems facing our city schools need new frontiers if we are going to overcome deprivation. No longer can we rely on outdated methods and ideas generated during the period when immigrants from the old orders of Europe were coming to America's shore. The new emigrants of today to the big cities have their own particular educational expectations. The educational needs will flourish in a school system that incorporates the values of openness, wide involvement, increased public control and compassionate sensitivity to the needs of every pupil in the big city school system. School decentralization is advanced by proponents as a most promising system to fulfill these needs.

The social-political dimensions of decentralization are the most positive strengths for school governance in our democratic society. Yet, several conflicts that have surfaced in two demonstration decentralized districts in New York City indicate that modifications of the complex school systems must be organized and protected within the structure of enlightened legislation. We can only wait and see what the prospects of school decentralization will be in America's big cities. Hopefully, the movement will be deliberate, rational, and evolutionary—anything else would be detrimental to pupils, professionals, parents, and the community.

NOTES

1. National Society for the Study of Education, *Metropolitanism: Its Challenge to Education,* The Sixty-seven Yearbook, Part 1 (Chicago: The University of Chicago Press, 1968).
2. Francis S. Chase and Edgar L. Morphet, *The Forty-Eight State School Systems* (Chicago: Council of State Governments, 1949), p. 192.
3. National Education Association, *NEA Research Bulletin* (Washington, D.C.: Research Division, National Educational Association), 46 (March, 1968), No. 1, p. 14.
4. Fred Hechinger, "Rescue Operation for the Urban School," *The New York Times,* July 16, 1967, Section 4, p. 7.
5. Jack Shepherd, "Cities the Word on Schools," *Look* (June 11, 1968), No. 12, p. 73.
6. M. A. Farber, "Professor Scores 'Nonresponsible' Critics of Big-City Schools," *The New York Times,* January 28, 1968, p. 56.
7. *Report of the National Advisory Commission in Civil Disorders* (New York: Bantam Books, 1968), p. 433.
8. New York City Board of Education, *Facts and Figures* (Brooklyn: 110 Livingston Street, April 1, 1967).
9. Russell Baker, "Observer: The New Leftspeak Examinations," *The New York Times,* May 28, 1968, p. 46.
10. Philip M. Katz, "A Proposed Structure for Urban School Systems," *Phi Delta Kappan,* 48 (March, 1967), No. 7, p. 325.

11. Herbert A. Thelen, "Urban School Systems (A Response to Mr. Katz),"
    Phi Delta Kappan, 48 (March, 1967), No. 7, p. 327.
12. Irving Kristol, "Decentralization for What?," *The Public Interest* (New
    York: National Affairs, Inc., Spring, 1968), No. 11, p. 25.
13. Peter Kihss, "Moynihan Deplores Ethnic Quota Idea," *The New York
    Times,* June 5, 1968, p. 1.
14. John T. Walhquist, *et al., The Administration of Public Education* (New
    York: The Ronald Press Company, 1952), p. 95.
15. New York State Senate Act. No. 4622 (Albany, New York, March 30,
    1967).
16. Board of Education, City School District of the City of New York,
    Statement of Policy, Decentralization (Brooklyn: April 19, 1967),
    p. 1.
17. Mayor's Advisory Panel on Decentralization of the New York City
    Schools, *Reconnection for Learning—A Community School System for
    New York City* (New York: 477 Madison Avenue, November 9,
    1967), p. III.
18. John V. Lindsay, "Letter to Governor Nelson A. Rockefeller, Members
    of the State Legislature and Members of the Board of Regents" (New
    York: Office of the Mayor, January 2, 1968), p. 2.
19. Editorial, "The Bundy Challenge—II," *The New York Times,* Decem-
    ber 29, 1967, p. 26.
20. M. A. Farber, "Plan to Reorganize City Schools Assailed by Board and
    Parents," *The New York Times,* February 8, 1968, p. 34.
21. United Federation of Teachers, AFL-CIO, *The United Federation of
    Teachers Looks at School Decentralization* (New York: 260 Park
    Avenue South, N.Y., 1968).
22. Sydney H. Schanberg, "Decentralization Dispute," *The New York Times,*
    May 20, 1968, p. 16.
23. Mayor's Advisory Panel on Decentralization of the New York City
    Schools Report, *op. cit.,* p. 4.
24. Theodore R. Sizer, "Report Analysis, Reconnection for Learning: A
    Community School System for New York City, Report of the Mayor's
    Advisory Panel on Decentralization of the New York City Schools,"
    Harvard Educational Review, 38 (Winter, 1968), No. 1, pp. 176–184.
25. Sandra Feldman, *Decentralization and the City Schools* (New York:
    League for Industrial Democracy, 1968), No. 12.
26. John B. King, "Overcoming Problems of Bigness in Our School System,"
    High Points (New York: Office of Educational Publications, Board
    of Education of the City of New York, Spring, 1967), p. 3.

20 DEVELOPING ALTERNATE STRATEGIES FOR A LEARNING ENVIRONMENT

RAYMOND S. KLEIN

The Schools and Society Today

Realization of the American dream has come to be equated with the quality of education. Though evidence exists that changes within the educational industry are taking place, pertinent statistics leave a great deal to be desired. For example, how can we evaluate the effectiveness of programs when comparable data do not exist. The statistics available are related to the school environment without necessarily having any pertinence to society. Measures of quality are needed. There is a need to think through and identify educational indicators so that the effectiveness of the programs may be judged.

School programs develop in many situations that are not reflective of the changes occurring within the society. Students who have successfully moved through the system find that their rights of passage into a productive role are not necessarily assured.[1] In recent years there has been an increasing attempt to bridge this gap. Enrichment programs on all levels can be seen today. However, as evidenced by the residual, there remains a great deal to be accomplished. If these challenges are to be met, business education and community planners must in fact greatly increase their interaction.[2] Although indicators show the acceleration of technology that suggests individuals will be employed in many roles during their life, the schools have been slow to introduce programs that would permit the transition to be smoother.

The obligation goes beyond providing twelve years of learning. What is needed is for our schools to equip students with basic skills that have wide application, along with fostering attitudes that encourage flexibility. In the planning of programs, the child

Unpublished paper. Reprinted by permission of the author.

and his environment must be considered.[3] With the absence of these bonds, meaningful interactions are infrequent, or occur by chance in few situations. The purpose of this paper is to examine selective factors influencing the education of the disadvantaged and to describe approaches that are aimed at improving the effectiveness of a learning environment. It is not enough for our educational system to provide basic education; it must provide for continuous learning activities at all levels.[4] Otherwise, there is a waste of human potential. In the United States, when one considers all forms of learning experience, both in school and out of school, millions of individuals are involved. With this tremendous investment in human development, it appears that the time has come to obtain a better assessment of how effective inputs are in relation to development.

This is especially important, for education is a growth industry that continues to command a higher percentage of the Gross National Product (GNP). Currently, 6.5 percent can be attributed to the educational industry. If the trend continues, it is not unlikely that 8.5 or even 10 percent of the GNP may be devoted to education.[5] With new programs in evidence directed towards the disadvantaged populations, the time has come when we must make an assessment to ascertain those inputs that will return the greatest educational yield. We cannot continue on a feeling basis indefinitely. Good things become better when they can be measured and assessed so that steps may be taken to assure a better yield.

Programmed instructional material, increased utilization of audiovisual equipment, and the computer are tending to provide the instructor with soft- and hardware that will improve the learning experience, but tools alone cannot do the job. With the age of computers, the schools now, for the first time, are in a position where individualized instruction could become a reality. Along with the inventory of reams of paper purchased should be a cumulative profile of the student as he journeys in the land of discovery. A profile of this nature in the hands of a skillful educator could become a powerful diagnostic tool. This profile could be matched against different resources of given degrees of difficulty, enabling infinite combinations that would not be otherwise possible. Such case histories would be invaluable in planning special treatments for individual students. One sees the development of learning materials at various levels so that a student with a given profile could be matched with a learning experience of a given degree of difficulty. In this way, not only would measures of quantity be possible; that is, the school graduates so many annually, but the important dimension of quality could be introduced and assessed, for differential measures would be feasible. To accomplish this will require breaking down many traditions. A learning team is required that will introduce greater flexibility into scheduling and increase the meaningfulness of materials used in learning situations.

Other considerations that must be included deal with the requirements of the school as mandated by law. Are the laws that require certain subjects to be taught for a period of time in phase with the needs? This requires a careful analysis of existing laws and regulations. It should be made part of an ongoing review in order to assess the validity of such inputs. Another area of concern is the availability and use of resources. Adequate resources must be placed at the disposal of the educational institutions so that curriculum may be improved, so that the quality of education may be enhanced and innovations attempted. The development of support personnel to produce learning materials is needed. The teacher of a disadvantaged child faces different problems. However, the tools that he has to work with have been designed for a different population. These resources need to be brought into phase with the situation.

The schools must equip individuals with the necessary tools to achieve independence. The degree to which this has been accomplished will reflect the success of the program. In addition, there are a variety of social and human values and attitudes that help provide the cement that holds the society together. The dignity of the family and the worth of the individual are basic building blocks. These also must be taken into consideration in any assessment of the quality of learning. If the teacher treats students in an inferior manner, this results in inferior accomplishments. Evidence exists which reveals that in every state in the Union the test performance on the Armed Forces qualification examinations was significantly higher for whites than for Negroes. The point of quality also is reflected in the fact that average Negroes who fail this examination have had more than one additional year of schooling than whites who fail the test.[6]

Traditionally, educators have been trained to instruct in various subject-related fields. The training in many instances failed to instill a philosophy required of professionals, which reflects a need to continuously update one's skills. Reliance on colleges and universities to accomplish this has not been completely satisfactory, for these institutions tend at times to be theoretical in areas where clinical application is required. Industry has long recognized that in order to maintain its competitive position, it has to institute training. If meaningful activities are to be implemented, the design of the programs must provide for in-service development; otherwise, a transition will not occur. With increased investments in closed circuit television, systems now can be instituted that would provide improved communication among the teachers, thus enabling a sharing that otherwise would be prohibitive in relation to time and costs. The practice of education in most schools serving the disadvantaged does not allow for adequate exchanges among teachers. Common problems can be shared and solutions worked through when there is improved communication among teachers. Closed circuit techniques have been used in conjunction with continuation education programs for physicians. Some of these networks have involved several states. Companies have placed learning programs on computers to enable their staffs to take courses during slack periods. A time-sharing computer system would make such a service practicable for our teachers as well as their students.

Another difficulty that must be overcome is the failure on the part of the system to engage in research and evaluation programs that are aimed at improving the various educational processes. Without adequate measures of effectiveness, teaching has tended to remain more of an art than a science. Without these measures, there cannot be meaningful refinement in the system. Although a trial and error approach has its place, one may question the degree of its application in today's schools.

The research that has been accomplished fails to be disseminated, for there is a dichotomy among those who produce research and those who are consumers of the product. The time has come to include statistical reasoning programs in the lower grades and require that educators be exposed to inferential as well as multi-variate concepts. The lack of understanding of probability theory creates a time lag between the uncovering of significant relationships and their application. For this reason, there is need for an increased investment in what might be referred to as a middleman. This person would be responsible for the translation of research findings into materials that are readily understood by educators. Through such translations, a language barrier would be crossed. The findings of the research in effect could be packaged in such a way that it gains acceptance. For example, multivariate behavioral research monographs could be written in a manner that would make their application by the teacher at least as important as an antiperspirant. In other words, research needs to uncover what teacher characteristics can be employed to improve communications between the practitioner (the teacher) and the researcher. Teachers of the disadvantaged would apply the findings of the researchers if they were presented in a nonthreatening form. This in turn would improve instruction.

Generations may pass before there is evidence of change. In today's world, these delays can no longer be tolerated. However, societies, like children, must grow and mature. At times there has been increased statements regarding the failures of the school to effectively bring about change. Evidence exists that shows that basic patterns of performance in school are in fact set prior to the child's entrance into the formal program. Our traditional concepts of school have to be changed when it comes to serving populations that have not had an experience which permits readiness for learning.[7] In areas where there is a large concentration of disadvantaged children, special programs might be instituted that would be aimed at providing the parents of these children with insights so that readiness may occur. For example, a small group of residents could be trained, and these in turn could train others who would be responsible for visiting with parents to discuss problems and to plan ways of resolving them. These indigenous workers could become the link between the institutions of our society and the people who need services. It may be possible to train welfare recipients to do this work.

Although the process of education requires considerable investments, little evidence is seen to indicate that this is occurring.

Our planning tends to create edifices to the mythical god of learning, but such temples alone will not bring about change. Today, considerable opportunity exists in the schools through the use of computers to study the flow processes that make up an educational experience. Critical points of go and no-go need to be determined, and accurate measures of these steps of achievement need to be recorded. If the teacher of the disadvantaged had such tools, he would be in a better position to adjust his learning approaches to the needs of the child. Although all of these things are desirable, given the current level of functioning with the resources that are available, it is impossible for the school to accomplish these tasks. Without the appropriate ancillary staff, this development cannot proceed at a rapid pace. A paradox exists that is reflected in the fact that there is a student-teacher ratio which needs to be replaced by an efficiency ratio that spells out yield in relation to outputs divided by inputs.

The problems of educators of children from disadvantaged homes cannot be overcome by the schools alone. Deprivation resulting from poverty and discrimination cannot be solved merely by improving the information retrieval systems of the institution. If the curriculum of the school is to have meaning for the children of such families, it must be related to programs that meet other basic needs. Consumer education, job related programs, health and nutrition activities and services should be expanded. Learning experience developed by the teacher must take into account these basic needs. The illustrations used should be of such a nature that there is application possible. For example, a unit that requires children to do comparative pricing could be interwoven with the learning of basic number skills.

The schools today train workers, but there is little or no effort directed towards entrepreneurship. This seems rather strange, for our whole system is based on this concept. The schools do not truly provide experiences that would permit a larger number of individuals from adequately assuming these roles. This is important for the disadvantaged because it will lend a greater identification with society which in turn will result in gains for all. Ownership has a way of generating this feeling.

The schools fail to take into consideration the environment and to devote energies that may improve such environments. The fact remains that in many urban settings, the staff is there by day and gone by night. There is little or no identification with the area, nor is there understanding of the problems that exist. Families in these areas are less mobile, some might even be considered to be imprisoned within their habitat. Programs of the school that open up new horizons through visitations may provide beginnings of some linkages that are necessary for development to occur. The selection of such experiences must be carefully thought through. For example, introduction to community services through visitations might in the long run be more helpful than visiting a museum. Para-professionals could be employed to a greater extent in these ancillary areas.

It is difficult for the schools to assess what they are doing, for the information is not readily available in small enough units, such as the individual school within the system or a regional grouping of schools serving a community. Records tend to conform to the requirements for fiscal accountability rather than for learning and development. Little or no data are kept to show relationships that could help to explain if certain techniques are indeed effective. If the teachers of the disadvantaged had such information, they could stress those factors that tend to bring about growth. As things stand today, every item has equal weight. All stocks do not represent good growth prospects any more than do all learning experiences. Furthermore, investments in different kinds of learning experiences bring about different results. One child may respond to visual materials, another through another sense. How can instruction be meaningful to each student when the needs of each child are not always considered in the learning situation.

The schools themselves are not capable of coping with the total problem. Proportionately, children from disadvantaged homes come from families that show a greater tendency towards instability and reflect economic resources that are significantly less than is true for the general population. In the main, these families have had less formal education, and therefore, the principal breadwinners perform in occupations that are less remunerative. In addition, because of a combination of factors, their patterns of expenditures tend to be ineffective. It is a chain of reactions that suggest that the handicaps are cumulative in nature.[8] Duncan states that the chain of events that tends to maintain these populations in their treadmill results from poverty as well as segregation, results from poorer and less schooling, results from job discrimination and inequality in employment in the labor market, results from differential pay salaries and low job security, which in turn limits income and ability to gain access to credit, which in turn reduces buying power. Even when equality of education and occupational achievement is reached, the social status in which these populations are held tends to inhibit development.[9]

In order to cope with the conditions that exist, the programs in the school, as well as other inputs from without, must be directed to an all-out attack on these problems. Teachers must be aware of these cycles and consider their effects on the learning environment. Teachers have a major responsibility in equipping youth with the attitudes and positive self-images that can be employed to build a better society. The realization that the resolution of these problems are in fact the basic requirements for the survival of this society has been witnessed by the events of the time.

An Approach for Improving the Learning Environment

Variations from the norm become the standards when one considers the needs of youth who have come to be referred to as "the disadvantaged." Yet, it is precisely these deviations that provide the instructor with an exciting milieu to work in, one of unlimited challenges. This requires communication among people, which is difficult even when parties have similar understandings and values.

Meaningful programs can be witnessed only when there is growth and development on the part of the students. This occurs when there is support brought about by acceptance of the student for the teacher. What makes one classroom environment conducive to development, whereas another is not? How can the stage be set so that institutions of learning are continuously releasing creative energies that result from significant experiences? If a business is to be successful, it must meet customer demands. Changes in the market are considered, and these developments are reflected in product and practice. The key is competition (interaction) as well as a reward system that is motivational.

If the programs offered by the schools are to succeed, the needs of youth must be identified and followed up by a treatment plan designed to achieve objectives. These programs must be coupled with appropriate rewards. In the same fashion that a business sets a target or a goal, so schools must understand their mission in terms that can be translated into systems capable of achieving the desired outcomes. Rewards for such achievement must be suitable and presented when deserved. In one setting, students receive time units for success. These can be traded for extra time in gym or in other activities of the student's choosing. (Experimental class in the Guilderland Public Schools, New York State.)

The key to this process of growth is pertinent interaction among the players (the students, the family, and the community of which the school is part). The separation of these components reduces the effectiveness of school programs. Isolation is a fantasy —interdependency is reality. Yet, the schools today tend to function in an atmosphere of isolation. This reinforces what has happened in the past and fails to consider the needs of today. Educators tend to compartmentalize learning. In the process, teachers tend to stress knowledge of the "facts" instead of providing opportunities for the student to acquire developmental skills.

In areas where readiness for learning has been an integral part of the home, the role of the school and identification of its mission are reinforced by the family. In areas where populations are disadvantaged, the readiness process may not have preceded the child's entrance into school. When school age is reached, the program of the school and the needs of the child are not in phase. Techniques that can be utilized by the teacher to determine the degree of readiness for learning should be used to test preschool children. When variations occur, treatments should be instituted. Preschool clinics are an example of such treatments. If children are not ready for the work in the first or second grade, other activities should be substituted to enhance readiness. Mental maturity varies with each individual so teachers should vary learning experience accordingly. The school has always considered homework for the child. It is also possible to tie into this activity an active role for the parents. The idea of a joint learning experience should be used to a far greater degree than it is used today.

For example, this may necessitate a new type of program involving the parents and their children in a participatory learning environment.

The following general description is presented with the view that curriculum planning must be made a continuous component of a school system.[10] Developing alternatives requires the breaking of "set," a feat that is not simple, for there is a basic need to bring an equilibrium to any system. If growth is to occur, there must be the upsetting of this tendency but in a planned manner. Fundamental to this process is the recognition that approaches that are held in reverence may not be the most effective way of meeting needs. Approaches aimed at decentralizing the schools have this in mind. The movement to have a voice in policy making may see dramatic changes in curriculum. Such subjects as African languages and Puerto Rican history may be taught in the public schools of New York as a result of such participation in the near future. Systems tend to create their own dogma. Failure to accept the dogma often results in severe penalties to the participant (students as well as staff). When a school system introduces procedures that reward change and experimentation, this will tend to release a chain of energies that will be directed with a primary focus on the development of the child. For example, merit awards have been an attempt in this direction.

There is the tendency on the part of society to see children from disadvantaged backgrounds as if they were infested with some communicable disease. This in turn sets up feelings and attitudes that reinforce the image. These children have similar needs (recognition, status, belonging, etc.) and respond positively when these needs are met. When they feel rejection, they respond appropriately. When they receive acceptance, their eyes glow. To increase that glow, alternative strategies need to be formulated. This requires planning to uncover and evaluate a series of approaches to arrive at the best possible system that will achieve a goal. In this process, the first step is to state all goals in terms of desired outcomes. After this has been accomplished, there is a need to review the current systems to see if they are designed to accomplish these goals. In this process, some assessment as to the degree of effectiveness of the current system should be obtained. In addition, problems and/or needs will emerge that may provide cues that suggest reasons for the concerns. Sometimes the causative agent is uncovered. In other instances, further exploration, including testing, may be required. To the extent that needs have been identified, it is possible to look at the current system and decide what might be accomplished to achieve the goal or to suggest several alternatives that are worthy of exploration and testing.

During the developmental stage, decisions must be made and guidelines and methodology established. The following outline attempts, in a modified sense, to provide a frame of reference from which solutions to problems may emerge. It is not intended to specify all of the steps, but merely suggest some critical items for consideration:

1. Goals have to be stated, and the reasons for them have to be indicated.

2. Criteria (standards) need to be identified that can be used to evaluate the degree to which the goal is achieved. (Measures need to be obtained based on the criteria that describe the relative success that the system is having in achieving the goal.)

3. Questions need to be raised to ascertain if the system is or is not achieving its objective. This will identify problems that can be handled either through recommending changes that are predictable, or recommending changes that may require some testing and further evaluation.

The carrying out of these steps may be referred to as a systems analysis. Sophisticated statistical techniques are not always required in such an undertaking. There is still considerable merit in using a "think" process.

In attempting to search for answers to the problems which have been identified, certain essential information gathering and analysis are required. These include: obtaining data that describe the problem; some indication as to whether it is a problem of a continuous nature or unique to the situation; what has been done about the problem or what is being planned; how have others handled this problem and what success or failures have they had; is this problem part of a series of concerns, and if so, how do they relate; are there times when the problem is more noticeable; what happens because the problem has not been resolved?

Answers to the above questions will lead to other questions that are concerned with arriving at solutions. These include: with the systems available, what modification might bring about the desired outcomes; if additional systems are needed, what is required to bring about the goal; for each of the alternatives suggested, what are some of the problems to be resolved to achieve the new approach; are there other problems which can be resolved through similar approaches; of the alternatives suggested, which seems, through experience and knowledge, to be the most effective, which is the most efficient, what appears to be most feasible; what are the benefits and costs associated with each of the alternatives; what approaches are recommended, and in what sequence should they be instituted?

In essence, the process described reflects the need to identify the extent that problems exist, as well as the probable reasons for their cause. It requires a thought process aimed at identifying possible solutions. It permits the identification of a series of alternatives from which a workable alternative may be identified— the alternative that is most effective, most efficient, and most feasible to achieve the desired goal at a particular time. The present attempt to decentralize large urban schools could be used to illustrate the approach. There is need, for example, to identify overall goals and objectives for the schools and to establish standards to ascertain the degree to which these goals have been met. Once this is known, alternatives can be worked out which are aimed at improving the schools in relation to these stated goals. These goals are comprised of items that are mandated by law and those determined by the policies of the board. The central administration should be charged with the responsibility of clarifying these objectives and communicating them to local school administrators. It should be the responsibility of the local administration, working with their staffs and community, to translate these into operational terms so that the process of education will be in tune with local needs. Teachers working with curriculum specialists need to develop and refine approaches that will achieve these results. In industry, for example, it has been found that smaller units that have specific responsibilities are more effective than one large system attempting to accomplish a goal. Economists have long recognized the concept of marginal utility which has the effect of reducing the efficiency of systems as they grow larger. If the schools could have a team of specialists responsible for certain activities, it is felt that the efficiency and effectiveness would increase. Because of the varied needs of youth in deprived areas, a multi-discipline approach is indicated.

When designing programs for the disadvantaged, other concepts need to be considered. There is expended annually, tremendous energies to have the child meet the requirements of the school. The need is for the school to meet the requirements of the child. It calls for sharing of success. Students need to teach each other to an extent far greater than is in evidence in schools today.[11] For example, older children could assist the teachers of younger children with the teaching of basic skills. Children who present learning problems to teachers in the upper grades (a case in point would be a socially aggressive youth) can be of assistance to other teachers in the lower grades. In the first instance, the younger child who already identifies with the older child may find it easier to accept instruction from him, and thereby overcome his own learning difficulties. The older child is rewarded through recognition and status and the feeling that positive accomplishments bring. In other words, instead of the teacher punishing the sixth grade child for acting out, she would be using his energies constructively. This in turn should result in better adjustments on the part of the older as well as the younger student. This requires a different focus. As one begins to assess needs and establish plans for implementation, what was once a static environment can become a dynamic learning situation. By definition the disadvantaged are atypical; it then follows that standard procedures will not achieve the development that is desired. Differences in values and attitudes lead to communication problems which also tend to reduce the effectiveness of the learning environment. Learning in this instance means an ability to break set and to assimilate new perceptions. If the teacher does not actively support this view in all of its undertakings, then how can he expect the child to develop the skills and understandings necessary to make these transformations? A creative environment fostered by the policies of the board and translated through leadership of the administration and staff is essential. This reference to creativity needs additional clarification.

In the context stated it means a significant interaction that results in the achievement of an objective, which in this instance is the growth and development of the child. This calls for participation, not role playing. This implies that a learning environment must generate a kind of energy only possible when there is a deep involvement and a commitment to creative development. The community, the board, the administration, the teacher and the students must work together not only to achieve understanding of what is, but to use knowledge as a creative force that leads to new frontiers, new heights, new accomplishments. This occurs in a setting where students and teachers learn not only about the world but about each other and themselves. It occurs in an environment that expresses acceptance, a place where the children know they have an identity, where someone cares.

The planning of schools of the future will require a variety of ancillary services. The investment in plant must be returned to the community in a variety of ways. There is no good reason why such a facility cannot be used for activities other than education. Future planning must include the concept of a school as a multipurpose center.[12] The activities that could be incorporated in such a resource might well be integrated with such programs as health, welfare, and employment. In the formulation of plans, the multipurpose concept could be so designed to improve the delivery of many services that are necessary to maximize the investment in learning. This requires identification of local needs and the planning of systems to adequately accomplish the mission. The school could take an active part in such developments. Many of the related activities in such endeavors provide teachers and students with excellent learning opportunities, and these experiences help to make constructive changes possible. This calls for program assessment followed by implementation and the testing of plans. Through this approach important gains may be realized.[13] With an ever increasing competition for the tax dollar, due consideration to this multi-service approach should be given.

Many benefits are achieved as the school actively engages in the planning endeavor. Problems can be identified and alternatives considered before decisions have to be reached. The associated planning activities help to create synergisms, that is, a releasing of creative energies that are greater than the inputs. These activities help to establish an atmosphere that is conducive to change.[14] Participation of all the staff is essential if such endeavors are to have lasting effects. Staff energies need to be harnessed. One way to accomplish this is through curriculum committees made up of teachers.

Considering the special needs of disadvantaged youth, certain additional aspects need to be considered. North and Buchman [15] found that teachers' attitudes have a direct effect on the learning process. Where teachers tended to express negative feelings about the children they worked with, their ability to be effective with them diminished. Positive attitudes were found where teachers were judged to be effective. A study conducted by Greenberg and Gerver [16] found that it was essential to take the attitude of the learner into consideration when planning programs. They found that children from deprived backgrounds, who were underachieving, did not tend to be reality-focused. Their study reveals that the children tended to lack critical ability as well as self-confidence. Assuming that the teacher of such children might expect a reality focus, it is possible that a stressful situation would result. The school, in this instance, may do well to provide programs that emphasize attitude development so that at a later stage the learning of skills can be accepted. Teachers need to be trained with understandings of the needs of disadvantaged students, and they must be made aware of how their own attitudes affect learning.

The complexities of our society involve forces outside of the school that must be considered in any learning situation. Some of these forces the school has little control over, and in other cases, the school would do well to take a more active role. An illustration of this point is the current public policy in the area of welfare that forces males out of many homes. Sandbon and Wesson [17] found that children from fatherless homes exhibited a consistently lower IQ than was found in the general population. This points out that social policy may well be a deterrent to effective school planning effort. It is for this reason that teachers must not only be concerned with the learning act, but in some manner must consider other forces that relate to the curriculum.

Conclusion

Planning efforts cannot be put into practice without a considerable investment in time, funds, and energy. In order to reach the deprived populations, alternative designs must be identified and need to be tested. The traditional teacher-class ratio cannot continue to prevail. The tendency for schools to be subject minded must also see a transition. In areas where the curriculum exhibits little relevance in relation to the needs of the child, how can there be hope for growth and development? Of what value is a report card system that substitutes symbols for reality? Certainly, a description of the child in relation to goals that are to be achieved has greater meaning for the child, his parents, and the teacher. Criteria can be spelled out and assessments can be made that help the teacher to judge the degree to which the standards have been achieved. An accumulative record of this nature could be used both to indicate special treatments for the child as well as for the school program. With school systems investing in computer hardware, such inventories are now feasible. Planning endeavors in part could be used to assist in the development of criteria in behavioral terms that might be used for such evaluation purposes. The principle of feedback has major importance in this situation.

The basic thesis which has been expressed is that true growth and development can only occur through meaningful interactions. This calls for the translation of theory into operational terms that can be measured. The schools have been unsuccessful in working with the disadvantaged because they are currently not equipped to handle the job. In many instances *institution* comes before *organization*. This simply reflects the phenomenon that results when values are accepted as fact.

Economists use the term *value added by manufacture*. Educators need to think in terms that measure the value added by their programs. Sensitivity to needs, coupled with the knowledge that there is accountability that goes along with any effort, is essential if the schools are to meet challenges that exist. Teachers cannot do this alone, nor can they remain alone in what they are doing. The challenges that lie ahead will test the most dedicated, but the goal of equality of opportunity through education can be achieved if creativity is given priority over conformity.

NOTES

1. Solon T. Kimbol, "Culture, Class, and Educational Congruency," Stanley Elam and William P. McLure (eds.), *Educational Requirements for the 1970's* (New York: Praeger Press, 1967), pp. 6–26.
2. Wilbur J. Cohen, "Education and Learning," *Social Goals and Indicators for American Society: II, The Annals,* Volume 373 (September 1967), p. 82.
3. Susan S. Stodolsly and Gerald Lesser, "Learning Patterns in the Disadvantaged," *Harvard Educational Review,* Volume 37, No. 4 (Fall 1967), pp. 546–593.
4. Cohen, *op. cit.,* p. 84.
5. Leonard Leacht, *Goals, Priorities and Dollars: The Next Decade* (New York: Free Press, 1966).
6. Richard D. E. Neufvill and Caryl Connor, "How Good Are Our Schools?", *American Education,* Volume 2 (October 1966), p. 4.
7. Benjamin Bloom, *Stability and Change in Human Characteristics* (New York: John Wiley, 1964).
8. Rashi Fein, "An Economic and Social Profile of the Negro American," *Daedalus,* Proceedings of the American Academy of Arts and Sciences (Fall 1965), pp. 815–846.
9. Otis Dudley Duncan, "Discrimination Against Negroes," *Social Goals and Indicators for American Society: I, The Annals,* Volume 371 (May 1967), pp. 85–103.
10. Edward A. Karg and Associates, *Administrative Curriculum Planning* (New York: Harper and Row, 1956).
11. Kenneth B. Single, Donald A. Davis, and Albert Maze, "Interpersonal Effects on Underachievers," *The Journal of Educational Research,* Volume 61, No. 5 (January 1968), pp. 208, 210.
12. Henry Saltzman, "The Community in the Urban Setting," A. Harry Passow (ed.), *Education in Depressed Areas* (New York: Teachers College, Columbia University, 1963), pp. 322–331.
13. Edwin C. Coffin, "Designing an Administrative Structure for a Changing Educational System," *Journal of Secondary Education,* Volume 43 (January 1968), pp. 26–29.
14. Harold G. Shane and June Grant Shane, "Future Planning and the Curriculum," *Phi Delta Kappan,* Volume 49 (March 1968), pp. 372–377.
15. George E. North and O. Lee Buchanan, "Teacher Views of Poverty Area Children," *The Journal of Educational Research,* Volume 61, No. 21 (October 1967), pp. 53–58.
16. Judith W. Greenberg, Joan M. Gerver, Jeane Chall, and Helen H. Davidson, "Attitudes of Children from a Deprived Environment

Towards Achievement-Related Concepts," *The Journal of Educational Research,* Volume 59 (October 1965), pp. 57–62.

17. Marshall P. Sanborn and Robert M. Wesson, "Guidance of Students with Special Characteristics," *Review of Educational Research,* Volume 36 (April 1966), pp. 308–326.

Part Three

WHAT PREPARATION DO TEACHERS OF DISADVANTAGED YOUTH NEED?

If the problems of educating disadvantaged America are to be solved, it will be largely through the efforts of capable, understanding, and imaginative teachers. Teachers in the ghettos, as well as in the impoverished rural communities, must be adequately prepared to do the job that society expects them to accomplish. Teacher education programs cannot afford to be as archaic as the "horse and buggy" on Madison Avenue. The graduates of these programs must begin their careers with optimum competence and confidence.

Philip D. Vairo and William Perel call for a dialogue on some of the "nuts and bolts" issues of teacher education programs. The overall strengthening of university and college programs is a requisite to meeting the educational needs of our disadvantaged population. The authors have directed attention to three areas: 1) the relationship between the arts and sciences faculty and the education faculty; 2) the professional interests and experience of the educational faculty; and 3) the student teaching internship experience.

Preparing teachers for urban areas is one of the most difficult challenges that face our institutions of teacher education. Harry N. Rivlin proposes a new pattern for urban teacher education. He points out that unless urban schools develop the expert teachers they need, our nation will be headed for a great disillusionment. The question he attempts to answer is how can we prepare teachers so that they will be competent when they begin to teach and then mature as experts and members of a profession.

David E. Hunt presents a model for analyzing the training of

345

training agents which is applicable to the assessment, training, and placement of teachers, psychotherapists, social workers, and allied personnel. Training-agent effectiveness is defined by Hunt as the capacity to radiate a wide variety of environments, to select from this variety a specific environment to be radiated toward a particular person or group with the aim of producing a particular behavioral outcome, and to shift from one environment to another under separate circumstances.

Frank Riessman presents a fivefold plan for the training of both preservice and inservice teachers of urban disadvantaged children. His plan includes: 1) building teacher respect for disadvantaged children and their families; 2) supplying teacher experiences with the disadvantaged; 3) general guides for teaching the urban poor; 4) a teaching technology appropriate for low-income youngsters; and 5) the development of a variety of teacher styles.

Alvin P. Lierheimer's remarks are concerned with the preparation of teachers for urban schools. He points out that the problems of teaching in disadvantaged schools fall into two areas: 1) inability to be precise in analyzing, carrying out, and evaluating the teaching act; and 2) failure to demonstrate in a classroom warmth and psychologically astute support. The author emphasizes the importance of a cooperative venture between college faculties and state education departments.

21 PREREQUISITES FOR THE PREPARATION OF TEACHERS OF DISADVANTAGED YOUTH

PHILIP D. VAIRO AND WILLIAM PEREL

During the last decade a great deal of the professional literature has focused on the problems of the disadvantaged. Special programs, inservice institutes, workshops, and so forth, have been designed for the preservice and inservice training of teachers to work with the underprivileged citizens of the inner city as well as of the rural sections of our nation. However rewarding we believe these programs have been, there is one underlying assumption which, in essence, has been ignored. Can specialized programs for the disadvantaged be effective, with the lack of the basic ingredients that are so necessary for sound preservice and inservice training programs for teachers?

Because it would indeed be an impossible task to attempt to explore all the facets of teacher training that are in dire need of improvement, the authors in this paper have limited their scope to three areas: 1) the relationship between the arts and sciences faculty and the education faculty; 2) the professional interests and experience of the educational faculty; and 3) the student-teaching internship experience.

Only when these "nuts and bolts" issues have been crystallized, and only then, can we really make a breakthrough in the specialized programs designed for disadvantaged youth. There is no point talking about using the total resources of the university to fight poverty and assist the underprivileged when in reality the faculty of arts and sciences and the education faculty do not communicate with each other. To complicate matters, when senior professors of education consider supervising student teachers the least important function and the most undesirable assignment, and junior faculty view a promotion as a chance to

This paper draws on three previous writings of the authors.

escape from involvement with teacher training, the most imaginative program supported by adequate funds will result in frustration.

Our thesis is simply to point the finger at three important areas that need to be revitalized before a meaningful program designed to assist teachers and students alike who teach and live in our urban ghettos and impoverished rural communities can be implemented.

Needed: Dialogue between Professors of Education and Academicians *

At the outset, the authors raise the question of what is the most important duty of a university. Immediately, the training of scholars is mentioned, and perhaps, rightly so. Nevertheless, the university is a proper place for the training of teachers of teachers and the training of teachers for all levels: kindergarten, elementary, secondary, and college or university. It is indeed one of the tragedies of American higher education that liberal arts and teacher education faculties have not been able to communicate, or at least have a tolerant understanding of each other's goals. Perhaps, in the last analysis, the liberal arts faculties have been primarily responsible for this wasteful conflict because the job of training teachers was rejected by them many decades ago.

Although new approaches to teacher education and in particular the disadvantaged have been reported, they still follow, in general, the traditional patterns. There has been a general reluctance on the part of both the education faculty and the faculty of other disciplines within our universities to depart from the traditional ways of preparing teachers. Innovating programs for the disadvantaged community are needed if really significant changes in the training of teachers are to be made. It would seem obvious that these changes can come only after considerable discussion among all of those persons charged with the responsibility of educating teachers. Certainly, the academic departments of the university will continue to instruct prospective teachers in those

---

* William Perel and Philip D. Vairo, "Needed: Dialogue between Professors of Education and Academicians," *Liberal Education* (December 1966), pp. 470–478. Reprinted by permission of the authors and publisher.

subjects that the prospective teachers will be expected to teach in addition to providing them with what is usually called a liberal education. However, even about carrying out this most basic duty, there is room for discussion. For example, elementary school teachers are now expected to teach mathematics, general science, social studies, and language arts.

However, in many universities there are no courses in precisely these areas. For example, the prospective teacher may study chemistry, physics, biology, geology, and so on, but usually there is no room in the curriculum for all of these. Yet, in most universities, there is no course of a general nature in science that would provide the teacher with the necessary integrated subject matter background. Is there any discussion concerning the feasibility of such a course of study? In most universities there is not.

What about social studies, at either the elementary or secondary level? In most universities there is no such thing as a course in social studies; indeed, "social studies" usually aroused no enthusiasm in professors of history, political science, and so on. Can we expect the teacher to take courses in political science, history, sociology, economics, and other so-called social sciences and thus obtain a broad, general knowledge of social studies that he can impart to students? It seems most unlikely, even when the student has found time to take separate courses in each of these areas. Why is there no discussion of the possibility of other curricular experiences for prospective teachers?

In mathematics, we must ask whether the usual freshman and sophomore courses, with their enrollment often dominated by science and engineering majors, are appropriate curricular experiences for the prospective elementary school teacher. The Committee on the Undergraduate Program in Mathematics (CUPM) of the Mathematical Association of America has made an exhaustive study of this problem and published its recommendations, but these recommendations have been implemented in only a handful of universities. Of course, these recommendations may be surrounded with controversy, but it is the authors' opinion that this controversy is not being aired and that mathematics faculties and education faculties not only are not discussing these recommendations, but in many cases are not even aware that they exist.

Another area of common concern and interest should be the professional education of the prospective teacher. Why should such course work as educational psychology, sociology of education, history of education, educational statistics, and so on remain the exclusive province of the professors of education? Why should our future teachers be insulated from exposure to other students, by studying so-called specialized courses within a school of education? Cannot these courses best be handled cooperatively by the respective departments of psychology, sociology, history, and mathematics and the education faculty? When will our academic departments assume their responsibility in the preparation of teachers?

The faculty of education can often claim with some justice that history departments are not usually interested in teaching the history of education, that sociology departments are not interested in teaching the sociology of education, and that psychology departments would often rather not involve themselves with the education of teachers. Still, it is not common for education faculties to urge these courses upon the departments that ought to teach them. At least, one would hope that there would be some dialogue about the content of these courses with persons from other departments trained specifically in the disciplines involved. The isolation from the rest of the university in which such courses are usually taught lends weight to the often false charge that these courses, as taught by professors of education, have little content and low standards. And certainly, it seems strange to find a professor of education teaching a graduate course in statistics on a campus which has available a professor holding a doctorate in statistics.

We all believe or pretend to believe that one of the advantages of university education is the contact students have with each other. Students do learn from one another. Why should not the prospective teacher take his history from a professor of history while seated beside an English major? Why should he not learn his statistics from a statistician while seated beside a sociology major? Many university faculty members, as well as the authors, are asking these questions.

The most important part of the professional training of a teacher ought to be his training in methods, followed by his student teaching experience. How tragic it is that use is not made of those persons on the faculty of a university who have had excellent training in their respective disciplines and years of experience teaching them! Why should not the professors of English, history, and mathematics, for example, cooperate with the teacher education faculty in methods courses and in the supervision of student teachers in their areas of competence? A fuller discussion of this point will be made later in this paper.

It is unfortunately true that professors in the academic departments have only rarely had experience as elementary or secondary school teachers. Furthermore, the authors have found, incredible as it may seem, that professors having such experience often seek to keep it hidden, fearing loss of status within the academic community. On the other hand, no attempt is being made by the education faculties to reach those academic professors willing to admit to such experience. It is not our purpose to urge that the student-teaching experience be put under the charge of a faculty member who is himself without teaching experience at that level. But there is no valid reason why a faculty member with experience and training in the discipline could not cooperate with a faculty member having elementary or secondary school teaching experience, as the case might be, in the evaluation of the efforts of a student teacher. However, in many universities, academic faculties avoid contact with professors of education and some may even go so far as to reject the idea that teacher education is a legitimate function of a university.

One solution to the problem of communication herein presented is a university committee on teacher education. Such a committee would normally consist of one member from each of the academic departments involved plus one or more members of the education faculty. Such committees do exist in some universities, but not in many others. Even where such a committee does exist, its value is often limited by the persons who compose it. If membership on this committee is regarded by an academic department as a chore, to be foisted on the least influential or most junior member of the department, one cannot say that communication has taken place. Although ideally a mathematics department might have a member trained in mathematics education who could well serve on this committee besides assisting in other ways with the training of mathematics teachers, there is no academic home for the person trained in science education or social studies education. Persons trained in science education, for example, are not usually welcomed as members of a chemistry or physics department, and they do not really belong there. It must also be admitted that persons trained in mathematics education are not often welcomed as members of a mathematics department, and if allowed as members, seldom have much influence with their departmental colleagues.

While a committee on teacher education is then, a step in the right direction and a step that ought to be attempted in those universities that lack such a committee, it cannot be hoped that such a committee will be a real benefit unless there is a real change in attitude on the part of both academicians and professors of education.

Such accrediting agencies as the National Council for Accreditation of Teacher Education (NCATE) and many state departments of education are requiring as a prerequisite for accreditation that teacher education be recognized as an institution-wide function and receive full cooperation, support, and constructive participation from every department and division. Conant says:

> If the institution is engaged in educating teachers, the lay board of trustees should ask the faculty or faculties whether in fact there is a continuing and effective all university (or inter-departmental) approach to the education of teachers; and, if not, why not.[1]

At times one cannot help but wonder how important the teacher training function of a university is regarded by the university administration and board of trustees. Surely, a sympathetic and enlightened administration and board could play an important part in establishing the means of communication, whether through a teacher education committee, a conference on teacher education, or by some other means. It is not enough for the board of trustees to pass a resolution that states that teacher education is a major function of the university that it governs.

Basically the difficulty is one of isolation—geographic isolation and ideological isolation. Within big universities, education is often a separate college or school, with its own building and its own structure of graduation requirements, departments, and rules of procedure. If its building is located at some distance from the academic buildings, as is often the case, more particularly, if its building has its own faculty lounge, separate and distinct from the lounge used by other faculty members, a lack of communication is certain to follow. The authors recognize that the problem of geographic isolation is one which besets a faculty at any large university and that a less than adequate program in teacher education is only one of the drawbacks of such isolation from the total university educational program. However, such isolation does exist, and it would seem clear that conversations between professors of education and other professors are not going to take place by accidental meetings on a campus with thousands of students and several hundred faculty members.

If innovations for the teaching of the disadvantaged are going to be explored, new techniques developed, and inservice programs for university faculty implemented, the authors call, then, for a dialogue between professors of education and the other professors on every university campus. Teacher education is a university enterprise and all segments of the academic community must make a concerted effort in solving the problems of the disadvantaged.

Probably, a beginning must be made by the professors of education. Because the education faculty has the primary responsibility for coordinating the campus-wide effort in teacher education, it follows that they must initiate the articulation between themselves and the other departments. The authors believe that communication can be established if the professors of education remember that the training of teachers is a university function, and not solely their private preserve. We said earlier that students learn from one another. Let us hope that faculties also can learn from one another.

Professor, Is Your Experience Outdated? *

It is never easy or simple to identify two or three factors as panaceas for a profession's shortcomings. However, how can we rebuild the teaching profession if we ignore or remain passive

* Philip D. Vairo and William Perel, "Professor, Is Your Experience Outdated?," *Educational Forum* (November 1968), pp. 39–44. Reprinted by permission of the authors and publisher.

toward the very people who are responsible for the training of teachers, the college professors?

There is indeed a need for dialogue on the role of the college professor in teacher training. For a starter, the authors raise the question: why are professors of education held in low repute by their colleagues in the liberal arts?

Professors of education are frequently held in low repute by faculty members of the academic departments because it is believed that professors of education teach students how to teach. It is an interesting observation on academic attitudes that any program that is intended to teach students how to do something is held in low repute. Thus, Phi Beta Kappa, the most prestigious honor society of Academia, will not consider courses in engineering, accounting, and education because these courses are felt to be "how to do something" as opposed to being "about something." The general public also believes that the education faculty of a university devotes itself to the training of prospective teachers, and regards such training as the proper and appropriate role of the education professors within a university.

However, many professors of education are not involved at all with the training of teachers, nor do they want to be involved. Since professors of education have often been the scapegoats of the academic faculty, sometimes justly so, they have tended to play down the practical aspect of their teaching experience and focus their attention on the so-called theoretical questions of the day. As an education professor gains experience and rises in rank and seniority at his institution, there is a tendency for him to become further and further removed from the teacher training role of his institution and to become more and more involved with course work in philosophy and history of education, counseling psychology, school administration, and educational psychology, and so on. Particularly is the above true if the professor devotes more and more of his time to graduate instruction.

Because our society needs teachers and because departments, schools, and colleges of education are expected by society to prepare the needed teachers and were created for that purpose, let us accept that role. Let us accept it, not as a necessary chore, but as one of the oldest and most honored purposes of college or university education. It is very unfortunate that any university faculty member regards involvement with the training of teachers as degrading. But for a professor of education to seek to remove himself from this aspect of higher education is intolerable.

One of the major criticisms launched against teacher-training programs is that the personnel instructing the beginning teachers have had little or no teaching experience during the past five or ten years, on the level at which they are supposedly preparing teachers. To complicate matters, some of our elementary and secondary school administrators have proceeded on the naive assumption that new teachers who are employed know how to teach, or perhaps should learn on the job by a process of trial and error. School administrators have themselves often not actually taught for many years. However, serious as the latter problem is, it is our purpose to confine our attention here to the elementary or secondary school teaching experience of the professor of education.

It must be said that the college professor of methods and student teaching must be a person of sufficient competence and one who possesses sufficiently recent teaching experience, in view of the rapid changes in the profession, to be respected by those novice teachers whom he is preparing. Certainly, as a minimum qualification, we should demand that the professor return to full-time teaching, at the grade levels at which he prepares teachers, for at least one semester every five or six years. The professor should serve as an exchange colleague or as a visiting teacher in a secondary or elementary school, with his salary supplemented by his college or university, so that this exchange program would entail no financial sacrifice on the part of the professor. During this semester, the college professor should be actively involved in observation and interclass visitations in the school at which he is obtaining his in-service training. Teachers in the school should have an opportunity to observe demonstration lessons given by the more experienced teachers and supervisory personnel in the school. New media and teaching innovations should be introduced to the professor during his tenure at the school. Most of all, he should be encouraged to experiment and attempt to implement new ideas and practices in his daily lessons. In essence, on the job, in-service training should be a real and meaningful experience for the college professor.

It is unfortunately true that a college professor, because of his long absence from public school teaching, might be less competent than are some of the student teachers he is supervising. In such cases, the resentment toward and lack of regard for the college professor, on the part of the student, is readily understandable. Frequently, an apprentice teacher will say, "When was the last time Dr. Jones actually taught in a high school?" There is no substitute for actual classroom experience! Perhaps Dr. James B. Conant was justified in suggesting that there is a need for a clinical professor in education. It is not at all uncommon for the college professor to have been away from classroom teaching for more than fifteen years. It is easy to see why the student teacher may find it difficult to accept advice and criticism from the college professor, whom he cannot respect professionally.

Yet the very colleges and universities that are engaged in educating teachers provide no relief so that the college professor can return to the public school. Sabbatical leaves are seldom, if ever, available for this purpose. Even if they were, most professors probably would rather use their sabbaticals for purposes other than obtaining fresh experience in precollege teaching. Institutions not offering sabbaticals to their staffs, and there are a large number of such institutions, have not initiated plans, to the best of the authors' knowledge, whereby education faculty members could return to the public schools without substantial loss in salary. In no real sense can a professor of education give attention to improving his knowledge of teaching techniques at the elementary and secondary levels and broadening his horizons while he is teaching a full load of courses at his college or university.

Before we can develop expert teachers to deal effectively with the educational problems of our day, we are going to need to expose more of our trainers of teachers to up-to-date teaching experiences in our schools. The National Education Association [2] in a recent study pointed out three areas in which teachers were found lacking in their preparation. These are: (1) teaching methods (24 per cent); (2) classroom management, routines, and discipline (28 per cent); (3) use of audiovisual equipment and materials (49 per cent). All three of these areas are directly related to the instruction they received from the teacher education faculty. It can be readily recognized that the three areas mentioned above, because of their very nature, require recent teaching experience on the part of the college professor.

One of the greatest problems in education today is the education of the culturally deprived or disadvantaged youth. This problem is particularly acute in urban areas where some attempt must be made to bring young people out of the urban ghetto slums and into the mainstream of American life.

The crisis in the preparation of teachers in this area is due not only to inadequate resources on hand, but also to the professor's lack of familiarity and teaching experience with the under-privileged in our urban ghettos. Our universities and colleges will need to redesign their teacher education programs and recruit staff who can prepare teachers in up-to-date methods and media so that they can teach the children of poverty.

Dr. J. C. Sitterson, Chancellor of the University of North Carolina at Chapel Hill, reported in the *Southern Education Report* that teacher education graduates from his institution "are far less prepared to teach disadvantaged children than we'd like them to be or feel they should be." This comment is typical of those from many institutions.

It is often claimed that teachers are members of the middle class, almost by definition. Even those teachers who grew up in slums seem to enter the middle class at the same time they receive their teaching certificates. A great deal that is written on this subject puts too much emphasis on what must be done to assist the prospective teacher in obtaining knowledge and understanding of the disadvantaged. Too little emphasis is placed upon improving the understanding of these problems upon the part of the professors of education. If teachers in the elementary and secondary schools are middle class, surely the professors in the colleges and universities are middle or upper middle class.

Dr. Herbert Scheuler, president of Richmond College of the City University of New York, in a book recently published by *Phi Delta Kappan, Improving Teacher Education in the United States*, says that a teacher education program for the underprivileged and the children of poverty "cannot be developed in an ivory tower apart and remote from the people it is intended to serve." The fashioners and builders of teacher education curricula must go back to the schools and re-orient themselves.

The National Council on Education for the Disadvantaged recently singled out the attitudes of teachers as the crucial ingredient in success or failure in teaching culturally deprived youth. Only by actual contact with the children of the poor can the professor readily appreciate their problems and be able to share his experience with his own students. The professor must recognize that the children of poverty in the urban ghettos have special problems and special needs. It is insufficient to just read about their problems in professional literature, for very frequently the authors who purport to be experts on these problems have themselves never taught in a school serving the children of poverty.

Professors of education, in general, have had little experience with culturally deprived students. Thus, a cycle is begun whereby professors with little experience in or knowledge of the problems of teaching the culturally deprived, teach prospective teachers, who, in turn, will not be properly prepared to teach the children of the poor, the disadvantaged, and the culturally deprived people of the urban slums. It is pointless to attempt to assess blame or to heap recriminations upon the heads of professors of education or other professors. But it needs to be said over and over again that most people in teacher education have virtually no real first-hand experience in the problems of educating culturally disadvantaged youth. With this fact society must deal. If we are to take decisive steps, which will break this cycle, then a beginning must be made with the preparation of teacher education professors and with in-service education that consists of real experience on the levels on which they are preparing teachers.

Much could be written about the problems of educating culturally deprived youth. However, it is our purpose here only to to call for continuing contact between elementary and secondary schools on the one hand and colleges of education on the other. Cultural deprivation, curricular change, and changes in methods of instruction are only some of the problems of the schools in which those who teach teachers need to keep constantly in mind.

Hopefully, professors of education, if not other academicians, will keep in mind that their primary function is to prepare teachers and they will regard this function as fully worthy of their attention and interest. Particularly as a professor of education rises in rank and seniority and becomes more and more involved with the graduate program of his institution, with all of the prestige and fringe benefits usually associated with involvement with graduate programs, he will still maintain an interest and involvement with this primary function of his discipline.

Once the idea of continued involvement with the training of teachers is reestablished, surely it is only logical that the idea of periodic returns to secondary and elementary school classrooms by professors of education can gain acceptance.

Is Student Teaching Bankrupt? *

Unfortunately, the most important aspect of teacher training, the student teaching internship, has taken on an unpleasant connotation. The colleges and universities, the public schools, and the profession as a whole have given this matter very little, if any, serious consideration. Little or no effort has been made to develop an internship for the prospective teacher that represents a well-planned program. On the whole, attempts have been feeble and unworthy of the profession. There is no comparison, for example, between the professional experience required by a medical intern and that required of the student teacher. At best, student teaching is a superficial exposure. The short duration of the internship plus inadequate supervision and first-hand experience does little to prepare students for classroom leadership. For these and other reasons, the authors say that student teaching is bankrupt and needs a total reevaluation.

Some of our schools have proceeded on the naive assumption that students sent to them by the colleges and universities for student teaching already know how to teach or will learn on the job by a process of trial and error. Student teaching programs are often haphazard affairs with a minimum amount of direction and coordination. Although there is a need to reduce the faculty-student teacher ratio considerably, many colleges have a student-teacher ratio of at least twenty to one during student teaching.

Often during his internship the student teacher is overwhelmed

* Philip D. Vairo and William Perel, "Is Student Teaching Bankrupt?," *Clearing House* (April 1968), pp. 251–258. Reprinted by permission of the authors and publisher.

with many chores which divert his attention from real teaching and which complicate and frustrate the objectives of the experience. The cooperating teacher also has many demands placed upon him. He is expected to be chaperon, a public relations man, a personal friend, and an excellent teacher. There is urgent need for clarification of the role of the cooperating teacher. Should he not be considered a member of the college faculty? His duties are certainly vital to the teacher education program. Why not recognize the cooperating teacher as a professional colleague in fact as well as in spirit?

It must be said that the cooperating teacher must be a person of sufficient competence to be respected by those student teachers whom he is to supervise. Certainly, as a minimum qualification, we should demand that a cooperating teacher hold a master's degree with subject matter concentration as well as education courses and have at least three years of teaching experience. Further, he ought to have received some relatively recent training through workshops, institutes, or short courses. Such programs supported by the National Science Foundation or by the Office of Education are now fairly common, and there is no reason why teachers with such experiences would not be available in most areas. The supervising teacher ought to have a sufficiency of both subject matter knowledge and teaching techniques to enable him to make constructive suggestions to the young novice. Unfortunately, it sometimes happens that the cooperating teacher is less competent than are some of the student teachers he is expected to supervise. In such cases the resentment of the student teacher being supervised is readily understandable.

Further, to give a teacher the title *cooperating teacher* and then give him no reduction in his own teaching load or additional compensation is to pretend that the student teacher does not need special help which is time-consuming for the cooperating teacher. In such cases, the cooperating teacher is only a device by which the college administration and the public schools can relieve themselves of some of the details of student teacher supervision. In no real sense can a cooperating teacher give attention to the supervision of a student teacher within his classroom, while he is himself teaching a full load of courses! Remuneration without a course load reduction is not the answer either, as there are only so many hours in each day. The failure to recognize the efforts of the co-operating teacher often leads the cooperating teacher to adopt a cynical attitude, and simply use his student teachers to divest himself of some of his work load. Why should we expect a teacher who has not received special training in supervision, and who is not regarded by either his superiors or by the college authorities as one who is making an important contribution to teacher education, to regard his role as sufficiently important to give it his fullest attention?

Another stumbling block has been that mutual observation among student teachers and experienced teachers has run head-on into our tradition of respecting the so-called privacy of the teacher in his classroom. Older teachers and departmental chairmen should be encouraged to visit the classes taught by the student teacher, and the student teacher should be encouraged to visit their classes. The authors have found this practice to be the exception rather than the rule.

One of the basic principles of supervision is that it assists a teacher in utilizing to the maximum his abilities and resources. There is little doubt that every teacher possesses strengths and capabilities of which he may not even be aware that are not integrated fully into the teaching situation. With professional guidance and direction the student teacher can identify and assess his strengths and resources. Helping the young teacher to develop a sense of security and a realistic self-appraisal are essential attributes of the cooperating teacher and college supervisor. However, as long as the student teacher is assigned a grade for the experience, a strange relationship exists between supervisor and student. Why must a grade be assigned? Would not pass or fail suffice? Physicians are required to complete an internship as a condition for licensing, but they are not assigned grades.

The cooperating teacher and college supervisor must have the capacity for professional interpretation to the teacher. Student teachers may not be psychologically ready to explore their own resources, and the cooperating teacher and college supervisor will both need to relate in a positive, constructive fashion if they are to help the student teacher's functioning. Needless to say, it is not their function to provide wholesale recipes for classroom situations and techniques of teaching. Present supervisory practices, such as the convenient "check list," in many instances are as archaic as would be the horse and buggy on Madison Avenue.

If the "Big Brother" attitude conveyed by Carbone [3] exists in most supervisory situations, which the authors have some serious reservations about, there is little doubt that supervision is not providing the necessary ingredients to assist either the classroom teacher or the student teacher. Although perhaps exaggerating the point, Carbone suggests that teachers tend to think that the supervisor is always trying to check up on them—even going so far as to tune in their classes on the intercom system. This negative attitude towards supervision is often conveyed to the student teacher by the experienced teachers. In a recent popular novel, set in a New York high school, the teachers referred to the possibility of visits by their department chairmen with the phrase, "the ghost walks." Such attitudes seem to be fairly common in real life, as well. But only with proper supervision and understanding may a student teacher develop into an adequate teacher, and a mediocre teacher develop into an outstanding classroom performer. The authors believe that the present practices do not lend themselves to a wholesome professional experience.

During the student teaching experience, while the tyro is subject to the supervision of a cooperating teacher, much improvement ought to be possible. But most cooperating teachers have had no special training in supervision, not even so much as one course. Why should not some course work in supervision be part of the master's program for a teacher who, having earned a master's degree, should be in a position to offer leadership in teaching. If the cooperating teacher has only a bachelor's degree and only two or three years of teaching experience it is very common to find that the student teacher, having more recent training, and perhaps at a superior university or college, knows a great deal more about his subject than does the cooperating teacher. If, then, the cooperating teacher knows neither more about the subject nor more about the teaching nor anything about supervision, it is not surprising that he is not respected by the student teacher who has been put in his charge. Under such circumstances, the student teacher will find it difficult to accept such advice and criticism as he is given. Even worse, the cooperating teacher may be so insecure himself that he will not be able to offer any advice or criticism.

Student evaluation should also be very much a part of the student teaching experience. How can it be ignored? Although it is conceded that some students lack the necessary judgment, this limitation does not offset the fact that student responses can be helpful in many ways. The student teacher and cooperating teacher can get some ideas about the attitudes and reactions of the students. We seldom consult the students who, after all, are the very reason we are attempting to improve instruction. Evaluation often comes from some administrative source. The students, even those in the early grades, can offer valuable suggestions. Student opinion on the quality of instruction is valuable only if properly interpreted, however. But in any program of student ratings, care must be taken to avoid giving the students the impression that a student teacher obtains his grade at their pleasure. Surely students can be shown that their opinions are valued and respected, without turning the school over to student control.

If the role of the cooperating teacher in the student teaching experience is less than satisfactory, and if the students being taught are given no role at all, what of the role of the university professor who is assigned to observe student teachers? Many of these professors consider the function of observing student teachers as not worthy of their professional time. Particularly, as a professor rises in rank and seniority and becomes more and more involved with graduate programs, with all of the prestige and fringe benefits usually associated with such involvement, he tends to lose interest and concern in actively participating in this primary function of his discipline, preparing teachers.

The college supervisor's purpose would be to assist the student teacher in improving his teaching, rather than simply to rate the teacher for the purpose of assigning a grade. Care should be taken not to interrupt or embarrass the student teacher in any way. Frequent, informal, short visits are to be preferred to a few very long visits. Usually, more information may be obtained by weekly visits than by even all day visits at less frequent intervals.

Let us attract the most qualified of our teacher education faculty to serve as college supervisors and not rely upon graduate assistants and young, inexperienced faculty for this important work.

Also, colleges and universities should select with care the cooperating teachers. Often the cooperating teacher is selected by a school principal, without prior consultation with the college supervisor. And in some cases the cooperating teacher is required to accept the student teacher. For much too long, we have set our professional sights too low. The time has arrived for us to broaden them and develop a student teaching program of the first order.

The authors believe that the present status of the student teaching experience is so seriously deficient as to warrant the word *bankrupt*. Unless considerable improvement can be made in the existing pattern, the time will come when we must consider changing the pattern altogether. Already, some criticism has been leveled at the present method of giving prospective teachers their practical experience. Perhaps the solution to the problem is to abandon student teaching as part of the undergraduate training of a prospective teacher. Perhaps the schools themselves must take a larger role in the training of teachers and provide something more like the one-year internship now required of physicians. If the teaching profession is ever to be accorded the respect now given to the other professions, perhaps the time will come when teachers are required to complete a full year of practical experience beyond their education.

The authors do not advocate so drastic a step as the abolition of the student teaching program, as it is now known. Before any thought can be given to abandoning the procedures now in use, a great deal of thought and study and effort should go into an attempt to make the present procedures work. What is advocated for the present is recognition that student teaching in its present form is bankrupt and that study, thought, and experimentation are vitally needed to remedy the most important gap in the entire teacher training program. We believe that student teaching can be made to work in the present framework. But unless those in authority recognize that it has not been working satisfactorily in the past, we shall either continue to produce unsatisfactorily trained teachers for the schools at a time when education is becoming vitally important to our national survival, or society will demand that drastic and perhaps dangerous re-evaluations of the entire teacher education program be made.

Concluding Remarks

Although there are no panaceas, first and foremost the authors contend that if the economic sector of our society does not provide the necessary mobility and opportunity so frequently promised to our less privileged citizens, whatever attempts are made by the school will be minimized. We can no longer look to just one social institution, let it be church, state, or school for solution of the multitude of problems in our complex society.

As the battles of our generation rage about and around the school and the university, without there being much action or reaction by these educational institutions, it is not surprising that the school has become the symbol of the *status quo* to many of our disadvantaged citizens. Clearly, the school ought to be the symbol of progress and change. We must quit talking about how nice it was in the old days when all students were so much better motivated, so much more eager to learn (or so we are told), and start talking about how to motivate children from the ghetto, how to deal with all of the problems that beset mid-twentieth century America.

In the last analysis, well trained teachers are the essential ingredients if the cultural and educational level of all our citizens is to be raised. If decisive steps are to be initiated to break the cycle of cultural deprivation, the logical place to begin with is the training of teachers and those who train teachers.

NOTES

1. James B. Conant, *The Education of American Teachers* (New York: McGraw-Hill Book Co., 1963), p. 110.
2. Hazel Davis, "Profile of the American Public School Teacher, 1966," *NEA Journal*, 56 (May 1967), p. 12.
3. Robert F. Carbone, "Big Brother is in the Office," *Phi Delta Kappan*, 57 (November 1965), pp. 34–37.

22 A NEW PATTERN FOR URBAN TEACHER EDUCATION

HARRY N. RIVLIN

Teaching is difficult, and teaching people how to teach in an urban school is one of the most difficult of all kinds of teaching. Teaching is a skill, but unlike many other skills, it cannot be learned solely by an apprenticeship. Teaching is based on scholarship, but enriching the teacher's scholarship does not assure effective teaching, for unless the teacher can communicate his scholarship to his students and arouse their zest for learning, he is not teaching. Similarly, teaching is in part an interrelationship between teacher and students, but preparation for teaching is more than learning how to get along with people.

The problems which urban schools face are often only an accentuation of those which confront all American schools, but sometimes they are so much more acute they look entirely different. City teachers must be able to retain their own individuality and respect their students as individuals, even when schools and school systems are so huge that the individual seems to be lost in an organization chart. The schools must be prepared to teach children from widely different social backgrounds and must know how to teach those who suffer from social discrimination and economic handicaps. The teachers must be skilled in working with both the academically talented and those with little interest in or background for academic success. The schools have to be able to correct educational handicaps without watering down the curriculum, lest parents who are concerned with the quality of education withdraw their children from public and enroll them in private schools, thereby making school integration a cruel hoax as a new kind of segregation develops.

Harry N. Rivlin, "A New Pattern for Urban Teacher Education," *Journal of Teacher Education* (Summer 1966), pp. 177–184. Reprinted by permission of the author and publisher.

There is general agreement that student teaching is a most valuable part of preparation for teaching. Nevertheless, student teaching, as it is generally conducted, is far from adequate for urban teachers; and it needs more than patchwork changes to make it adequate. There is just too big a gap between the limited experience and responsibility of a student teacher and the full responsibilities of a classroom teacher, which the new teacher is expected to be able to shoulder the minute he is appointed. It is not enough to recruit new teachers and let them sink or swim, for too many refuse to get their feet wet, and some do not even go near the water.

How can we prepare teachers so that they will be competent when they begin to teach and then will mature as experts and members of a profession?

Preliminary Studies. The major part of the proposed plan begins when the prospective teacher is a college senior or a college graduate. Prior to his admission into the program, the student can follow the usual liberal arts college program, including study in depth in the subject matter areas in which he plans to teach. As part of his undergraduate program, there should be courses in anthropology, sociology, and psychology and as much work in speech and written English as the student needs. If he is an undergraduate who plans to get his degree within the usual four-year period and also prepare for teaching, he will have to attend one or two summer sessions in anticipation of the reduced number of academic credits he will earn in his senior year.

The liberal arts program for prospective teachers must be sufficiently thorough to give the new teacher the mastery of subject matter every teacher needs before he dares presume to teach others. In all too many instances, a principal or superintendent who is desperately trying to staff his classes has appointed inadequately prepared teachers on condition that they take the courses they need within a stated period of time. Such an arrangement is grossly unfair to the children. It is slight comfort to a student to know that within two or three years his teachers will understand what they were trying to explain this morning. No one, neither an undergraduate nor a college graduate, should be appointed as an assistant teacher unless he has the necessary subject matter background.

Included within this preparatory period there need be only one course designed specifically for prospective teachers, even though it could be taken to good advantage by those who have no thought of ever becoming teachers. This course should give students an overall view of American education and of its practices and problems. Inasmuch as an increasing percentage of our children will be enrolled in schools in metropolitan areas, this course should pay considerable attention to urban schools and should help students understand that city schools are not all slum schools and that slum children can be educated. As they take this course, students should have firsthand experience with children and with schools by part-time service as school aides and as assistants in social service agencies dealing with school children and their families.

The Assistant Teacher. As college senior or as college graduate, the prospective teacher should be appointed by a school system and assigned to a selected classroom teacher or to a teaching team. For four hours a day he should assist the teacher with his clerical and teaching responsibilities and should get experience in working with individuals, groups, and the class as a whole. The assistant teacher should also have opportunities for observing the other teachers in the school and for gaining some understanding of the operation of the school as a whole. Approximately 30 percent of a teacher's first-year salary may be an appropriate stipend for the assistant teacher.

All assistant teachers will enroll in a major education course for the full year (6 or 8 credits each semester) which will use their background in psychology and sociology as well as their experience as assistant teachers as the basis for their study of curriculum and methods of teaching; they should not be permitted to enroll in any additional college courses at this time. The college instructor in this course should be responsible for supervising the assistant teachers in his class, helping them to interpret and to deal with the conditions they face in their schools and aiding the classroom teachers to use assistant teachers wisely. Enrollment in a section of this course should be limited to about fifteen, and the responsibility for teaching and working with the assistant teachers is demanding enough to constitute a full instructional schedule for the instructor. If several sections of this course are being offered at an institution, the instructors should get together to discuss their plans and procedures.

There are many reasons for suggesting that assistant teachers be paid for their services. First, they can help improve the quality of education by relieving the teacher of many of his nonteaching clerical duties and by working with individuals and small groups who need special help. We have already learned that assistant teachers are indispensable in early childhood classes, but we have not yet begun to use them in elementary and secondary education on a comparable scale.

Second, when assistant teachers are paid, they become part of the school staff rather than visitors from a college for whom the school accepts little direct responsibility.

Third, we shall be able to recruit better prospective teachers, both mature college graduates and capable undergraduates, when we pay assistant teachers. If the proposed pattern of teacher education is educationally sound, we must make it practicable for prospective teachers to enroll in it. We must not forget that education is now competing with other fields of advanced study that offer many scholarships and paid assistantships to college graduates. Many undergraduate students, moreover, will be reluctant to sacrifice summer employment in order to attend summer sessions to make up for the reduced number of college credits they will earn in their senior year, and many college graduates who would become highly competent teachers cannot afford to give up their jobs to prepare for teaching without some kind of subsidy. Why not let them earn that subsidy by serving as assistant teachers? We certainly cannot afford to waste money preparing prospective teachers only to find that they feel so overwhelmed by the difficulties of their first full teaching appointment that they soon resign from teaching.

This program should not become part of an academic lockstep, but should be adjusted to the assistant teachers' individual differences in ability and background. Those assistant teachers who are ready to advance to greater responsibility after only one semester should be permitted to do so. On the other hand, some who need to be assistant teachers for a year and a half before they are ready to start teaching their own class should get that additional experience. The education course, moreover, is planned as a large block of time and credit so that it can be adjusted to the needs of the group rather than split up into two or three credits of this and two or three credits of that.

The Beginning Teacher. Those who have satisfactorily completed their services as assistant teachers and have been graduated from college are ready to be appointed as teachers, but only as beginning teachers. They are not full-fledged professionals available for assignment wherever a teacher is needed, and they cannot be expected to meet all of the classroom problems which an experienced teacher can face. If they are to develop into capable and experienced teachers, they need a first year of teaching in which the responsibilities are in proportion to their abilities. The beginning teacher should have an assignment he can fill successfully. How the teaching assignment should be adjusted for the beginning teacher will vary from school to school. In some instances, he will have a regular program but with smaller classes; in others, his classes will be of the usual size, but he will have fewer classes than a regular teacher; in still other schools, he will have the usual instructional program but will get more assistance from helping teachers and supervisors.

All beginning teachers should be required to enroll in a graduate course concerned with such problems as the improvement of teaching skills, class management, and discipline as they arise in the beginning teacher's classroom. The instructor for this course should also be available in the schools to help the beginning teachers in their own classes. He may come from either the college faculty or the school staff, but he must be a person who can deal constructively with the problems discussed.

Having selected members of the school system conduct the course for beginning teachers and help them in their classrooms may be one way of profiting from the skill and insight developed by experienced teachers and may offer them an avenue of professional advancement that keeps them in the classroom, or close to it. There is no reason for assuming that only college professors can conduct such a course or that one must have a doctorate before being qualified to help beginning teachers. Yet, classroom teaching is not enough, not even successful classroom teaching, for the experienced classroom teacher who is working with beginning teachers is likely to deal with each problem by indicating what he would have done in that instance. If members of the school staff are to be assigned to work with beginning teachers, they will have to be selected and prepared so that they have a broader background than comes from experience in a single school system. To be sure, the instructor in this course must be able to deal with the specific problems that arise, but he must also help the beginning teachers to develop insight into teaching and learning so that they will be able to deal with other problems in the future.

Although most beginning teachers will serve in that capacity for a full school year, the length of service should be flexible so that the unusually skilled person can be appointed as a regular teacher after only a half year and those who need continued help may serve for a year and a half. Of course, there may be some who do not merit reappointment at all.

The Second Year of Teaching. Those who have served satisfactorily as beginning teachers should be ready for a full teaching assignment. They should continue, however, to have ready access to the instructor who helped them as beginning teachers and should be permitted, if they wish, to enroll in the course planned for beginning teachers without additional college credit.

Once service as a beginning teacher has been completed, or even during the summer prior to appointment as a beginning teacher, teachers should enroll in a graduate program leading to a master's degree, preferably attending summer sessions full time. This graduate study should be tailored to fit the individual teacher's background and needs. In general, it should include advanced courses in his field or specialization, other courses he may need to fill gaps in his preparation, and professional courses in education.

Some of the more advanced subject matter courses which a college senior takes will mean even more to him if studied after he has started teaching. Thus, a social studies or English teacher who takes advanced courses in his field will see applications to his own teaching that would not have occurred to him had he taken the same course as an undergraduate. The graduate year should also enable him to take some subject matter courses that are not advanced. For example, if an elementary school teacher finds that his background in mathematics or science is inadequate, he should be encouraged to take some elementary or intermediate courses in these areas even if he does not have the prerequisites for admission to advanced courses that are planned for predoctoral students in these subjects. He will also need professional education courses if he is to understand the *why* as well as the *how* of teaching. It is when he has had some classroom experience that a course like comparative education or the philosophy of education becomes most meaningful. The very courses in education that seem to be only words and more words to the undergraduate have substance when the student has a background of experience to give meaning to these words. A discussion of individual differences or of the problems of dealing with an emotionally disturbed child, for example, means much more to a teacher than it does to a student at college.

The Third Year of Teaching. In his third year of teaching, the teacher should be treated as a full-fledged member of the school staff, ready to be assigned anywhere, and receiving only such supervisory assistance as all other teachers receive. After all, he will ordinarily be eligible for reappointment with tenure upon completion of three years of teaching and should demonstrate that he can serve as a teacher.

If he has spent his summers enrolled in a graduate program, he should receive a master's degree and a tenure appointment when he starts his fourth year. There should be an appropriate increase in salary at this point.

The Continuing Education of Teachers. No program of teacher education can be defended if it presumes to give a beginning teacher all the knowledge and all the skill he will ever need to have. Nor does any school system ever get all the expert teachers it needs. Schools do not get expert teachers—they develop them.

Unless adequate provision is made for professional growth, teachers can become less effective with the passage of time rather than remain on the level of effectiveness of beginning teachers. Thus, any science teacher who was graduated from college ten years ago and who knows only the science he learned at college is unfit to teach science. Similarly, in every other subject matter area and on every level of education, it is essential that even a well-prepared new teacher keep up with developments in his field and in teaching if he is to continue to function effectively.

Most existing in-service programs are weak because they tend to stress regulations and procedures and lose sight of the basic purpose. The major goal of continuing education is to help teachers and administrators become increasingly successful as experts and professionals and to enjoy the feeling of achievement that comes from the realization that they are indeed experts and professionals. It is important, therefore, that schools create a climate in which professional growth is encouraged and that facilities for such growth are made available.

Schools must learn that the cost of the continuing education of teachers is part of the price that must be paid for good education. When an industrial concern changes its practices, it does not ask its employees whether they would like to stop by on Thursday on their way home after a full day's work and take a course on how the new process operates. Industrial concerns know that keeping their staffs up to date is an essential part of the cost of operation; the schools can do no less.

Few changes in educational practice are as likely to lead to immediate improvement in the quality of instruction as the provision of sabbatical leaves with pay for full-time university attendance. Conant has suggested that new teachers who are studying for the master's degree be granted a paid leave of absence for a semester so that they may attend a university full time rather than take part-time or extension courses. If such full-time attendance is valuable for a young teacher who has been away from a campus for just a year or two, how much more important is it for teachers who were graduated ten or twenty years ago? When teachers enroll in late afternoon or evening courses while they are carrying a full teaching program and also have personal and family responsibilities, it is hardly likely that they can engage in academic activities on a level of excellence required for advanced studies.

This proposal is not revolutionary. The New York State Department of Education, for example, has a program of professional development and education leaves, including tuition reimbursement, with leaves for one year at half salary or six months at full salary for employees with six years of service. Fortunately some of the federal funds now available can be used to subsidize such full-time study by members of school staffs.

There is much more that urban schools can do to stimulate professional development. Most city school systems are excessively inbred. Few city principals, for example, have ever taught in any other school system than their own. Can teachers and principals be encouraged to visit other school systems and even some of the schools in their own system to see other approaches to education? Is more support needed for the school's professional libraries, and can important materials be purchased by the school system for the teacher's personal professional library?

In a large urban school system, it is easy to develop a bureaucratic hierarchy in which the importance of the individual teacher is almost forgotten. Changes are sometimes introduced with too little thought of the teacher who finds chore added to chore until he has little time or zest for teaching. Even the most conscientious teacher is likely to become unenthusiastic and frustrated if the school does not help him to continue feeling successful and appreciated. How can we retain respect for the teacher and concern for his continuing to find teaching stimulating and satisfying?

The program of continuing education for teachers should recognize the different but complementary roles of in-service education and graduate study. When a school system introduces a new curriculum, it may have to arrange a program for preparing teachers to use it effectively. For this reason, it may need a program of in-service courses, lectures, demonstrations, workshops, and other activities that may be most useful but are not necessarily part of an advanced program leading to a graduate degree. On the other hand, a university degree program may include advanced study in an academic discipline and courses that will deepen a teacher's insight into basic educational problems without immediately affecting his day-to-day classroom performance.

Of course, the dichotomy is not always so clear. Thus, a committee that is preparing a new science program for a school may examine the basic issues in science education and evaluate existing and proposed programs in many parts of the country and in other countries. Such a committee may thus be engaging in a professional assignment on a level of intellectual activity that well merits academic recognition. On the other hand, some of the graduate courses in which a teacher enrolls may have a direct bearing upon what he does in the classroom.

When the different functions of in-service and graduate study are recognized, they can be combined into a program that improves professional competence and both satisfies and whets the teacher's intellectual appetite. Failure to recognize the distinction leads to the situation in which badly needed in-service activities are not conducted unless some university accepts them for graduate credit; and some university courses, in order to meet a pressing in-service need, do not rise above the how-to-do-the-same-thing-better level. Undue reliance on graduate courses, moreover, sometimes leads to educational hypocrisy by calling any course taken by a teacher a graduate course, regardless of the intellectual demands made upon him.

Changing the Pattern of Teacher Education. Because schools and colleges vary, it would be unfortunate if the program described here were to be adopted *in toto* on a nation-wide scale. Parts of the pattern may be used even if other suggestions prove not to be feasible at the time. For example, a school system that is not ready to grant its teachers paid leaves of absence for university attendance may be able to accept the assistant teacher-beginning teacher sequence, and schools that cannot pay assistant teachers may be able to salvage some of the value of having them even if they are not paid.

The pattern is more important than the details, and the details can be modified to adjust to local needs. Thus, in one situation, it may be better to have the assistant teachers taught and supervised by a member of the college faculty; in another case, the best person for this assignment may be a member of the school system. Similarly, in some instances, the beginning teacher can be given smaller classes to teach, while in other schools it may be better to keep class size constant but provide additional help for him. Of course the program for educating teachers has to be different for a college that works with small schools scattered throughout an entire state than it is for another college that works closely with large schools in a metropolitan area.

If we are to change the pattern of teacher education, we shall also have to strengthen the state education departments so that they can stress their role as catalysts for change instead of being largely administrative and regulatory agencies. We shall also have to modify certification procedures so that they stress competence rather than courses. It would be inappropriate here to indicate in detail what should be done to modify state education departments or certification procedures, but these phases certainly deserve consideration.

There are those who pronounce *era* as though it were *error*. If we are to have a new era in urban education rather than just a new error, we must have expert teachers. Unless the urban schools do develop the expert teachers they need with the increased funds that are available, we shall be headed for a great disillusionment, with disastrous results for the schools, the cities, and the nation.

23 A MODEL FOR ANALYZING THE TRAINING OF TRAINING AGENTS

DAVID E. HUNT

Education, psychotherapy, social case work, and child-rearing are typically treated separately rather than considered similar. However, a teacher, a psychotherapist, a social worker, and a parent share at least one common feature: each provides an interper-sonal *environment* for the person or group with whom he interacts. In analyzing the effect of teachers, psychotherapists, social work-ers, and parents upon personality development, the author and his co-workers previously described such persons as *training agents* to emphasize this generic similarity (Harvey, Hunt, and Schroder, 1961). Use of the term, training agent, in analyzing environ-mental influence upon the developing child permits coordinating those environmental conditions which a child encounters in the home, school, and clinic by use of a common descriptive language.

In this paper we shift perspective from analyzing how the en-vironments radiated by training agents affect the course of de-velopment to analyzing how these training agents learn to radiate environments. We use the term, *radiating environment,* to de-scribe the training agent's behavior as it impinges upon the person with whom he interacts. A teacher radiates an environment through the way a lesson is presented, e.g., highly structured; a therapist radiates an environment through his general mode of reaction, e.g., permissive acceptance. (The training agent is not necessarily aware of the environment he radiates.)

A better understanding of how to prepare training agents should facilitate the application of the Conceptual Systems change model (Hunt, 1964) since an agent must be capable of radiating the specifically prescribed environments. A model for analyzing the training of training agents is also potentially valuable for

David E. Hunt, "A Model for Analyzing the Training of Training Agents," *Merrill-Palmer Quarterly* (April 1966), pp. 137–156. Reprinted by permis-sion of the author and publisher.

illuminating the general training of professional workers whom we will refer to as trainees. Training procedures are typically aimed toward the trainee's becoming better able to radiate environments which will induce certain changes in a person or group. Therefore the model is primarily applicable to the training of persons such as teachers, psychotherapists, social workers, Peace Corps volunteers, and probation officers. But there is no reason that it could not be applied to the training or re-education of parents (cf. Brim, 1959).

Questions in the training of professional workers abound: under what conditions is learning by imitation most effective? Is awareness of one's role as an environmental influence necessary? Under what conditions is role playing valuable? What is the appropriate pacing of "intellectual understanding" and direct experience? Is direct feedback more valuable early in training or later after forming categories within which the feedback can be processed? What is the most appropriate synchronization between the learning of specific environmental tactics and the learning of long term strategy?

Before these questions can be answered, the job for which the trainee is being prepared must be described. We will set forth a specific job description of a training agent and specify the components of agent effectiveness in operational terms much as an industrial psychologist might analyze the job of a factory worker. The objectives of training must be described before one can analyze the effectiveness of the training process. If the present objectives of agent effectiveness are unacceptable, then the model is not relevant, but this does not minimize the necessity for explicating the objectives.

In presenting this training model, we first specify the objective or desired state by defining agent effectiveness. Next, we describe the specific skills necessary for a trainee to accomplish this objective. After describing each skill we describe assessment methods and procedures most likely to facilitate the trainee's learning this skill. The training model is very similar in form to the Conceptual Systems change model (Hunt, 1964) which analyzed the process of personality development by specifying the desired state of abstractness, setting forth the stages of conceptual development through which progress toward this state occurs, and finally prescribing those environmental conditions most likely to produce such progression. Another link between the two models is the use of those specific environments prescribed in the change model as examples of environments to be learned by trainees (although the training model should also be applicable to the learning of environments outside the Conceptual System's theoretical domain). The present model differs from the change model in that the procedures proposed for producing skill acquisition and the hierarchical order of skill components are set forth, as areas to be investigated rather than as theoretically derived assertions. The purpose of this training model is not to provide answers directly, but to provide a framework within which studies can be designed to investigate the many unanswered questions.

The Desired State: Agent Effectiveness

Agent effectiveness is presently defined as the capacity to radiate a wide variety of environments, to select from this variety a specific environment to be radiated toward a particular person or group with the aim of producing a particular behavioral outcome, and to shift from one environment to another under appropriate circumstances. In education, for example, the teacher's capacity to present the same lesson in a variety of educational environments, to select and use that specific educational environment most appropriate to produce a specific learner outcome with a particular group of students, and to shift to a new form of educational environment when appropriate would constitute the operations for teacher effectiveness. In a similar way, the effectiveness of a social worker is defined in terms of his capacity to relate to a client in a variety of environmental forms, to use that specific treatment environment most likely to produce a particular client outcome upon a specific kind of client, and to shift to a different treatment stance when necessary.

Kurt Lewin's classic formula—B $= f(P,E)$, or ("Behavior is a function of the Person and the Environment")—is a useful way to conceptualize differential treatment or differential intervention from the viewpoint of the developing child, the student or client (Hunt, 1964). From the standpoint of the training agent who controls only one factor in this relationship—the Environment—let us restate the formula to read $E: P \rightarrow B$ ("Environment radiated toward a Person leads to Behavior"). The effective agent specifies a desired behavior B for a person P and then selects from his repertory of environments that specific one E most likely to produce the desired result. A teacher wishing to induce critical thinking (B_1) from an inquisitive child (P_1), for example, might select and radiate a reflective environment (E_x) in order to produce this result.

To perform such complex activity successfully requires many skills. The agent must have an available armamentarium of environments and be capable of selecting and radiating the most appropriate one. To use the most appropriate environment he must understand the differential use of environments in relation to long-term objectives and to the intermediate steps toward this objective. Agent effectiveness therefore includes both his *ability* to radiate specific environments and his *understanding* of when to utilize a specific environment or shift to another. Professional schools differ considerably in the order and emphasis in conveying such skill and knowledge to trainees. Whether theory should precede, accompany, or follow specific skill acquisition is an empirical question which needs exploration.

In order to explore such problems we need to specify the components underlying agent effectiveness which are summarized in Table 1.

In Table 1 we use the three factors in the relationship—Environments, Behaviors, and Persons—as the basic units in describing the components underlying agent effectiveness.

Table 1 sets down the organization to be followed in this paper in that we will discuss each of these skills in turn. After describing the skill we will suggest methods for assessment and procedures for training. In the present initial statement we will set forth these skills as necessary components which a trainee may possess in varying degree. However, from the viewpoint of training, these skill components will likely be viewed as intermediate steps toward the desired state of agent effectiveness. We will present the skills in a general order from the more simple to the more complex, but the optimal sequence to be employed in the actual training of such skill acquisition remains an empirical question.

TABLE 1

SKILL COMPONENTS OF TRAINING AGENT EFFECTIVENESS

Type of Skill	Components of Training Agent Effectiveness		
Skill in flexible modulation from one environment to another	To shift from one environment to another under appropriate circumstances (Time 1) E_x: $P_1 \rightarrow B_1$ (Time 2) E_x: $P_1 \rightarrow B_3$		
Skill in radiating environments	To radiate a variety of environments E_x: E_y: E_z:	To radiate that environment which will produce a specific behavior $E_x: \rightarrow B_1$ $E_y: \rightarrow B_2$	To radiate that environment which will produce a specific behavior from a particular person $E_x: P_I \rightarrow B_1$ $E_y: P_{II} \rightarrow B_1$
Skill in discrimination	To discriminate between environments $E_x/E_y/E_z$	To discriminate between behaviors $B_1/B_2/B_3$	To discriminate between persons $P_I/P_{II}/P_{III}$

Skill in Discrimination

To Discriminate Between Environments ($E_x/E_y/E_z$)

Before a trainee can learn to radiate a variety of environments, he must be aware of the differences between these environments and be capable of accurately classifying them. For example, consider the following teacher comments which may be viewed as environmental stimuli to be classified:

1. "I'm disappointed in you."
2. "That's right."
3. "That's interesting—any other ideas?"
4. "How could you go about checking on your ideas?"

Teacher comments 1 and 2 might be classified together as representing teacher-centered reactions, and thus discriminably different from 3 and 4 which might be classified as being reflective or student-centered.

A basic discrimination to be learned by psychotherapy trainees is between directive and nondirective therapeutic environments. From the present viewpoint, the trainee's learning to make this discrimination and learning to classify therapist comments into one of these two categories is an essential skill regardless of which therapeutic environment the trainee may ultimately utilize. Implicit in the present approach is the belief that the controversies between directive and nondirective therapy are not very fruitful because a well-trained psychotherapist should be capable of radiating either therapeutic environment and to see its utility in different contexts.

To Discriminate Between Behaviors ($B_1/B_2/B_3$)

The trainee needs to be capable of discriminating accurately between the various behavioral outcomes he will encounter. The domain of behaviors to be discriminated will obviously be those responses made by persons with whom the trainee works so that the domain of behaviors will vary from teacher to social worker to psychotherapist. For example, a teacher trainee needs to have available a taxonomy of student behavior within which he can discriminate among occurrences of student behavior. Let us consider the following student behaviors as stimuli to be classified:

1. "The square root of 49 is 7."
2. "*Hamlet* is a tragedy written by Shakespeare."
3. "I have a hunch about the main character in this story."
4. "Maybe we should consider the effect of rainfall on the kind of house they build."

The teacher trainee may place the first and second together as assertions of fact, discriminating them from the last two categories as hypothesis formation. Unless the teacher trainee can quickly and accurately classify student responses, he will not be in a position to evaluate the effect of the environment he radiates. The taxonomy devised by Bloom represents test exercises for learning to make such discrimination (Bloom, 1954, pp. 17–32).

For a social worker the behavioral stimuli may be client remarks such as the following:

1. "It isn't my fault I got in trouble."
2. "No matter what I do, things still turn out the same."
3. "Maybe if I try this, then that might improve things."
4. "I can see where part of this may be my fault."

Here the social worker trainee is likely to classify the first two as negation or denial of responsibility and thus discriminate them from the last two which may be classified as acceptance of responsibility or internal causality. The classification system will vary with the theoretical orientation, but the trainee's task is to learn to use whatever system of classification is appropriate in order to discriminate between client reactions, and to classify them reliably. The trainee should be capable of classifying behavioral outcomes as rapidly as he sorts objects into classes according to their size or color.

To Discriminate Between Persons ($P_I/P_{II}/P_{III}$)

In teacher training this skill might be included in the study of individual differences or "understanding the child" while in psychotherapy training such skill acquisition might be considered diagnostic ability. Among the very large number of classification methods available, the most promising appear to be those based on intervention-relevant differences between persons (cf. Hunt, 1964). We may simply ask the question: does the differential discrimination of persons in this classification system carry with it a differential prescription of effective environments? If not, the classification of persons has little or no function. The system developed by Warren and her associates (1964) exemplifies a functional classification system in which they have developed a typology of classifying delinquent youths directly related to a pattern of differential treatment. Using this system, the agent who knows the · person's position in the classification system immediately has available knowledge of what form of therapeutic intervention is most likely to be effective. Such functional classification is in sharp contrast to the frequently dysfunctional utility of the Kraepelinian diagnostic classification system which was developed in a static typological framework.

The importance of "sizing up" the person with whom one communicates is nicely illustrated in a study by Flavell (1963), who was interested in investigating the role of children's discrimination of "role attributes of another person, that is, the person's disposition, capabilities, and limitations" in order to communicate more effectively. Using the stimulus variation of blindfolded vs. sighted persons, Flavell found that such discriminative capacity increased with age, e.g., older children are more likely to vary or modulate the communication to fit the characteristics of the person.

The trainee must learn to classify the person with whom he is working in some functional system of classification. Such skill is considered to be a higher-level version of skill in classifying behaviors, since the person's behavior provides an important part of the discriminative classification. Research in the area of person perception and impression formation provides one useful methodology for measuring how effectively a trainee can make discriminations between persons. A more complex component of skill in sizing up the person with whom one works is the capacity to evoke cues from the person which will permit classification, and this skill may also need to be acquired.

Assessment of Discriminative Skill

The procedures for assessing how effectively a trainee can discriminate in each of these three areas are generally similar. The only difference lies in the stimuli presented: Behaviors, Environments, or Persons. In all three cases the stimuli can be presented on paper (as in examples above), on tape, film, or hypothetically through role-playing. Obviously, the more adequately the mode of presentation represents the actual Behavior, Environment, or Person, the more precise will be the measurement.

Response form of the method may vary also from a free response as above ("Which ones go together? Why?") to requesting the trainee to classify according to predetermined dimensions or categories. The free response form is similar in some ways to the "discovery" method in that the trainee must generate his own dimensions along which he will make discriminations, while the latter form is more structured in that he must make his discriminations along already specified dimensions. For different purposes each may be appropriate.

Davitz (1964) has developed methods for assessing a person's sensitivity to emotional expression which illustrate the form of such assessment methods. In one method subjects were asked to listen to the same statement presented several times in different emotional contexts. The subject was given a list of ten emotions which might be expressed upon which he was to record his judgment of each of the different presentations. Assessment of discriminative skill was based on how well the subjects' judgments agreed with judgments made by a large group of trained judges who had agreed on a veridical classification. Davitz also followed a similar procedure using stimuli of drawings and musical sounds, illustrating the possible range in mode of presentation. Although his purpose was slightly different from the present one, the generic assessment approach is identical.

A method for assessing skill in discriminating environments is readily available since several coding systems for classifying teacher behavior (e.g., Joyce, 1964) or therapist reaction have been devised. Thus one may simply use as stimuli, pre-coded environmental events (teacher or therapist reaction)—with instructions for the trainee to code these environmental occurrences according to the manual provided. Discriminative skill thus becomes identical to rater reliability in relation to some pre-established norm.

Kahn and Cannell (1957) have developed an ingenious method for coding the environment radiated by an interviewer. In their approach the trainee is requested to code the interviewer's reaction (Environment, in present terms) on three dimensions: acceptance (support vs. reject respondent), validity (unbiased vs. biased), and relevance (toward vs. away from desired objective). Although this approach involves a multidimensional classification of the stimuli, the classification is functionally related to later skill acquisition of the interviewer trainee.

If measures of each of these three discriminative skills are available, they serve several purposes. At the beginning of training, a base rate profile spotlights areas of deficiency in which training is needed. Conversely, if a trainee has a high skill level in one or more areas, then there is no particular value in exposing him to training to increase that specific skill. Thus, one purpose is to maximize training efficiency by discarding the traditional lock-step training program and substituting a more individually tailored program designed according to the differential skill profile of each trainee. A second purpose is achieved if the measures are administered after training so that some index of skill acquisition may be derived and the differential effectiveness of various training procedures evaluated.

Procedures for Training Discriminative Skill

Much more is presently known about how to assess variation in discriminative skill than about what techniques are likely to increase the level of such skill. For example, after outlining in detail several methods for assessing emotional sensitivity, Davitz concludes his book by stating that we need to learn more about "the development of effective training procedures to increase sensitivity" (Davitz, 1964, p. 202).

Two approaches appear potentially valuable for suggesting procedures for increasing discriminative skill. The first is the area of traditional psychophysics in which considerable empirical knowledge is available regarding how the skill in discriminating physical objects can be acquired or increased. This literature should prove quite useful in providing leads regarding the optimal order of presentation, importance of anchoring effects, etc. The second approach is that of the sensitivity training employed in T-group training (Bradford, Bibb, and Benne, 1964) which deals directly with the enhancement of interpersonal discrimination. Once the skill has been described objectively then experimentation may proceed toward evaluating which procedure will be most effective in enhancing discriminative skill. Also implicit in our use of examples is the belief that a side benefit of viewing teacher trainees, psychotherapy trainees, and social work trainees generically as trainees is the possibility of cross-stimulation between the professional schools in these various disciplines.

Skill in Radiating Environments

To Radiate a Variety of Environments (E_x:, E_y:, E_z:)

Once the trainee has learned to discriminate between environments radiated by others, he needs to learn to radiate these environments himself. Trainees initially vary considerably in their preferred environmental style—e.g., teaching style, therapeutic style, etc.—and it is important to measure this preferred style or styles at the beginning of training. Teacher trainees entering training may exhibit preferred styles ranging from directive to supportive to reflective. The trainee who is primarily supportive will therefore need to learn to radiate directive and reflective environments. Ideally, he should be able to convey the same lesson topic through different environmental contexts when appropriate.

Skill in radiating a variety of environments is purely a performance skill much like playing a role on command. We intentionally distinguish this performance skill in which the trainee is instructed to radiate a specific environment from the skill in which the trainee must "size up" the situation himself, come to some conclusion about the most effective environment, and then radiate it. The distinction seems useful because a trainee may fail at the more complex task either because of his inability to size up the situation or in his ability to radiate the prescribed environment.

Although we are presently contending that capacity to radiate a wide variety of environments is an important skill component, it should be noted that certain rather specific jobs may require only a limited repertory of environments. In such cases it may be more efficient to *select* for agents who already have available the requisite environmental skill as part of their preferred style than to attempt to produce such skill through training.

The preferred style of a teacher trainee just entering training is likely embedded in a value matrix of how learning occurs, and what is the best way to induce such learning through teaching procedures. For example, consider the following responses given by two Peace Corps trainees about to enter teacher training to the statement, "The most important thing in teaching is":

Trainee A: "Interest in subject matter and accomplishment in subject matter. If one is devoted to this, one can perhaps indirectly surmount the problem of personal relationships with the students."

Trainee B: "To develop creativity and critical thinking. It is *not* the rote memorization of facts and formulas. I feel that creativity and critical thinking can be developed in the ordinary classroom situations if the teacher emphasizes them."

It seems quite clear that the preferred teaching styles which these trainees bring to the training situation will reflect these value beliefs and will probably be very different from each other. Therefore, in attempting to extend the trainee's behavioral repertory of environments he can radiate, it is most important to present the environments in a non-value-laden context insofar as possible. The trainee should think about variations in environmental contexts, much as he thinks about variations in media—TV, radio, newspapers—that is, as alternative, potentially interchangeable means of conveying information.

To Radiate That Environment Which Will Produce a Specified Behavior ($E_x: \rightarrow B_1$)

Just as skill in radiating environments requires a capacity to discriminate between environments, so does the manipulation of behavior by environmental control require skill in radiating environments. In this component the trainee is given the task of producing a specific behavior (from an unspecified person) and he must then radiate an environment which will produce this result. Obviously, this is a two-phase process. The new component

involved here is learning the E: → B relations. The trainee entering this phase of training is confronted with what Tolman has
called learning "what leads to what" or more specifically, what
environment produces what behavior.

The trainee may learn E: → B relations in a mechanical "push-
pull, click-click" fashion or he may learn these relations as part
of a highly complex theoretical network. However, the skill itself
involves simply the capacity when confronted by a particular
desired behavioral outcome to radiate the environment most likely
to produce such behavior. The behavior to be produced varies
between trainees in education, therapy, and social work so that
the range of behaviors may be large in some cases and quite
limited in others.

It is possible that this component will turn out to be only
useful in the hypothetical case of deriving components since
trainees may find it exceedingly difficult to perform with an unspecified person (or people-in-general) instruction. Put another
way, from a practical viewpoint, the E: P → B relation may be
the only meaningful condition for trainees to deal with, in which
case the present E: → B relation becomes only a hypothetical component. This is an empirical question.

Ideally, the trainee learns these E: → B relations as a number
of causally related connections with a minimum of value judgment. The trainee can assimilate these E: → B relations through
a process of intellectual curiosity, e.g., "I wonder what behavior
results from a highly directive environment? Hmm . . . What do
you know . . . that produces a reliable routine behavior pattern . . . that's interesting!" De-emphasis of value association with
certain environments or certain behaviors in the intermediate steps
is critical because the trainee should later learn to see various
environments as *differentially* valuable and to see various behaviors as differentially desirable at various phases in the learning or therapeutic process. If the E: → B relations are learned in
a neutral way much as one views a candy machine ("If I pull
this, I'll get a chocolate bar and if I pull this, I'll get a peanut
cluster"), then the possibility is open later to use these relations
as required in a more objective fashion. Insofar as possible, therefore, the acquisition of E: → B relations should be in the spirit of
knowledge for its own sake.

*To Radiate That Environment Which Will Produce a Specified
Behavior from a Particular Person* (E_x: $P_1 \rightarrow B_1$)

In this skill the trainee is given information about the behavior
to be produced and some information about the person, and his
job is to select and radiate that environment most likely to produce such a desired result. This skill differs from the "push-pull"
skill in that it must take account of differential effectiveness as a
function of the person with whom one is working. We have intentionally placed this skill *after* the trainee has learned to radiate a
variety of environments because variation in environmental radiation is the one means which the trainee or agent has available for
control. He cannot usually control the kind of person with whom
he works, but must modulate to the characteristics of that person
in his choice of environment. However, he cannot modulate if he
has not already learned to vary the environment he radiates.

Some training programs begin with understanding the person
and on the assumption that person discrimination and individual
modulation to persons should be given priority. In the present
view we hold that to give trainees a great deal of information
about differential accessibility of persons without an already
present armamentarium of functionally related environments will
simply lead to trainee exasperation and disappointment. He will
sense the differences between the persons with whom he works
but be unable to do anything about it. However, as with many of
the present assertions, the relative merits of these two sequences
should be empirically evaluated.

Although it is probably possible to learn E: $\rightarrow$ B connections
in a mechanical fashion, it seems less likely that trainees can so
acquire knowledge about E: P $\rightarrow$ B relations simply because of
the complexity involved. Therefore, such learning will be facili-
tated if embedded in some theoretical network which gives some
process justification for the E: P $\rightarrow$ B relations (cf. Hunt, 1964).

Assessment of Skill in Radiating Environments

Although the three skills just described vary in complexity, the
task of assessment has one common characteristic: the coding of
the kind of environment which the trainee radiates. Once a reliable coding manual for classifying environments is available

(e.g., Joyce, MS., 1964), then this system can be used to classify the environment radiated by the trainee. Let us assume that we wish to assess the variety of environments that a trainee can radiate. In a teaching trainee context, for example, we might instruct a trainee to teach a particular lesson (keeping content constant) in a structured environmental context and then code the trainee's performance under these instructions. A similar procedure would then be followed for a supportive environmental context and a reflective environmental context. Each of these performance efforts would be coded to determine how closely the trainee did in fact radiate the prescribed environment. These presentations should also be analyzed to note how *distinct* one was from the other. During the training process a trainee may have difficulty, for example, in presenting two environments, e.g., supportive and reflective, in distinctively different fashions. Such difficulty may represent some remaining confusion in discriminating between these environments, or it may represent difficulty in extending these cognitive discriminations to behavioral referents.

In assessing the preferred environmental style of incoming trainees we know that preferred style is significantly related to conceptual level of the trainee in that the higher the trainee's conceptual level (CL), the more likely he is to radiate a reflective environment as a preferred style (Hunt and Joyce, in press). It is tempting to conclude from this trainee personality-preferred style relation that higher CL trainees have more potential but, while this *may* be so, it is nonetheless true that it may be as difficult to make structured environmental radiation available to high CL trainees as it is to induce the availability of more reflective environmental radiation in low CL trainees.

In assessing skill in E: → B as well as producing specific behaviors it will be useful to obtain an independent measure of the trainee's understanding and planning of the E: → B connection as through a lesson plan or some explication of intended strategy. The assessment of E: → B skill will likely take the form of a profile in that certain trainees will be proficient in producing certain forms of behavior (either through proficiency in radiating the requisite environment or in the ease with which they grasp the connection, or both) while they may be quite deficient in producing other forms of behavior. Thus, this assessment will depict a profile of skills over the relevant domain of E: → B possibilities.

Assessment of skill in the E: P → B realm becomes more complex and also necessarily more job-specific. If the trainee is to work entirely with withdrawn, mentally defective youngsters then there is no reason for assessing (or training competence in) working with aggressive, acting-out delinquents.

We have recently developed a prototype for assessing such E: P → B skill (Hunt, MS., 1965) in relation to the assessment of Peace Corps trainees (Hunt, Joyce and Weinstein, MS., 1965). This method consisted simply of obtaining a 15-minute behavior sample of the way in which the trainee communicated (conveyed through an environmental context) some information (in this case, the historic concept of the balance of power in our Federal Government) to a specified person (a not-too-bright Venezuelan immigrant who hoped to become a citizen) with the behavioral purpose of increasing his understanding of the concept of checks and balances. Each trainee was given information on the topic, information about the person and the aim, time to prepare a brief lesson plan or strategy, and finally he attempted to communicate this to a person who played the role of the Venezuelan. During the 15-minute presentation, the role player systematically presented obstacles to effective communication in the form of misunderstanding, impatience, erroneous understanding, etc. The trainee's behavior was coded along several dimensions to assess how effectively he took cognizance of the person's frame of reference and modulated ("flexed") to this frame of reference, how effectively he dealt with various obstacles, etc. We view this behavior sample as representing one E: P → B component which for Peace Corps volunteers as well as most teachers is very important. In order to obtain a representative picture of agent effectiveness, one needs to apply this assessment prototype to other E: P → B demands in addition to that tapped in the communication method, a task which has been taken up by Weinstein (MS., 1965) who designed a task sampling how effectively a trainee can control and regulate a teaching situation.

Weinstein was interested in assessing persons who were applicants to be trained for teaching culturally deprived children. Experience in training such teachers has indicated that unless the trainee can establish a routine or a line of march, and let the students know initially that he is in fact in charge, that he will be in continual difficulty no matter how many other skills he may possess. Therefore, in this task, the persons were three sixth-grade students (role players) in a culturally deprived school and the desired behavior was to let them know the rules for the coming semester and to become acquainted with the teacher. Here again, the role players introduced systematic obstacles to the purpose of the trainee, and the environment radiated by the trainee during the fifteen minute period was coded on relevant dimensions. These two tasks illustrate the flexible possibilities of this assessment prototype. It is important to note that skill in the communication task is not necessarily highly correlated with skill in the control task. As we have suggested earlier, such knowledge of relative strengths and weaknesses will provide the basis for pinpointing training resources.

Procedures for Training Skill in Radiating Environments

The specific question of how to induce a response which we have called "radiating an environment" can be viewed generally as the problem of how any response becomes acquired. From a theoretical view, this question is enormously complex, and from the practical side, since training institutions spend months and even years attempting to accomplish this goal, we can only touch on a few of the key issues.

Campbell (1961, pp. 103–106) has distinguished six modes of response acquisition which can be applied to acquisition of skill in radiating environments:

1. Learning, blind trial-and-error, or locomotor exploration.
2. Perception.
3. Perceptual observation of the outcomes of another person's trial-and-error exploration.
4. Perceptual observation of another person's responses.
5. Linguistic instruction about the characteristics of objects.
6. Linguistic instruction about responses to be made.

Let us consider these procedures in relation to a trainee's attempting to acquire the response skill of radiating a reflective environment. The first two procedures are probably used least frequently in most current training programs. Learning to radiate a reflective environment only through the trial-and-error method, for example, would presumably also involve some differential reinforcement so that the trainee's random efforts to radiate the "correct" environment would be gradually shaped or molded. As Bandura (1965) observed, the use of "shaping" responses is highly inefficient when one is attempting to induce complex patterns of response, e.g., driving a car. The third and fourth procedures represent reliance on modeling and imitation. In training terms, these procedures consist of the teacher trainee watching another novice trainee make mistakes (procedure No. 3) or observe an experienced teacher (procedure No. 4). Watching films or listening to tape recordings of other persons radiating environments are also examples of this type. For some purposes, the person being observed may exemplify high skill or very poor performance in attempting to execute the desired response pattern. The last two procedures represent the more symbolic modes of response induction in which the trainee is acquainted with the response pattern through verbal description. Most training procedures rely on a combination of these various techniques, e.g., begin with "#6, Linguistic instruction," then use "#4, Perceptual observation of another person's response" and finally use "#1, Learning." However, this taxonomy of procedures is potentially helpful for analyzing various forms of training.

The response of radiating a specific environment is considerably more highly skilled and complex than the responses which Campbell described. Therefore, it seems likely that the trainee will need to spend considerable time in attempting to execute the response pattern and in profiting from his own mistakes through some confrontation with his performance. For example, there has been considerable interest recently in procedures which confront the trainee with his own performance efforts either through films, e.g., video feedback, or through tape recordings. From the present viewpoint we would contend that the usefulness of procedures such as video feedback will depend in large part upon how well the trainee has previously learned to discriminate between environments. In order for a therapy trainee to profit from viewing or listening to his efforts at radiating environments toward a patient, he needs some system of classifying or coding his own environmental radiation in order to evaluate it and, if need be, make appropriate modification. This contention could be translated into an empirical investigation by simply observing two groups of trainees who receive video feedback training, one group having been trained early in discriminative skill in classifying environments and the other group not having received such discriminative training, we would predict that the former group would profit more from the feedback experience than the latter group.

Training for skill in E: → B is somewhat more complex. Procedures for producing such skill vary along a dimension ranging from mechanical "push-pull" to a highly theoretical conception of the organism and its relation to environmental pressures. For most readers, the suggestion that the trainees may acquire E: → B skill through a mechanical notion of how an environment produces a behavior is likely to be seen as impractical and perhaps nonhumanistic. We would contend that these procedures deserve a try mainly because we know that many trainees are simply incapable of learning a great deal about the complexities of personality organization required to understand thoroughly why certain E: → B combinations occur. Therefore, we make the suggestion that the mechanical attempt deserves a try on a pragmatic basis, not necessarily because we feel it will be superior to the more comprehensive theoretical understanding.

One intermediate procedure for training E: → B (in this case the behavior of generating hunches is encouraged by a reflective environment) was used in a pilot study by Hunt, Joyce, and DelPopolo (MS., 1964). In this investigation, a small group of sophomore teacher trainees were seen in a brief workshop. The teacher trainees took the role of students while one of the investigators taught three brief lessons in each of three areas: mathematics, social studies, and English. The teacher intentionally radiated a highly reflective environment in all three lessons during which the students were encouraged to generate hunches about the material in the lessons. After each lesson, the teacher trainees discussed their own experiences and feelings during the lesson. They were encouraged to verbalize how they felt—e.g., "I was afraid I would make a fool of myself if I said that," or "one of my ideas seemed so silly"—and also to describe how the environment which they encountered fostered their bringing their hunches out in the open despite these reservations. During this discussion, the teacher trainees also discussed how they might have reacted if the environment had been very directive, and why they would not have felt comfortable in bringing out new hunches in such an atmosphere. Although the results of this pilot investigation were inconclusive, the general approach illustrates one possible method in which the trainee becomes aware of the E: → B connection through his own experience and later verbalization of the process which he experienced.

Many of the questions to be answered in relation to the most effective training procedures are concerned with the *order* or sequence of procedures rather than with the procedure as such. For example, there is little question that a trainee who can verbalize (i.e., is aware of) E: → B relations is more likely to be capable radiating differential environments to produce differentially specified behaviors than a trainee who is unaware of such relations, but this does not necessarily mean that the process of arriving at such skill involves a training sequence in which he first learns to be aware of such relations. It is possible that the training procedure in which he first learns to execute the performance of a particular environment and note its behavioral effects without any necessary conceptual apprehension of the basis for the relation *may* be more effective.

Procedures for training E: → P relations are likely to be somewhat more complex and, as implied earlier, it seems less likely that such relations can be learned in a mechanical fashion. If the trainee has learned several E: → B relations for "people in general" it may be that something similar to a "cognitive conflict" training procedure may be used. The trainee might be confronted by a person (or small number of persons, perhaps in a "micro-teaching" situation) for whom this particular E: → B relation does not work. After the trainee has used the particular environment which was supposed to produce the desired behavior and finds it unsuccessful, he can then attempt to puzzle out why this environment did not work for this person. In order for a trainee to learn E: P → B skill it seems necessary that he become aware of how earlier learned distinctions between persons have relevance for differential reaction. We have found in in-service teacher training procedures that discussing differences between students in relation to their having different "channels" or being differentially accessible may be somewhat helpful. Once the trainee can radiate different environments, it seems likely that the most effective means for him to learn E: P → B relations is through some grasp of a theoretical model which provides a conceptual basis for these complex relations (e.g., Hunt, 1964; Warren et al., 1964).

Skill in Flexible Modulation from One Environment to Another

Up to this point the skills discussed have been aimed to produce specific behaviors, but no attention has been devoted to the cumulative or sequential relations between behaviors over a period of time. For example, a teacher with a group of culturally disadvantaged students whose personality orientation is predominantly what we have described as Sub I (Hunt, 1964) must initially radiate an environment which is highly structured, somewhat controlling, and also accepting. However, if the teacher is capable only of radiating strength and power in establishing initial structure and is incapable of modulating to other, more effective environments once the routine has been established, he is unlikely to be very effective. (Conversely, of course, the teacher who cannot initially radiate control in order to establish a line of march will also be ineffective but for very different reasons.)

In order to acquire skill in flexible modulation (or what we have called "flexing") the trainee probably needs to acquire some temporal perspective—e.g., in education this may be a developmental perspective while in psychotherapy it may be a therapeutic perspective. In discussing this question, Lippitt, Watson, and Westley (1958, p. 289) put the issue as follows: "We suggest again that no change agent can control the dynamic process of change unless he knows what has happened and what is happening. The techniques which enable him to find out what has happened and what is happening are therefore exceedingly important."

Some training agents can learn E: P → B relations for a particular group quite effectively, but be incapable of flexible modulation. For example, we found (Hunt, 1964) in an exploratory application of the Conceptual Systems change model that some teachers could learn the "recipe" that Stage I students were initially receptive to consistent environment which involves some competition. Such teachers begin to use procedures (e.g., debates), which are functionally very facilitating for these students. However, such environments, though effective in facilitating present functioning, may if not modulated, ultimately produce arrestation. Therefore, we attempted to convey the notion that although debates, for example, may be initially effective for Stage I students, the teacher should gradually introduce (modulate) to an environment which attempted to foster student distinctions within the pro vs. con dichotomy of debates so that the students could learn to appreciate distinctions in viewpoints within those students who all happen to be for a particular issue. Only through encouraging such distinctions can the Stage I person be encouraged to develop more autonomy and independence. This distinction is essentially the functional vs. developmental distinction, and it is a vital one for trainees to learn. As was the case with the learning of E: P → B relations, learning to modulate to another environment once one behavior has been evoked probably occurs most effectively when the trainee is provided with some theory which deals with how these behaviors are organized and how they go together into a course of continuous development (cf. Hunt, 1964).

Flexible modulation of environments may be called for within a single lesson or therapeutic session, it may be called for in dealing with heterogeneous groups as a special case of the differential receptivity of persons to environments, or it may be called for in the long-term planning of strategy for change. In any case, flexible modulation requires that the trainee be capable of the three sub-skills described in the preceding section in skill in radiating environments.

Skill in flexible modulation also requires the explication of the desired behavioral or organizational changes which the training agent is attempting to produce, e.g., goals of education, goals of therapy, etc. For example, if the accepted goal of education is simply to increase scores on objective achievement examinations, then such a limited goal may not be fostered by encouraging conceptual development since we know (Hunt, 1964) that Stage I students score higher on objective examinations than Stage II students do. However, if we are aiming for more critical thinking and creativity, then environments which will facilitate conceptual progression are appropriate. Put another way, when one analyzes the role of the training agent in terms of flexible modulation, then it becomes critical to establish the desired behaviors toward which such modulation is aimed. Thus, the present explication of the training process cannot proceed effectively unless one has also explicitly acknowledged the goals of the change process within which the training agent is working.

Assessment of capacity to modulate flexibly is conducted with procedures very similar to those described in the previous section. However, when assessing capacity to modulate, the person with whom the trainee is working (i.e., role player) must change his behavior systematically in order to observe how effectively the trainee can "flex" in relation to such a change since this capacity is the crux of this adaptive skill.

Summary

We have presented a model for analyzing the training of training agents which is applicable to the assessment, training, and placement of teachers, psychotherapists, social workers, and other training agents whose function is to provide an interpersonal environment to other persons, e.g., Peace Corps volunteers. Training agent effectiveness was defined as the capacity to radiate a wide variety of environments, to select from this variety a specific environment to be radiated toward a particular person or group with the aim of producing a particular behavioral outcome, and to shift from one environment to another under appropriate circumstances. Using a variation of the Lewinian $B = f(P, E)$ formula, we considered the job of the training agent in terms of E: $P \rightarrow B$ (or the Environment directed toward a Person produces a Behavior). Specific skill components underlying agent effectiveness—discriminative skill, skill in radiating environments, and capacity to shift from one environment to another—were described, techniques for assessing such skill considered, and procedures for training these skills discussed.

If the present definition of agent effectiveness is accepted, this model provides the basis for designing investigations to learn more about how such skills can be acquired most effectively. The assessment of trainees in terms of differential skills should also provide a means for making training procedures more efficient. Finally, it is hoped that viewing teachers, therapists, social workers, and Peace Corps volunteers as generically similar has the potential advantage of increasing knowledge about training procedures through interprofessional cross-stimulation.

NOTES

Bandura, A. Behavioral modification through modeling procedures. In L. Krasner & L. P. Ullman (Eds.), *Research in behavior modification.* New York: Holt, Rinehart & Winston, 1965.

Bloom, B. S. (Ed.). *Taxonomy of educational objectives.* New York. Longman, Green, 1954.

Bradford, L. P., Gibb, J. R., & Benne, K. D. *T-group theory and laboratory method.* New York: Wiley, 1964.

Brim, O. J. *Education for child rearing.* New York. Russell Sage, 1959.

Campbell, D. T. Conformity in psychology's theories of acquired behavioral dispositions. In I. A. Berg & B. M. Bass (Eds.), *Conformity and deviation.* New York: Harper, 1961. Pp. 101–142.

Davitz, J. *The communication of emotional meaning.* New York: McGraw-Hill, 1964.

Flavell, J. H. Developmental studies of verbal communication skills. Paper read at Soc. Res. Child Develpm., Berkeley, California, 1963.

Harvey, O. J., Hunt, D. E., & Schroder, H. M. *Conceptual systems and personality organization.* New York: Wiley, 1961.

Hunt, D. E. A Conceptual Systems change model and its application to education. Paper presented at Office of Naval Research conference, "Flexibility, adaptability, and creativity: nature and developmental determinants," Boulder, Colorado, March 19–21, 1964.

Hunt, D. E. A behavioral method for assessing effectiveness of interpersonal communication derived from a training model. Unpublished MS., Syracuse University, 1965.

Hunt, D. E. & Joyce, B. R. Teacher trainee personality and initial teaching style. *Amer. educ. res. J.,* in press.

Hunt, D. E., Joyce, B R., & DelPopolo, J. An exploratory study in the modification of students' teaching patterns. Unpublished MS., Syracuse University, 1964.

Hunt, D. E., Joyce, B. R., & Weinstein, G. Application of communication task in the assessment of Peace Corps trainees. Unpublished MS., Syracuse University, 1965.

Joyce, B. R. A manual for coding teacher communications relevant to Conceptual Systems theory. Unpublished MS., University of Chicago, 1964.

Kahn, R. L. & Cannell, C. F. *The dynamics of interviewing.* New York: Wiley, 1957.

Lippitt, R., Watson, Jeanne, & Westley, B. *The dynamics of planned change.* New York: Harcourt Brace, 1958.

Warren, Marguerite Q., Palmer, T., & Turner, J. K. Community treatment project: an evaluation of community treatment for delinquents. CTP Research Report No. 5. Sacramento, California, 1964.

Weinstein, G. A method for assessing ability to control and regulate classroom behavior. Unpublished MS., Syracuse University, 1965.

24   TEACHERS OF THE POOR: A FIVE-POINT PLAN [1]

FRANK RIESSMAN

Introduction

There are numerous paths to improved education of the educationally deprived, culturally different child: the curriculum, parent involvement, school administration. The teacher and his approach stand at a central point; moreover, in the present hopeful atmosphere, the teacher is more open to change than ever before. However, it would be naïve to suppose that teacher change can occur independently of other relevant variables, particularly administration.[2] Presented below is a fivefold plan for the training of both preservice and in-service teachers of urban disadvantaged children:

1. Building teacher respect for disadvantaged children and their families. This involves attitude change and a proposed method of producing it.

2. Supplying teacher experiences with the disadvantaged.

3. Some general do's and don'ts in teaching the urban poor.

4. A teaching technology appropriate for low-income youngsters.

5. The development of a variety of teacher styles through integrating other parts of the plan with the idiosyncratic potential of each teacher. This concerns the *art of teaching* and how it can be developed and organized.

1. Attitude Change Through Interest

Many people stress the importance of respecting disadvantaged children as the key to their education, but the secret of respect for someone is to know his positives, his strengths. Unfortunately, too many who talk of respecting these children really see nothing

Frank Riessman, "Teachers of the Poor: A Five-Point Plan," *Journal of Teacher Education* (Fall 1967), pp. 326–336. Reprinted by permission of the author and publisher.

to respect. Hence, it is crucial for teachers to know such positives in the culture, behavior, and style of the disadvantaged as the cooperativeness and mutual aid that mark the extended family; the avoidance of the strain accompanying competitiveness and individualism; the equalitarianism, informality, and humor; the freedom from self-blame and parental overprotection; the children's enjoyment of each other's company and lessened sibling rivalry; the security and traditional outlook found in an extended family; the enjoyment of music, games, sports, and cards; the ability to express anger; the freedom from being word bound; and finally, the physical style involved in learning.

These positives must be spelled out in detail lest they become vague, romantic, sentimental, and demagogic. We need clear vision regarding the positives in people who cope with a difficult environment, who can express their anger toward the school, and who are disturbed at being discriminated against. The point is that you cannot have respect in a general way. To have genuine respect, you must know the culture and its positives, you must appreciate how these people cope with their environment, and how in coping with it, they have built their culture.

However, it is not enough to build respect and knowledge; teacher attitudes must also be changed. This is not so difficult as may be imagined; the most important element is to *interest* the teacher in disadvantaged people and their culture. Generally, school personnel have not been especially interested in the make-up of the disadvantaged; the poor, for the most part, are seen as an undifferentiated, drab mass. Surprisingly, providing teachers with sociological analyses of disadvantaged groups, though valuable, is not sufficient to develop deep interest and excitement. Oscar Lewis' literary anthropology is more useful, but it is still not enough; the time has come for teacher preparation to include the novels, films, art, dance, and music of low-income groups, particularly Negro and Spanish. Discussion around books such as *The Cool World* [3] and the movie made from it are more helpful and stimulating than any anthropological text.

Contrasts and issues can be stimulated by books and movies about the disadvantaged elsewhere, such as the British *The Sporting Life* and *Saturday Night and Sunday Morning*.[4] Such films and literature offer prospective teachers a different perspective and a closer feeling for these cultures. Valuable, too, is the study of Negro history and Negro contributions in science, art, and engineering.[5] Discussion of "hip" language may help overcome the stereotype of the nonverbal, inarticulate poor! A look through *Hiptionary* [6] is especially valuable in creating a feeling for the language of certain disadvantaged groups; it reveals their wonderful ability to verbalize and destroys the absurd illusion that they lack verbal ability. They have a highly imaginative language, though they are limited in its formal structure, and the school should certainly work on this need. The first area in the proposed program, then, is to build teacher respect for these people by developing interest and excitement in their psychology and culture.

2. Prepared Exposure

The second area considers appropriate laboratory experiences for teachers. Several programs are emerging in this area: one is the Hunter College preservice program described in *The Culturally Deprived Child;* [7] another is the Mobilization for Youth inservice program in New York City. Such programs stress visiting the homes and neighborhoods of the poor. Many people think that this *exposure* will prove positive in and of itself; actually, simple exposure may only reinforce existing stereotypes. Teachers, like everyone else, see selectively what they want and expect to see; consequently, what is needed is a carefully directed, prepared exposure showing *what* to look at and *how* to look at the culture. Instead of merely a broken home, they see an extended female-based family which may be highly organized, although in ways very different from the traditional nuclear family. They learn to see how functions are delegated and organized, how child rearing is handled, how cooking is assigned, how members of the family care for the house, how some go to work, and how responsibility is divided.

Teachers can learn not to confuse the normal with the pathological. The normal female-based family is not pathological, although pathology may occur in some families. The difference may be clarified by a look at the middle-class family. In some middle-class strata, child rearing includes parental overprotection and overindulgence. This is the norm, just as less intensive loving is normative in lower socioeconomic groups. But neither pattern by itself is abnormal, even though pathologies in both classes may well be related to the norm, reflecting it in an extreme form or expressing the constitutional reactions of particular children. What teachers need is an emphasis on the understanding of the basic culture (the norm) rather than on pathology. They should not focus on the environment as such (the crowdedness, the lack of privacy, the lack of economic security) but upon how these people struggle with their environment, how they have thereby forged a culture, and how this culture can be utilized in the school. It is clear, then, that we cannot simply call for tours and home visits. Teachers must be carefully prepared to look beyond the environment and the surface behavior in comprehending the meaning of the life and behavior of the poor.

3. Some General Do's and Don'ts

The third area briefly considers some do's and don'ts in teaching educationally deprived children. Consistency, structure, and order are fundamental. *Informality and authority are not seen as contradictions, and the poor like both.* Extrinsic rewards and punishments are understood, but brutality is strongly rejected. The teacher should be straightforward, direct, and should clearly define what is to be done. *Values related to order, tardiness, or aggression should be strictly oriented toward their usefulness in learning.* (We can't conduct a class if children fight, come late, walk around, etc. This does not mean that fighting is "bad.")

Goldberg states:

The successful teacher meets the disadvantaged child on equal terms, as person to person, individual to individual. But while he *accepts, he doesn't condone.* He sets clearly defined limits for his pupils and will brook few transgressions. He is aware that, unlike middle-class children, they rarely respond to exhortations intended to control behavior through invoking feelings of guilt and shame. He, therefore, sets the rules, fixes the boundaries, establishes the routines with a minimum of discussion. Here he is impersonal, undeviating, strict, but never punitive. Within these boundaries, the successful teacher is business-like and orderly, knowing that he is there to do a job. But he is also warm and outgoing, adapting his behavior to the individual pupils in his class. He shows his respect and liking for his pupils and makes known his belief in their latent abilities.[8]

Different stages of the teaching process should also be considered. There are two crucial stages: first, achieving contact; and second, developing educational power. In the contact stage, comes the special "breaking through" to the child, winning his attention, etc.; although this problem is sometimes exaggerated, it is nevertheless a definite issue in preparing teachers who must develop effective techniques. Unfortunately, a good many teachers who succeed at the contact stage (maintaining orderly, attentive classes) are unable to move on to the next stage and develop educational power. They have done well to achieve the contact stage, but to stop short of the next and most crucial stage is indeed unfortunate.[9]

4. Appropriate Teaching Technology

Listed below are a number of approaches that may have special value for low-income children:

(1) The "organics" approach of Sylvia Ashton-Warner [10] should be especially valuable in utilizing the interests and strengths of the youngsters and should guard against their being "acted upon." (The latter is the current trend in many programs designed for the disadvantaged, who are supposedly deficit-ridden.)

(2) The Montessori System, which envisions a 35 to 1 ratio of children to teacher, may provide valuable leads. The stress on sensory materials and on order in this approach should be particularly congenial to low-income children.[11] (Dr. Ronald Kregler, a neuropsychiatrist at the University of California, Los Angeles, is experimenting with a Montessori nursery program for disadvantaged children.)

(3) Various game techniques may be valuable: In the Manner of the Adverb, Robbins Auditory Set Game, etc.[12]

(4) Senesch's techniques for teaching economics to first- and second-graders seem promising.[13]

(5) *Scope,* the new magazine published by Scholastic Magazines, is particularly attuned to teaching the disadvantaged.

The Special Significance of Role Playing.[14] Role-playing techniques have long been popular with blue-color workers in labor unions and industry. Experiences at Mobilization for Youth and various community organizations also indicate an exceptionally positive response to role-play technology by low-income people. Although more systematic research is needed regarding these observations, it would appear that this technology is very congenial to the low-income person's style—physical (action-oriented, doing rather than talking); down to earth, concrete, problem-directed; externally oriented rather than introspective; group-centered; gamelike rather than test-oriented, easy, informal in tempo.

Miller and others,[15] on the basis of investigations, concluded that an outstanding characteristic of the low-income person's style is an emphasis on the physical, especially the motoric (the large muscles involved in voluntary action). They prefer to do rather than to talk. It is not simply that the poor *are* physical: that their labor is characterized by working with things, that their child rearing typically utilizes physical punishment, that their religious expressions more often include physical manifestations of emotion such as handclapping, that when they become mentally ill they appear more likely to develop motoric symptoms such as conversion hysteria and catatonia (disorders involving malfunctions of the voluntary muscles), that they are strongly interested in sports, that they are especially responsive to extraverbal forms of communication such as gestures; [16] the significant factor from the point of view of style is that low-income people tend to *work out mental problems best when they can do things physically*. This is their *habit* or style of work, and it appears when they work on academic problems, personal problems, or whatever.

Role playing appears admirably suited to this physical, action-centered, motoric style that requires a wholistic doing or acting out of situations, a mode of problem solving that low-income males, and young males in particular, find attractive. They frequently have a strong dislike for talk, especially talk that is isolated from experience; they want action and prefer talk that is related to action. They also like vivid (e.g., hip slang), down-to-earth, situationally rooted talk; and this, too, is more likely to emerge in the role-play format. Role playing is much more lively, physical, and active than the typical interview.

There are numerous other dimensions of role playing which are congruent with various aspects of the low-income person's style:

Low-income groups typically do not like the traditional test format, and this limits diagnostic work with them. The requirements of their style seem to be better met by gamelike atmospheres and situational measures, both of which are found more readily in role-play technology.[17] They are generally less introspective, less introverted, and less concerned with self. They respond more to the external, to the outside, to action. They are more likely to see the causes of their problems in external forces; they project more and tend to externalize their guilt.[18] Kohn notes that their child-rearing patterns center on conformity to external prescriptions in contrast to the self-direction focus of the middle class.[19] He relates this, in part, to the fact that working-class occupations require that one follow explicit rules set down by an authority; middle-class positions are more subject to self-direction.[20]

Although the style of the poor probably includes a strong emphasis on informality, humor, and warmth, the disadvantaged also like a content that is structured, definite, and specific. It is often assumed that role playing is highly unstructured, open, and free. In part, this is true, particularly in the early phase of setting the problem and mood; but in the middle and later phases (especially the role-*training* stage), where the effort is made to teach very specific behaviors, role playing can be highly structured, reviewing in minute detail the various operations to be learned (such as how to run a meeting, organize a conference, talk to a housing manager). Educationally disadvantaged people appear to prefer a mood or feeling tone that is informal and easy but a *content* that is more structured and task-centered. Role playing may suit both needs.

A Route to Verbalization. In role-playing sessions we have had occasion to observe that the verbal performance of deprived children is markedly improved in the discussion period following the session. When talking about some action they have seen, deprived children are apparently able to verbalize much more fully. Typically, they do not verbalize well in response to words alone. They express themselves more readily when reacting to things they can see and do. Words as stimuli are not sufficient for them as a rule. Ask a juvenile delinquent who comes from a disadvantaged background what he doesn't like about school or the teacher and you will get an abbreviated, inarticulate reply. But have a group of these youngsters act out a school scene in which someone plays the teacher, and you will discover a stream of verbal consciousness that is almost impossible to shut off.[21]

Role playing can have various beneficial results in the teaching of academic material in the school. Considerable excitement is added to a lecture when the instructor illustrates a point this way; for example, if an inquiring student should wonder what Abraham Lincoln would think of our present civil rights policy, let Lincoln and Johnson stage a debate enacted by two students! The impossibilities of time and space are eliminated, and the civics lesson will be well remembered.

The Use of Hip Language—A description of the use of hip language (combined with role playing) in teaching disadvantaged children in the Madison Area Project in Syracuse was given in the *Syracuse Herald-Journal* of November 11, 1963.[22]

A teacher had complained to Gerald Weinstein, curriculum coordinator of the Madison Area Project, that her students "practically fell asleep" while she was reading poems from a standard anthology. He responded by distributing to the class copies of "Motto," a poem by the Negro author Langston Hughes:

> I play it cool and dig all jive.
> That's the reason I stay alive.
> My motto, as I live and learn,
> Is: Dig and Be Dug in Return.

After the students had read the poem, there was a long silence, followed by exclamations, such as, "Hey this is tough"; "Hey, Mr. Weinstein, this cat is pretty cool"; "It's written in our talk." However, when asked the meaning of "playing it cool," the students had difficulty in verbalizing the idea, but a boy volunteered to act it out, with Mr. Weinstein taking the part of the teacher.

During the discussion of the phrase "dig all jive," Weinstein was able to impress upon the class that, in addition to understanding their own jive, their chances of "staying alive" would be infinitely increased if they also understood the school jive.

The enthusiasm of the students for "Motto" led them into more of Hughes' poetry. Later they moved into other kinds of literature, written in more conventional language. But the students were not the only ones to learn from that exciting class. Weinstein learned too: he learned the advantage of being familiar with the language of the children you are teaching and establishing a rapport with them. If a teacher doesn't "start where the child is," Weinstein says, he only reinforces the failures and frustration that have become the normal pattern for disadvantaged students.

Exposure to the best cultural works produces no magical results, and the phony literature that often characterizes school readers, especially in the lower grades, is even less effective. Exposure must begin "where the child is" and proceed to other varieties of art forms. The method applies to all kinds of students, Weinstein says; for the student who has read Shakespeare but has not read Langston Hughes, for example, is also disadvantaged.

It should be clear that we are *not* suggesting that teachers employ hip language in normal conversation with underprivileged youngsters. It is not intended as a device for attempting to be friendly with the child through imitating his culture; this would indeed be patronizing and dangerous. Rather the use of hip materials in a formal lesson plan can become an excellent avenue to the style and interests of the disadvantaged and contribute to the development of their verbalization.

Recently in tutoring a disadvantaged high school student in English, I employed a hiptionary in a completely systematic and formal fashion. The first and rather immediate result was that the student learned a great many new English word definitions for the hip words with which she had been familiar: [23]

Hip Word	*Definition*
"bug"	to disturb, bother, annoy
"cop out"	to avoid conflict by running away, not considered admirable or honorably accepted
"cool it"	to be quiet, peaceful, tranquil
"far out"	not comprehensible
"weak"	inadequate, inappropriate

Words such as *tranquil, inappropriate,* etc., were unknown to this youngster, but through use of the hip word game, she quickly became familiar with them and derived great pleasure from a new-found use of various "big" words. I then used the hiptionary to clarify the meaning and significance of the metaphor (e.g., the hip phrases for bisexual are *AC-DC, switch hitter,* and *swings from both sides of the fence*). Similarly, many other linguistic concepts can be introduced by utilizing hip language in this word game.

In addition to teaching technology, there is great need for curriculum materials that appear to promise success with disadvantaged youngsters. Both the Bank Street College of Education, through its proposed Educational Resources Center, and Mobilization for Youth have been developing such curriculum laboratories, which should be closely related to the teacher institutes and should contain not only materials but also reports (and films)[24] of positive experiments in the teaching of the disadvantaged, functional illiterates, etc.[25]

5. Effective Teacher Styles

There is some tendency to develop a hypothetical model of the ideal teacher. We tend to assume that effective teachers must be healthy and well adjusted. I seriously question this idea. I am not suggesting, of course, that we look for sick people and make them teachers; what I am suggesting is that we think about the development of individual teacher styles, and some of these may have significant nonhealthy components. There appear to be many styles that function well with low-income youngsters; teachers succeed in different ways. In visits to schools in low-income areas in over thirty-five cities, I have always found at least one teacher in a school who, it was agreed by everyone (children, parents, colleagues, and administrators), was an effective teacher, but the personality of each of these teachers, the manner of approach, and point of view were vastly different.[26]

For example, there is the fussy, compulsive type, whom I find it difficult to query, who teaches things over and over, is very concerned that I understand him, and treats me like a child. But, actually, in the classroom the behavior that annoys me can be quite effective. This kind of person might well be called a "sublimated compulsive"; he directs his compulsivity into the functional order and structure which disadvantaged children like.

Another type of teacher is the "boomer." He shouts out in a loud, strong voice: "You're going to learn. I'm here to teach you, and there is no nonsense in this classroom." He lays the ground rules early, and the kids know immediately that there is a point beyond which they cannot go. They may not like him, but they learn. Some psychologists and educators might call this person hostile; yet he has learned to use this quality effectively in the classroom.

Another kind of teacher might be called the maverick. Everybody loves him but the boss. He upsets everything because he's always raising difficult questions and presenting ideas that disturb. This teacher is convinced that ideas are meant to stir people up, and consequently he develops a close link with his young and eager students. He is as surprised and curious as they at each turn of mind, each new discovery, and it is this fresh quality that comes through to them.

Then there is the coach. He is informal, earthy, and may be an athlete, but in any case, he is physically expressive in conducting his dialogue with the world. Many low-income youngsters like this. Coming from homes characterized by activity and motion, they connect with this quality quickly and naturally.

In sharp contrast is the quiet one. This teacher accomplishes much the same goal by sincerity, calmness, and definitiveness. His essential dignity pervades the situation and commands both respect and attention.

We also have the entertainer, colorful, melodramatic, and most importantly, not afraid to have fun with the children. He may make mistakes through his sheer flair for the comic, but he is free enough to laugh with the children at his own blunders. His inventiveness may furrow his supervisor's brow, as when he has children make western hats from a paper-reading assignment about cowboys. But they learn more about cowboys than if a traditional method had been applied. This teacher actively involves the children—their opinions count, and they know it.

A striking example of another teacher style is the secular. This fellow is relaxed and informal with the kids, may have lunch with them, or use their bathroom. You would be amazed at how many children do not *really* believe that teachers eat and sleep and go to the bathroom like other people! This fellow is comfortable talking turkey with the kids.

There are many other styles, but I will cite just one more—the secular intellectual. He is not academic, but he is interested in knowledge and its transmission to youngsters. He is really interested in the substance and not just the academic correctness of the material. He doesn't like classical music because he is supposed to but because he likes all types of music; and it so happens that he also likes blues, jazz, and popular music. He really has *broader* horizons. One such person I met was especially interested in hip language, which he was learning from the youngsters—a normally unwise action against which I would warn most people. However, this teacher, because of his deep interest in all language, could show a genuine interest in hip language without being false or condescending.

Teacher preparation should include learning about these types of teachers, with films and observation of them in action, but above all, with an opportunity for student teachers to play each type. Each student should develop his repertoire by trying out the roles in permissive, unthreatening situations in his own group; he should play the classroom and the different problems that arise. Out of this role play, he develops his own repertoire. No matter what is talked about in general, he must formulate these things in his own individual way for his own specific personality. He needs more than practice teaching for this, since the actual classroom cannot allow full experimentation. He needs a practice situation —experimental and permissive—in which he can actually try out various techniques and approaches, experiment with different styles, see which ones fit, blend them to his personality, and develop his own strengths.

Organization of the Teacher Institutes

Without detailing the methods whereby teachers would receive the training proposed in the five-point plan, a number of general principles can be outlined:

Where possible, teachers themselves (master teachers, consulting teachers) should do the teaching or group leading. It may be necessary first to hold master institutes where teachers who would later train other teachers would be exposed to the five-point program. At a later point, these master teachers would be supervised as they translated the program for their local schools. The master institute could call on all kinds of specialists, including sociologists, psychologists, Montessori specialists, role-playing leaders, etc. The institutes could be introduced as special courses in pre-service training (in regular sessions or summer sessions) as well as for in-service programs.

Training that is provided close to the operations in which it will be utilized will be most effective.[27] Teachers, for example, should be worked with around their specific school and classroom problems and the trainers should visit the classrooms, observe the teachers closely, and discuss problems and suggestions with them in considerable detail. The ideas embodied in the five-point plan would thus be selectively applied in relation to on-the-job problems experienced by the teacher trainees. An interesting variant of this approach is to be found in the Bank Street College proposal for an Educational Resources Center which will be de-voted to "development, collection and dissemination of new in-structional materials, new teaching methods, and curriculum in-novations specifically designed to raise the achievement of the educationally handicapped minority group child."

Teachers and their pupils selected for demonstration will actually move into the Center for a designated period—say three weeks—where they will receive special instruction from master teachers and other spe-cialists. When the class returns to its home school following the instruc-tion period at the Center, the teacher will continue to use methods and skills acquired at the ERC and will also consult frequently with spe-cialists from the Center who will visit the school. Eventually it is hoped that each school will boast a number of teachers who, with their classes, have had instructional periods at the Center.[28]

A group or team approach should be a central feature in the training, with a strong emphasis on building esprit de corps in the groups. The group experience would be examined and utilized for the development of concepts, understanding of group process, etc. (T (training)-group approach).

Full participation of the trainees should be intensively solicited with regard to encouraging them to formulate their needs, the way they see their problems, and their suggestions for meeting these problems. Hence, small teacher meetings should be organ-ized to discuss (and role play) ways of meeting classroom difficulties, teaching techniques, and approaches. In this context, the trainers would offer for discussion techniques that have evolved elsewhere.

In order to have the training become a part of neuromuscular make-up of the trainees, a variety of techniques should be instituted: supervisory conferences, role-playing films, demonstrations, quizzes, intensive brief reading, small group discussions, lectures, debates, and the writing of a paper. This methodology is based on two principles: (a) People learn through a variety of styles—some learn best from doing (e.g., role playing), others from lectures, still others from films, etc. (b) In order to internalize material taught over a relatively short period of time, it is necessary to provide as much active practice and involvement as possible, along with corrective feedback from the supervisory staff; hence the emphasis on role playing and supervisor's sessions. In addition, having the learner teach the material to other trainees appears to be an excellent device for the development of deep learning.

There is constant criticism today of education in the United States—the school system, the curriculum, the teachers, and the administration. There are constant attacks by authors such as Paul Goodman, Edward Friedenberg, and others upon the conformity of the system and the lack of any real learning. There is also constant, powerful criticism of the middle class in our country by authors like Erich Fromm and Paul Goodman, who see the middle class as conformists who have lost their spontaneity and inner convictions. Yet, although this criticism is very widespread, it is rarely applied to the teaching of disadvantaged children, who, apparently, are to adapt to the oft-criticized school and be made into middle-class people by its culture. When we talk about disadvantaged children, we seem suddenly to acquire an idealized picture of the school and the middle-class life for which these children are to be prepared, even though many of us might agree with the David Riesmans, Paul Goodmans, and Erich Fromms that a great deal must be done to change both the middle class and the school. Disadvantaged children have much to contribute to this needed change; their culture, their style, and their positives can aid greatly in the remaking of our middle-class society.[29]

NOTES

1. Prepared for presentation to the Syracuse University Conference on Urban Education and Cultural Deprivation, July 15–16, 1964.
2. It is striking that significant teacher improvement in morale and performance appears to have taken place in the Banneker District in St. Louis where Assistant Superintendent Samuel Shepard has introduced marked administrative modifications vis-à-vis the teaching staff.
3. Miller, Warren. *The Cool World*. Boston, Mass.: Little, 1959.
4. Sillitoe, Alan. *Saturday Night and Sunday Morning*. New York: Knopf, 1959.
5. See *Negro Heritage*, published monthly in Chicago.
6. Horne, Elliot. *The Hiptionary: A Hipster's View of the World Scene*. New York: Simon & Schuster, 1963.
7. Riessman, Frank. *The Culturally Deprived Child*. New York: Harper, 1962, pp. 118–19.
8. Goldberg, Miriam. "Adapting Teacher Style to Pupil Differences." A paper delivered at Teachers College Conference on Disadvantaged Children, July 1963, p. 9.
9. For a fuller discussion of these stages, see Riessman, *op. cit.*, pp. 94–95.
10. Ashton-Warner, Sylvia. *The Teacher*. New York: Simon & Schuster, 1963.
11. See Mayer, Martin. "Schools, Slums, and Montessori." *Commentary* 37: 33–39; June 1964.
12. Riessman, *op. cit.*, pp. 84–85.
13. Senesch, Lawrence. "The Organic Curriculum: A New Experiment in Economic Education." Reprint Series No. 22. Lafayette, Indiana: Purdue University, School of Industrial Management.
14. The following discussion of role playing is taken from Riessman, Frank, and Goldfarb, Jean. "Role Playing and the Poor." *Group Psychotherapy*, Vol. 17, No. 1, 1964.
15. Miller, D. R., and others. *Inner Conflict and Defense*. New York: Holt, 1960, p. 24.
16. For a discussion of many of these items see Miller and others, *op. cit.*
17. Becker, Jerome, and others. "Situational Testing of Social Psychological Variables in Personality." *Mental Health of the Poor: New Treatment Approaches for Low-Income People*. (Edited by Frank Riessman and others.) New York: The Free Press, 1964.
18. Miller and others, *op. cit.*, p. 396.
19. Kohn, Melvin L. "Social Class and Parent-Child Relationships: An Interpretation." *American Journal of Sociology*, 68: 471–80; January 1963.
20. *Ibid.*
21. Riessman, *op. cit.*, p. 77.
22. Kanasola, Robert. "Students Dig Jive When It's Played Cool." *Syracuse Herald-Journal*, November 11, 1963.

23. The words in this list were taken from a hiptionary entitled "The Other Language" developed by Anthony Romeo at Mobilization for Youth, January 1962.

24. The Lincoln Filene Center of Tufts University and McGraw-Hill Publishing Company are jointly preparing three films related to the teaching of disadvantaged children.

25. An illustration would be the Bank Street experiment conducted in the summer of 1963 where disadvantaged youngsters showed marked academic and emotional improvement as a result of a special one-month program. Shepard's project in the Banneker District of St. Louis is another illustration. Shepard's program is especially noteworthy because he has demonstrated that disadvantaged youngsters at the elementary and junior high school levels can be quickly improved to grade level. Much more comprehensive efforts than Shepard's might very well produce even more startling results. It is time to put an end to the tendency toward educational surrender on all but preschool disadvantaged children.

26. The discussion of teacher types that follows is based on a joint unpublished paper with Arlene Hannah entitled "Teachers of the Poor," 1964.

27. This proposal, called site training, as well as a number of other proposals in this section were developed for the Rutgers University Training Center, a grant for which has been requested from the President's Committee on Juvenile Delinquency.

28. *Bank Street Reporting,* Vol. 1, No. 1, 1964.

29. For an excellent discussion of the Negro contributions to our age, see Killens, John Oliver. "Explanation of the 'Black Psyche.' " *New York Times* Magazine Section; June 7, 1964, p. 37.

25 PROBLEMS RELATED TO TEACHER PREPARATION

It does seem to me that the subject of urban teaching has had more than its share of contemplation and discussion. Apparently, however, demonstrably successful programs do not yet form a model or pattern. Ed Gordon and Doxey Wilkerson of Yeshiva University affirm this in their recent book, *Contemporary Education for the Disadvantaged.* They state that, "Despite all of our current efforts, tremendous gains are not being achieved. We are probably failing because we have not yet found the right answers."

What we're really saying is that *no* teaching is done very well; it's still mostly teacher-talk and textbooks. But its failure shows up more on the disadvantaged child. Teacher preparation had always assumed that children bring a motivation to school: they *want* to learn. Teachers have been taught to build on that motivation and perhaps to remove or repair some minor impediments. But when we look at the cross section of cultures in urban communities, we see that this built-in motivation is not only lacking but in its place may be an active hostility or at least indifference to the middle-class values of teachers. Mind you, it's not that *education* is not held in high regard among the disadvantaged population, it's the *schools* that are depreciated. . . .

Our concern with education of youngsters should not blind us either to the mammoth problems of housing, employment, and family structure that bear particularly on inner-city families. It may be that education alone just isn't the answer to it all, that we must expect progress to be linked closely with movement in these other areas. . . . What I have to say concerns the necessary inter-

Alvin P. Lierheimer, "Problems Related to Teacher Preparation," *Conference Journal, The City College School of Education and the Urban Community* (New York: The College of the City of New York, 1967), pp. 27–38. Reprinted by permission of the author and publisher.

relationship of schools, colleges, and state education departments. I can only claim to have some expertness in this latter category as it relates to the first two. Few people have included in their thinking and writing the role of a state education department as it pertains to teacher training or teacher education. There are many writings about the proper role of the schools in teaching disadvantaged youngsters and there are numerous articles on how to prepare teachers for classroom responsibilities in the urban schools. Some pieces have concerned themselves with the necessary interrelationships of school and college programs, for example, internships and student teaching. But few of them bring in the third party.

Let me review some of the problem areas in urban education to reveal my own biases and then suggest some of the solutions that are beginning to appear. As I proceed I will identify how these might involve state education departments.

Isn't it disconcerting to realize that . . . tomorrow professors will be facing a class of youthful faces who will be in full teaching bloom in 1984, that mystical year foretold by George Orwell? If we *are* preparing teachers who will be in mid-career in 1984, we should give some thought to the major problems these teachers are likely to face. And it is not difficult to predict what some of them will be.

A concern for the future of teaching was expressed eloquently in a speech made by Professor William Arrowsmith of the University of Texas at the recent meeting of the American Council of Education. His concerns pervade the other problems I'll mention. He comments on the "takeover" by scholarship and research interests in the university and the abandonment, in his eyes, of the fundamental purpose of education, one of *molding men* rather than *producing knowledge*. The university he says, "has disowned what teaching has always meant, a care and concern for the future of man, a platonic love of the species not for what it *is* but for what it *might be*." While his remarks were aimed at the college and university community in general, his call to greatness sounds hollow for teachers who have not confronted the realities of intergroup differences and worked through that confrontation to a point of acceptance and outgoingly constructive help to students. Hilda Taba's remarks add to this dimension: "There is a need for emphasis on emotional content in curriculum; materials, which make an impact on feelings, which generate insight into values, and which permit an analysis of human factors and relationships in events of life. The treatment of such materials for the purpose of altering personal feelings and of cultivating sensitivity requires teaching strategies for which teachers tend to be the least prepared."

One is reminded, in reviewing the extensive writing and research activities in the field of education for depressed areas, that we still don't know how to make teachers behave toward children in ways that reflect the goals we have always had for education, e.g., dignity, justice, freedom.

In their simplest form, the problems of teaching in disadvantaged schools fall in two areas:

1. Inability to be precise in analyzing, carrying out and evaluating the teaching act, and

2. Failure to demonstrate in a classroom the warmth and psychologically astute support that appears in articles and speeches.

A. I place a high value on all-university responsibility and involvement in teacher education for reasons that more nearly resemble those in Professor Arrowsmith's paper than for those which James B. Conant has identified. The involvement of scholars in all fields of the university is important for teacher education, whether it is for urban schools or for other schools, not because these scholars have the life-blood of knowledge to drip into the teachers and which might conceivably be of help, but because only by exposure to such a broad range of knowledgeable and committed individuals, wherever they may be, can prospective teachers see and have as models many styles of human existence, many approaches to the problems of living. I do not believe teacher behavior is changed by courses or textbooks, but that it may be changed by the lives of professors with whom they identify because of their concern with the human condition. No single department or school of education can encompass the diversity of human beings that exemplify and indeed inspire greatness and concern for man. It is for these reasons that I would place an exceptionally high value on intra-institutional involvement in teacher education.

There are, of course, the usual reasons also to encourage intra-university involvement in teacher preparation; its value is so apparent one wonders why highly educated people have not practiced it more assiduously. The resources of the social sciences —psychology and sociology in particular—are especially applicable to the clarification and solution of human problems in the city; conversely the inner city provides the laboratory for both education and social science faculties to develop and test theoretical models.

B. On a more mundane level, I am concerned with the problem of the teacher shortage even though we have very little formal information to describe that shortage. For the most part it consists of reports from employers reflecting their difficulty in the competitive market of today. We don't know, for instance, very much about the shifting percentages of teachers going from urban to suburban schools or indeed between the schools within a given city. We don't know why teachers choose one kind of school over another. We can guess that something will have to be done to increase the attractiveness of teaching in the urban schools. It may take a differential in pay. It also may be that we can't throw neophytes into the most difficult schools and expect them to be transformed into giants. Yet it is also likely that the urban school is the best training laboratory for teachers in exemplifying so many of the problems that apply to *all* students. The urban school could become a laboratory experience sought after by the best teachers.

We don't know what difference it makes when auxiliary personnel or para-professionals are used. Conceivably, such use would affect the teacher shortage itself. Some experience with urban schools suggests that the use of these auxiliary personnel is particularly important for the additional opportunity it provides for a one-to-one relationship between students and adults. Benne and Birnbaum have suggested a few interesting kinds of para-professionals that might be tried, e.g., Teacher Guidance Specialists to help a teacher "understand the dynamics of the classroom group better and to understand her own dynamics in relation to students, individually and collectively within the teaching-learning situation." There are many others.

C. Then there is the problem of dropouts. I am not referring to teenage dropouts but rather to the dropouts from teacher education itself. Stanford University, for instance, reports that half of those who get certified in June aren't teaching two years later. The figures elsewhere would be similar. We need to know why this dropout occurs. We need to try some programs that might make a difference. During the recent campaign Governor Rockefeller announced a Teachers Reserve and our office is developing such a program. Programs may be developed which would cut down on the fearful loss of teachers, especially women, who graduate from college, and then do not enter the teaching force or enter it for only a brief time. For instance, teachers who are not planning on entering the classroom upon graduation might be signed up in the Reserve and provided with a variety of continuing education opportunities through correspondence, television, home study, or other types of work during their non-working years so that they would be better able to re-enter the classroom at a later date. We will also use the Reserve to explore possible uses of a variety of para-professional positions. Another response to the dropout problem is reflected in Harry Rivlin's proposal for urban teacher preparation that provides for a smoother transition between the training program and the induction period.

D. Preschool programs are important not only as compensatory education but as an aid to motivational growth; they're here to stay. Those who could afford good preschool programs knew their value long ago. How should we staff these programs in light of the teacher shortage? There is little doubt that experiences in these formative years are crucial. Isn't something like 50% of intelligence developed by the age of three? But we need to test the general acceptance of the notion that "the earlier we do something the better" or that "doing something is better than doing nothing." Some think that by starting early we ignite growth and then simply stand back and watch the flames spread. Such a thought suggests that we start at as early an age as possible and give as much stimulation as possible. That's pretty risky! There is a million-dollar fund in the Department for prekindergarten programs and I hope at least some of it is finding its way into university-school investigation of these and other basic problems.

E. Much is written about the implications of new technology for education, e.g., programmed study, educational TV, etc. But relatively little solid information is available from which to prepare a program for teachers who will themselves be supervising other teachers at the turn of the century. Our office has been developing a program to demonstrate the uses of computer-assisted instruction in the in-service education of teachers using remote terminals with a variety of visual and auditory displays. The thought occurred to me in watching a computer-assisted program providing practice in writing German that the infinite patience and encouragement built into the program was probably warmer and more encouraging for the learner than the ministration of a caustic and harried housewife-teacher whose husband started her off on the wrong foot in the morning. So far, higher institutions haven't displayed much interest in the Department's activities on this front. Some of that blame will have to be accepted as a result of our failure to make loud noises about the program.

F. One of the problems that appears to be sharper for the schools with large numbers of disadvantaged students than it does for other schools is the establishment of clearcut instructional objectives. Most schools lack a systematic means for determining which of today's current problem areas have curriculum implications for local programs. Where have you seen high school courses of study designed around poverty, pollution, or population, for instance? Worse yet, in approaching the teaching process itself, how well are teachers taught to select *desired* pupil behavior against which to judge *learned* pupil behavior? Do teachers establish objectives and then select activities to produce the desired behavior? Do they measure what pupils have actually learned, comparing *learned* behavior with *desired* behavior? And if they fall short, do they select a better set of instructional experiences? Brickell calls this a "control loop" and says that it is absolutely essential for making instructional decisions systematically. But if so, why don't we see teachers doing it more often?

G. The rising educational level in laymen who control the schools will be an even more important factor in the future than it is now. And I remind you of my earlier observation that the disadvantaged population frequently holds *education* in high esteem, it's the *schools* they dislike. Persons with expertness in areas that impinge upon the schools will begin to ask embarrassing questions such as "how much does it cost to get a child with normal intelligence to the third grade reading level?" This cost factor becomes important as the price of education goes up.

In looking at school programs today one must admit that there is not an awful lot of difference from the classrooms of a generation ago. There may be a revolution in education seen by the popular press but there is still peace and quiet in many, many classrooms. We might consider for a moment what would happen if a school were established in conjunction with a university where *real* experiments could take place. In this school all State and local regulations would be called off, necessary resources from all levels would be poured in, and children would volunteer for a school experience where we tried our best hunches on effective teaching. The cooperation of a state agency would be necessary as would be its support. If only one or two such truly *experimental* schools were in operation, perhaps a number of others could be designated as *demonstration* schools where some of the successful experiments could be shown to larger numbers of teachers in a setting more nearly like their own. I must say parenthetically that campus schools I've seen in New York State do not appear to be doing either of these two jobs at this time. The partnership to make such a program possible includes local schools, university faculty and state education department.

H. Still another problem area continues to be the distance between what the schools think teachers need *to begin work* and what colleges think they must provide *before graduation*. A teacher's training should be subject to the continuing scrutiny of his colleagues both in the schools and in the colleges. We hear increasingly that experienced teachers will play a stronger role in preparing the coming generation of teachers. Some of you will recall that Harry Rivlin suggested a program of teacher preparation that begins with an assistant teacher getting school-based, paid experience working with individuals and groups as well as observing classrooms. His assistant teacher takes some consolidated and highly relevant course work and advances in succeeding semesters to a position of greater responsibility as a beginning teacher. To me, the attractiveness of Dean Rivlin's proposal for a new pattern of urban teacher preparation was not so much in the details which he outlined but rather in his implication that we could indeed break the current pattern of teacher education without serious loss. He says himself that "parts of the pattern may be used even if other suggestions prove not to be feasible at the time." In a similar proposal, Robert Bush of Stanford University suggests that we "make all beginning teaching positions of such a junior level that only a limited amount of training would qualify a person to enter, leaving much more of the demanding and extensive training for career teaching to take place after the first few years on the job." Both of these approaches to teacher preparation are especially realistic in dealing with the problems of urban schools. They also address the problem of the teacher-dropouts. Perhaps we should postpone and make more functional the extensive training for teachers who will "stay with it."

Proposals such as these need the support and cooperation of the State Education Department. Nothing sound has been proposed yet which could not be accommodated, either under existing rules or under regulations which are themselves subject to change on the basis of good advice. But before some of these articulated programs become operational, there will need to be a decrease in the alienation that appears between educators at all levels including state departments, schools, universities, federal and foundation officials, commercial agencies with educational interests and the like. Unfortunately, each of us thinks of cooperation as a situation where *you* co- while *I* operate.

The Functions of the State Education Department

New faculty members in some higher institutions are told by their more experienced colleagues that any course variations in teacher preparation would never be approved by the Department —don't propose any. In other colleges, the new faculty member is told to go ahead and change but don't tell the Department. This latter approach works well sometimes but it can also lead to compromising situations where a student's right to teach is concerned.

Let me give you an example of the Department's role along these lines. We asked five New York State institutions preparing teachers if they would participate with us in an exploration of all-university approaches to teacher education and certification. We offered freedom from State regulation or requirement and further, we secured funds for the release of faculty time to do the necessary intra-institutional planning. The Five College Project has been operating for about a year now. Skeptics have said that the money will be used up and little will be accomplished. And it *will* be hard to pin down significant learnings for teacher education at first. But one should note carefully that it was the Department itself, created as a regulatory body, which divested itself of that function for the purpose of exploring new approaches to teacher education and certification.

College faculty members frequently are active in professional associations which encourage the Department to alter certification requirements in one way or another. This usually takes the shape of a resolution passed at a state-wide meeting and transmitted to the Commissioner. What typically is missing is a coherent justification of why the proposal would be desirable. The impact of recommended changes in certification would be far greater if such statements were well developed and convincingly stated. It would then be appropriate to have consideration given to these proposals by an advisory board and a recommendation put before the Commissioner and the Regents. Parenthetically one must observe a certain ambivalence on the part of professional groups which request additional categories of certification and at the same time criticize the Department as excessively regulatory.

The very meaning and function of certification itself has never been explored in any depth by university scholars so that certification might come to mean *competence* rather than *exposure to courses.*

Suppose the State stopped mandating courses and mandated instead specific learnings, that is, what a prospective teacher would have to be able *to do.* Suppose further that prospective candidates for a certificate had to demonstrate their ability to perform within a period of years before certification was granted on the basis of a school-college recommendation. If certification were based on demonstrated ability to perform and have command of certain understandings, the State could give full freedom to teacher preparatory programs. Think of the scramble to find ways of producing the teaching behavior determined to be a minimum desirable essential!

This type of approach is in the discussion stages right now and the idea didn't come out of a school of education! But if alternatives to the unhappy course-counting approach to certification are ever to become a reality, we're going to need help.

Whether in seeking variations from existing course requirements or in developing alternative patterns to certification, the Department depends heavily on evidence that a university faculty has thought through the problem sufficiently and supports a request with cogent documentation. Many so-called experimental programs are withdrawn once probing questions are asked by the Department. It is hard to believe that we are either so devastating in our criticism or so repulsive in our search for assurance.

But the Department also functions to provide outright encouragement and assistance to programs of pre- and in-service education teachers. Funds are granted each year by the Legislature and while they are always of limited amount, frequently we have been able to lead applicants to alternate or additional sources of support for promising programs. Most activities that involve the Department either financially or for purposes of approval have their origin in a school or college although some programs are initiated by the Department.

We are making plans for a spring conference, for instance, at which colleges will exchange their experiences in programs for teachers of the disadvantaged. Out of a conference of this sort might develop teams of school and college people who could travel to interested institutions to describe and demonstrate their programs in detail.

We have provided stipend support to preservice programs for teachers who themselves come from disadvantaged backgrounds and wish to prepare to teach in those areas. We have supported summer programs for critic teachers who will supervise student teachers.

The variety of viable programs is limited only by the availability of faculty time and immediate sources of funding. A school and college might plan jointly, for instance, a program to select promising teachers to spend a year at developing methods, materials and programs for teaching things such as human relations, reading skills, etc. in urban schools. After such a year's study, these teachers could form a demonstration team moving from district to district.

Another example: principals are frequently considered a key to educational change. Collegiate programs might provide for key administrators in urban schools to deal with problems solicited from the participants in advance. Such a program would get away from the usual concept of graduate study and its relation to a predetermined discipline and would concentrate instead on pre-identified problems to which the resources of the entire university would be brought. Attention would be given to both emotional and cognitive training and follow-up sessions would be planned with teachers working for these principals.

It has been proposed, for instance, that the State provide stipends for Negro and Puerto Rican educators to pursue doctoral level study in the field of educational administration. When opportunities are available in these areas, it is often difficult to find Negroes or Puerto Ricans with the appropriate training to fill them. Specially developed cross-departmental programs might capitalize on the unique backgrounds, insights, and resources which such groups could bring to schools in urban areas.

Many other in-service possibilities could be devised to address problems identified earlier in these remarks even with our limited knowledge of answers for all of them. I have suggested only a few and this I do with the fear that someone will shortly tell me that just such a program as I describe has indeed been operating for the past three years and our money would be very welcome!

Conclusion

I have tried to indicate some of the major problem areas in teacher education, some of the proposed solutions for pieces of those problems, and also the unique role of the State Education Department, not only as a regulatory agency but also as a supporting partner in improving educational opportunities for all children. . . .

The solution to the practical problems of training teachers will not come from a Department regulation or indeed from a Department-originated program. Such solutions will come from college faculties with the support and encouragement of the State

Education Department. The Department's unique role as arbiter between school and college as well as its financial resources make it a partner that should not be overlooked.

They say that everybody has his price. The Department's price is the convincing argument that a proposal lends real hope in providing improved educational opportunity for children whose opportunities have been limited or denied. It is the very regulatory function given to the Department by statute that enables us to gain sufficient confidence in higher institutions that we can encourage them to step far beyond the minimum requirements and indeed step out in new directions which will provide more realistically useful teacher preparation.

INDEX

A